*A Reader's Guide
to the Short Stories of*
WILLA CATHER

A
Reference
Publication
in
Literature

Everett Emerson
Editor

A Reader's Guide
to the Short Stories of
WILLA CATHER

Sheryl L. Meyering

G.K. Hall & Co.
An Imprint of Macmillan Publishing Company
New York

Maxwell Macmillan Canada
Toronto

Maxwell Macmillan International
New York   Oxford   Singapore   Sydney

G.K. Hall & Co.
An Imprint of Macmillan Publishing Company
866 Third Avenue
New York, NY 10022

Maxwell Macmillan Canada, Inc.
1200 Eglinton Avenue East
Suite 200
Don Mills, Ontario M3C 3N1

Macmillan Publishing Company is part of the Maxwell Communications Group of Companies.

Library of Congress Catalog Card Number: 93-10381

Printed in the United States of America

Printing number
 2 3 4 5 6 7 8 9 10

Library of Congress Cataloging-in-Publication Data

Meyering, Sheryl L.
    A reader's guide to the short stories of Willa Cather : Sheryl L. Meyering.
       p.   cm.
    Includes bibliographical references and index.
    ISBN 0-8161-1834-5 : (alk. paper)
    1. Cather, Willa, 1873–1947—Criticism and interpretation. 2. Short Story. I. Title.
PS3505.A87Z7425 1994
813'.52—dc20   93-10381
                                                                    CIP

The paper used in this publication meets the minimum requirements of American National Standard for Information Sciences–Permanence of Paper for Printed Library Materials. ANSI Z3948-1984. ∞ ™

To Wesley

Contents

The Author

Sheryl L. Meyering received her Ph.D. in English from Michigan State University in 1986. She is the author of *Sylvia Plath: A Reference Guide, 1973–88* (G. K. Hall, 1990) and editor of *Charlotte Perkins Gilman: The Woman and Her Work* (Ann Arbor: UMI Research Press, 1989). Meyering's work has appeared in several collections of essays and in such scholarly journals as *American Literature*; her subjects include Nathaniel Hawthorne, Louise Glück, Carolyn Cheesebro', and Aimee Semple McPherson. Meyering has presented papers on topics ranging from nineteenth-century American literature to Sinclair Lewis to popular culture. She has taught at Michigan State University and is currently Assistant Professor of English at Southern Illinois University at Edwardsville and Associate Editor of the journal *Papers on Language and Literature*.

Preface

This book is intended as a complete reference source for readers of Willa Cather's short fiction. Although many critics have preferred to concentrate on Cather's novels, most students approach Cather for the first time through one of her anthologized short stories. Further, Cather was a writer of short stories years before she became a writer of novels, and she continued to publish short fiction throughout her career. Because only three or four of Cather's stories—"Paul's Case," "Neighbour Rosicky," "The Sculptor's Funeral," and recently "Old Mrs. Harris"—have been consistently anthologized, many readers will be surprised to learn that Cather published over sixty short stories, and that many of them are equal in quality to the ones that have found their way into anthologies over the years.

Each of the following chapters is devoted to one story and consists of five parts. The first, publication history, lists when, where, and how many times the story has appeared. The second section provides information about the circumstances of the story's composition. Biographical details, such as where the story was written and what significant events in Cather's life at the time influenced the story, are provided when they are available and pertinent, as are all significant literary and cultural sources.

Each of Cather's short stories is in some way connected to her other work—a novel, an essay, or another story. The third section of each chapter in this book, then, addresses these connections, which often take the form of shared settings or themes, frequently used symbols, or common narrative strategies.

The fourth section of each chapter provides an overview of the various readings each story has received from Cather's critics. I have tried to organize these often diverse discussions into as coherent a form as possible, presenting the opinions of those critics who have similar interpretations first, then those whose readings are noticeably different. Frequently, however, there is no easy way to group the various responses, and in those cases, I have simply presented them serially and have made the transitions from one reading to the next as smooth as possible.

The last section of each chapter provides a list of the works cited in that chapter. In addition to giving credit to the articles and books from which I quote, this section is intended to refer the reader to valuable sources for further study.

I wish to thank Southern Illinois University at Edwardsville for giving me two grants that helped defray the cost of my research, which always amounts to more than any scholar expects at the outset, and for granting me a sabbatical leave to prepare the book.

I am grateful to my friends and fellow scholars Maria Bruno, Guillermina Elissondo, and Diana Pingatore, who believe that books like this one are valuable—that they "count"—and who listened over the telephone to my expressions of frustration without hanging up on me; to Cathy Davidson and Linda Wagner-Martin, who after all these years are still my role models; and especially to Brian Abel Ragen, the most incredible font of knowledge I have ever known, who through it all gave me sanctuary, support, solace, and often dinner.

Finally, I owe an immeasurable debt to my parents, who believe I am perfect, and to my husband, who knows I am not but endures anyway.

Introduction

Willa Cather's status as one of the great American authors of the twentieth century is now secure. Cather's work appears in every anthology of American or modern fiction, and at least one of her short stories is certain to be found on the syllabus of even the most basic course in American literature. Each year scholars add more bricks to the already vast edifice of critical commentary. And she has been enshrined in what is closest to an official pantheon of American letters, the Library of America. All this aside, she is still not quite part of the mainstream of American culture—and her enthusiasts as much as her detractors are responsible for her equivocal position. Earlier in the century, while Modernism reigned and every author was expected to be a disillusioned expatriate, Cather seemed to be continuing a part of the much-despised genteel tradition. She was a mere regional writer—perhaps the finest guide to Nebraska or the Southwest, but that was not saying much in the heyday of Hemingway. When scholars began to pay her fresh attention (not to rediscover her, for her books always elicited critical attention), she was fitted into almost equally restrictive categories. Feminists championed her books, and she became a "woman writer"—in the minds of many, even a "lesbian writer." The first label, at least, was as true as that of "regionalist," but also as unfairly limiting. She is a writer of great scope. The commentators on her, alas, have explored only a small part of her range.

There are several reasons for the odd imbalance in Cather criticism. To begin with, scholars have concentrated mainly on the novels and neglected the large body of shorter fiction. In part, this focus is the result of the common prejudice of critics, who take the novel more seriously than the short story—just as their predecessors in earlier ages took the epic more seriously than the lyric poem. But in part it is Cather's own responsibility. In fashioning her career, Cather tried to present herself as a novelist and in many ways tried to deny her career as a writer of short fiction. Much of her earlier work was never reprinted in her lifetime, and although she did collect a few stories, she refused to allow most of them to be reprinted in anthologies. Many of the earlier stories were thus consigned to oblivion.

Even now, one might easily think that Cather wrote only three or four short stories. The many collections of American short fiction always seem to include the same ones. "Paul's Case" appears most often. "Neighbour

Rosicky" is a close second, and "The Sculptor's Funeral" is occasionally found, usually in collections intended for high schools. These are all fine stories, but many equally good ones never appear. Recently, anthologists have evidently noticed that all three are male-centered, and so have begun selecting another of her stories that focuses on a woman—"Old Mrs. Harris." To try to show Cather's range and dispel the notion that all her stories are male-centered is a laudable objective. Unfortunately, current anthologists seem to be making the same mistake as their predecessors—they all choose the *same* story, so that "Old Mrs. Harris" is in danger of becoming the "Paul's Case" of the 1990s. It is not just students whose experience of Cather is limited by this narrow range of selections; most critics of American literature have the same limited view of Cather's work because the vast majority of critical commentary is directed at these same few popular stories.

Since Cather was first described as a lesbian writer in the 1970s, the question of her sexuality and its influence on her fiction has become the focus of almost all Cather criticism. Some writers simply assume her homosexuality and use it as the key to all ambiguities in her works. Some insist that since there is no hard evidence that Cather was a lesbian—unless the term is so broadly defined as to include women who are not sexually involved with other women, but whose primary emotional attachments are to women—to make such an assumption is irresponsible. Others insist that the author's sexual orientation is simply irrelevant. But almost none of Cather's recent commentators has, in fact, been able to ignore the question of homoerotic elements in her work.

Sharon O'Brien's work on Cather, culminating in *Willa Cather: The Emerging Voice* (1987), is the most powerful body of criticism that deals with Cather as a woman—and lesbian—writer. Using Nancy Chodorow's feminist psychoanalytical theories on the relations between women and their mothers, O'Brien attempts to show how the roles of woman writer—which Cather acknowledged—and of lesbian writer—which she attempted to hide—shaped her fiction. O'Brien's work, which is both solid scholarship and a startlingly new way of viewing an established reputation, has provoked a great deal of commentary itself. It has, in fact, become the work in Cather studies that cannot be ignored, requiring even those who disagree with O'Brien's conclusions to come to terms with the arguments she presents and the evidence she marshals.

Although the author's sexuality has recently become the centerpiece of Cather criticism, scholars have explored many equally interesting aspects of her work. One that is sometimes related to Cather's sexuality is her idea of what art exacts from the artist. Cather believed a devotion to art required the artist—especially the woman artist—to forego emotional attachments. The work is all-demanding, and the woman artist seduced by love or romance would soon cease to be an artist. Some recent critics have argued that this principle applied only to heterosexual relationships, which, because of the power imbalance between the sexes, place women in a position in which artistic effort is impossible. Male egotism and the responsibilities brought by children, not emotional attachment itself, make it impossible for a woman to continue as an artist. Others suggest that in Cather's view art requires an even greater self-denial—that any romantic attachment weakens the artist's devotion to her art and enfeebles her work.

As Cather grew older, however, her earlier faith in the religion of art seems to have wavered. Her later career was shaped, not so much by sexual conflicts, as by her realization that art itself would not supply the meaning or comfort she needed. Indeed, since art and literature seemed, in Cather's view, to have become debased, she sought more traditional repositories of meaning. In the preface to her 1936 collection of essays, *Not Under Forty*, Cather says "the world broke in two in 1922 or thereabouts. . . ." Exactly what she meant has never been perfectly clear to her readers, but the likely explanation is that in many ways she felt beaten by life and disillusioned about art's ability to order or give meaning to existence. One of the most significant blows Cather endured was her separation from her dear friend Isabelle McClung, who moved to Europe permanently with her husband in late 1921. Further, it was around 1922 that Cather began to feel the effects of the very things that made so many of her contemporaries become expatriates: she saw American culture as more and more given over to materialism and vulgarity, and modern American life as disgusting. She attributed this in part to deteriorating manners; to be in vogue, one had to be informal, irreverent, and disrespectful. Just as much as the high modernists, Cather was disillusioned by the aftermath of World War I, which brought, not a new era of peace, but new threats of chaos. Unlike the expatriate modernists, however, she did not ascribe the deterioration of society to the bankruptcy of traditional values; rather, she blamed society for abandoning the values that had served it well.

Cather was equally troubled by new trends in the world of writing. She was appalled by the growth of creative writing programs on college campuses. Despite—or perhaps because of—her stint as an instructor at Breadloaf in 1922, she believed that neither the students nor the teachers had a solid command of the English language, and that trying to teach such people to write was putting the cart before the horse.

Finally, in 1922 she visited her parents in Red Cloud, Nebraska, and helped them celebrate their fiftieth wedding anniversary. This trip was more than a reunion with her family: it also marked Cather's public acceptance of organized Christianity. Along with her parents, Cather was confirmed in Red Cloud's Episcopal Church on December 27. Cather had not come from a rigidly religious family, and in her youth she proclaimed herself an atheist. At this point in her life, while still struggling with unbelief, she looked to both the Catholic and Episcopal churches for the solace she no longer found in art alone.

Sorrow continued to dog Cather in the years that followed. After her father's sudden death in the spring of 1928, Cather again returned to Red Cloud. After the funeral she spent several weeks in Nebraska and seems to have drawn sustenance from reestablishing connections with the past. Later the same year, her mother suffered a stroke while visiting her son in California. In 1938, both Cather's brother Douglass and Isabelle McClung died. After the death of her remaining brother, Roscoe, in 1945, Cather gave up writing. The more misfortune she suffered, the more she turned to tradition (in the forms of old friends and those institutions, like the church, that preserve tradition) for support. Art seemed no longer to suffice.

In any case, from about 1922 on, there is often a sense of disillusionment and regret in Cather's work, especially in her last stories. In many of these, Cather so mercilessly attacks every aspect of the modern world that many of her critics accuse her of escaping into a romanticized past in order to avoid facing the problems of the present. They argue that her work becomes merely nostalgic and that she abandons the complexities of the present for the simplicities of the past. She is even linked with T. S. Eliot as an author who chooses the order and decorum of the Anglican Church over the wasteland. Although these critics may overstate the case, Cather was certainly repulsed by the vulgarity and shallowness she saw in contemporary American life. Still, her attacks on the present do not necessarily imply the kind of sappy nostalgia she is accused of. She indicts what she feels is modern America's tendency to cheapen everything, to lower everything to the same standard of mediocrity, and to diminish the importance of quality in every area of life. Her later work cannot fairly be called either escapist or nostalgic; it is as legitimate a response to the chaos and vulgarity of society that she observed between the wars as any other. And it is free of the stylistic or political posturing that mars so much of the fiction of the 30s.

Cather is still read, appropriately, as a regional writer. The limited number of stories that are often read, however, has produced quite a skewed version of her view of Nebraska. Thanks to "Neighbour Rosicky" and several novels, it has been possible to see Cather as a writer who consistently celebrates the simple life on the plains. But Cather only came to love Nebraska in later life—and from a distance. In her earlier work, such as "On the Divide" and "A Wagner Matinée," she harshly—even cruelly—attacks the provinciality and coarseness of the Nebraska farm country. She did eventually come to appreciate the people of the plains, who gave her the subjects for much of her best work—but it is significant to note that she never chose to live there again; instead, she celebrated Red Cloud from Pittsburgh, Paris, and New York.

It is striking how pervasive the biographical impulse is in Cather studies. Those articles that address the question of technique are often limited to discussions of Cather's tendency to use male narrators. What we find most often in articles on Cather are discussions of her "finding a voice." We hear a good deal about her early respect for and imitation of Henry James, and her later admiration of and friendship with Sarah Orne Jewett, and about how her relationship with Jewett changed her writing. But Cather's development at this time is rarely treated as a series of artistic choices—the selection of techniques appropriate to the subject. Rather it is presented as her discovering the possibility of writing in a woman's voice without being sentimental. The same is true in many discussions of her coming to terms with Nebraska: the subject is not artistic choices, but the biographical reasons for them.

All too few of the many articles on Cather's fiction treat the stories as skillfully made objects—as works of art. It would perhaps be good if more critics were willing to treat them as such, rather than as documents to be weighed in a biographical study. Not only would this approach be fairer to the works themselves—and truer to Cather's own desire to be regarded as an artist— but it would counter the still-pervasive idea that in art, form and technique are male interests, while feeling and personality are female. In any literature worth reading, an author transforms what she takes from her life through her mastery of her craft. Cather's life has filled the pages of journals for years now. Her craft deserves equal attention.

The Affair at Grover Station

Publication History

This story was first published in *The Library* in two installments on June 16 and 23, 1900 (1:3–4; 14–15) under the name Willa Sibert Cather (Faulkner 1970, 593). It was reprinted by the Lincoln *Courier* on July 7, 1900 (15:3–5, 8–9) (Faulkner 1970, 593). It was reprinted again in 1957 by Dodd, Mead in *Early Stories*, and in 1965 by the University of Nebraska Press in *Willa Cather's Collected Short Fiction, 1892–1912*.

Circumstances of Composition, Sources, and Influences

Written shortly after Cather had resigned from the Pittsburgh *Leader* where she had been an editor of wire copy, this story is the first of many in which the railroad figures prominently. Bennett quotes Cather's sister as saying, "Yes, the story about Grover Station is the one that I remember. . . . Willa worked that one out with [her brother] Douglass. She always worked anything that she wrote about the railroad out with him" (1957, 239). Douglass Cather had left high school early to take a job on the Burlington line. After doing railroad work for two years, he returned home, finished school, and went back to work, the Burlington having put him in charge of their Cheyenne station, where he stayed for several years. His railroad expertise allowed him to provide his sister with several of this story's details (1957, 239).

Bennett sees the influence of Henry James in Cather's use of a ghost in her plot, but not in the themes she uses that device to explore (Bennett 1957, 239).

Relationship to Other Cather Works

Bennett notes that the opening scene of the story is similar to that of *My Ántonia*, and that the portrayal of Larry as a well-liked, intelligent man makes him very much like Reggie in "'The Fear That Walks by Noonday'" and like Jay in "Tommy, the Unsentimental," although Larry is responsible and Jay is not (1957, 240, 243). Arnold connects the story to *My Ántonia* in a slightly different way: like that novel, it uses a framing narrator who recounts another

1

character's story, and like the novel it opens with a scene on a train (1984, 35–36n).

Interpretations and Criticisms

Instead of drawing on her Nebraska roots, Cather explores a subject that would be important in her final novels—the grotesque (Woodress 1987, 146). Most critics agree that this story is much more skillful than her first attempt at a ghost story, "'The Fear That Walks by Noonday'"; nevertheless, it is still second-rate and "artificial" compared with those stories that are Nebraska-based (O'Brien 1987, 269).

Arnold finds the story to be especially graceful, the first sentence being "nearly perfect as the narrator of the frame story sets the stage. . . . No laborious dredging up of suspense here, no self-conscious storytelling; only the solid, but plastic, style of a teller sure of his tale and a writer sure of her craft"; Cather is measured, careful, and restrained in her development of character, mood, and plot progression (1984, 27–28).

Works Cited

Arnold, Marilyn. 1984. *Willa Cather's Short Fiction*. Athens: Ohio University Press.

Bennett, Mildred, ed. 1957. *Early Stories of Willa Cather*. New York: Dodd, Mead.

Cather, Willa. 1957. "The Affair at Grover Station." In *Early Stories*. Ed. Mildred Bennett. New York: Dodd, Mead, 239–56.

———. [1965] 1970. "The Affair at Grover Station." In *Willa Cather's Collected Short Fiction, 1892–1912*. Ed. Virginia Faulkner. Lincoln: University of Nebraska Press, 339–52.

Faulkner, Virginia, ed. [1965] 1970. *Willa Cather's Collected Short Fiction, 1892–1912*. Lincoln: University of Nebraska Press. Reprint. Lincoln: University of Nebraska Press.

O'Brien, Sharon. 1987. *Willa Cather: The Emerging Voice*. New York: Oxford University Press.

Woodress, James. 1987. *Willa Cather: A Literary Life*. Lincoln: University of Nebraska Press.

Ardessa

Publication History

This story was first published under the name Willa Sibert Cather in the May 1918 issue of *Century* (96:105–116) (Faulkner 1970, 597). It was reprinted in 1973 by the University of Nebraska Press in *Uncle Valentine and Other Stories: Willa Cather's Uncollected Short Fiction, 1915–1929* and in 1992 by Literary Classics of the United States in *Cather: Stories, Poems, and Other Writings*, a volume in the Library of America series.

Circumstances of Composition, Sources, and Influences

By the time this story was written, Cather had been making her living solely by writing fiction for nearly six years, and most critics agree that this is one of the tales she wrote simply because she knew what would sell easily to the slick magazines of the day. Also, she was still plagued by money worries and was working diligently to finish her novel *My Ántonia* when she sent the story to *Century* via her literary agent, Paul Reynolds. In her accompanying letter, she suggested to the editor of *Century*, Douglas Doty, that he publish a series of stories under the general title "Office Wives." Doty thought the series would work and was willing to publish the stories in the magazine and later as a book (Woodress 1987, 286).

Most critics also agree that the character of O'Mally is based closely on S. S. McClure, publisher of *McClure's* magazine, where Cather worked as editor (and for a time as managing editor) from 1906 until 1912. (For a discussion of Cather's years on the magazine's staff, see the chapters below on "The Namesake" and "The Sculptor's Funeral," under the "Circumstances of Composition, Sources, and Influences" section.) McClure was a muckraking pioneer—boisterous, innovative, and, in Cather's estimation, congenial. Not all of his staff on the magazine agreed, however. He was gifted at identifying a potential great talent and had published such eminent authors as Twain, Stevenson, Conrad, Crane, Kipling, Anthony Hope, Arnold Bennett, and Jack London. In 1903 McClure virtually made the magazine's name by assigning Lincoln Steffens to probe political corruption. Because Cather was interested more in fiction than in social/political reform, she was in some ways a misfit at *McClure's*. Her lack of sympathy for the reformist pieces *McClure's* was

3

publishing may explain the "caustic" attitude toward muckrakers so evident in "Ardessa" (Lee 1989, 63, 65).

Cather also draws on her journalistic experience before *McClure's* for this story. She was managing editor of *Home Monthly* magazine during 1896–97 and spent several years on the staff of the Pittsburgh *Leader* before that. The character of Becky Tietelbaum has a good deal of Willa Cather about her: she works harder and more skillfully than almost anyone else, and, like Becky, Cather often was forced to do others' work without being acknowledged for it (Slote 1973, xii–xiii). Arnold, on the other hand, believes Cather herself is more closely associated with "the capable but humane" character of Rena Kalski than she is with Becky Tietelbaum (1984, 102).

Relationship to Other Cather Works

Uncle Valentine and Other Stories contains five stories under the heading "New York Stories" and two under the heading "Pittsburgh Stories." As one of the "New York Stories," "Ardessa" is most often linked with the others under that heading: "Consequences," "The Bookkeeper's Wife," "Her Boss," and "Coming, Eden Bower." These stories may be read as period pieces, for each depicts women working in the typical women's jobs of that time—jobs as disparate as that of secretary and actress. Yet these stories, which are little more than the usual offering of the slick magazines of the time, provide ample evidence that Cather was a real magazine editor, and that she had a knack for providing her readership with what it wanted (La Salle 1987, 169).

Arnold maintains that Cather is making the same point she does in the "The Old Beauty," a much later story. She sympathizes with a character who has perpetuated a class system that must eventually fall, and whose collapse will destroy her. Despite the author's sympathy for the character, however, she does imply that Ardessa will learn and grow from her experience of loss. In other words, unlike Gabrielle Longstreet of "The Old Beauty," Ardessa "may learn to live in the present" (1984, 103).

Interpretations and Criticisms

Arnold sees the main conflict of this story as one between the old order, represented by Ardessa, and the new, represented by O'Mally. Even though the editor-owner is a grand old man, he is nevertheless "brimming over with new methods and new ideas while Ardessa still lives in the old century, a vestige of a sterile brand of gentility that can leave character virtually unimproved over an entire lifetime" (1984, 103). Although Ardessa may deserve our pity, nothing can stop change, and it would be to her advantage if she could learn to adjust to the new world, where the protection of "ladies" is no longer valued.

Cather does not mourn the loss of "a set of empty rituals and gestures which are never the true values of the past" (1984, 103).

In Ryder's opinion, in this story Cather is simply describing the common evils of the workplace—"complacency and misuse of power. Ardessa's overbearing nature and pride are no defense against the efficiency and modesty of a younger staff member" (1990, 165). To Brown, the story is built on Cather's fond memories of her time on the staff of *McClure's*, where men sat in private offices pondering the best way to expose some metropolitan vice ([1953] 1964, 128).

Bloom and Bloom read "Ardessa" as part of Cather's attack on the American trend toward standardization. Cather despised the sameness of everything in America and often complained that advertisers brainwash the public into believing that this kind of deadly, uniform mediocrity is desirable. "Ardessa," then, is a relentless attack on commercial propaganda (1962, 86).

Works Cited

Arnold, Marilyn. 1984. *Willa Cather's Short Fiction*. Athens: Ohio University Press.

Bloom, Edward A., and Lillian D. Bloom. 1962. *Willa Cather's Gift of Sympathy*. Carbondale: Southern Illinois University Press.

Brown, E. K. Completed by Leon Edel. [1953] 1964. *Willa Cather: A Critical Biography*. New York: Knopf.

Cather, Willa. 1973. "Ardessa." In *Uncle Valentine and Other Stories: Willa Cather's Uncollected Short Fiction, 1915-1929*. Ed. Bernice Slote. Lincoln: University of Nebraska Press, 99-115.

———. 1992. "Ardessa." In *Cather: Stories, Poems, and Other Writings*. New York: Literary Classics of the United States, 167–84.

Faulkner, Virginia, ed. [1965] 1970. *Willa Cather's Collected Short Fiction, 1892–1912*. Lincoln: University of Nebraska Press. Reprint. Lincoln: University of Nebraska Press.

LaSalle, Peter. 1987. Review of *Uncle Valentine and Other Stories*, by Willa Cather. *Studies in Short Fiction* 24:169–70.

Lee, Hermione. 1989. *Willa Cather: Double Lives*. New York: Pantheon.

Ryder, Mary Ruth. 1990. *Willa Cather and Classical Myth*. Lewiston, NY: Edwin Mellen Press.

Slote, Bernice. 1973. Introduction to *Uncle Valentine and Other Stories: Willa Cather's Uncollected Short Fiction, 1915–1929*, by Willa Cather. Lincoln: University of Nebraska Press.

Woodress, James. 1987. *Willa Cather: A Literary Life*. Lincoln: University of Nebraska Press.

Before Breakfast

Publication History

Completed in 1944 and signed "Willa Cather," this story did not appear in print until 1948 when a posthumous collection of short stories, *The Old Beauty and Others*, was published by Knopf; Vintage Books put out a paperback reprint of the collection in 1976. In 1992 the story was reprinted by the Literary Classics of the United States in *Cather: Stories, Poems, and Other Writings*, a volume in the Library of America series.

Circumstances of Composition, Sources, and Influences

From 1921 on, Cather spent at least part of most summers on the Canadian island of Grand Manan. According to Cather's longtime companion, Edith Lewis, Cather felt that the island was a wonderful place to write. During the years 1943–1946, however, Cather was unable to go there because the war had depleted the island of all its workmen. She chose Northeast Harbour, Maine, as a replacement, and it was there in the summer of 1944 that she wrote "Before Breakfast" (1953, 192–96).

Woodress believes that the bleakness of the mood in this story grew out of Cather's outrage over the role played by science and technology in bringing humanity close to annihilation (1970, 266). It was wartime, and Cather had written to a friend in February 1944 that she had been mourning over the destruction of the familiar world she had assumed was permanent. She wondered why beautiful old cities had to be destroyed and why whole countries had to disappear from the map (1970, 266–67).

Woodress and Butcher both point to Grand Manan Island as the setting of the story (Butcher 1948, sec. 4, p. 5; Woodress 1970, 267), but O'Brien feels the story owes more to Lavandou, the small fishing village Cather and her friend Isabelle McClung visited during Cather's first trip to Europe in 1902. It was a spot Cather had drawn on for settings before; the landscape of Lavandou reappears in the Panther Canyon sequence of *The Song of the Lark* and again in *My Mortal Enemy* and "Before Breakfast" (1987, 254). Cather also drew on her memories of Lavandou for the setting of "Eleanor's House" (see the "Circumstances of Composition, Sources, and Influences" section for that story).

According to Thurin, in this story Cather suggests the importance of all the life—human and nonhuman—that covers what was once a bare globe. The story's fusion of the cold heavenly Venus and the nurturing Mother Earth has its source in Lucretius's *De rerum natura*, as do many of the ideas in the story. Cather's familiarity with the works of Lucretius is made explicit by a reference she makes to him at the end of Book One of her novel *The Professor's House* (1990, 361, 363).

Although the influence of Henry James on Cather had largely disappeared by this stage in Cather's career, Wasserman sees a bit of James's John Marcher of "The Beast in the Jungle" in this story: there is "the same obstinate fidelity to an obscure desire for fulfillment and the same blindness to the figure in the carpet that is pointing the way he should go" (1991, 20).

Relationship to Other Cather Works

Arnold draws parallels between this story and *The Professor's House* in that Grenfell's inner conflict is the same one that torments Godfrey St. Peter—both characters want at once to be involved with other human beings and to have nothing to do with them—to interact with nature alone. The resolution of Grenfell's struggle, however, is much happier than St. Peter's (1984b, 168). Daiches, too, sees similarities between the two works. Cather has reversed the roles of the professor and the businessman: "This time it is the businessman who reads Scott and Shakespeare and is disturbed by the cold brilliance of his academic son as well as by his socially superior wife" (1962, 172).

According to Thurin, the story is also reminiscent of Cather's earlier story "Coming, Aphrodite!" especially during the scene where Grenfell watches Miss Fairweather through the trees. The scene is very similar to the one in the earlier story where Don Hedger spies on Eden Bower through a knothole. Furthermore, Cather's allusion to the birth of Venus echoes "her 1896 review of a performance of Massenet's *Eve* in which Cather at one point transforms the vision of the mother of mankind into a vision of 'the mother of all things-to-be opening her eyes upon her world—Aphrodite rising from the foam of the sea'" (quoted in Thurin 1990, 361). In that same review she also quotes from Massenet's libretto something that sounds very much as though it came from the text of "Before Breakfast": "A pure light is spread over creation, and from the new-born earth light vapors illumined by the sunrise on the horizon. A soft breeze undulates the flowers of the field and the waves of the sea" (quoted in Thurin 1990, 363).

Interpretations and Criticisms

Most Cather authorities agree that this story is a natural product of that stage in the author's life when she faced change, upheaval, and the deaths of several people she loved. Arnold notes "Henry Grenfell's resourceful frog" specifically as a symbol of Cather as survivor (1984a, 243). Like the frog, Cather has adapted to the vicissitudes of life, and in finding a way to endure has found rejuvenation. The story underscores both her commitment to and her propensity for recoiling from life (Arnold 1984a, 243).

The question Cather deals with in the story is massive, according to McFarland—one that much modern literature has attempted to answer: What is man's place in the unfathomably vast universe? But despite its seriousness, Cather handles her subject "lightly" and with "an ironic, whimsical tone that exactly matches Grenfell's character" (1972, 134).

Grenfell, who all his life has strived for power, suddenly finds himself "being mocked by the impersonal universe around him which will claim him in death" (Stouck 1975, 236). Thus, his despair results from an awareness of his own puniness and insignificance in the face of the natural world, which has existed for millions of years. The simple sight of a young woman "pitting herself gamely against the vast ocean" allows Grenfell to come to the understanding that anything that has "courage and the will to survive, proves humanity's value and life's value" (Arnold 1984a, 243–44).

Wasserman believes that in this story Cather is illustrating the balance between "the cold, heavy weight of scientific time—the glacier, the eons of time—[and] the force, the energy, flowing through both matter and spirit: Venus (star, girl, and myth), the evolving sea creature, the story of the Pilgrim seeking perfection, the girl's courage" (1991, 19). Ryder, on the other hand, maintains that in Grenfell's "resurrected spirit," Cather has depicted a situation that "lends itself readily to the Christian myth," although the story's "dominant imagery" comes from classical myth (1990, 280). When the narrator speaks of Grenfell's sharpened appetite, we are to infer that this appetite is not merely physical. Through the classical figures of Aphrodite and Venus, Grenfell has been given a renewed "eagerness for life"; thus, "the implications of Cather's story assume both mythic and religious proportions" (Ryder 1990, 280). Thurin pointedly disagrees, arguing that the story absolutely ignores the Christian tradition. Aphrodite, in the form of the geologist's daughter, does inspire Grenfell and thus "establishes the triumph of myth and symbol over science," and there can be no doubt that Cather's argument is, in part at least, antiscience (1990, 362). It is interesting to note, however, that in the end Grenfell accepts rather than rebels against science. In Thurin's view, Cather explicitly links the concept of evolution with Grenfell's "vision of Miss Fairweather. . . . In this way, Venus becomes . . . a symbol not only of beauty encouraging the propagation of the species but of life's urge to rise toward higher forms of beauty"; that Cather should use the Aphrodite image so successfully can be seen as "both a final confession of faith . . . and a final vindication of her poetic-symbolist approach to the art of fiction" (1990, 362).

Works Cited

Arnold, Marilyn. 1984a. "Cather's Last Three Stories: A Testament of Life and Endurance." *Great Plains Quarterly* 4:238–44.

———. 1984b. *Willa Cather's Short Fiction*. Athens: Ohio University Press.

Butcher, Fanny. 1948. "Three Long Short Stories by Willa Cather." *Chicago Daily Tribune*, 12 September, sec. 4, p. 5.

Cather, Willa. 1948. "Before Breakfast." In *The Old Beauty and Others*. New York: Knopf, 141–66.

———. 1976. "Before Breakfast." In *The Old Beauty and Others*. New York: Vintage Books, 141–66.

———. 1992. "Before Breakfast." In *Cather: Stories, Poems, and Other Writings*. New York: Literary Classics of the United States, 645–727.

Daiches, David. [1951] 1962. *Willa Cather: A Critical Introduction*. Ithaca, NY: Cornell University Press; London: Oxford University Press. Reprint. New York: Collier.

Faulkner, Virginia, ed. [1965] 1970. *Willa Cather's Collected Short Fiction, 1892–1912*. Lincoln: University of Nebraska Press. Reprint. Lincoln: University of Nebraska Press.

Lewis, Edith. 1953. *Willa Cather Living*. New York: Knopf.

McFarland, Dorothy Tuck. 1972. *Willa Cather*. New York: Frederick Ungar.

O'Brien, Sharon. 1987. *Willa Cather: The Emerging Voice*. New York: Oxford University Press.

Ryder, Mary Ruth. 1990. *Willa Cather and Classical Myth*. Lewiston, NY: Edwin Mellen Press.

Stouck, David. 1975. *Willa Cather's Imagination*. Lincoln: University of Nebraska Press.

Thurin, Erik Ingvar. 1990. *The Humanization of Willa Cather: Classicism in an American Classic*. Lund, Sweden: Lund University Press.

Wasserman, Loretta. 1991. *Willa Cather: A Study of the Short Fiction*. Boston: Twayne.

Woodress, James. 1970. *Willa Cather: Her Life and Art*. New York: Pegasus.

Behind the Singer Tower

Publication History

This story was first published under the name Willa Sibert Cather in the May 1912 issue of *Collier's* (49:16–17) and was reprinted in 1965 by the University of Nebraska Press in *Willa Cather's Collected Short Fiction, 1892–1912*.

Circumstances of Composition, Sources, and Influences

Cather wrote this story while she was living in New York and working as managing editor of *McClure's* magazine, one of the premier muckraking journals of the day. The magazine frequently published accounts of industrial accidents, many of which included with added irony the death of the rich as well as of those they exploited. Cather was undoubtedly so accustomed to reading these articles that her choice of subject matter for this story comes as no surprise (Haller 1990, 40–41). Furthermore, at the time the story was written, Cather was polishing her first novel, *Alexander's Bridge*, which was to be published the next year in *McClure's* (Woodress 1987, 216).

Most scholars agree that Cather used both the biblical story of the Tower of Babel and Flaubert's novel *Salammbô* as foundations for this piece. Haller is perhaps the most explicit in describing the parallels between this story and *Salammbô*. While she was still living in Pittsburgh, Cather reread Flaubert's novel with her friends Mr. and Mrs. George Seibel, who regularly met to read French literature. Flaubert's novel is "an imaginative reconstruction of the war waged by mercenaries against their former masters after the First Punic War. In other words, Flaubert wrote about the assault of the cheated and deprived upon an arrogant city," and the issues he raised were still fresh in Cather's mind when she wrote her story (1990, 41). The "verticality of New York skyscrapers" in "Behind the Singer Tower" corresponds to that of Flaubert's "towers, Baalim, engines of war, terraced buildings, [and] aqueducts" (Haller 1990, 43). Her New York is very like his Carthage in "its decadence, its sadistic violence, its verticality, its absence of conventional domesticity" (Haller 1990, 46). And just as the soldiers' hands are severed by cutlasses in Flaubert's work, the tenor's hand is severed *as if* by a cutlass in Cather's story (Haller 1990, 52).

Several other critics have suggested, however, that this mutilation of the hand may have its roots in an incident in Cather's childhood in Virginia. Edith Lewis, Cather's companion for over forty years, explains that when Cather was five years old, the "half-witted" son of one of the servants threatened to cut off Cather's hand with a knife he was holding at the time. Even though she diverted the boy's attention and escaped injury, the incident traumatized her, and she was somewhat preoccupied with mutilation—especially of the hand—forever after (1953, 10).

Cather also draws on Conrad's "Heart of Darkness" for the setting of this story. Her narrator, like Conrad's Marlow, recounts to a group his awful story about a pleasure boat. Using this allusion to the frame of Conrad's famous "tale of the unspeakable, Cather was preparing not only for 'the horror' to be found in her story but also perhaps for a fear that her ambition to become a great artist in New York was hubris approaching the scale of Kurtz's" (Haller 1990, 47).

Bennett believes this story was suggested to Cather by the Windsor Hotel fire of March 17, 1899 (1970, xli). Haller, on the other hand, maintains that the more likely sources were a 1912 fire at the Equitable Building and a fire at a Columbia University fraternity house that had been described in *McClure's* (1990, 47).

O'Brien points to a poem by Allan Updegraff, which was published in the February 1911 issue of *McClure's*, as a possible source for some of the themes and images in the story. In that poem "four people are 'reading' the New York skyline, the first three seeing fame, wealth, and power, while the fourth sees 'shame'" (1987, 400n).

Relationship to Other Cather Works

This story is sometimes linked with Cather's first novel, *Alexander's Bridge*, because both works feature "an engineer and the failure of a great architectural structure," and each is concerned with the issue of inferior workmanship and materials and the general lowering of quality in order to keep costs down (Arnold 1984, 92). To Arnold, however, the central conflict in *Alexander's Bridge* is internal to Bartley Alexander, who stands poised between youth and approaching middle age. In "Behind the Singer Tower" the conflict is between two systems of values, which are embodied in Fred Hallet and Stanley Merryweather (1984, 92).

Stouck pairs the story with Cather's later novel, *One of Ours*, in that the ending of "Behind the Singer Tower" contains a "vision of evolutionary purpose behind the dynamic processes of the city": the men ponder "what new 'Idea' will be born into human history from their civilization on Manhattan Island," just as, in the novel, David Gerhardt contemplates the possibility that there is some hidden purpose "behind the devastation of the war" (1975, 77–78). Cather explored the same theme—"those who gain by corruption and the misuse of others"—in the much earlier story, "El Dorado: A Kansas Recessional," which portrays exploitative western land speculators in much the same way that exploitative New York builders are depicted in "Behind the Singer Tower" (Slote 1970, 11).

O'Brien likens the story to the earlier "The Enchanted Bluff." In both Cather describes how the competition common in America is responsible for "the destruction of the communal ideal" (O'Brien 1987, 383). Also viewing the story as social criticism, Thurin sees it returning to the concerns of Cather's early work, such as "Lou, the Prophet" and "The Clemency of the Court" (1990, 157n).

Bennett groups this story with others that contain Oriental, or otherwise exotic characters, such as Yung, the Chinese in "A Son of the Celestial," and Freymark, the son of a French soldier and a Chinese slave girl in "The Affair at Grover Station." In "Behind the Singer Tower," the half-Oriental Stanley Merryweather "is a forerunner of Louis Marsellus of Cather's novel *The Professor's House*. Louis has been in China [and] has a brother there engaged in the silk trade" (1982, 46–47).

Interpretations and Criticisms

In her attack on the exploitation of human beings for profit, Cather associates the Singer Tower with Moloch, a comparison that is appropriate because of its "evocation of child sacrifice," and Cather consistently stresses the fact that the workers, especially Caesarino, are extremely young and small in size (Haller 1990, 43). Haller believes that Moloch's presence is implied by the many lives that are sacrificed first in construction accidents and then in the hotel fire. The 300 deaths in the Mont Blanc hotel fire are foreshadowed by the death of Caesarino while its foundations are being laid (1990, 43–49). Although fire does not kill Caesarino, "Cather emphasizes the extraordinary heat of the summer night intensified by the steam engines in the hole. His birth on a volcanic island further reinforces this pattern" (Haller 1990, 45).

As one of the central images of the story, however, fire represents "the flame of desire, the almost gaudy glare of accomplishment, [as well as] the consuming blaze of destruction" (Arnold 1984, 96). Similarly, as Arnold argues, the skyscraper can be a symbol of both human aspiration and ruin; Cather uses the Singer Tower to represent the former and the Mont Blanc to represent the latter. The human need that is expressed by the construction of tall buildings cannot be denied; not everyone is a Stanley Merryweather; the Hallets of the world realize that "the seeds and the fruition of both thrusts, the creative and the destructive, are embedded in the past—in old

MacFarlane's dream and in young Caesarino's death, to be released again and again through succeeding generations of dreamers, builders, and unsuspecting martyrs" (Arnold 1984, 96–97). Thus, despite the enormous cost of the New York dream, there is nobility in some of the men who pursue it. Old Hughie MacFarlane, for example, had a vision of what Manhattan would become years before it actually happened. Cather sees him as sharing the nobility of the pioneers and the first railroad builders, whose successors also lost sight of the dreams and principles that inspired their enterprise (Arnold 1984, 92–93). Of course, by the time of the Mont Blanc disaster, the dream has been thoroughly corrupted, so much so that the people who perish are seen as expendable because they are largely foreign-born fur and garment workers. Hallet's cruel attack on Zablowski may be read as his own articulation of personal pain and rage that comes from his awareness that "Zablowski can be the butt of such jokes as his, . . . that the immigrant comes to this country and naively offers himself as a sacrifice to the inhuman, if compelling, New York idea" (Arnold 1984, 93–94).

Woodress agrees that the Mont Blanc hotel and the Singer Tower represent "destructive forces" and "vitality," respectively, but he argues that as symbols they are unconvincing (1987, 216). Cather's description of the Singer Tower as a "Jewy-looking thing" is one of many anti-Semitic remarks in Cather's work, often directed at a Jewish doctor (Woodress 1987, 216) (for a discussion of Cather's possible anti-Semitism, see the section "Relationship to Other Cather Works" for "The Marriage of Phaedra" chapter).

Bradford sees no such dual message in this story, viewing it instead as Cather's utter rejection of "the American scale of values," which she embodies in the skyscraper (1955, 546). The story shows that Cather shared more with her muckraking colleagues at *McClure's* than most have believed (Bradford 1955, 546–47). Gerber, too, reads the story as a straightforward indictment "of the national emphasis upon a brick and steel facade that acts as a cosmetic to disguise illness of the spirit" (1975, 98).

In Haller's view, Cather does include a bit of "redemptive kindness" into her bleak depiction by suggesting that the remedy for the ruthlessness depicted in the story is in friendships like the one between Hallet and Caesarino (1990, 50). Further, "Cather takes Caesarino's case to remind us of the qualitative difference affection makes to perception": despite Cesarino's insignificance as only one among the multitude of Italian immigrants, Cather's clear message is that each has a unique story to tell (Haller 1990, 51).

O'Brien connects this story to "Cather's own 'perpendicular' desire to rise as a novelist, going beyond both her editorial work and the short story"; she thought of this move in terms of an upward thrust and also associated her ambitions with masculinity: "Leaving the modest, and female, genre of the short story for the individualistic and male genre of the novel, she was also scaling heights from which she might fall" (1987, 384). This fear may explain her inclusion of "a gruesome punishment in [this story] for the woman novelist's literary crime" (O'Brien 1987, 384). The severed hand of the singer is another example of Cather's obsession with hand injuries, a fixation that "reflects her literary anxieties" (O'Brien 1987, 384). Each skyscraper itself may be seen as a metaphor for the long story Cather wanted to write, as well as the dangers that such an endeavor involved: "The taller the building, the deeper the foundation; the longer the story, the deeper the descent into [the self] and the greater the possibility of self-exposure" (1987, 384–85).

Works Cited

Arnold, Marilyn. 1984. *Willa Cather's Short Fiction*. Athens: Ohio University Press.

Bennett, Mildred. [1965] 1970. Introduction to *Willa Cather's Collected Short Fiction*. Ed. Virginia Faulkner. Lincoln: University of Nebraska Press. Reprint. Lincoln: University of Nebraska Press, xiii–xli.

———. 1982. "Willa Cather's Bodies for Ghosts." *Western American Literature* 17:39–52.

Bradford, Curtis. 1955. "Willa Cather's Uncollected Short Stories." *American Literature* 26:537–51.

Cather, Willa. [1965] 1970. "Behind the Singer Tower." In *Willa Cather's Collected Short Fiction, 1892–1912*. Ed. Virginia Faulkner. Lincoln: University of Nebraska Press, 359–79.

Faulkner, Virginia, ed. [1965] 1970. *Willa Cather's Collected Short Fiction, 1892–1912*. Lincoln: University of Nebraska Press. Reprint. Lincoln: University of Nebraska Press.

Gerber, Philip. 1975. *Willa Cather*. Boston: Twayne.

Haller, Evelyn. 1990. "'Behind the Singer Tower': Willa Cather and Flaubert." *Modern Fiction Studies* 36:39–54.

Lewis, Edith. 1953. *Willa Cather Living*. New York: Knopf.

O'Brien, Sharon. 1987. *Willa Cather: The Emerging Voice*. New York: Oxford University Press.

Slote, Bernice. 1970. "Willa Cather as a Regional Writer." *Kansas Quarterly* 2:7–15.

Stouck, David. 1975. *Willa Cather's Imagination*. Lincoln: University of Nebraska Press.

Thurin, Erik Ingvar. 1990. *The Humanization of Willa Cather: Classicism in an American Classic*. Lund, Sweden: Lund University Press.

Woodress, James. 1987. *Willa Cather: A Literary Life*. Lincoln: University of Nebraska Press.

The Best Years

Publication History

Completed in 1945 and signed Willa Cather, this story did not appear in print until 1948, when the posthumous collection of short stories, *The Old Beauty and Others*, was published by Knopf. It was reprinted in 1956 by Vintage Books in *Five Stories*; in 1976 by Vintage Books in a paperback edition of *The Old Beauty and Others*; and in 1992 by Literary Classics of the United States in *Cather: Stories, Poems, and Other Writings*, a volume in The Library of America series.

Circumstances of Composition, Sources, and Influences

Since 1921, Cather and her longtime companion Edith Lewis had summered on the Canadian island of Grand Manan, but when World War II interrupted this tradition, Cather chose to spend her summers at Northeast Harbour, Maine (see the "Circumstances of Composition, Sources, and Influences" section in the chapter "Before Breakfast"). She wrote this story, the last work she ever completed, during her third summer at Northeast Harbour (Lewis 1953, 196). The story was meant as a tribute to her younger brother, Roscoe, whom Cather had visited in California three years before. Her intention was to send the story to him as a reminder of their happy childhood in Red Cloud, but shortly after she had completed it, she received the news of his death. It was a devastating blow from which Cather never fully recovered.

For both setting and characters, Cather draws heavily on her childhood in Red Cloud for this her last story. Miss Knightly is based on a teacher Cather had during her second year in Red Cloud, Evangeline King. Cather called that year "one of the happiest she had ever spent" and remembered Miss King's "mirthful eyes and . . . kind, sympathetic manner"; the teacher was "the first person she had ever cared for deeply outside her own family" (O'Brien 1987, 88). The model for the protagonist, Lesley Ferguesson, could be Cather's brother Roscoe himself. While Cather was attending the University of Nebraska, Roscoe, like Lesley, taught school in order to help the family financially (Woodress 1987, 500). Mr. and Mrs. Ferguesson are portraits of Cather's parents, Charles and Virginia Cather (Murphy 1984, 15). Lesley's family home is nearly identical to the Cather family home in Red Cloud, which had a long attic room where Willa and her brothers shared a common bedroom: although there was plenty of room for separate bedrooms, Cather and her siblings, like the children in this story, wanted to be together so that they could share in one another's experiences (Robinson 1983, 25).

Relationship to Other Cather Works

Cather deliberately treats death differently in this story from the way she treated it in another story in the same collection, "The Old Beauty." Here, death is seen as natural, not tragic. It is significant that the cemetery is "a prominent feature of the landscape," placed close to the school, and that the children are not the least afraid of it (Arnold 1984a, 242). In "The Old Beauty" there is an almost morbid focusing on the actual corpse, but in this story "Cather mutes the effects of young Lesley's death by announcing it in a conversation, almost as if it were an afterthought by the speaker, several days after its occurrence" (Arnold 1984a, 242). Miss Knightly and the Ferguessons represent endurance, love, and warmth. They are very unlike Gabrielle Longstreet with her complaints, weariness, and longing for the past (Arnold 1984a, 242).

Arnold maintains that in many of Cather's earlier stories and novels, the death of a character was often accompanied by a "gesture of reconciliation toward death" made by a grieving survivor (1984b, 174). The murders of Emil and Marie in *O Pioneers!* for example, are accompanied by "the recognition that death is, in some respects, a charitable release from what could have been a lifetime of unremitting agony" (1984b, 174). In *One of Ours*, Mrs. Wheeler describes Claude's death as his merciful deliverance from "postwar disillusionment"; Professor St. Peter (*The Professor's House*) expresses a similar sentiment about Tom Outland's death in Europe (1984b, 174). In "The Joy of Nelly Deane," Margaret finds some solace in the fact that a part of Nelly still lives in her children, while in *Lucy Gayheart* Harry Gordon comes to a partial acceptance of Lucy's death by recognizing that she at least had a chance to live the best third of her life. Nothing even remotely resembling these gestures appears in "The Best Years"; instead, Cather seems to be saying that death is "just something that happens, and there is sometimes nothing to redeem the loss" (Arnold 1984b, 174).

Burgess contrasts Lesley Ferguesson with Thea Kronborg (*The Song of the Lark*) and notes that although both works are autobiographical, the two protagonists are complete opposites, perhaps representations of Cather's own divided self: "Thea Kronborg is ruddy, strong, independent, ambitious, determined, defiant, inviolable, specially gifted, and passionately committed to her art. Lesley Ferguesson is pale, weak, childlike, generous, self-sacrificing, obedient, loyal, loving, and ardently devoted to her family" (1990, 52).

Interpretations and Criticisms

This story confirms that toward the end of her life, Cather found a way to accommodate two sides of herself that had clashed from the beginning and created the ambivalence she felt toward her family. One side of her was drawn irresistibly toward her home and family, preferring nothing to spending time with them and being of help to them; the other side was terrified of being absorbed or engulfed by the family, and thus denied the separate identity necessary to create art. In Burgess's view, "these two impulses in Cather are reflected in the very different ways in which Thea and Lesley experience homecomings. For Thea, coming home reinforces her sense of difference from the other Kronborgs; for Lesley, coming home is a celebration of connectedness" (1990, 54–55). For Cather herself, choosing one impulse over the other was not an option; instead, she tried to accommodate both, as evidenced by her "seesawing back and forth across the country" most of her life, until her two lives finally came to complement each other (Burgess 1990, 55).

The family life depicted in this story is a bit sentimentalized, especially when compared with Cather's earlier portrayals, which were "more complex and strenuous. All the same, [the tale] has an endearingly wistful tenderness for childhood" (Lee 1989, 373). Wasserman, whose opinion is similar, asserts that there is a "slackening into self-indulgence" in this story (1991, 64). In her earlier Nebraska-based fiction, Cather had depicted a grim, often implacable landscape, but here she has inserted simple "calendar scenes, . . . and the landscape feels dimmed into an idea" (Wasserman 1991, 64–65). Cather, however, may be trying to remind us of something more profound. Miss Knightly's story about the little Scottish girl is, perhaps, Cather herself, reminding the reader that "without those who, by a gift, see beneath simple figures into other forces . . . , personal memory, however loving, would dim into impotence" (Wasserman 1991, 65).

Stouck argues that one of the most important achievements of this story is that the "feeling of love and accord imaginatively achieved between mother and daughter is here consummated. Instead of writing a daughter's eulogy for her dead mother, Miss Cather reverses the situation and lets the mother speak words of love for her lost daughter" (1975, 237).

Murphy believes this story contains a religious theme—God's grace is shown through the children gathering the family together. The Christmas Eve scene is a testimony to the story's function as a "parable of grace": Hector acknowledges Lesley's kindness in her gift of an overcoat and vows to reciprocate as soon as he has become successful (1984, 15). When he thinks about Christ's birth, he ponders whether or not the angels celebrate the anniversary, and he remembers the picture of angels around the three crosses at Golgotha that hung in Lesley's bedroom: "The joyful family feast is thus transformed into its harsh outcome, that of Christ shedding blood, just as the

Ferguessons' perfect happiness is shattered by Lesley's death" (Murphy 1984, 15). In future years, the Ferguesson brothers make pilgrimages to Lesley's grave, confirming that she keeps them together in unity as she did when she was alive—just as Christ did for his followers (Murphy 1984, 15).

Thurin's reading is diametrically opposed to Murphy's: "The names given to the Ferguesson boys—Homer, Hector, Vincent, and Bryan—hardly suggest a preoccupation with the Christian faith," and although Cather mentions that Mr. Ferguesson attends church, the strong emphasis is on his political meetings. Twenty years after Lesley's death, her family honors and remembers her, but they do not seem to hope to see her again in heaven (1990, 356–57). Furthermore, Lesley is closely identified with Proserpine—a dead girl who lives on in the earth lives in the memories of her loved ones (Thurin 1990, 356–58, 359). Daiches also notices the Proserpine connection: "Like Ántonia, [Lesley] is a rustic goddess, but not an Earth Mother, not Ceres, but rather Proserpine. . . . She is the symbol of all the lost innocence that to Willa Cather in her last years seemed to have vanished from the earth, and the perfect affection which united the family gathered around her was similarly bathed in the glory of a lost world" (1962, 171). Unlike Thurin, however, Daiches does draw a slight correspondence between the story and the Judeo-Christian creation myth: twenty years after Lesley's death, the family, "rich, conventional, and uncomfortable, represents, one might almost say, man after the Fall, [while] the earlier scenes had a prelapsarian quality about them" (1962, 171).

Works Cited

Arnold, Marilyn. 1984a. "Cather's Last Three Stories: A Testament of Life and Endurance." *Great Plains Quarterly* 4:238–44.

———. 1984b. *Willa Cather's Short Fiction*. Athens: Ohio University Press.

Burgess, Cheryll. 1990. "Willa Cather's Homecomings: A Meeting of Selves." In *Willa Cather and the Family, Community and History: The BYU Symposium.* Ed. John J. Murphy. Provo, Utah: Brigham Young University, 49–55.

Cather, Willa. 1948. "The Best Years." In *The Old Beauty and Others*. New York: Knopf, 75–138.

———. 1956. "The Best Years." In *Five Stories*. New York: Vintage Books, 112–48.

———. 1976. "The Best Years." In *The Old Beauty and Others*. New York: Vintage Books, 141–66.

———. 1992. "The Best Years." In *Cather: Stories, Poems, and Other Writings*. New York: Literary Classics of the United States, 728–57.

Daiches, David. [1951] 1962. *Willa Cather: A Critical Introduction*. Ithaca, NY: Cornell University Press; London: Oxford University Press. Reprint. New York: Collier.

Faulkner, Virginia, ed. [1965] 1970. *Willa Cather's Collected Short Fiction, 1892–1912*. Lincoln: University of Nebraska Press. Reprint. Lincoln: University of Nebraska Press.

Lee, Hermione. 1989. *Willa Cather: Double Lives*. New York: Pantheon.

Lewis, Edith. 1953. *Willa Cather Living*. New York: Knopf.

Murphy, John. 1984. "Willa Cather's Children of Grace." *Willa Cather Pioneer Memorial Newsletter* 28:13–15.

O'Brien, Sharon. 1987. *Willa Cather: The Emerging Voice*. New York: Oxford University Press.

Robinson, Phyllis C. 1983. *Willa: The Life of Willa Cather*. Garden City, NY: Doubleday.

Stouck, David. 1975. *Willa Cather's Imagination*. Lincoln: University of Nebraska Press.

Thurin, Erik Ingvar. 1990. *The Humanization of Willa Cather: Classicism in an American Classic*. Lund, Sweden: Lund University Press.

Wasserman, Loretta. 1991. *Willa Cather: A Study of the Short Fiction*. Boston: Twayne.

Woodress, James. 1987. *Willa Cather: A Literary Life*. Lincoln: University of Nebraska Press.

The Bohemian Girl

Publication History

This story was first published under the name Willa Sibert Cather in the August 1912 issue of *McClure's* (39:420–43). It was reprinted in 1965 by the University of Nebraska Press in *Willa Cather's Collected Short Fiction, 1892–1912* and in 1992 by Literary Classics of the United States in *Cather: Stories, Poems, and Other Writings*, a volume in The Library of America series.

Circumstances of Composition, Sources, and Influences

In October 1911, Cather took a leave of absence from her job at *McClure's* magazine in New York City and with her friend Isabelle McClung spent three months in Cherry Valley, New York—the Finger Lakes region. While there, she revised her first novel, *Alexander's Bridge*, and wrote "The Bohemian Girl." All Cather authorities agree that these three months were perhaps the most important in all of Cather's career, for it was then that she made the break from journalism that was necessary if she were to devote herself fully to writing fiction. Further, the support of her dear friend contributed to Cather's creative process. Isabelle knew exactly what kind of space her friend needed in order to write, and it was she who selected the house they finally rented (Woodress 1984, 86). (For a discussion of the enormous positive influence of Isabelle McClung on Cather's creativity see the "Circumstances of Composition, Sources, and Influences" section in the chapter "A Wagner Matinée.")

Sometime in early 1912, Cather officially resigned from *McClure's*, which was then being managed by Cameron Mackenzie, son-in-law of the magazine's publisher, S. S. McClure. In February of that year, Cather met Mackenzie for lunch in New York. When he asked her if she had any new work to show him from her vacation, she replied that she did have a new long story, but that it was perhaps a bit highbrow for *McClure's*. She was referring to "The Bohemian Girl," and Mackenzie convinced her to let him read it. When she met with him the next day, he offered her the amazing sum of $750 for it. Knowing that *McClure's* never paid more than $500 for a short story, Cather refused his offer and insisted he pay her only that sum. Mackenzie relented, but made her promise to accept more money next time (Woodress 1987, 226).

As is typical in Cather's work, this story has its source partly in the author's own life and partly in other works of art. Brown explains that Clara's depression and sense of hopelessness in living on the Divide may be traced to a feeling Cather reported to her friend Elizabeth Shepley Sergeant at about the time she wrote the story, that whenever she returned to Red Cloud to visit her family, she was plagued by the irrational fear that she would die there. At the same time, however, a much more positive attitude about the Divide, expressed in the story by Nils Ericson, also accurately reflects Cather's feelings: the grandmothers' insistent praise irritates Clara, but Nils points out to her that when she looks back on the old ladies from foreign shores, she will appreciate them much more than she can imagine (1964, 163–64). Nils's opinion provides the "first strong evidence that the years in Pittsburgh, Boston, and New York, the travels in Europe, the association with artists and cultivated persons were qualifying Willa Cather for the profound aesthetic realizations of Nebraska which she was now on the eve of making" (Brown 1964, 164–65). Further, Nils's return to the Divide mirrors almost exactly Cather's own return (Gerber 1975, 57). Cather herself admits that the story was closely tied to her own life when she asserts that until "The Bohemian

Girl," she "had been trying to sing a song that did not lie in [her] voice" (Bennett 1961, 199).

Cather drew primarily from at least three artistic sources for this story. One is *Madame Bovary*: the account of the supper at the Ericson barn raising recalls, in its profusion of details, the wedding chapter in Flaubert's novel (Brown [1953] 1964, 164). Another, according to Giannone, is *The Bohemian Girl*, a nineteenth-century romantic opera by Michael Balfe, from which Cather borrowed her title and perhaps a bit of the story line (1968, 51). Giannone goes on to explain that in the opera, a Bohemian girl, the daughter of the Austrian Count Arnheim, is being attacked by a stag when she is rescued by Thaddeus, a Polish exile trying to escape the Austrian army and hiding himself in a band of gypsies. Eventually Thaddeus kidnaps the girl, Arline. Twelve years later, after Arline has fallen in love with Thaddeus and the gypsy life, her father confronts her once again and "restores her to her high rank," but she longs for Thaddeus, who, at great personal risk, seeks her out (1968, 55–56). Impressed by Thaddeus's courage, the Count gives the young lovers his blessing, and they run away together to live the gypsy life. Cather also included some of the music from this opera in her story: the song "I Dreamt that I Dwelt in Marble Halls" is actually "The Gypsy Girl's Dream" from the opera; "When Other Lips and Other Hearts," the song Nils plays when Joe requests Bohemian songs, is Thaddeus's sad goodbye to Arline, who will marry someone else; Clara's song, "The Heart Bowed Down," is actually the father's expression of grief for his lost daughter (Giannone 1968, 55–56). Woodress points out that another possible source for the story is Keats's "The Eve of St. Agnes" in which Porphyro steals his love, Madeline, from her family's castle and elopes with her (Woodress 1987, 227).

Relationship to Other Cather Works

According to Levy, this story celebrates "female biological identity and cultural memory as the forces that directly create a new, vital civilization"; as such, it prefigures other Cather works featuring a "nurturing, conserving mother" (1990, 163–64). Grandmother Ericson is linked to Mrs. Kronborg (*The Song of the Lark*), to Ántonia Shimerda (*My Ántonia*), Cécile Auclair (*Shadows on the Rock*), Old Mrs. Harris ("Old Mrs. Harris"), and to Alexandra Bergson (*O Pioneers!*) (Levy 1990, 164). They are all "vital, calm, guardians of 'our ways,' sensuous, stubborn, unimaginative, self-satisfied, industrious, and unconventional in matters of fashion" (Levy 1990, 164). The community and the land are the sources of their strength and of their ability to withstand the changes brought by the modern world. Clara is one of Cather's passionate women, and may therefore be grouped with Marie Shabata (*O Pioneers!*), Myra

Henshawe (*My Mortal Enemy*), and Lucy Gayheart (*Lucy Gayheart*) (Levy 1990, 164–65).

Bennett refers to Old Mrs. Ericson as "a female forerunner of Nat Wheeler in *One of Ours*; both are continually running about the county in an automobile tending to everyone else's business, [and both] represent forces which drive the most sensitive son away to Europe" (1982, 43). Olena Yensen, too, is connected to other Cather works, both earlier and later (Bennett 1982, 43). (For a discussion of this character as she appears in several Cather works, see "Relationship to Other Cather Works" for "On the Divide.")

Stouck maintains that this story is similar in structure to both *O Pioneers!* and "Eric Hermannson's Soul." All three combine a romance between a Scandinavian man and a vivacious woman with a passion for the land, especially for the prairie (1975, 20). Wasserman, too, pairs this story with "Eric Hermannson's Soul," arguing that the Norwegian immigrants who made up the congregation at Asa Skinner's revivals in "Eric Hermannson's Soul" have become the wealthy Ericson family of "The Bohemian Girl." Both pieces sound a bit like the popular journalism of the time, and both are overwritten (1991, 42, 44). Woodress agrees with Stouck that the relationship between Nils and Clara foreshadows the one shared by Emil and Marie in *O Pioneers!* Further, Nils's grasping, materialistic brothers become Alexandra Bergson's brothers in *O Pioneers!* eventually evolving into characters like the despicable Ivy Peters of *A Lost Lady*. Mrs. Ericson, on the other hand, becomes Alexandra Bergson herself (1987, 229).

Arnold agrees that the association between Clara Vavrika Ericson and Marie Shabata is intimate but points out that Clara may also be paired with Nelly of "The Joy of Nelly Deane" Both women marry men who are unable to appreciate them, who in fact resent them (1984, 86–87). Thurin compares Clara with Margie Van Dyke in Cather's "The Treasure of Far Island" in that Clara's internal resistance to and simultaneous desire for Nils resembles the "opposition of Aphrodite and Artemis" as does Margie's relationship with Douglass Burnham (1990, 155–56). Rosowski establishes correspondences between Johanna Vavrika and Lydia (*My Mortal Enemy*), the three guardians in "The Joy of Nelly Deane," and Mrs. Anderson in *The Song of the Lark*; all are examples of women who use others for their own purposes (1986, 147).

Interpretations and Criticisms

In this story Cather describes the land as both seductive and suffocating. Certainly it has been suffocating to Olaf Ericson, a man like the one in the gospel who builds a bigger barn for his enormous harvest and loses his soul in the process; Mrs. Ericson, too, has become crassly materialistic (Schneider 1967, 88). Through these characters, Cather is criticizing the second-generation pioneer "whose values represent a complete denial of the creative spirit, whose attitudes mark the resistance to that which does not have immediate utility," and who insist upon their own aggrandizement (Bloom and Bloom 1962, 10, 54). Nevertheless, this story signals Cather's return to her own roots for the material of her fiction. Despite its largely negative portraits of the West, "The Bohemian Girl" does allow the reader to appreciate the pioneer settlers of Nebraska from a distance: Cather needed to escape them in order to appreciate them (Bradford 1955, 540).

In Rosowski's opinion, Cather juxtaposes two worlds in this story: Nils's mother's world represents a reality that new ideas have not altered. Another world—that of imagination and ideas—represents salvation. This second world may be reached either by escaping from the first or by recognizing the "imaginative possibility within it" (1986, 39). The latter strategy is denied to Clara and Nils because they cannot be together in the place where Clara's husband lives. Clara's entry into the dream world of escape is symbolized in part by her ever-changing clothing: her black dress and riding costume reflect the austere life of her Nebraska marriage, while her white clothes signify a mellowing. Each successive scene moves the lovers gradually from the first world to the second (Rosowski 1986, 39–40).

Wasserman contends that Cather is making a conscious distinction between the West as a ravishing landscape and the West as mundane and narrow society. Only a handful of admirable people are able to appreciate the land without possessing it. Clara is one example: the land itself—not family or greed—has a hold on her (1991, 46). Mrs. Ericson, on the other hand, represents just the opposite. She is in league with the other materialists that Nils and Clara are fighting against. She does not love the land but merely wants to own it. Her primary fear is that Nils's reappearance will somehow cost her money (Arnold 1984, 89).

O'Brien connects this story to Cather's own reaction to her flight from the Nebraska of her past, and "Clara's response to Nils reflects Cather's response to the creative power she sensed was within her" (1987, 396). Arnold, too, believes that in some ways Clara is the younger Cather herself, who desperately desired both to leave Nebraska and to stay there. Nils represents a version of the older Cather, who loved to return for a visit, but always recognized the importance of leaving again (1984, 88). Lee's reading is similar: Cather's own ambivalence about Nebraska is seen in Clara's conflict between the earth and the man she loves; the power of the land must be resisted, escaped because the alternative allows the land to "metamorphose its inhabitants into passive parts of itself. . . . Marks, traces, shapes, have to be made, or the landscape will unmake all human life and turn it back to void and formlessness, like a genesis in reverse" (1989, 103).

Levy disagrees with these interpretations, maintaining that if Cather had identified herself with Clara, she would have made that character into a heroine, not just a female protagonist, but Clara is emphatically not a heroine—she "despises the housewifely arts, absents herself from the woman's community, spites her husband and his dour family to amuse herself, and exploits the labor of her simple aunt" (1990, 164). Although Clara is certainly not evil, her intensity and passion are destructive; further, fleeing into romantic love is always portrayed as a negative act in Cather's other works, and there is no evidence to suggest that this story is an exception. Cather would not have approved of any part of Nils and Clara's behavior: Nils carries off his brother's wife, Clara betrays her past and the land, and both choose immediate gratification over duty. This behavior is unacceptable to Cather. In fact, rather than portraying Cather's faith in her own "female artistry, this story suggests that she had yet to find the rationale for her own leave-taking from women's roles and from her own past, and may in fact have doubted the morality of it" (Levy 1990, 164–65). Cather's portraits of women involved in domestic work are always positive. These are the women who "provide inspiration for an American writing which can be at once heroic and female" (Lee 1989, 5). Clara can hardly be placed in this class, and thus it is unlikely that Cather holds an approving view of her.

Slote suggests that the story contains a number of gods and goddesses in human form. Clara, for example, "suggests Diana—the huntress riding at night, uneasy in domesticity, sitting in a white dress with a black cat at her feet. Clara's father suggests Bacchus—convivial, drinking rare wine, keeping a tavern" (1966, 98, 101). Many Cather specialists have noted Nils's resemblance to Pan, with his flute—another of Cather's many classical references (Thurin 1990, 155). Giannone goes further, pointing out that Cather may have had a purpose for including the flute other than its association with Pan: "The history of the flute . . . invariably connects the instrument with regeneration. Flutes are phallic. . . . [Thus,] in working out the strangely magnetic force of Nils, which can break the root-tight grip the earth has on Clara, Cather shows how Nils's flute-playing sensitizes Clara to his dominating vigor" (1968, 54).

Stouck points out that the romance between Nils and Clara contrasts sharply with the simple pioneer life, and it is "conducted in a spirit of irony and sophistication" (1975, 19). The story is also a pastoral inasmuch as Nils comes back from Europe to the countryside of his youth, and a reawakening of memories, scenes that create an "epic backdrop" against which the ironic romance is played out (Stouck 1975, 19–20). The affair itself is remarkable for its association of pleasure and pain, a pattern that is most discernible in the scene where Nils finally convinces Clara to escape with him, a scene "presented in an image of male sexuality that culminates in the motif of erotic pain," where Nils and his passion are compared to a knife and its sheath (Stouck 1975, 20–21). Ryder sees this encounter as another reference to classical myth—that of Pan's seduction of the moon goddess Selene in the woods. Clara is "psychologically raped" in a similar setting, a moonlit field near a straw stack (1990, 90).

Most critics agree that the scene inside Olaf's barn is very like a Dutch painting. Cather makes this particular display uniquely hers, however. It is a scene that is "straining against domesticity, the trademark of genre painting, and toward the heroic," with the heaps of food and the large, heroic women, whose "Herculean labors" have produced it (Rosowski 1986, 42). Despite the charming nature of this picture, however, this and other pastoral scenes in the story can be deceptive. The country is changing. As Lee points out, Mrs. Ericson owns both a telephone and a car, and in describing each tableau in such detail, "Cather is catching the moment of transition which perpetually fascinates her: Not yet homogenized into Americanness, each of the distinct immigrant groups has survived in the alien landscape by persisting in its cultural identity," but before long, these groups will be forced either to assimilate into their new culture or to return to Europe (1989, 102).

Works Cited

Arnold, Marilyn. 1984. *Willa Cather's Short Fiction*. Athens: Ohio University Press.

Bennett, Mildred R. 1961. *The World of Willa Cather*. Lincoln: University of Nebraska Press.

———. 1982. "Willa Cather's Bodies for Ghosts." *Western American Literature* 17:39–52.

Bloom, Edward A., and Lillian D. Bloom. 1962. *Willa Cather's Gift of Sympathy*. Carbondale: Southern Illinois University Press.

Bradford, Curtis. 1955. "Willa Cather's Uncollected Short Stories." *American Literature* 26:537–51.

Brown, E. K. Completed by Leon Edel. [1953] 1964. *Willa Cather: A Critical Biography*. New York: Knopf.

Cather, Willa. [1965] 1970. "The Bohemian Girl." In *Willa Cather's Collected Short Fiction, 1892–1912*. Ed. Virginia Faulkner. Lincoln: University of Nebraska Press, 3–41.

———. 1992. In *Cather: Stories, Poems, and Other Writings*. New York: Literary Classics of the United States, 89–132.

Faulkner, Virginia, ed. [1965] 1970. *Willa Cather's Collected Short Fiction, 1892–1912*. Lincoln: University of Nebraska Press. Reprint. Lincoln: University of Nebraska Press.

Gerber, Philip. 1975. *Willa Cather*. Boston: Twayne.

Giannone, Richard. 1968. *Music in Willa Cather's Fiction*. Lincoln: University of Nebraska Press.

Lee, Hermione. 1989. *Willa Cather: Double Lives*. New York: Pantheon.

Levy, Helen Fiddyment. 1990. "Mothers and Daughters in 'The Bohemian Girl' and *The Song of the Lark.*" In *Willa Cather and the Family, Community and History: The BYU Symposium*. Ed. John J. Murphy. Provo, Utah: Brigham Young University, 163–67.

O'Brien, Sharon. 1987. *Willa Cather: The Emerging Voice*. New York: Oxford University Press.

Rosowski, Susan J. 1986. *The Voyage Perilous: Willa Cather's Romanticism*. Lincoln: University of Nebraska Press.

Ryder, Mary Ruth. 1990. *Willa Cather and Classical Myth*. Lewiston, NY: Edwin Mellen Press.

Schneider, Sister Lucy 1967. "Willa Cather's Early Stories in the Light of Her 'Land-Philosophy.'" *Midwest Quarterly* 9:75–94.

Slote, Bernice, ed. 1966. *The Kingdom of Art*. Lincoln: University of Nebraska Press.

Stouck, David. 1975. *Willa Cather's Imagination*. Lincoln: University of Nebraska Press.

Thurin, Erik Ingvar. 1990. *The Humanization of Willa Cather: Classicism in an American Classic*. Lund, Sweden: Lund University Press.

Wasserman, Loretta. 1991. *Willa Cather: A Study of the Short Fiction*. Boston: Twayne.

Woodress, James. 1984. "Cather and Her Friends." In *Critical Essays on Willa Cather*. Ed. John J. Murphy. Boston: G.K. Hall, 81–95.

———. 1987. *Willa Cather: A Literary Life*. Lincoln: University of Nebraska Press.

The Bookkeeper's Wife

Publication History

This story was first published under the name Willa Sibert Cather in the May 1916 issue of *Century* (92:51–59) (Faulkner 1970, 597). It was reprinted in 1973 by the University of Nebraska Press in *Uncle Valentine and Other Stories: Willa Cather's Uncollected Short Fiction, 1915–1929* and in 1992 by Literary Classics of the United States in *Cather: Stories, Poems, and Other Writings*, a volume in the Library of America series.

Circumstances of Composition, Sources, and Influences

The story was the second Cather wrote after she had formally resigned her post as editor of *McClure's* magazine in 1912. However, in the three years between her resignation and the first short story she wrote thereafter, "Consequences," Cather produced three novels, *Alexander's Bridge* (1912), *O Pioneers!* (1913), and *The Song of the Lark* (1915). "The Bookkeeper's Wife" appeared one month after Cather's dearest friend, Isabelle McClung, married the violinist Jan Hambourg, an event that devastated Cather, who interpreted it as Isabelle's abandonment of her. Around this time, too, Cather signed on with the literary agent Paul Reynolds, who from then on became responsible for placing her short stories and arranging the serialization of her longer works (O'Brien 1987, 1309).

Slote detects the possible influence of Bunyan's *Pilgrim's Progress* on the story, which resembles a parable "in names like Stella (the star). . . . Percy is saved from disgrace by Oliver (the peacemaker) Remsen" (1973, xi). The presence of Melville's famous scrivener, Bartleby, is also just barely perceptible in Percy's total absorption in his books, although Percy himself has none of the mystery Melville's Bartleby has (Slote 1973, xi).

Relationship to Other Cather Works

The stories collected in *Uncle Valentine and Other Stories* are grouped under two headings—"New York Stories," of which there are five, and "Pittsburgh Stories," of which there are two. As one of the "New York Stories," "The Bookkeeper's Wife" is most often linked with the others under that heading—"Consequences," "Ardessa," "Her Boss," and "Coming, Eden Bower!" In LaSalle's opinion, all five are interesting as portraits of typical women's jobs at the time, but they are also the typical fare of the popular magazines that sold so well. Cather had learned how to appeal to popular readers (LaSalle 1987, 169).

Ryder draws parallels between Stella in this story and characters in other works—such as Myra Henshawe (*My Mortal Enemy*), Bertha Gray ("The Willing Muse"), Virginia ("The Profile"), and Marian Forrester (*A Lost Lady*)—who show a "callousness or viciousness [that] stems directly from disappointed passion" (1990, 240). In a similar kind of grouping, Arnold places the story with others that describe a sensitive man married to a cold wife, like Claude Wheeler in *One of Ours*, Jim Burden in *My Ántonia*, Doctor Archie in *A Song of the Lark*, and Valentine Ramsey in "Uncle Valentine." At the same time, however, the story resembles "The Profile" and "The Willing Muse" in which Cather displays her unwillingness to blame the man's sorrow on his wife (1984, 102).

Stouck pairs this story with "Ardessa," since both stories are drawn from Cather's actual New York life and both concern office workers—those who are little more than cogs in the city's great wheels, but who nonetheless suffer from the random nature of fate (1975, 78).

Interpretations and Criticisms

This story has elicited very little critical comment, probably because many Cather scholars view it simply as one of the stories Cather used to pay the rent while she was devoting the majority of her time and energy to writing novels. Stouck asserts that the interest of the story is almost entirely biographical (Stouck 1975, 78). Bradford labels it "a dry but telling" tale that portrays a typical "new woman," grasping and stony-hearted (1955, 546).

Arnold believes the story is not so simple, that it achieves at least a degree of complexity from the fact that Cather refuses to make the woman a mere scapegoat: when Stella demands that Percy tell her why he chose her in the first place, she is implying that he is as much to blame for their unfortunate marriage as she is. After all, he knew what both she and her mother were before the marriage, and he was aware that he did not make enough money for them; nevertheless, he insisted on possessing Stella, "the dazzling princess the other fellows dated for a whirl"; he won her hand by lying about his income and stealing from his company (1984, 102).

Slote notes that the "eviscerated Mission clock in his empty house is Percy's symbol: a hollow man, indeed, and years before Eliot's" (1973, xi). Stella is an even worse character, "capable, beautiful, and cold. She is one of the deadliest women—and wives—in Cather's fiction, slipping easily from one alliance to another, counting position and pleasure worth the sacrifice of any other life" (Slote 1973, xii).

Works Cited

Arnold, Marilyn. 1984. *Willa Cather's Short Fiction*. Athens: Ohio University Press.

Bradford, Curtis. 1955. "Willa Cather's Uncollected Short Stories." *American Literature* 26:537–51.

Cather, Willa. 1973. "The Bookkeeper's Wife." In *Uncle Valentine and Other Stories: Willa Cather's Uncollected Short Fiction, 1915–1929*. Ed. Bernice Slote. Lincoln: University of Nebraska Press, 85–97.

———. 1992. "The Bookkeeper's Wife." In *Cather: Stories, Poems, and Other Writings*. New York: Literary Classics of the United States, 154–66.

Faulkner, Virginia, ed. [1965] 1970. *Willa Cather's Collected Short Fiction, 1892–1912*. Lincoln: University of Nebraska Press. Reprint. Lincoln: University of Nebraska Press.

LaSalle, Peter. 1987. Review of *Uncle Valentine and Other Stories,* by Willa Cather. *Studies in Short Fiction* 24:169–70.

O'Brien, Sharon. 1987. Chronology to *Cather: Early Novels & Stories,* by Willa Cather. New York: Literary Classics of the United States.

Ryder, Mary Ruth. 1990. *Willa Cather and Classical Myth.* Lewiston, NY: Edwin Mellen Press.

Slote, Bernice. 1973. Introduction to *Uncle Valentine and Other Stories: Willa Cather's Uncollected Short Fiction, 1915–1929,* by Willa Cather. Lincoln: University of Nebraska Press.

Stouck, David. 1975. *Willa Cather's Imagination.* Lincoln: University of Nebraska Press.

The Burglar's Christmas

Publication History

This story was first published in December 1896 in *Home Monthly* (6:8-10) under the name Elizabeth L. Seymour (Faulkner 1970, 592). Cather very likely used the pseudonym to disassociate herself from a story she did not think was up to her standards. It appeared in the same issue as another Cather story, "The Strategy of the Were-Wolf Dog"(Lathrop 38). It was reprinted in 1965 by the University of Nebraska Press in *Willa Cather's Collected Short Fiction, 1892-1912.*

Circumstances of Composition, Sources, and Influences

This story is a seasonal piece of the type for which magazines like *Home Monthly* were famous. According to Arnold, the piece stands in the tradition of folk literature, "one of those Christmas stories of marvelous chance in which the deserving poverty-stricken lad is discovered by large-hearted persons willing and able to give him new life and new hope" (1984, 177n). One obvious model for the plot is the story of the prodigal son; in fact, Woodress effectively dismisses the piece by calling it "a feeble version of the prodigal-son story laid in Chicago" (1970, 82).

Stories centering on the mother–child relationship were common in the popular fiction of the time. Given the Victorian exaltation of motherhood, Cather's use of the prodigal son motif, in which she replaces father with mother, was an effective way to exploit popular sentiment and to appeal to the female readership of *Home Monthly* (O'Brien 1987, 52). Nevertheless, as O'Brien points out, the story can be said to have its roots in Cather's own life. Certain links between the author and her protagonist are undeniable: the name William and the nickname Willie are the same ones Cather adopted when she was young. William's other aliases reflect the several names under which Cather chose to write. Furthermore, William is about Cather's age and pursued the same path Cather did: dissatisfied and ambitious, he set out into the world and became a journalist (1987, 52). The story also reflects Cather's own fear of professional failure: William, a magazine editor, fails in the very area where Cather hoped for success (O'Brien 1987, 231).

O'Brien establishes connections between the mother–son conflict and resolution in this story and "the conflicting strains in Cather's bond with her mother, who . . . sought [both] to confine and to expand her daughter's imagination" (1987, 45). Some of Cather's memories of her childhood suggest that she rejected the image of Southern lady that her mother wanted her to adopt, signifying her need for self-definition and autonomy. At the same time, however, her desire for fusion or reconciliation with her mother is obvious in other recollections. This conflict found its way into much of Cather's fiction, including "The Burglar's Christmas" (O'Brien 1987, 42-48).

According to O'Brien, much earlier evidence of Cather's interest in the dynamics of mother–child relationships can be found in her 1891 college essay on *Hamlet*: Cather's "response to *Hamlet* was . . . filtered through her preoccupation with the mother's power to reduce a child . . . to silence" (1987, 207). Hamlet's discovery of Gertrude's guilt transformed what might have been a creative impulse into a thirst for revenge that overpowered every other motivation (O'Brien 1987, 207).

Relationship to Other Cather Works

O'Brien groups this story with "A Resurrection" and "On the Gulls' Road," both of which also portray selfless mothers who sacrifice everything for their children, denying almost completely their own needs (1987, 49). Other stories that focus on the mother–child bond include "The Prodigies," "Flavia and her Artists," and "The Profile"; however, instead of nurturing, self-abnegating mothers, these stories feature beautiful but cold mothers devoid of maternal affection who neglect or exploit their children (O'Brien 1987, 49).

The abandoned or lost child seeking the mother had appeared earlier as the character of Serge in "The Clemency of the Court," and both it and "A Burglar's Christmas" reveal the dangers and the attraction of going back to the mother (O'Brien 1987, 208). Other stories in which the mother–child bond is central—although hidden in some way—include "Peter," "Lou, the Prophet," and "On the Divide." Although these stories do not contain literal mother–child relationships, their central figures are seeking some "connection with a maternal presence, variously represented as a lover, a mother, a homeland, and a fertile responsive environment" (O'Brien 1987, 207).

Interpretations and Criticisms

Arnold believes the story addresses only one serious theme, the "capacity of love to reach out and embrace a lost child" (1984, 12). Woodress simply calls the story "feeble" (1970, 82). Benson judges it thoroughly formulaic (1981, 238), and Bennett excludes it entirely from her 1957 collection, *Early Stories of Willa Cather*.

Virtually the only critic who has accorded the story enough importance as part of the Cather canon to warrant serious critical analysis is Sharon O'Brien. She views the story as significant because it "reveals that the same psychodynamics arising from the mother–daughter relationship contributed to [Cather's] use of male narrators or centers of consciousness to confront maternal or erotic figures" (1984, 595). When they analyze her other fiction, many scholars focus on what they often see as Cather's troubling use of male narrators; thus, O'Brien's interpretation of "The Burglar's Christmas" may be viewed as a response to a common assumption among Cather specialists— that her "use of male narrators and centers of consciousness . . . signif[ies] her acceptance of patriarchal values or her continuing male identification," an assumption with which O'Brien disagrees (1984, 595).

O'Brien admits the story is "aesthetically crude" but also insists upon its relevance to the author's psychology and to the canon of her work: "This bizarre tale of the prodigal son . . . reveals the psychological conflicts central to the mother–daughter, not the mother–son bond" (1984, 595). When the mother declares to her son that she has known all his impulses—even lived all his life—she is actually describing the kind of connection Cather feared existed between her and her own mother. Creating a male character allowed Cather "to define ego boundaries by placing the barrier of gender between herself and the female presence that offered gratification and nurturance but also threatened to obliterate a separate identity" (O'Brien 1984, 595). Cather herself was terrified of being swallowed up in this way.

Works Cited

Arnold, Marilyn. 1984. *Willa Cather's Short Fiction*. Athens: Ohio University Press.

Benson, Peter. 1981. "Willa Cather at *Home Monthly*." *Biography* 4:227–48.

Cather, Willa. [1965] 1970. "The Burglar's Christmas." In *Willa Cather's Collected Short Fiction, 1892–1912*. Ed. Virginia Faulkner. Lincoln: University of Nebraska Press, 557–66.

Faulkner, Virginia, ed. [1965] 1970. *Willa Cather's Collected Short Fiction, 1892–1912*. Lincoln: University of Nebraska Press. Reprint. Lincoln: University of Nebraska Press.

Lathrop, Joanna. 1975. *Willa Cather: A Checklist of Her Published Writing*. Lincoln: University of Nebraska Press.

O'Brien, Sharon. 1984. "'The Thing Not Named': Willa Cather as a Lesbian Writer." *Signs: Journal of Women in Culture and Society* 9:576–99.

———. 1987. *Willa Cather: The Emerging Voice*. New York: Oxford University Press.

Woodress, James. 1970. *Willa Cather: Her Life and Art*. New York: Pegasus.

The Clemency of the Court

Publication History

This story was first published on October 26, 1893, in the University of Nebraska student journal the *Hesperian* (22:3–7) under the name W. Cather (Faulkner 1970, 591; Lathrop 1975, 117). In the spring of 1948, it was reprinted in *Prairie Schooner* (22:104–111) as part of "Willa Cather's Juvenilia," edited by James R. Shively (Faulkner 1970, 591). It was reprinted again in 1950 by the University of Nebraska Press in *Willa Cather's Campus Years* (69–79); in 1957 by Dodd, Mead in *Early Stories of Willa Cather*; and in 1965 by the University of Nebraska Press in *Willa Cather's Collected Short Fiction, 1892–1912*.

Circumstances of Composition, Sources, and Influences

This piece is one of the seven stories Cather wrote as an undergraduate at the University of Nebraska in Lincoln. The story reflects Cather's acquaintance with some Russian immigrants, whose enclave in the northwest section of Webster County, Nebraska, was relatively close to where her family lived (Bennett 1957, 36).

Bennett points out that the treatment the character Serge receives at the hands of Baba Skaldi, the Russian woman who raised him and fed him only that food her children refused to eat, is also reminiscent of that suffered by Cosette in *Les Miserables* (1957, 35). In addition, Cather was probably drawing on her reading of Turgenev, one of whose short story characters is a serf who smashes his master's head with an axe (Bennett 1957, 33). In the Turgenev story, "Old Portraits," Ivan the serf is a farmhand like Serge, who is treated badly in each place he works. The handling of the murder scenes in the Cather and Turgenev stories is very similar (Bohlke 1974, 136).

Another Turgenev serf character also finds his way into the character of Serge: in "Mumu," Turgenev creates the serf Gerasim, an enormously strong deaf-mute, who has been raised in the country and is ostracized by his neighbors because of his disabilities (Bohlke 1974, 137). Both Cather's Serge and Turgenev's Gerasim are disconcerted by the city, the latter displaying antisocial, even psychopathic behavior when he is taken to town, while Serge is so afraid of people that he hides behind his team of horses. When Gerasim loses his girlfriend to another man, he presents her with a kind of wedding gift, a red scarf he had bought for her some time before. On his way home, Gerasim finds a puppy desperately struggling to stay above the surface of the water of the Crimean Ford. He saves her, takes her home, and subsequently the two become utterly devoted to each other. Serge's relationship with his dog, Matushka, echoes this incident (Bohlke 1974, 137–38). The red silk handkerchief that Serge ties around Matushka's head before he buries the dog is one of the most obvious details pulled by Cather from the Turgenev story.

A scandal involving the Nebraska State Penitentiary at Lincoln in 1893 almost certainly supplied Cather with the material for Serge's treatment in prison. Bohlke has shown how Serge's experiences exactly parallel those of an actual Nebraska State Penitentiary prisoner named Abel Powell, as reported by the *Nebraska State Journal*. When Powell was found hanging in his cell, a coroner's jury initially ruled the death a suicide. Later it was discovered that one member of the jury had refused to sign the verdict because he believed the findings to be a cover up. Soon the newspaper received letters from two former prisoners, both of which recount specific instances of brutal, inhumane treatment suffered at the penitentiary, and a serious investigation into the events leading to Powell's death was begun (Bohlke 1974, 138–39). The vicious tongue lashing Serge receives from the guard at the beginning of Cather's story about the proper way to hoop barrels closely matches the information that came out of the investigation about Powell printed in the *Nebraska State Journal*—Powell's punishment resulted from his inadequate work hooping barrels. Further, the guard in Cather's story yells, "Damn you!" at Serge and threatens to send him to the dark cell of solitary confinement (Cather 1970, 515; Bohlke 1974, 139–40). Similarly, the second former convict wrote the *Journal* that the officers' most frequent expressions were, "Say, you damn — — you get on that work or I will send you down, God damn you" (quoted in Bohlke 1974, 140).

Bohlke reports that the most remarkable resemblance between the real tragedy at the penitentiary and Cather's fictionalized version of it is the punishment itself (1974, 141). The guards tied Serge's arms behind his back, then attached the rope to his neck so that if he allowed his arms to relax, he would choke. Cather's description shows an uncanny similarity to the following passage from a January 14, 1893, *Nebraska State Journal* article: "The prisoner's hands are handcuffed behind his back, a noose is placed around his neck and the end of the rope is drawn tightly around the handcuffs, thus bringing the hands and forearms up behind the back till the hands are nearly level with the shoulders. This position is maintained for the term of punishment except at an interval three times a day when the culprit is allowed a ration of bread and water. It is easily seen that if the muscles of the arms are relaxed the weight all comes upon the neck, tending to produce strangulation" (quoted in Bohlke 1974, 142).

Relationship to Other Cather Works

In this piece Cather uses the technique of the story within a story when the narrator relates a tale told by Baba Skaldi to her children about her brother, who had killed himself in prison by biting into one of the veins in his arm and bleeding to death. It is a device to which Cather returns often in her later fiction, such as *The Professor's House* (Bennett 1957, 36).

This story was one of the three Nebraska-based tales published in the *Hesperian*. Like "Peter" and "Lou, the Prophet," the other two stories published while Cather was a student at the University of Nebraska, this tale displays Cather's interest in the people from Europe who came to America to subdue the land (Jackson 1950, 22), who are often eventually defeated by "social, economic, or natural forces" (O'Brien 1987, 207). However, it is much darker and more frightening than the other stories—"a grisly . . . pathetic tale" (Woodress 1987, 79). Serge, the story's protagonist, is an immigrant overwhelmed by mysterious forces, becoming a murderer in an almost mechanical way. A version of this character reappears in *O Pioneers!* as Frank Shabata. However, although Serge has been unhappy all his life, Frank at least had a period of joy in his youth. That changes when he becomes aware of his failing marriage and begins to suspect his wife of something he cannot define (Bennett 1982, 42). When he discovers his wife in the orchard with another man, he murders them both in a kind of unconscious, impulsive action, in much the same trance-like way Serge commits his crime (Bennett 1982, 42). Although both characters end up in prison, Serge seems unaware that he has committed murder. Frank, on the other hand, is fully conscious of what he has done and thus is forced to live the rest of his days with the ghastly memories of his act (Bennett 1982, 42).

Cather returns to the subject of unpremeditated murder once more in *Death Comes for the Archbishop* (1927) in the incident that occurs when Ramon attends a cockfight, having entered his prize cock to fight the champion cock of Sante Fe. When Ramon's bird wins, the owner of the losing cock kills Ramon's bird, and Ramon kills the man instantly, just as Serge murders the killer of his dog (Bennett 1982, 42). Bennett points out that a similar incident occurs in *Shadows on the Rock*, when the character Bichet is hanged for stealing a couple of pots (1957, 33).

Brown finds several other elements in the story that re-emerge later in the Nebraska novels: the struggle of the troubled immigrant trying to conform to the ways of a new and largely unsympathetic country, Cather's identification with "people rooted to the land to whom confinement and city labors are intolerable," and her compassion for those, like Lou in "Lou, the Prophet," who are pressured by the community simply because their personalities are "essentially at variance with it and [have] a central core the community will never rightly value" (1964, 60–61).

Interpretations and Criticisms

Relatively few critics have commented on "The Clemency of the Court" in any depth. Generally it is viewed in much the same way as the rest of Cather's early stories: valuable as apprentice pieces that can be studied for the germs of themes and concerns that reappear in her later, mature, aesthetically successful fiction, or as clues to author's own psychology.

Schneider emphasizes the relationship of the land to liberation and fulfillment in this story, which "ranks as perhaps Willa Cather's strongest statement of the love of the land—as land—before *O Pioneers!*" (1967, 79). During Serge's imprisonment for murder, the most intense pain he suffers appears to be that of being deprived of the outdoors and of even seeing the fields that he so loved. "Serge responds to the plains and is fascinated by them because they correspond to his feeling of loneliness and symbolize a yearning for the transcendent which he feels but cannot express in words" (1967, 79).

O'Brien focuses on the "maternal subtext" of the story (1987, 207). Although she acknowledges that the piece represents "the immigrants' despairing response to the terrible Nebraska drought" and to a corrupt legal system that destroys people, O'Brien's main emphasis is on the story as a portrayal of the search for "a sustaining connection with a maternal presence," a presence that is presented in various ways throughout Cather's fiction—"as a lover, a mother, a homeland, and a fertile, responsive environment" (1987, 207). Like so many of Cather's other protagonists, Serge seeks a substitute for the maternal figures he has lost. In exile, and without his mother, "he transfers his affection to his dog, to whom he gives her name" (O'Brien 1987, 207). When the dog dies, Serge, following the same pattern, views the State as a mother who will protect him; ironically, then, "it is his mother who kills him"; in the "womb/tomb" where Serge is held and tormented, he "begins a regressive, self-destructive journey" (O'Brien 1987, 208). The guards restrict his movements so severely that he must be fed like a baby, and when he dies, he is in a fetal position (O'Brien 1987, 208). Thus, according to O'Brien, Cather has shown both the desire for and the danger of returning to the mother, or to any nurturing figure. As attractive as such a return seems to be, the result can only be death. "Serge progressively loses the power of language as he reverses the stages of human development in returning to his 'great mother'" (1987, 208). He becomes increasingly paralyzed and inarticulate, eventually able to produce only an infant's gurgling noises, and finally, like the narrators in Cather's "A Tale of the White Pyramid" and "A Night at Greenway Court," he is utterly silenced (O'Brien 1987, 208).

Works Cited

Bennett, Mildred, ed. 1957. *Early Stories of Willa Cather*. New York: Dodd, Mead.

Bennett, Mildred R. 1982. "Willa Cather's Bodies for Ghosts." *Western American Literature* 17:39–52.

Bohlke, L. Brent. 1974. "Beginnings: Willa Cather and `The Clemency of the Court.'" *Prairie Schooner* 48:133–44.

Brown, E. K. [1953] 1964. *Willa Cather: A Critical Biography*. New York: Knopf.

Cather, Willa. 1957. "The Clemency of the Court." In *Early Stories*. Ed. Mildred Bennett. New York: Dodd, Mead, 69–79.

———. [1965] 1970. "The Clemency of the Court." In *Willa Cather's Collected Short Fiction, 1892–1912*. Ed. Virginia Faulkner. Lincoln: University of Nebraska Press, 515–22.

Faulkner, Virginia, ed. [1965] 1970. *Willa Cather's Collected Short Fiction, 1892–1912*. Lincoln: University of Nebraska Press. Reprint. Lincoln: University of Nebraska Press.

Jackson, Joseph Henry. 1950. "Cather on the Campus." *San Francisco Chronicle*, 22 March, 22.

Lathrop, Joanna. 1975. *Willa Cather: A Checklist of Her Published Writing*. Lincoln: University of Nebraska Press.

O'Brien, Sharon. 1987. *Willa Cather: The Emerging Voice*. New York: Oxford University Press.

Schneider, Sister Lucy. 1967. "Willa Cather's Early Stories in the Light of Her 'Land-Philosophy.'" *Midwest Quarterly* 9:75–94.

Woodress, James. 1987. *Willa Cather: A Literary Life*. Lincoln: University of Nebraska Press.

Coming, Aphrodite!

Publication History

This story was first published under this title in Cather's second collection of short stories, *Youth and the Bright Medusa* (New York: Knopf, 1920, pp. 11–78) (Faulkner 1970, 597) under the name Willa Cather, the author's first use of this signature (Slote 1973, xvii). This collection was Cather's first volume to be published by Knopf. (For a complete explanation of the evolution of Cather's association with Knopf, see the "Publication History" section of the chapter "Scandal.") Earlier that same year, in August, an expurgated version of the story entitled "Coming, Eden Bower!" had appeared in *Smart Set* (92:3–25) under the name of Willa Sibert Cather (Slote 1973, xvii). Thus, the first version of the story was second to appear in print, having been rejected often, not because the piece was of poor quality, but because many editors were afraid of what they considered its risqué subject; both *Metropolitan* and *Century* had rejected it, the latter explaining that the story contained "too much criminal content"; the editor, Tom Smith, went on to say that "the Comstocks are in violent eruption, and the *Century* has been taking too many chances" (Woodress 1987, 315). This decision may seem like paranoia to contemporary readers, but Anthony Comstock's Society for the Suppression of Vice wielded a great deal of power in 1920 (Woodress 1987, 315). "Coming, Eden Bower!" contained several significant differences from "Coming, Aphrodite!" (Faulkner 1970, 597). Bernice Slote maintains that the version published for the English edition of *Smart Set* is "quite literally clothed for the censoring 'Comstocks' and the Watch and Warders," and that "the chief difference between the two versions is that the *Smart Set* printing has cuts in the more sexually explicit passages and variants that modify certain sensuous details." In "Coming, Aphrodite!" Don Hedger watches Eden Bower exercising nude, but in the bowdlerized "Coming, Eden Bower!" the title character's body is partially covered by a pink negligee, and the mention of specific body parts is avoided—she even refrains from looking at a mole under her arm (1973, xvii). On the contrary, in "Coming, Aphrodite!" Hedger and Bower are obviously lovers, and they leave the door that connects their apartments open, a fact that is omitted from the magazine version of the story (Slote 1973, xvii).

In spite of being compelled to sanitize the story, Cather was pleased with its acceptance. As Woodress explains, at the time, she was planning a trip to Europe, and although *Smart Set* did not pay the best rates, she needed whatever she could get. The magazine demanded two revisions: changing the title to avoid a libel suit (Aphrodite was identified with Mary Garden, who had sung the title role in Camille Erlanger's opera *Aphrodite*), and toning down the sexuality of the descriptions of Eden Bower. When *Century* had asked for similar changes, Cather had refused, so her acquiescence to *Smart Set* came as something of a surprise to her agent, Paul Reynolds. The most likely explanation is that Cather never placed much importance on magazine publications, only on the collected versions of her works, and since she needed money, she made the requested revisions. Nevertheless, a month before she was scheduled to depart for Europe, the magazine was still unsatisfied. Only after another round of changes was made did *Smart Set* pay Cather her $450 (Woodress 1987, 315–16).

The editor of *Smart Set*, H. L. Mencken, had established a relationship with Cather before he bought "Coming, Eden Bower!" for the magazine, and in an April 23, 1920, letter to Cather's friend Louise Pound, he referred to the story as "a capital novelette" (Slote 1973, xiv). Nevertheless, the *Youth and the Bright Medusa* version is the one that reappeared in volume six of the thirteen-volume library edition of Cather's work, *The Novels and Stories of Willa Cather* (Boston: Houghton Mifflin, 1937–1941, pp. 1–74) (Faulkner 1970, 598), and in a 1975 paperback edition of *Youth and the Bright Medusa* published by Vintage Books.

The *Smart Set* version ("Coming, Eden Bower!") was reprinted in 1973 by the University of Nebraska Press in *Uncle Valentine and Other Stories: Willa Cather's Uncollected Short Fiction, 1915–1929*. The *Youth and the Bright Medusa* version was reprinted in 1992 by Literary Classics of the United States in *Cather: Stories, Poems, and Other Writings*, a volume in the Library of America series.

Circumstances of Composition, Sources, and Influences

Although Cather wrote this story in 1920, she drew heavily on her trip to the Southwest in 1912 for one part of the tale. She had arrived in Winslow,

Arizona, in April of that year to visit her brother Douglass, who was working there on the Santa Fe railroad. While her brother was working, Cather's near-constant companion was a young Mexican man named Julio, who acted as something of a tour guide, showing Cather the Painted Desert and acquainting her with various Mexican songs and dances. It was Julio who told her "the grimly erotic story of an Aztec Cleopatra," which she inserted into "Coming, Aphrodite!" as "The Forty Lovers of the Queen" eight years later (O'Brien 1987, 404).

Cather's memories of her early years in New York when she worked on *McClure's* magazine also figure largely in the story's setting. (For a discussion of Cather's move to New York to work on S. S. McClure's magazine, see the "Circumstances of Composition, Sources, and Influences" section in the chapters "The Sculptor's Funeral" and "The Namesake.") In those days she roomed in a building near Washington Square, and her recollections of "the dingy apartment house, the life in the public square, the Brevoort Hotel, the scenes on lower Fifth Avenue, [and] Coney Island" are vivid, and they serve her well in this story (Woodress 1987, 313).

The protagonist's name, Eden Bower, may be calculated to put readers in mind of Eve in the Garden of Eden, but in fact it comes from Dante Gabriel Rossetti's poem "Eden Bower," and is therefore actually "an allusion to Lilith, the beautiful witch who according to a post-biblical legend was Adam's first wife . . . [and] plays a subsidiary role in the story as a reminder of the ambiguous and dangerous nature of the power of Aphrodite" (Thurin 1990, 224). Another unarguable source for the story is the then-famous singer, Mary Garden, who was very much on Cather's mind at the time. Another probable source was an adaptation of Louÿs's novel *Aphrodite* that had been performed on the New York stage in December 1919 (Thurin 1990, 225–26).

Petry argues that the idea for Don Hedger's dog, Caesar, may have originated in a Mary E. Wilkins Freeman short story "A New England Nun," in which the protagonist, Louisa Ellis, also has a dog named Caesar. Like Hedger, Louisa lives a solitary but contented life, and, also like Hedger, Louisa begins to share characteristics with her dog. In Freeman's story, as in Cather's, the protagonist's life is thrown into turmoil by the reappearance of her long absent fiancé, but contentment returns when the engagement is broken. The dog in Freeman's story symbolizes "the turmoil in Louisa's subconscious, in much the same way that Cather uses Caesar to suggest the degree to which Hedger is compromising his artistic integrity" (1986, 311n).

Relationship to Other Cather Works

Cather included this story in her second collection of short fiction, *Youth and the Bright Medusa*, and thus it is closely related to the other stories in that collection. (For a full discussion of the shared characteristics of the stories in

Youth and the Bright Medusa, see the "Relationship to Other Cather Works" section in the chapter "The Diamond Mine.")

Chaliff argues that Cather's belief in childhood as a time of innocence and vitality, and puberty as the beginning of decay and failure, is obvious in this story, as it is in *The Professor's House* and *O Pioneers!* In both "Coming, Aphrodite!" and *O Pioneers!* Cather juxtaposes "ancient myth and modern tale to make a point about the dangers implicit in mature heterosexual love" (1978, 66). She uses the story-within-a-story technique effectively in both novels, in "The Enchanted Bluff," and in "Coming, Aphrodite!" (Chaliff 1978, 67).

Arnold views the character Eden Bower as more complex than most of Cather's other heroines—"she is elemental, . . . sexual, and she is an artist"; nevertheless, she shares with Alexandra Bergson (*O, Pioneers!*), Thea Kronborg (*The Song of the Lark*), Ántonia Shimerda (*My Ántonia*), and Lucy Gayheart (*Lucy Gayheart*) a strong affinity with the "earth's natural rhythms," and although these others are not specifically referred to as goddesses of love, they are far from "immune to romantic passion" (1984b, 113). In Alexandra's case, this passion is represented by the man who, in her dream, carries her off in his arms. Ántonia's sensuality is mirrored in "her generous fertility," Thea's in her love for Fred Ottenburg, and Lucy's in her love for Clement Sebastian (Arnold 1984b, 113). Further, like the others, "Eden is associated with cosmic principles of light—stars, moon, and sun. . . . Like Lucy Gayheart and Alexandra, she is given to contemplating the stars, and like Lucy and Thea, she is associated with light and the moon" (Arnold 1984b, 116). Unlike the love interests of the others, however, Don Hedger's relationship with Eden is clearly sexual (Arnold 1984b, 114). There are other differences as well. The mutual attraction of Don Hedger and Eden Bower in many ways does not resemble the "shallow sentimentality of the nostalgic lover" in the early story "On the Gulls' Road," nor does it recall the kind of platonic love shared by Carl Linstrum and Alexandra Bergson, nor the "ethereal sexless love of Jim Burden for Ántonia, [nor] . . . the clandestine skirmishes of Marian Forrester" (Arnold 1984a, 251–52). Although a powerful sexual attraction is unquestionably a part of the relationship between Emil Bergson and Marie Shabata (*O Pioneers!*) and between Nils Ericson and Clara Vavrika ("The Bohemian Girl"), the forces that pull them together are not nearly as strong as those working on Don Hedger and Eden Bower (Arnold 1984a, 251–52).

O'Brien argues that in this story Cather is once again associating sexual and/or creative expression with punishment as she had in the early story "The Elopement of Allen Poole." In "Coming, Aphrodite!" the punishment is much more "brutally signified" than in the early tale; few penalties could be more ruthless than the "castration, muting, and [eventual] death" suffered by the princess's Captive in "The Forty Lovers of the Queen," the tale Don Hedger relates to Eden Bower (1987, 204).

Interpretations and Criticisms

Many have judged this story the best in the collection *Youth and the Bright Medusa*. One early reviewer sees it as an optimistic tale in which everyone wins: "The woman wins success with her hard ideal of it. Her very desires are utilized to an end—and in the end . . . her name blazons in electric lights. The man wins by being . . . original" (Field 1921, 73). Arnold praises the "grace and sensitivity" Cather displays in her description of the "elemental passion, the mystery of innate feeling between men and women . . . in the large contexts of art and earth and cosmos" (1984a, 248). Another reviewer says that Cather tells her story with restraint and without sentimentality, using the "deftest effects of descriptive incident. The two contrasted personalities are projected as firmly in a few strokes as if a whole novel had been filled with the details of their careers" (B. 1920, 286). In Wasserman's view, Cather's handling of "the game-playing tone, motifs from legend and myth, animal imagery (the identification of Hedger and his dog), and the context of sharply contrasting urban scenes—strongly identify her as an artist working in the idiom of her time" (1991, 41).

Most critics also agree that "Coming, Aphrodite!" is probably the most overtly sexual love story Cather ever wrote, the most sensuous scene being that of Hedger watching through a knothole as the nude Eden Bower does her exercises. According to Woodress, Cather presents Hedger's "voyeurism as an aesthetic experience," but that depiction does not prevent contemporary readers from understanding that "the explosive and gesture imagery suggests masturbation" (1987, 313–14). Wasserman, too, asserts that Cather is concerned only with the beginning of passionate love in this story, and that her great achievement is her ability to convey the growing intimacy of the two characters. It is not a one-sided courtship, but a kind of "mating ritual" in which each participant is involved equally (1991, 37, 39). Agreeing that this story is Cather's "most palpably erotic," Robinson suggests that the author's voice is more androgynous here than in any of her other stories: "Don Hedger . . . could as easily be a woman as a man. . . . [T]he male and female roles seem interchangeable and the ambiguity is underscored in the story within a story, . . . 'The Forty Lovers of the Queen'" (1983, 158). By this time in her career Cather had thoroughly mastered the ability to write from a "dual perspective. She had absorbed both the male and female roles, and her voice seems primitive and androgynous" (Robinson 1983, 159).

Arnold argues that Cather even allows something of the barbaric to creep into the attraction Hedger and Bower experience. For example, Hedger uses the legend of the Rain Princess as a weapon to get even with her for frightening him so by taking a trip in a hot-air balloon. He uses it to punish her, "almost barbarically making love to her at the same time—forcing her to submit to him" (1984a 254). Because Eden Bower and the Rain Princess are closely related (like Eden, the Rain Princess is associated with both mortality and the supernatural or otherworldliness, both are capable of destroying the higher good through the earthly desires of the flesh, and both possess gifts that draw men irresistibly to them), Hedger is clearly using the story "to expose Eden's ruthlessness, to uncover her essential self, and to reveal her own sexuality to her" (Arnold 1984a, 254). At the same time, though, he uses the story to express his rage over his own inability to control his love for this woman "who is somehow elemental woman and goddess of love as well as the singer from Illinois who lives next door" (Arnold 1984a, 254–55).

Chaliff explains Hedger's anger as a reaction to a heroine who is "transformed into the mythic archetypal woman who . . . threatens the very existence of men by her sexuality" (1978, 66). Hedger's only salvation is to disentangle himself from Eden somehow and return the abstraction of his art. The Aztec myth, then, becomes the central element in the story by "illuminating the unconscious meaning of the action. What Cather had learned to do was to exploit universal myth that speaks to the deepest level of the psyche so as to present her own peculiar version based on her individual psychological need," and to that extent "Coming, Aphrodite!" explains the author's own life (Chaliff 1978, 66–67). Lee, on the other hand, feels that Cather is somewhat more ambivalent about the conflicting desires of sexuality and "a chaste dedication to art"; the author "expresses herself both through the solitary, male . . . figure, his thwarted passions transferred into his powerful work, and the escaping, aspiring, woman artist" (1989, 163).

Gerber believes Cather comes down firmly on Hedger's side. He is the true artist who disdains the familiarity so cherished by the public: he paints for those few who will understand him. Eden Bower, on the other hand, thinks only about the wealth popularity will bring. In Cather's mind, Hedger serves genuine art, while Eden Bower serves the cheap imitation, acquiescing to the desires of her ignorant public (1975, 68–69).

Petry also believes that Cather's sympathies are with Hedger, arguing that it is through Hedger's dog, Caesar, that Cather reveals her position on the relationship between the artist and his society. Cather establishes clear correspondences between Hedger and Caesar early on—dog and man have established an affectionate bond (1986, 307–308). It soon becomes apparent, however, that Caesar also symbolizes the object of Hedger's worship—that is, his artistic sensibility; then Cather is able to show "Hedger's changing attitude towards and treatment of the dog as the story's most sensitive indicator of the degree to which the painter is—or is not—being faithful to his artistic ideals" (Petry 1986, 309). The more insistently Caesar tries to come between Hedger and Bower, the more harshly Hedger treats him. When Eden insists that Caesar be left at home while she and Don visit Coney Island, the implication is clear: Hedger "must choose between the glittering, sensual, but superficial life offered by Eden, and the more disciplined, ascetic, but satisfying life represented by Caesar" (Petry 1986, 310–311).

Ryder takes a similar position, characterizing Eden Bower as a devouring Medusa with purely selfish motives. Hedger is the noble disciple of art and embraces the values Cather respects—values rejected by Eden. As a representative of both Lilith and Eve, Aphrodite and Artemis, Eden is to be both feared for her evil and destructiveness and loved for her beauty and chastity. Hedger becomes a representation of Hephaestus, whose love for Aphrodite was not returned. Hedger's room is grim and dark like Hephaestus's underground forge, and Hedger is physically strong like Hephaestus. Even their backgrounds are similar—both were rejected by their mothers. In both cases, the woman the man loves proves too strong for him, despite his attempts to subdue and control her. It is only when Eden goes to Europe and leaves Hedger's life that he begins slowly to disentangle himself from her grip on him (1990, 170–80). Ryder's conclusion is that in this story Cather meant to suggest that civilization was in real danger of being destroyed by "the dominance of Aphrodite whose Medusan lures of beauty become the ugliness of unrestrained or misdirected passion" (1990, 180).

In Thurin's view Cather deliberately parades these gorgeous mythic and literary women in front of the reader in order to create the impression that the heroine possesses "a primordial, impersonal quality. . . . The element of impersonality in Hedger's approach to Eden Bower doubtless has something to do with the artist's eye. But above all there is the desire to subsume all the instances of mortal beauty under the image of Aphrodite" (1990, 223–24). It is, however, Aphrodite's actual body that Eden represents, and Hedger is "basically a follower of the higher and celestial Aphrodite," although, on first reading Cather seems to be saying just the opposite (Thurin 1990, 226). Through her balloon ride, Bower is associated with height, light, and open spaces; Hedger, on the other hand, is associated with women of the lower classes and "tends to favor basement restaurants serving lobster and oysters and other things from the depth of the sea" (Thurin 1990, 226–27). Here Cather is suggesting the "contrast between the light-weight and the heavy-weight, between superficiality and depth, between centrifugal and centripetal activity" (Thurin 1990, 227).

Arnold does not confer so much significance on the differences between Bower and Hedger. The light and dark represented by Eden and Hedger, respectively, simply underscore the notion that opposites attract. The implication is that "human aspirations toward art and self-realization" are always threatened by romantic/sexual relationships, and conversely, art threatens the "basic humanness and sexuality" just as much as those earthly desires threaten artistic achievement (1984a, 257–59). Hedger and Bower are both winners and losers—Hedger is left in his dark solitude and Bower has learned that her realization of a successful career has taken its toll. "Coming, Aphrodite!" contrasts two views of success: "Hedger's private search for a new art, always changing, rarely profitable; Eden Bower's commitment to fame and money" (Slote 1973, xx).

Not all critics, however, see Bower's focus on financial security as a prostitution of her art. Giannone, for example, argues that her good head for business may be seen as simply a sign of her more highly refined perceptions about life. From her perspective, Hedger is an unrealistic dreamer, whose irresponsible behavior in financial matters she finds unattractive (1968, 104–105).

Works Cited

Arnold, Marilyn. 1984a. "Coming, Willa Cather!" *Women's Studies* 11:247–60.

———. 1984b. *Willa Cather's Short Fiction*. Athens: Ohio University Press.

B., E. A. 1920. Review of *Youth and the Bright Medusa*, by Willa Cather. *The Freeman*, 1 December, 286.

Cather, Willa. 1973. "Coming, Eden Bower!" In *Uncle Valentine and Other Stories: Willa Cather's Uncollected Short Fiction, 1915–1929*. Ed. Bernice Slote. Lincoln: University of Nebraska Press, 143–76.

———. 1975. "Coming, Aphrodite!" In *Youth and the Bright Medusa*. New York: Vintage Books, 3–63.

———. 1992. "Coming, Aphrodite!" In *Cather: Stories, Poems, and Other Writings*. New York: Literary Classics of the United States, 357–96.

Chaliff, Cynthia. 1978. "The Art of Willa Cather's Craft." *Papers on Language & Literature* 14:61–73.

Faulkner, Virginia, ed. [1965] 1970. *Willa Cather's Collected Short Fiction, 1892–1912*. Lincoln: University of Nebraska Press. Reprint. Lincoln: University of Nebraska Press.

Field, Flo. 1921. "Willa Cather's *Youth and the Bright Medusa*." *Double Dealer* 1:73–74.

Gerber, Philip. 1975. *Willa Cather*. Boston: Twayne.

Giannone, Richard. 1968. *Music in Willa Cather's Fiction*. Lincoln: University of Nebraska Press.

Lee, Hermione. 1989. *Willa Cather: Double Lives*. New York: Pantheon.

O'Brien, Sharon. 1987. *Willa Cather: The Emerging Voice*. New York: Oxford University Press.

Petry, Alice Hall. 1986. "Caesar and the Artist in Willa Cather's 'Coming, Aphrodite!'" *Studies in Short Fiction* 23:307–14.

Robinson, Phyllis C. 1983. *Willa: The Life of Willa Cather*. Garden City, NY: Doubleday.

Ryder, Mary Ruth. 1990. *Willa Cather and Classical Myth*. Lewiston, NY: Edwin Mellen Press.

Slote, Bernice. 1973. Introduction to *Uncle Valentine and Other Stories: Willa Cather's Uncollected Short Fiction, 1915–1929*, by Willa Cather. Lincoln: University of Nebraska Press.

Thurin, Erik Ingvar. 1990. *The Humanization of Willa Cather: Classicism in an American Classic*. Lund, Sweden: Lund University Press.

Wasserman, Loretta. 1991. *Willa Cather: A Study of the Short Fiction*. Boston: Twayne.

Woodress, James. 1987. *Willa Cather: A Literary Life*. Lincoln: University of Nebraska Press.

Consequences

Publication History

This story was first published under the name Willa Sibert Cather in the November 1915 issue of *McClure's* (46:30–32, 63–64) (Faulkner 1970, 597). It was reprinted in 1973 by the University of Nebraska Press in *Uncle Valentine and Other Stories: Willa Cather's Uncollected Short Fiction, 1915–1929*, and again in 1992 by Literary Classics of the United States in *Cather: Stories, Poems, and Other Writings*, a volume in the Library of America Series.

Circumstances of Composition, Sources, and Influences

This story was the first Cather wrote after she had formally resigned her post at *McClure's* magazine, and the next-to-last one she would ever write for that publication. Like the rest of the pieces she wrote between 1915 and 1920, this story draws on her New York experiences rather than on her earlier life, and was written primarily to make money (Stouck 1973, 329).

In Arnold's opinion, Cather's use of an alter ego or double in this story suggests several possible literary sources: Wilde's *Picture of Dorian Gray*, Poe's "William Wilson," and the most obvious of all, James's "The Jolly Corner." There are several examples of doubles in Cather's previous work, also. In most cases, however, the double is a part of the character himself. Jim, in "The Sculptor's Funeral," displays a double nature, as do many characters in the novels (Arnold 1984, 100).

Relationship to Other Cather Works

Besides the obvious New York connection between this story and the other New York tales Cather wrote between 1915 and 1920—"The Bookkeeper's Wife," "Ardessa," "Her Boss," and "Coming, Eden Bower" (later changed to "Coming, Aphrodite!")—the story is easily linked to Cather's first novel, *Alexander's Bridge*. In both works the themes of marriage and infidelity figure prominently; also, both Bartley of *Alexander's Bridge* and Kier Cavenaugh of "Consequences" try to achieve anonymity by melting into a crowd (Oehlschlaeger 1986, 196–97).

In Stouck's view, the old man who haunts Cavanaugh—a death figure among other things—prefigures the character James Mockford (*Lucy Gayheart*), who embodies impending death. Both Mockford and the figure in this story dress like members of a theatrical group. The story's dance of death theme is also found in *Lucy Gayheart* (Stouck 1973, 329–30). Many of Cather's characters are caught in the dance of death; for example, she "refers the title of *Death Comes for the Archbishop* to Holbein's *Dance of Death*. There is the image of the runners in 'A Death in the Desert'; and . . . the rude carvings Canute Canuteson makes on the window sills and boards of his house all depict designs from a Dance of Death" (Stouck 1975, 239n).

Arnold draws parallels between this story and "Uncle Valentine," in which Roland is the ghost of Valentine in the future. Like Kier Cavenaugh, Valentine is afraid of what he might become (1984, 125). Slote notes that both "Consequences" and "The Bookkeeper's Wife" have the "flat ending, the throwaway last line, that in context restores perspective" (1973, xi).

Interpretations and Criticisms

Few commentators have written on this story, perhaps because many believe it to be little more than one of Cather's early and rather desperate efforts to make her living solely by writing fiction. Later, as she became more confident, her writing improved. Woodress says the story is told by "inference and indirection," which suggests that beneath Cather's "calm, well-organized exterior there were doubts and uncertainties" (1987, 275).

All critics agree that Cather has reverted here to her old habit of imitating Henry James. Arnold points out, however, that although "Consequences" is undeniably similar to James's "The Jolly Corner," there are some striking differences as well. For one thing, the ghost who haunts James's Spencer

Brydon never becomes actual flesh, and unlike Cavenaugh, who wants only to escape from his ghost, Brydon makes contact with his, surviving the encounter and realizing in the end that the ghost is not himself, but a stranger. Brydon, then, is victorious and survives, whereas Cavenaugh is destroyed (1984, 100).

Slote identifies the main concern of "Consequences" as "cause or chance, [and] the moral question one of self-determination. Why do some men commit suicide?" (1973, x). The story is heavily theatrical, conveyed in scenes reminiscent of *Don Quixote*, from the first rainy scene near the Flatiron Building, to the one describing the "stunned chauffeur surrounded by luggage and his master dead just at the hour of departure for Montana" (Slote 1973, xi).

Arnold suggests that Cather deliberately sets up contrasts between Cavenaugh and the "literal-minded Eastman" in order to highlight Eastman's blindness (1984, 101). The lawyer simply dismisses Cavenaugh and therefore the entire event has passed over him unnoticed, because for Eastman no mysteries exist—the only truths are empirical facts. Eastman is interested in nothing beyond routine days spent at his office. He is portrayed as a man without depth or imagination (Arnold 1984, 101).

Rosowski sees Eastman as a storyteller whom Cather uses to frame the story and ease the reader's transition from the everyday to the uncanny. Eastman is simply a reporter of a neighbor's story (1986, 212).

Oehlschlaeger explains Kier Cavenaugh in terms of R. D. Laing's definition of ontological insecurity. According to Laing, the ontologically insecure person is unable to maintain his or her identity without the presence of other people. At the same time, however, this desperate need for others "threatens the self with engulfment," forcing the person to retreat into complete solitude (1986, 191). For this individual, "the poles of existence cease to be separateness and relatedness"; instead, they are absolute solitude on the one hand, and complete engulfment on the other (1986, 192). In Oehlschlaeger's opinion, the reason that suicide is connected in some way to marriage in this story is that through marriage one partner may easily be absorbed by the other or, just as easily, feel in utter isolation if the relationship ends (1986, 195). Dudley is an example of the latter; Captain Jack, of the former (Oehlschlaeger 1986, 196).

Works Cited

Arnold, Marilyn. 1984. *Willa Cather's Short Fiction*. Athens: Ohio University Press.

Cather, Willa. 1973."Consequences." In *Uncle Valentine and Other Stories: Willa Cather's Uncollected Short Fiction, 1915–1929*. Ed. Bernice Slote. Lincoln: University of Nebraska Press, 65–84.

————. 1992. "Consequences." In *Cather: Stories, Poems, and Other Writings*. New York: Literary Classics of the United States, 133–53.

Faulkner, Virginia, ed. [1965] 1970. *Willa Cather's Collected Short Fiction, 1892–1912*. Lincoln: University of Nebraska Press. Reprint. Lincoln: University of Nebraska Press.

Oehlschlaeger, Fritz. 1986. "Willa Cather's 'Consequences' and *Alexander's Bridge*: An Approach through R. D. Laing and Ernest Becker." *Modern Fiction Studies* 32:191–202.

Rosowski, Susan J. 1986. *The Voyage Perilous: Willa Cather's Romanticism*. Lincoln: University of Nebraska Press.

Slote, Bernice. 1973. Introduction to *Uncle Valentine and Other Stories: Willa Cather's Uncollected Short Fiction, 1915–1929*, by Willa Cather. Lincoln: University of Nebraska Press.

Stouck, David. 1973. Review of *Uncle Valentine and Other Stories*, by Willa Cather. *Southern Humanities Review* 9:329–30.

————. 1975. *Willa Cather's Imagination*. Lincoln: University of Nebraska Press.

Woodress, James. 1987. *Willa Cather: A Literary Life*. Lincoln: University of Nebraska Press.

The Conversion of Sum Loo

Publication History

This story was first published in *Library* magazine on August 11, 1900 (1:4–6), under the name Willa Sibert Cather (Faulkner 1970, 593). It was reprinted in 1957 by Dodd, Mead in *Early Stories* and in 1965 by the University of Nebraska Press in *Willa Cather's Collected Short Fiction, 1892–1912*.

Circumstances of Composition, Sources, and Influences

The story was published four months after Cather's last piece appeared in the Pittsburgh *Leader*, where she had worked for three years (1897–1900). For several months following her resignation, Cather contributed her stories and poems almost exclusively to *Library* magazine. Bennett reports that "The Conversion of Sum Loo," one of five Cather stories to appear in *Library*, was written after Cather had interviewed a man named Lee Chin, who was "the leading Chinese importer of Pittsburgh, whose first wife had committed suicide because she could not return to the United States with him after his annual trip to China to visit her, and whose second wife had a mental breakdown" (1957, 265).

Another suggestion by Bennett is that the story may have had its roots in Cather's aversion to Christian missionary efforts in China. One of Cather's Red Cloud acquaintances was a young woman who became a missionary to China and years later returned to America with several souvenirs that Cather suspected she had acquired by dealing in a dishonest way with the natives. Cather believed that "the ancient civilization of China could get along quite well without [America's] cultural interference" (1961, 136).

Stouck believes Cather's source for both this story and the earlier "A Son of the Celestial" (1893) is literary, specifically the literature of nineteenth-century America. He points out that several American writers of the period such as Bret Harte, Frank Norris, and Mary Austin wrote short stories about the Chinese in California. These stories contain some of the same conventions Cather uses in her story: "the inscrutable protagonist, the bartered bride, the opium den, the joss house, and the numerous devils of the spirit world. Of central importance is the detached, tourist-like narrator who submits the Oriental characters to occidental scrutiny" (1979, 2–3). In fact, this story is uncannily similar to Mary Austin's tale of almost the same name, "The Conversion of Ah Lew Sing," an 1897 story published in *Overland Monthly*, a periodical with which Cather was familiar and in which her own story "On the Divide" had appeared in 1896. According to Stouck, both the Austin and Cather stories are about first-generation Chinese shopkeepers in California. In each, part of the plot concerns acquiring a wife and establishing an American family, the involvement of a female missionary, and the conflict of two very different religious traditions. Further, in both cases the conversion mentioned in the title is used ironically—it never actually occurs (1979, 2).

Relationship to Other Cather Works

Although Cather was always interested in the immigrant experience, only two of her stories deal specifically with Chinese immigrants, this one and "A Son of the Celestial." The two stories are "different in plot and circumstance, but Cather quotes almost verbatim from 'A Son of the Celestial' for filler material describing Sum Chin's early life in 'The Conversion of Sum Loo'" (Arnold 1984, 6). Faulkner even refers to this story as a reworking of "A Son of the Celestial" (1970, 481). However, Bennett points out that in the paragraph lifted from the earlier story, Cather has added "the Oriental conception of filial duty and the idea of ancestor worship," subjects that did not appear in "A Son of the Celestial" (1957, 268).

Cather's outrage about religious evangelism and hypocrisy reappears in her novel *One of Ours*. As Bennett puts it, "she reached the climax of her disgust in the character of Enid, the religious hypocrite in *One of Ours*" (1961, 136–37).

Interpretations and Criticisms

Woodress feels that none of the five *Library* stories, including this one, is very important. In the case of both Cather's stories about Chinese immigrants, he suggests that Cather would have been wise to stick to subjects she knew something about: the setting of the story is San Francisco, a city Cather never visited, and the story itself is too similar to "A Son of the Celestial": "The pathos is feeble, and the story is certainly one of Cather's bad apples" (1987, 146).

Stouck argues that this story shows "Cather's talent did not lie in plot making: the baby dies and the story ends melodramatically with Sum Loo burning her New Testament and the nun, in tears, withdrawing her application to do missionary work abroad"; nevertheless, Cather does "observe a proper distance between the narrator and the subject matter, which resonates not with condescension but respect" (1979, 3).

Works Cited

Arnold, Marilyn. 1984. *Willa Cather's Short Fiction*. Athens: Ohio University Press.

Bennett, Mildred, ed. 1957. *Early Stories of Willa Cather*. New York: Dodd, Mead.

Bennett, Mildred R. 1961. *The World of Willa Cather*. Lincoln: University of Nebraska Press.

Cather, Willa. 1957. "The Conversion of Sum Loo." In *Early Stories*. Ed. Mildred Bennett. New York: Dodd, Mead & Co., 265–75.

———. [1965] 1970. "The Conversion of Sum Loo." In *Willa Cather's Collected Short Fiction, 1892–1912*. Ed. Virginia Faulkner. Lincoln: University of Nebraska Press, 323–31.

Faulkner, Virginia, ed. [1965] 1970. *Willa Cather's Collected Short Fiction, 1892–1912*. Lincoln: University of Nebraska Press. Reprint. Lincoln: University of Nebraska Press

Stouck, David. 1979. "Mary Austin and Willa Cather." *Willa Cather Pioneer Memorial Newsletter* 23:2–3.

Woodress, James. 1987. *Willa Cather: A Literary Life*. Lincoln: University of Nebraska Press.

The Count of Crow's Nest

Publication History

The first part of this story was published in the September 1896 issue of *Home Monthly* (6:9–11) and concluded in the October issue (6:12–13; 22–23). Both installments were under the name Willa Cather (Faulkner 1970, 592). The story was reprinted in 1957 by Dodd, Mead in *Early Stories* and in 1965 by the University of Nebraska Press in *Willa Cather's Collected Short Fiction, 1892–1912*.

Circumstances of Composition, Sources, and Influences

Cather was offered $100 for this story by Harold Dundy of *Cosmopolitan*, but she could not sell it to him because she was at that time still primarily responsible for filling the pages of *Home Monthly*. However, she was encouraged by Dundy's offer, which reassured her about the progress of her career (Bennett 1957, 115).

According to Slote, the story owes a good deal to John Esten Cooke's 1880 novel *The Virginia Bohemians*, in which an odd mix of travelers lodge at a place called the Crow's Nest (1966, 42). Moreover, the character of Count de Koch may have been suggested to Cather by a newspaper article about Baron Constantine de Grimm that appeared in May 1896. Both the Baron and the Count were Europeans in America, had known royalty, and had won the Iron Cross on the field of Gravelotte (1966, 84). The piece also draws heavily on Anthony Hope's *The Prisoner of Zenda* (Bennett 1970, xxviii).

Most Cather scholars, however, focus on the heavy influence of Henry James that is obvious for the first time in this piece. Bohlke believes Cather draws on James's "The Real Thing" (1974, 135), while others see in the subject matter of the story a resemblance to James's 1888 novella *The Aspern Papers*, which centers on the attempts of an American editor to acquire the letters of the poet Jeffrey Aspern to his mistress. Besides the similarity in plot, Cather's handling of point of view is very close to that of James: the reader hears the story from "an observer who sympathizes with the Count's stubborn integrity" (O'Brien 1987, 232). The old man's decision to put honor above all is one that many of James's characters would make (Arnold 1984, 69). This story represents Cather's first use of such an observer figure, and she handles the technique rather ineptly here. She returns to it in "Eleanor's House" and "The Willing Muse," but only after she had thoroughly mastered James's technique could she use it deftly for her own purposes, as she would in *My Ántonia*, *A Lost Lady*, and *My Mortal Enemy*, where "the observer's acknowledged and unacknowledged investment in the subject is the story itself" (O'Brien 1987, 310).

Despite the obvious shadow of Henry James, according to Mildred Bennett much of the material in the story comes from Cather's own experience. The point of view, for example, is that of the twenty-two-year-old Cather herself. The character of Buchanan finds himself in a situation similar to Cather's at the time she wrote the story: when Buchanan recognizes both his gifts and his immaturity, and acknowledges the barriers between himself and success which time must clear away, his comments sound very much like the things Cather was saying about herself in letters to her friends about the same time (Bennett 1957, 116). Not only is Buchanan's situation close to Cather's, but he also expresses some of Cather's opinions, notably that deep relationships between two people inevitably weaken over time. Cather felt much the same way, especially about the marriage relationship. In another example, Buchanan's professed inability to meet the taste of the masses represents almost exactly Cather's attitude about her position on the staff of *Home Monthly* (Bennett 1957, 122, 138).

When the Count prefers the indefinite to the definite and illusion to fact, he is giving a particularly Catherian response (Arnold 1984, 12). The statement closely resembles Cather's theory of art outlined in her "The Novel Demeuble": "Whatever is felt upon the page without being specifically named there—that, one might say is created. It is the inexplicable presence of the thing not named, of the overtone divined by the ear but not heard by it, the verbal mood, the emotional aura of the fact or the thing or the deed, that gives high quality to the novel or the drama, as well as to poetry itself" (Cather 1936, 50).

Relationship to Other Cather Works

The Count's daughter prefigures "Cather's later exploiters of the West, exemplifying the worst imaginable in blatant materialism and shabby art," and in this she is very close to Ivy Peters in *A Lost Lady* and Bayliss Wheeler in *One of Ours* (Arnold 1984, 11). Arnold sees the story as an echo of what Cather was writing about art in her newspaper columns at the time: "Helen, who sings 'floridly' but does not 'have perception enough to know it,' represents all that is vulgar in third-rate art" (1984, 12).

The steel box in this piece, connected as it is to clandestine sex, convinces O'Brien that this story is one of several in which Cather uses the box as "a female symbol suggesting both Pandora's box of sexuality and the container of unexpressed but potential creativity" (1987, 201). Other stories containing symbolic boxes include "A Son of the Celestial," "The Burglar's Christmas," "El Dorado: A Kansas Recessional," "The Treasure of Far Island," "The Namesake," and "On the Gulls' Road" (O'Brien 1987, 201).

Bennett emphasizes the thematic similarity of this piece and some of Cather's later work. Buchanan's hesitancy about developing an attachment to the Count, for example, can be seen in the absence of intense feelings between the professor and his wife in *The Professor's House*. Another subject Cather favored was that of the charlatan or shabby artist contrasted with the authentic master. In "The Count of Crow's Nest" Cather clearly sympathizes with the man and his reverence for his past. We see this same kind of character later in *The Professor's House*—figures who feel somehow out of place within humanity (1957, 122, 125, 127). Chicago musicians reappear in later works, too, such as *The Song of the Lark* and *Lucy Gayheart*, but the harsh attitude Cather displays toward them in this story has softened somewhat by then (Bennett 1957, 131).

The story's preoccupation with artists who struggle against a hostile society foreshadows the theme of much of Cather's later work (Robinson 1983, 88). In fact, the story's treatment of the place of art in the world foreshadows the main themes of *The Troll Garden*, and those themes can also be seen in two other stories describing singers that were published in *Home Monthly*— "The Prodigies" and "Nanette: An Aside" (1983, xii).

Interpretations and Criticisms

Virtually all the critics who have commented on this story agree that its value lies in the evidence it provides of a young artist who is still writing rather derivative material, but who is struggling to assimilate her mentors' influences enough to make them serve her own purposes.

O'Brien groups the story with others that use the imagery of a box to signify the danger of self-disclosure. In that way, the story is one of several that reveal to one degree or another the psychology of the author (see the "Relationship to Other Cather Works" and "Interpretations and Criticisms" sections in the chapter "A Tale of the White Pyramid"). The fear of self-disclosure is made perhaps more personal in this story by the central conflict, which concerns whether or not to make public a package of personal letters. Cather herself asked that her letters be destroyed. Furthermore, her will stipulates that no surviving letters may be quoted. It is significant that in this story we are able to see the twenty-two-year-old Cather already beginning "to put up fences around her personality" (Bennett 1957, 126).

Thurin discusses the significance of the classical references in the story, all of which appear in dialogue and are "to some extent . . . used simply to suggest sophistication on the part of Paul de Koch and Buchanan" (1990, 100). They are also included to help differentiate between the two contrasting attitudes about the duties of life (Thurin 1990, 100). This story, Thurin goes on to argue, "is noteworthy as a fictional illustration of the connection between Cather's espousal of aristocratic values and her use of decadent Rome as an analogue of modern vulgarity" (1990, 100). She suggests that the real decadence can be seen "in the plebeian greed developed by Helena," who seems to believe that a classical reference will help her obtain Buchanan's assistance in getting her father's papers (Thurin 1990, 100). When Buchanan refuses to help her on ethical grounds, she replies, "That all may be, but when we are in Rome we must be Romans or provincials," and then, "You must give the people what they want" (Cather 1970, 464). Such a comment reflects the mediocrity and crass "consumerism" taking over America that Cather herself so loathed (Thurin 1990, 100).

Works Cited

Arnold, Marilyn. 1984. *Willa Cather's Short Fiction*. Athens: Ohio University Press.

Bennett, Mildred, ed. 1957. *Early Stories of Willa Cather*. New York: Dodd, Mead.

———. [1965] 1970. Introduction to *Willa Cather's Collected Short Fiction*. Ed. Virginia Faulkner. Lincoln: University of Nebraska Press. Reprint. Lincoln: University of Nebraska Press.

Bohlke, L. Brent. 1974. "Beginnings: Willa Cather and 'The Clemency of the Court.'" *Prairie Schooner* 48:133–44.

Cather, Willa. 1936. "The Novel Demeuble." In *Not Under Forty*, by Willa Cather. New York: Knopf, 43–51.

———. 1957. "The Count of Crow's Nest." In *Early Stories*. Ed. Mildred Bennett. New York: Dodd, Mead, 115–45.

———. [1965] 1970. "The Count of Crow's Nest." In *Willa Cather's Collected Short Fiction, 1892–1912*. Ed. Virginia Faulkner. Lincoln: University of Nebraska Press, 449–71.

Faulkner, Virginia, ed. [1965] 1970. *Willa Cather's Collected Short Fiction, 1892–1912*. Lincoln: University of Nebraska Press. Reprint. Lincoln: University of Nebraska Press.

O'Brien, Sharon. 1987. *Willa Cather: The Emerging Voice*. New York: Oxford University Press.

Robinson, Phyllis C. 1983. *Willa: The Life of Willa Cather*. Garden City, NY: Doubleday.

Slote, Bernice, ed. 1966. *The Kingdom of Art*. Lincoln: University of Nebraska Press.

Thurin, Erik Ingvar. 1990. *The Humanization of Willa Cather: Classicism in an American Classic*. Lund, Sweden: Lund University Press.

Woodress, James. 1983. Introduction to *The Troll Garden*. Ed. James Woodress. Lincoln: University of Nebraska Press.

The Dance at Chevalier's

Publication History

This story was first published in *Library* magazine on April 28, 1900 (1:12–13) under the name Henry Nicklemann (Faulkner 1970, 593). It was reprinted in 1957 by Dodd, Mead in *Early Stories* and in 1965 by the University of Nebraska Press in *Willa Cather's Collected Short Fiction, 1892–1912*.

Circumstances of Composition, Sources, and Influences

Cather resigned from her editing position on the Pittsburgh *Leader* in 1900, her last contribution having appeared in April of that year. Woodress reports that the publication of "Eric Hermannson's Soul" in *Cosmopolitan* gave her the confidence she needed to leave the grind of daily journalism. She had, however, taken another job with a weekly called the *Library* even before her final piece appeared in the *Leader* (Woodress 1987, 146). The *Library* existed only six months before it ran out of funds, but in that time Cather contributed "The Dance at Chevalier's" and four other new stories ("The Sentimentality of William Tavener," "The Diamond Mine," "The Conversion of Sum Loo," and "The Affair at Grover Station"), sixteen articles, and seven poems. An additional three Cather stories were published in *Library*, but these were reworkings or reprintings of formerly published work: she revised "Peter" for that story's third appearance in print; "A Night at Greenway Court" was reprinted; "A Singer's Romance," a reworked version of "Nanette: An Aside," was also printed there. According to Woodress, Cather was paid fairly for her work at *Library* (1987, 146).

Cather used her real name for all *Library* stories except "The Dance at Chevalier's." Robinson states that Cather may have been slightly embarrassed by the quality of the story, but that the more probable explanation is that she did not want to deflect attention from one of her other stories, "Eric Hermannson's Soul," which appeared the same month in the much more prominent magazine *Cosmopolitan*. She signed that story Willa Sibert Cather (1983, 101).

Cather's love for France and everything French is obvious in several of her writings. In one of her early articles she declares that "most things come from France, chefs and salads, gowns and bonnets, dolls and music boxes, play and players, scientists and inventors, sculptors and painters, novelists and poets. It is a very little country, this France, and yet if it were to take a landslide in the channel some day there would not be much creative power of any sort left in the world" (quoted in Curtin 1970, 223). Gervaud argues that Cather's childhood had much to do with her idealization of France. One of her neighbors, a Mrs. Wiener, who was of French descent, acquainted Cather with French literature. Cather also often visited French-Canadian settlements, where she listened to sermons in French and danced and sang to French music. All of these experiences later appear in "The Dance at Chevalier's" (Gervaud 1974, 67).

At least two characters' names are directly connected to real people from Cather's life. Bennett reports Cather's sister Elsie as saying that Alplosen de Mar was actually a pupil of Cather's brother Roscoe, and that one of Cather's great-great-uncles had married a French woman named Severine; further, a family named Chevalier lived in Nebraska fairly close to the Cathers (1957, 217).

Bennett sees the clear influence of Alexandre Dumas's *Marguerite de Valois* in this story, especially in the poisoning scene, but also in Severine's behavior: in *Marguerite de Valois*, Dumas's heroine, who is nearly dead herself, embraces her dying lover's head and presses onto it a holy kiss (1957, 229).

Relationship to Other Cather Works

Most Cather specialists notice the similarity of "The Dance at Chevalier's" to "Eric Hermannson's Soul," which appeared at about the same time. Even though Cather signed her real name to the latter and a pseudonym to the former, it is obvious that the two were written by the same author. "Eric Hermannson's Soul," however, is the more sophisticated work; "The Dance at Chevalier's" is heavily melodramatic (Robinson 1983, 101).

Like Eric, Denis is a big, handsome "artist in the rough" who is in danger of being ruined by civilization (Bennett 1957, 19). His experience of passion with Severine, where he is "seized and mastered and borne away by that floodtide of tenderness which we can know but once in our lives" is nearly identical to Eric Hermannson's experience with Margaret; both are examples of Cather's "one-great-moment theory of love" (Bennett 1957, 227).

One of the characters who makes a reappearance in this story is Peter Sadelack, the violinist. He originated in Cather's first published short story, "Peter" (1892), which she revised as "Peter Sadelack, Father of Anton" for publication in *Library* in 1900 (Bennett 1957, 223). In the first story we are told that Peter had been a member of a theatre orchestra in Bohemia, until he suffered a paralytic stroke that left his arms so weak that his bowing was no longer certain. The identical information about him is given in "The Dance at Chevalier's." This kind of intertextuality is also obvious in "Eric Hermannson's Soul," where the dances at Chevalier's are mentioned (Bennett 1957, 223).

Not all the characters in this story are such exact duplicates of those in other works; some merely share certain similarities. For example, the Mexican in "The Dance at Chevalier's" is "a spiritual brother to Freymark in 'The Affair at Grover Station' who killed Larry O'Toole, another engaging Irishman such as Denis" (Bennett 1957, 219).

Arnold focuses on Cather's use of dancing in the story to establish correspondences between it and two others—"Eric Hermannson's Soul" and "The Affair at Grover Station." Each of the three dances represented in these stories is "conducted at a different level of social sophistication," moving from the most primitive—the Norwegian dance in "Eric Hermannson's Soul"—to the light airiness of the French dance in "The Dance at Chevalier's," and finally to the height of sophisticated elegance in the Anglo-Saxon–style inaugural ball of "The Affair at Grover Station" (1984, 26). The French dance specifically foreshadows the festive Catholic fair the French immigrants arrange in *O Pioneers!* (Arnold 1984, 26). Further, Cather's interest in French settlements in general led directly to her novel *Shadows on the Rock* (Bennett 1957, 224).

Interpretations and Criticisms

The idea that "love and the destruction of that love are collateral truths" appears often in Cather's fiction, and in this story that view is bluntly stated by the Signor when he tells his lover that he likes to kill the things he loves (Bloom and Bloom 1962, 149). According to Bloom and Bloom, although such a declaration is melodramatic, it does echo the artist's instinct Cather frequently portrays: in much of her fiction creative people suffer unhappy personal lives as well as the loneliness that comes from being social outsiders (1962, 149). "Even the titles of some of the stories—'The Sculptor's Funeral' and 'A Death in the Desert'—suggest the self-destructive element both physically and spiritually" (Bloom and Bloom 1962, 149).

Robinson reads the entire story as "pure melodrama" (1983, 101). Arnold agrees but also maintains that the story might have worked better if treated only as a folktale (many of the elements in the story, including the slow-acting poison concocted by a native of Guinea's Gold Coast, are borrowed from folk literature). Unfortunately, "Cather does not sustain the story's oral folk atmosphere; the storyteller tends to drift in and out, now controlling the narrative, now relinquishing control" (1984, 27).

Two critics have mentioned the troubling presence of racist elements in the story, undoubtedly much more readily apparent to today's readers than they were to Cather's contemporaries. Bennett acknowledges that the character Harry Burns exposes his prejudice when he refers to Mexicans as a "nasty lot" of "Greasers" and wonders aloud why Chevalier would continue to keep one of them in his employ; yet if Cather herself were biased, she obviously revised her position before writing *The Song of the Lark* and *Death Comes for the Archbishop*, where many of her characters are Spanish-American (1957, 220).

Arnold finds racist overtones in Cather's narrator's insistence that the people at the Chevalier dance are not pure French at all. The narrator's implication that they are impure or polluted by an infusion of "Canadian and Indian ('red squaw') sources" (1984, 26) elevates the status of the white race, enshrines the racist idea of "pure blood," and denigrates all others—especially mixed-race people. While conceding that these comments are read as blatantly racist today, Arnold exonerates Cather by arguing that such portrayals were common among the early realists. Later in her career, Cather's references to racial stereotypes diminish in number. In fact, in many works she is sympathetic to European immigrants, Mexicans, and Native Americans; in some cases, however, Cather's portraits of Jews do invite accusations of anti-Semitism (1984, 35).

Works Cited

Arnold, Marilyn. 1984. *Willa Cather's Short Fiction*. Athens: Ohio University Press.

Bennett, Mildred, ed. 1957. *Early Stories of Willa Cather*. New York: Dodd, Mead.

Bloom, Edward A., and Lillian D. Bloom. 1962. *Willa Cather's Gift of Sympathy*. Carbondale: Southern Illinois University Press.

Cather, Willa. 1957. "The Dance at Chevalier's." In *Early Stories*. Ed. Mildred Bennett. New York: Dodd, Mead, 217–29.

———. [1965] 1970. "The Dance at Chevalier's." In *Willa Cather's Collected Short Fiction, 1892–1912*. Ed. Virginia Faulkner. Lincoln: University of Nebraska Press, 547–55.

Curtin, William M., ed. 1970. *The World and the Parish: Willa Cather's Articles and Reviews, 1893–1902*. Lincoln: University of Nebraska Press.

Faulkner, Virginia, ed. [1965] 1970. *Willa Cather's Collected Short Fiction, 1892–1912*. Lincoln: University of Nebraska Press. Reprint. Lincoln: University of Nebraska Press.

Gervaud, Michel. 1974. "Willa Cather and France: Elective Affinities." In *The Art of Willa Cather*. Ed. Bernice Slote and Virginia Faulkner. Lincoln: University of Nebraska Press, 65–81.

Robinson, Phyllis C. 1983. *Willa: The Life of Willa Cather*. Garden City, NY: Doubleday.

Woodress, James. 1987. *Willa Cather: A Literary Life*. Lincoln: University of Nebraska Press.

"A Death in the Desert"

Publication History

This story was first published in the January 1903 issue of *Scribner's* (33:109–121) without the quotation marks (Faulkner 1970, 594). In 1905, Cather included the story in her first collection, *The Troll Garden* (New York: McClure, Phillips, pp. 111–54) (Faulkner 1970, 594). According to Faulkner, this version of the story included "ninety-eight substantive changes including twenty-five deep cuts, mostly descriptive passages," but there were also many changes in spelling, capitalization, and punctuation; also, the character of Windermere Hilgarde becomes Everett Hilgarde (1970, 594).

The story was reprinted in Cather's second collection, *Youth and the Bright Medusa* (New York: Knopf, 1920, pp. 273–303), with "one hundred and seventy-nine substantive changes from the 1905 version" (Faulkner 1970, 594). In 1961, the story was included in a Signet Classics paperback edition of *The Troll Garden*, where it "carries no note on the editing and thus is presumably a reprint. [However,] a comparison of the text with that of the original 1905 edition shows several alterations," mostly in punctuation and spelling, "but in a few cases words have been omitted or added, or another word substituted" (Faulkner 1970, 589).

In 1965, the 1905 version was reprinted by the University of Nebraska Press in *Willa Cather's Collected Short Fiction, 1892–1912*, and in 1983 it was republished by the same press in *The Troll Garden*, edited by James Woodress; in 1987 it was published by Literary Classics of the United States in *Cather: Early Novels and Stories*, a volume in the Library of America series, and again in 1992 by that press in another volume of the series, *Cather: Stories, Poems, and Other Writings*.

Circumstances of Composition, Sources, and Influences

The story's title comes from Robert Browning's poem of the same title, a dramatic monologue in which the dying apostle John addresses the few faithful friends who attend him (Woodress 1983a, xxi). According to Bradford, Cather's borrowing this title is significant because "the implied reference to Browning's poem . . . indicate[s] that attending an artist is as destructive of one's personal life as attending a saint" (1955, 544).

This, the earliest of the *Troll Garden* stories, was written while Cather was living with Isabelle McClung and her family in Pittsburgh. (For a discussion of the significance of Cather's friendship with Isabelle McClung and its influence on Cather's work, see the "Circumstances of Composition, Sources, and Influences" section in the chapter "A Wagner Matinée.") The story is a tribute of sorts to Cather's friend, composer Ethelbert Nevin, whose family owned the Pittsburgh *Leader*. Cather met Nevin in 1898, and three years later in 1901, he died at the age of thirty-eight. His death was a severe blow to Cather, who had spent many Sundays listening to music with him and "grew to worship the man she considered the greatest American composer" (O'Brien 1987, 263). He is undeniably the model for many of the androgynous men who appear in Cather's work (O'Brien 1987, 262–63). He was certainly the model for Adriance Hilgarde in "'A Death in the Desert,'" which was probably written the year following Nevin's death (Woodress 1970, 114).

As strong an influence on the story as Cather's grief may have been, in Lee's opinion "the strongest emotion in the [story] is the dying singer's yearning for a world elsewhere" (1989, 77). In that case, the source would be Cather's own life, for Katharine, having tasted fame, success, and the excitement of the musical world, has lost it all and has been forgotten, dying "like a rat in a hole"—a description that articulates Cather's fears about her own life (Lee 1989, 77). The train on which Everett Hilgarde is traveling at the beginning of the story is following the same route that Cather traveled with her brother on a trip in 1898 (Woodress 1983b, 126).

Cather reworked this story several times, but all her critics and biographers agree that although this was the first story she ever reprinted, she was never truly happy with it. Eventually she gave up on it completely and dropped it from Houghton Mifflin's library edition of her work, *The Novels and Stories of Willa Cather (1937–1941)*.

In his notes to the text, Woodress explains many of the story's allusions: Katharine's Camille entrance is a reference to Alexandre Dumas's *La dame aux camélias*, a nineteenth-century play Cather admired. Katharine's mention of the feet of passing runners is probably an allusion to Lucretius's *De rerum natura*, which Cather had certainly read, along with a good deal more Latin literature (1983b, 126). When Katharine quotes, "'and in the book we read no more that night'" (Cather 1987, 79) she is giving a "free translation of Francesca da Rimini's account of her tragic love affair with Paolo in *The Divine Comedy, Inferno* 5.138": While the two lovers were reading a book describing the affair between Lancelot and Guinevere, Paolo suddenly kissed Francesca passionately—the end of their reading and the beginning of their own affair (1983b, 126–27).

Stouck points out that the title "The Baggage Coach Ahead" mentioned in the story is not fictitious, but was "a popular song composed by the black songwriter and railroad porter Gussie L. Davis in 1896," which was actually entitled "In the Baggage Coach Ahead" (1984, 278). Its sentimental lyrics tell the story of a grieving widower and his child who are riding the train that is also carrying the body of their loved one. "Cather's mortally ill heroine is rejecting such sentimentality" (Stouck 1984, 278).

Relationship to Other Cather Works

As in "The Bohemian Girl," *Alexander's Bridge*, *O Pioneers!*, and *A Lost Lady*, the basic plot structure of this story is "the eternal triangle" (Woodress 1987, 222). Since Cather included this story in her first collection of short stories, *The Troll Garden*, however, its ties to the other stories in the book ("Flavia and Her Artists," "The Sculptor's Funeral," "The Garden Lodge," "The Marriage of Phaedra," "A Wagner Matinée," and "Paul's Case") are clear and strong. Arnold sees them as stories that "deal with human values and relationships played against genuine art as an index of value" (1984, 45). Edward A. Bloom and Lillian D. Bloom view each story as presenting part of "an extended colloquy between the artist as hero and a personified middle-class society as the villain" (1962, 117).

More than anything else, the two epigraphs Cather chose for *The Troll Garden* help explain not only the placement of the stories within the collection, but also the ways in which the stories are bound together thematically. One of the epigraphs is taken from the poem "Goblin Market" by Christina Rossetti—"We must not look at Goblin men,/ We must not buy their fruits;/ Who knows upon what soil they fed/ Their hungry thirsty roots?" The other is from Charles Kingsley's *The Roman and the Teuton*— "A fairy palace, with a fairy garden; . . . inside the trolls dwell, . . . working at their magic forges, making and making always things rare and strange." In

Brown's view, "[t]he fairy palace and the fairy garden are the preserves of art; and the trolls are artists or persons with artistic temperament" ([1953] 1964, 115). The plot of each *Troll Garden* story somehow sets the trolls (artists) against the goblins, "those who live outside the preserves of art or trespass upon them. . . . [T]hose who venture into the goblin market . . . risk eating of the poisoned fruit. . . . The sensuous fruits of life and of luxury can be tainted with evil. Success somehow exacts an ominous price" (Brown [1953] 1964, 115).

Rossetti's poem tells the story of Laura and Lizzie, two sisters who live in a fairyland, where each day goblin men come out of a nearby, evil vale and try to convince the girls to taste their delicious and tempting, but forbidden, fruit. Laura succumbs to temptation. After eating the fruit, she sickens—and can no longer hear the cries of the goblin fruit sellers. Lizzie, however, can still hear the men's entreaties and is determined to save her sister's life. When she offers to buy the goblins' fruit but refuses to eat it, the men become enraged, pelt her with fruit, and try to force it into her mouth. Covered with the juice of the goblins' fruit she hurries home to Laura and asks her to "eat me, drink me, suck my juices" (Rossetti 1970, 106). Laura kisses Lizzie, and the juice of the fruit, now bitter to the taste, restores her to health. The poem has received many readings, and though Rossetti clearly had the eucharist in mind, "Goblin Market" has also been seen as a lesbian work.

According to Woodress, "the fruits of the goblin men are related in Cather's mind to the magical things rare and strange made by the trolls in the garden. The things desired are not only delightful and marvelous but also dangerous and capable of corrupting" (1983a, xvii). Although Cather was utterly committed to art and had sacrificed much in its service, "she also was aware that in the pursuit of any religion she might mistake false gods for the true one" (Woodress 1983a, xvii).

O'Brien interprets Cather's choice of Rossetti's poem in another way: Cather connected the goblin men's fruits with "the fruits of the creative imagination, but in her *Troll Garden* stories aesthetic fruits grow from male—not female—writers' imaginations, just as the fruit belongs to the goblin men" (1987, 275). Women artists who rely heavily, if not solely, upon artistic fathers—the male tradition—lose their identities as artists, and "in making aesthetic desire a female/male drama Cather was drawing directly on her own experience as the bond slave of A. E. Housman and, more pertinent to this collection, as the servant of . . . Henry James" (O'Brien 1987, 275).

Wasserman's explanation of the title and the epigraphs is that they "suggest certain dangers in art, the work of not-quite-human trolls, fascinating to forest children peeking into their garden. . . . Cather made these dangers more puzzling and ominous by [the] second epigraph," the one by Rossetti (1990, 122).

Slote considers the "basic contrasts" of the epigraphs to be "the Trolls inside and the Forest Children outside, the Romans and the Barbarians, Palace-Garden and Wood-Country, and the cyclic movements of decaying civilization and reconquering nature" (1966, 95). The genuine and the false may be found everywhere—even in the world of art. *"The Troll Garden* is about corruption, the distortion of values; in every human sense there may be goblin fruit to desire, and Trolls who guard their riches" (Slote 1966, 95–96). Cather located *"*A Death in the Desert'" in the middle of the book because it is the only story that contains all the themes from both Rossetti and Kingsley (Slote 1966, 95–96).

Woodress believes Cather's reason for placing this story in the middle of *The Troll Garden* is that it deals with three different artists, each with different careers. Viewing the characters in terms of the epigraphs, Katharine may be said to be a forest child who is destroyed when she enters the garden. Everett Hilgarde longs to be an artist but has not enough talent. Adriance is the only forest child who has survived in the garden of the trolls. Of the three, Everett is the least important—in Henry James's term, a "'ficelle,' a character invented by the author as a convenience to the narrative structure"; the other two are actually "two sides of the same coin: [Ethelbert] Nevin in his prime and Nevin who died at the age of thirty-eight" (1983a, xx).

Because the art in this story is music, the story may be grouped with the many other stories Cather wrote about musicians, especially singers. Some are *Troll Garden* stories, others are not: "Nanette: An Aside," "A Singer's Romance," "A Wagner Matinée," "The Garden Lodge," "The Diamond Mine," "A Gold Slipper," and "Uncle Valentine" all deal with the music world and the musicians who inhabit it, as do two later novels, *The Song of the Lark* and *Lucy Gayheart.* O'Brien argues that these works are evidence of the strong influence music had on Cather. It "offered her the fusion of passion and form she valued in great art, presenting a symbolic as well as experiential reconciliation of the tension between disorder and order, emotion and control, desire and limitation" (1987, 170).

Another way of grouping this story with other Cather works is to see it in relation to those other *Troll Garden* stories—"Flavia and Her Artists," "A Garden Lodge," and "The Marriage of Phaedra—in which Cather "seems to be speaking in another's voice—whether that of Henry James, Edith Wharton, or of genteel magazine fiction of the day" (O'Brien 1987, 280).

Thurin contends that one of Cather's allusions in the story—Katharine's reference to the figure of Diana on the Garden Theatre—is "a poignant anticipation of the successful use of Saint-Gaudens' sculpture as a symbol of female aspiration in *My Mortal Enemy*" (1990, 127).

Interpretations and Criticisms

Some Cather scholars view Katharine as the center of this story. She is the character who symbolizes the great heart of the artist who despite society's hostility toward her, remains benevolent toward everyone (Bloom and Bloom 1958, 283). Katharine is a part of the "selfish, sensual world of song"; she is dying but "will get up and come back to the footlights if there is the slightest applause" (DuBois 1905, 613). The tragedy of the artist is Katharine Gaylord's tragedy: her "ruined, living body . . . becomes the personification of the artist's . . . sacrifice to an ideal," and like all Cather's artist characters, Katharine cannot have a happy personal life because she is so thoroughly generous of spirit that she becomes incomprehensible to ordinary, self-centered individuals (Bloom and Bloom 1962, 149).

In an opposing view, Gerber sees Katharine's story as anything but tragic, "if tragedy springs from character" (1975, 71). O'Brien sees Katharine's consumption as "a symbolic disease—the sign . . . of her subservience to male power: in this case, consumption is the fitting result of her infatuation with composer Adriance Hilgarde, the absent male artist who consumes her imagination" (1987, 274). The fact that the male artist *is* absent is important, O'Brien continues, as it suggests Cather's developing interest in "women who possess creativity—albeit creativity that is denied, distorted, or repressed" (1987, 277). The failure of the women characters suggests that Cather was aware of the formidable task facing them—"confronting a patriarchal artistic tradition (suggested by the absent or dead male artists in the stories)" (O'Brien 1987, 277). Cather's portrayal of these women as having artistic sensibilities at all, however, suggests her "awareness that women are not innately limited as artists, an insight that can be connected with her development of her own creative powers and growing artistic self-confidence" (O'Brien 1982, 277).

Arnold maintains that the story is less about Katharine than it is about "the tragedy of a man's being subsumed in the identity of a famous brother whom he has the misfortune to resemble" (1984, 54). Katharine's story merely provides an opportunity and a backdrop against which "Everett's bitter lifelong eclipse can be revealed"; the story turns on Everett, just as the Robert Browning poem turns on the person who takes care of the dying man, not the dying man himself (Arnold 1984, 54). "Katharine's death . . . has momentary significance chiefly as it affects and elucidates Everett's life. Everett's death is continual" (Arnold 1984, 54).

Thurin believes Cather's handling of classical references in the story is inept and thus diminishes the overall effectiveness of the piece. Katharine's mention of runners passing by her is a reference to "Lucretius' discussion of permanence and mutability [which] fits the theme of the story well, but the effect is marred by the theatrical-hysterical atmosphere" (1990, 127). Other classical references include Adriance's cantata entitled "Proserpine," Katharine's memory of a contralto who had expressed her certainty that the shepherd boys of the Vale of Tempe resemble Adriance, Adriance's library of Latin books, and Everett's comparison of Katharine to a Greek goddess. All of these references are calculated to lend the story sophistication (Thurin 1990, 126–27). Nevertheless, "even a classical scholar may not be happy to see the author throw in—for good measure, as it were—some lines from Shakespeare's *Julius Caesar* and having Katharine bid Everett farewell in the words with which Brutus says goodbye to Cassius before Philippi" (Thurin 1990, 127).

Cather herself was less than pleased with this story in her later life. In fact, in a letter of response to Edward Wagenknecht, who was interested in reprinting some of her early fiction, Cather scolded him, asking whether, if he wanted evidence of the limitations of her talent, "A Death in the Desert" was not bad enough. By this time she felt that the story had some honest feeling of a youthful kind, but not much more (Woodress 1987, 180).

Woodress reports that Cather's friend Dorothy Canfield Fisher evidently did not agree with Cather's negative assessment of this story. Fisher herself reviewed Cather's second short story collection, *Youth and the Bright Medusa*, in which this story reappeared (1970, 115). She compared the original version with the later and recommended that anyone who wished to learn how a real artist "smooth[s] away crudeness without rooting out the life" should examine the alterations carefully. "To see her do it gives me complete and rounded pleasure that only fine craftsmanship can give" (quoted in Woodress 1970, 115).

Works Cited

Arnold, Marilyn. 1984. *Willa Cather's Short Fiction*. Athens: Ohio University Press.

Bloom, Edward A., and Lillian D. Bloom. 1958. "Willa Cather's Portrait of the Artist." *University of Toronto Quarterly* 27:273–88.

———. 1962. *Willa Cather's Gift of Sympathy*. Carbondale: Southern Illinois University Press.

Bradford, Curtis. 1955. "Willa Cather's Uncollected Short Stories." *American Literature* 26:537–51.

Brown, E. K. Completed by Leon Edel. [1953] 1964. *Willa Cather: A Critical Biography*. New York: Knopf.

Du Bois, Bessie. 1905. "Miss Cather's *The Troll Garden*." *Bookman* 21:612–14.

Cather, Willa. 1961. "'A Death in the Desert.'" In *The Troll Garden*. New York: Signet Classics, 65–86.

———. [1965] 1970. "'A Death in the Desert.'" In *Willa Cather's Collected Short Fiction, 1892–1912*. Ed. Virginia Faulkner. Lincoln: University of Nebraska Press, 199–217.

———. 1983. "'A Death in the Desert.'" In *The Troll Garden*. Ed. James Woodress. Lincoln: University of Nebraska Press, 57–76.

———. 1987. "'A Death in the Desert.'" In *Cather: Early Novels and Stories*. New York: Literary Classics of the United States, 61–82.

———. 1992. "'A Death in the Desert.'" In *Cather: Stories, Poems, and Other Writings*. New York: Literary Classics of the United States, 512–29.

Faulkner, Virginia, ed. [1965] 1970. *Willa Cather's Collected Short Fiction, 1892–1912*. Lincoln: University of Nebraska Press. Reprint. Lincoln: University of Nebraska Press.

Gerber, Philip. 1975. *Willa Cather*. Boston: Twayne.

Lee, Hermione. 1989. *Willa Cather: Double Lives*. New York: Pantheon.

O'Brien, Sharon. 1982. "Mothers, Daughters, and the 'Art Necessity': Willa Cather and the Creative Process." In *American Novelists Revisited: Essays in Feminist Criticism*. Ed. Fritz Fleischmann. Boston: G.K. Hall, 265–98.

———. 1987. *Willa Cather: The Emerging Voice*. New York: Oxford University Press.

Rossetti, Christina. 1970. "Goblin Market." In *Selected Poems of Christina Rossetti*. Ed. Marya Zaturenska. New York: Macmillan, 93–109.

Slote, Bernice, ed. 1966. *The Kingdom of Art*. Lincoln: University of Nebraska Press.

Stouck, David. 1984. Review of *The Troll Garden,* by Willa Cather. *Great Plains Quarterly* 4:278.

Thurin, Erik Ingvar. 1990. *The Humanization of Willa Cather: Classicism in an American Classic*. Lund, Sweden: Lund University Press.

Wasserman, Loretta. 1990. "Is Cather's Paul a Case?" *Modern Fiction Studies* 36:121–29.

Woodress, James. 1970. *Willa Cather: Her Life and Art*. New York: Pegasus.

———. 1983a. Introduction to *The Troll Garden*. Ed. James Woodress. Lincoln: University of Nebraska Press.

———, ed. 1983b. *The Troll Garden,* by Willa Cather. Lincoln: University of Nebraska Press.

———. 1987. *Willa Cather: A Literary Life*. Lincoln: University of Nebraska Press.

The Diamond Mine

Publication History

This story was first published under the name Willa Sibert Cather in the October 1916 issue of *McClure's* (67:7–11) (Faulkner 1970, 597). Cather included it in her second short story collection, *Youth and the Bright Medusa* (New York: Knopf, 1920, pp. 248–72). (For a complete explanation of the way Cather's association with Knopf began, see the "Publication History" section for the chapter "Scandal.") The story reappeared in volume six of the thirteen-volume library edition of Cather's work *The Novels and Stories of Willa Cather* (Boston: Houghton Mifflin, 1937–1941, pp. 75–140) (Faulkner 1970, 597). It was reprinted in 1975 by Vintage Books in a paperback edition of *Youth and the Bright Medusa*, and again in 1992 by Literary Classics of the United States in *Cather: Stories, Poems, and Other Writings*, a volume in the Library of America series.

Circumstances of Composition, Sources, and Influences

This story is the last that Cather ever placed in *McClure's* magazine, where she was once managing editor. (For a discussion of Cather's years on the magazine's staff, see the "Circumstances of Composition, Sources, and Influences" section for the chapters "The Sculptor's Funeral" and "The Namesake.") As Ryder explains, it was also the first story handled by her new literary agent, Paul Reynolds, with whom she remained for ten years. Cather admitted that she herself would never have tried to sell "The Diamond Mine" because its length, content, and narrative style were inappropriate for magazine publication. Nevertheless, Reynolds sold it to *McClure's* for $600, although not without some difficulty. He had been turned down by both *Century* and the *Smart Set,* before approaching McCLure's. H. L. Mencken, then editor of *Smart Set* refused to publish it because of his concern that the story might be considered libelous—the main character was closely based on Lillian Nordica, the American Wagnerian soprano, "whose last husband, George Young, is very thinly disguised in the story as the unscrupulous, mercenary character Jerome Brown" (1990, 168). Cather's novel *The Song of the Lark* had been published the previous year, so that opera singers and the world of music in general were probably still very much on her mind as she wrote this story (Ryder 1990, 168). Woodress reports Cather's admission that Nordica was the inspiration for the story, but that in this case fiction was much less odious than fact and that only two incidents in the story—the shipwreck and the contested will—even resemble the facts. All the same, George Young threatened to sue if the story was published but never carried out his threat. Most readers recognized Nordica in the story, and a short time after it appeared in *McClure's*, the *Musical Courier* printed an article responding to it. Lillian Nordica was undeniably famous in her day; while studying in Europe, she had "attracted the attention of Cosima Wagner, who made her a star at Bayreuth," and when she returned to America, she became "one of the workhorses at the Met. She died in 1913 after a shipwreck in the East Indies while on a world tour. She had a great voice, almost no temperament, and several husbands" (Woodress 1987, 278–80).

Wasserman says that another source for the story is George du Maurier's *Trilby*; the control Poppas holds over Cressida certainly recalls the powers of du Maurier's Svengali (1991, 33). In du Maurier's novel Svengali's death causes the singer to lose her voice; in "The Diamond Mine" the author reverses the situation. When Cressida dies, Poppas retires and moves to central Asia, where, supposedly, the hot, dry weather will cure his headaches (Wasserman 1991, 33–34).

Another possibility, according to one Cather biographer, is that Poppas owes his existence to "the residue of anger [Cather] felt toward Jan [Hambourg] that she could not express in more direct ways" (Robinson 1983, 207). Hambourg had married Cather's dearest friend, Isabelle McClung, six months before "The Diamond Mine" appeared in print, and Cather was devastated. Feeling abandoned and lost, she told several of her acquaintances that she did not much care for Hambourg, but then it is doubtful that she would have been capable of liking anyone who married Isabelle. Hambourg had taken from her "the most important person in her life" (Robinson 1983, 205). (For a discussion of the enormous positive influence of Isabelle McClung on Cather's creativity see the "Circumstances of Composition, Sources, and Influences" section for the chapter "A Wagner Matinée.") Robinson points out that Hambourg "came from a family of Russian Jews, . . . [and Cather] had always seen Jews as intruders and despoilers," and although Hambourg was clearly neither of these things, Cather was unable to be objective about him (1983, 205). She continued to see his relationship with Isabelle as a desecration of her own intimate friendship with Isabelle, whom Cather had always been able to rely on for support and for a safe haven when she returned to Pittsburgh. After Isabelle's marriage, however, Cather "was faced abruptly with the necessity of altering her working patterns and, more acutely, her habit of emotional dependency on Isabelle" (Robinson 1983, 206).

Relationship to Other Cather Works

For her second collection of short stories, *Youth and the Bright Medusa* (Knopf, 1920), Cather reprinted four of the stories from the earlier collection *The Troll Garden*: "Paul's Case," "A Wagner Matinée," "The Sculptor's Funeral," and "'A Death in the Desert.'" To these were added four newer works, "Coming, Aphrodite!" "A Gold Slipper," "Scandal," and "The Diamond Mine," the earliest of the four. The title of the collection suggests the theme that binds all eight stories together. As she had done for *The Troll Garden*, Cather chose a classical image for *Youth and the Bright Medusa* as a way of tying the stories together thematically. (For a complete explanation of the thematic relationship of the *Troll Garden* stories to the epigraphs Cather chose for them, see the section "Relationship to Other Cather Works" for the chapters "'A Death in the Desert'" and "A Wagner Matinée.") What the image has in common with the epigraphs of *The Troll Garden* is the notion of "life's incompatibility with art. . . . The chief difference between the two books is that the incompatibility of life and art is not in 1920 suggested in terms of an opposition between the dangerous sophistication of the metropolis and provincial naiveté" (Thurin 1990, 221). Instead, Cather articulates the contrasts between the vibrant energy of youth and the regrets and often the pessimism of age: "Age—not necessarily old age—is a kind of petrifaction in itself even when death does not immediately supervene" (Thurin 1990, 221). The Medusa myth is also used "to explain the hypnotic attraction of the arts for youth," but instead of focusing on the legend itself—about a grotesque monster who is nevertheless also mesmerizingly beautiful—Cather concentrates on the Medusa tale in its "beginning when the Gorgon was a beautiful young woman devoted to and associated with the earth goddesses. . . . In the myth itself lay expression of the conflict Cather observed in the post-war society. The matriarchy had fallen to a masculine possessor, and the demise of beauty was imminent" (Ryder 1990, 167). Thus, all the stories in the collection are related in that they all illustrate this view in one way or another. According to Ryder, "The Diamond Mine" is particularly close to "Scandal" and "A Gold Slipper" because in all three stories Cather places a male enemy in a woman's way (1990, 167).

Arnold explains the title of the collection as an expression of the conviction that "anyone who looked upon the Medusa, the Gorgon, would be turned to stone. Anyone who pursues art will become its captive" (1984, 106). Woodress maintains much the same thing (1970, 186), but Stouck believes that by Medusa Cather means only commercial success. Sometimes the artist is victorious, but at other times, he or she is "at the Medusa's mercy, a victim of the financial bonanza that success brings" (1975, 200).

Giannone recognizes the correspondences between the four stories reprinted from *The Troll Garden* and the other four in *Youth and the Bright Medusa*, which were published after *The Song of the Lark*: "In both groups the artist confronts possible misunderstanding by the public, exploitation in personal affairs, professional failure, and the inevitability of death. The stories from *The Troll Garden* stress defeat or death" (1968, 100). To some extent the newer stories contain the same element of pessimism, but the agony is somewhat relieved by "the artists' resignation to pain and impermanence. The earlier stories vent outrage and bitterness; the later ones express courage, assurance, and forgiveness" (1968, 100). Brown says that in "The Diamond Mine," "A Gold Slipper, " and "Scandal," Cather shifted the focus from "the greatness, growth, or decline of a talent" to "the kind of relationships artists have with those who are not artists but are brought into contact with them" ([1953] 1964, 210–11).

Arnold groups the story with others in which Cather depicts a talented woman who sacrifices everything for her art. Such a woman was first portrayed in "Nanette: An Aside," but she reappears in "A Gold Slipper," "Scandal," "Coming, Aphrodite!," and *The Song of the Lark* (1984, 106). Cather's view that marriage and art are utterly incompatible is also evident here, as it is in many other works—"Nanette: An Aside," "A Singer's Romance," and even "Paul's Case," where "the actresses whom Paul admired . . . were typically supporting shiftless husbands" (Arnold 1984, 107). Woodress's interpretation is similar: sometimes the heroine does not marry, but usually she does, and she suffers for it. Cather's opinion on this subject was so strong that in one of her short stories, "Uncle Valentine," she borrows details from the marriage of her musician friend Ethelbert Nevin—a perfectly happy union—and turns it into a destructive and sad fictional one (1970, 87). (For a discussion of Cather's friendship with Nevin, see the "Circumstances of Composition, Sources, and Influences" section for the chapter "'A Death in the Desert.'")

"The Diamond Mine" shares a few more minor elements with other stories as well. For example, like "Scandal" it contains a portrait of a Jew that, in Robinson's opinion, "can only be described as an outburst of anti-Semitism" (1983, 207). Field says that both "The Diamond Mine" and "The Sculptor's Funeral" "strike the note of the tragic humor in the Every Day" (1921, 73–74). Bloom and Bloom see similarities between this story and "The Sculptor's Funeral" in the isolation endured by the fictional artists (1962, 151).

Interpretations and Criticisms

This story is seen by some critics as an indication of Cather's maturing views of the artist in society. Brown notes that in "The Sculptor's Funeral" (1905), Cather made clear her opinion that if an artist's friends and family failed or refused to understand him or her, the result was catastrophic to the artist, but by the time she published "The Diamond Mine" eleven years later, Cather had come to realize her mistake. Having watched artists of many kinds, she came to see that the artist was not as fragile as she had thought: genuine artistic talent survives even when powerful forces are arrayed against it (1964, 211–12). Thus, although Cather's "tone is ironical and melancholy, [it is] not in the least cynical," and the absence of cynicism may be the result of Cather's having outgrown her need to compare the artist's life with the nonartist's life (Daiches 1962, 156–57).

Ryder would not agree that Cather's view of the artist became optimistic. On the contrary, by 1920 "Cather had come to believe that even the most res-olute women of artistic sensibilities would find their dreams thwarted by a mercantile, masculine society" (1990, 170). Although they were attracted by the "allure of beauty" as much as the female artists before them were, "the pursuit of the ideal" would transform them into Gorgons, and they would "lose an essential humanity in their efforts to repulse new Poseidons, new possessors of mother earth" (Ryder 1990, 170).

The character of Cressida Garnet has elicited various comments from Cather specialists. Arnold maintains that Cressida is not quite the blameless victim she appears to be at first glance. She is, in fact, to some extent guilty of corrupting her family by allowing them to use her. Her portrayal as the inno-cent victim of exploitation indicates that the narrator herself is "as blind to the singer's faults as Cressida's family is to her virtues" (1984, 108–109). Ryder says that Cressida's struggle for recognition and her failed attempts at successful marriage have made her bitter. The artist herself is aware of this hardness, realizing that "her plight is Medusa's—an inability to share herself with other people" (1990, 169–70). Wasserman asserts that in order to under-stand Cressida, the reader must take a serious look at her Svengali, Miletus Poppas. When he sends Carrie a German verse, the content of which sug-gests his selfless sacrifice to Cressida, "the fairy-tale substructure of this story emerges. Poppas is the hidden gnome with the secret, the Rumpelstiltskin who can help the poor man's daughter spin the raw material of straw into the gold of art. He is Cressida's submerged self, in charge (bizarrely) of her very memories" (1991, 34). Given his positive role in the story, the reader must necessarily question Cather's motives for making Poppas a Jew and for using stereotypical notions in her portrait of him. She may be evoking "ancientness [and] timeless endurance" by making Poppas appear as "'old as Jewry,'" or perhaps she is using the fact that he is a Greek Jew to link the "twin roots of Western myth, the classical and the Hebraic." Her description of him may also be seen as anti-Semitic, "a view that obscures her many hints that Poppas represents the deep psychic levels that must be plumbed—mined, rather—before the diamond of art can be achieved" (Wasserman 1991, 34).

Some critics give this story short shrift, viewing it as one of Cather's poor-er efforts. Stouck says that despite the "genuine pathos" of Cressida's search for love, the story is "curiously flat," since the "narrator never enters into the story's imaginative design" (1975, 201). Thurin says the story's "burlesque" ending is jarring; it does not fit with the rest of the tale (1990, 221). Williams considers the story a good idea that fails in the telling. Cather has enough material in this piece for a novel, but she falls very far short of having written it (1920, 890).

Works Cited

Arnold, Marilyn. 1984. *Willa Cather's Short Fiction*. Athens: Ohio University Press.

Bloom, Edward A., and Lillian D. Bloom. 1962. *Willa Cather's Gift of Sympathy*. Carbondale: Southern Illinois University Press.

Brown, E. K. Completed by Leon Edel. [1953] 1964. *Willa Cather: A Critical Biography*. New York: Knopf.

Cather, Willa. 1975. "The Diamond Mine." In *Youth and the Bright Medusa*. New York: Vintage Books, 67–120.

———. 1992. "The Diamond Mine." In *Cather: Stories, Poems, and Other Writings*. New York: Literary Classics of the United States, 397–432.

Daiches, David. [1951] 1962. *Willa Cather: A Critical Introduction*. Ithaca, NY: Cornell University Press; London: Oxford University Press. Reprint. New York: Collier.

Field, Flo. 1921. "Willa Cather's *Youth and the Bright Medusa*." *Double Dealer* 1:73–74.

Faulkner, Virginia, ed. [1965] 1970. *Willa Cather's Collected Short Fiction, 1892–1912*. Lincoln: University of Nebraska Press. Reprint. Lincoln: University of Nebraska Press.

Giannone, Richard. 1968. *Music in Willa Cather's Fiction*. Lincoln: University of Nebraska Press.

Robinson, Phyllis C. 1983. *Willa: The Life of Willa Cather*. Garden City, NY: Doubleday.

Ryder, Mary Ruth. 1990. *Willa Cather and Classical Myth*. Lewiston, NY: Edwin Mellen Press.

Stouck, David. 1975. *Willa Cather's Imagination*. Lincoln: University of Nebraska Press.

Thurin, Erik Ingvar. 1990. *The Humanization of Willa Cather: Classicism in an American Classic*. Lund, Sweden: Lund University Press.

Wasserman, Loretta. 1991. *Willa Cather: A Study of the Short Fiction*. Boston: Twayne.

Williams, Orlo. 1920. "Paul's Case." *Athenaeum*, 31 December, 890.

Woodress, James. 1970. *Willa Cather: Her Life and Art*. New York: Pegasus.

———. 1987. *Willa Cather: A Literary Life*. Lincoln: University of Nebraska Press.

Double Birthday

Publication History

This story was first published under the name Willa Cather in the February 1929 issue of *Forum* (81:78–82, 124–28) (Faulkner 1970, 598). It was also chosen for inclusion in *Best Short Stories of 1929*, edited by E. J. O'Brien (New York: Dodd, Mead, pp. 60–85) (Faulkner 1970, 598).

The story was reprinted in 1973 by the University of Nebraska Press in *Uncle Valentine and Other Stories: Willa Cather's Uncollected Short Fiction, 1915–1929*, and again in 1992 by Literary Classics of the United States in *Cather: Stories, Poems, and Other Writings*, a volume in the Library of America series.

Circumstances of Composition, Sources, and Influences

The story was written in 1928, probably during the summer while Cather was living in her newly built cottage on Grand Manan Island in the Bay of Fundy. According to Woodress, however, that year was not a very productive one for Cather. Her father had died of a heart attack in March, and she had stayed on at the family home in Red Cloud, Nebraska, for more than a month after the funeral. She went to Grand Manan partly to recuperate from the trauma of her father's death and also from a bout with the flu and other physical ailments (1987, 413–15).

Like "Uncle Valentine," this story grows directly out of Cather's memories of her Pittsburgh years, 1896–1906. Judge Hammersley is certainly based on Isabelle McClung's father, who was also a judge, "and his daughter Marjorie is probably Cather's view of what Isabelle would have become had her circumstances been the same as Marjorie's" (Woodress 1987, 418). The Hammersley's home is also very similar to the McClungs' (Slote 1973, xxviii), and like Judge McClung, Judge Hammersley is "a stern old traditionalist, dedicated to a life of order"; while he was on the bench, in fact, Judge McClung "had given the harshest possible sentence to an anarchist friend of Emma Goldman's, Alexander Berkman, for trying to shoot Henry Clay Frick after Frick had broken the '92 Homestead steel mills strike" (Lee 1989, 57–58). (For a discussion of the significance of Cather's friendship with Isabelle McClung and its influence on Cather's work, see the "Circumstances of

Composition, Sources, and Influences" section for the chapter "A Wagner Matinée.") The house where the two Alberts live is nearly an exact replica of the apartment where George and Helen Seibel, two more of Cather's Pittsburgh friends, lived at the time Cather was staying with the McClungs: "the little two story brick house on a dingy street, the upstairs apartment reached by going down a paved alley and climbing an outside flight of wooden stairs at the back" (Woodress 1987, 419).

Albert Englehardt, too, is drawn from life, but from Cather's life in Lincoln, Nebraska, not Pittsburgh. He is a tribute to Dr. Julius Tyndale, whom Cather had known since 1893, when both the young Cather and Tyndale, a man of fifty, worked as newspaper drama critics for the Lincoln papers. Albert Engelhardt is so closely modeled on Dr. Tyndale, in fact, that Cather wrote to her friend during the winter of 1928–29, evidently concerned that her fictional portrait of him would be recognized and perhaps not appreciated. Tyndale's reply reassured Cather that he would be not only unoffended, but flattered (Slote 1973, xxviii–xxix). According to Stouck, however, the great sadness of Doctor Engelhardt's life comes not from something in Dr. Tyndale's life, but from Cather's own obsession with physical decay and death at the time (1975, 162).

Relationship to Other Cather Works

Stouck sees connections between this story and Cather's novels *My Mortal Enemy* (1926), *Death Comes for the Archbishop* (1927), and *Shadows on the Rock* (1931). In all three Cather "explore[s] through Christian imagery and myth the full range of the moral universe, . . . the whole spectrum of man's capacity for good and evil" (1975, 115).

Slote groups the story with Cather's later Nebraska tales—"Neighbour Rosicky," "Old Mrs. Harris," and "Two Friends." Cather's use of doubleness in this story is also present in some of her other works. For example, the Alberts, who share a birthday, bring other pairings to mind: Valentine and Charlotte ("Uncle Valentine"), Eden Bower's double face ("Coming, Aphrodite!"), Paul Wanning ("Her Boss") and the youthful self he remembers while writing, and in "Consequences" three people—"Kier Cavenaugh, his future self, and his dead twin brother. . . ." (1973, xxix–xxx).

Marguerite's similarity to other female characters in Cather is also striking. Cather was intrigued by beautiful, talented women who die young, such as Katharine Gaylord ("'A Death in the Desert'"), Alexandra Ebbling ("On the Gulls' Road"), Nelly Deane ("The Joy of Nelly Deane"), Marie Shabata (*O Pioneers!*), Cressida Garnet ("The Diamond Mine"), Lucy Gayheart (*Lucy Gayheart*), and Lesley Ferguesson ("The Best Years") (Stouck 1975, 167n). Marguerite is also explicitly connected to Thea Kronborg in that both women were singers who were given confidence by an older doctor who believed in their talent (Arnold 1984, 127).

Thurin says that both this story and "Uncle Valentine" hark back to "the troll-garden or Medusa theme," and as in those earlier stories the central concern is the struggle of the artist (1990, 320). (For an explanation of the ways in which the stories in *The Troll Garden* and *Youth and the Bright Medusa* are held together thematically, see the "Interpretations and Criticisms" section for the chapters "'A Death in the Desert'" and "Relationship to Other Cather Works" for "The Diamond Mine," respectively.) Arnold notes that in this story Cather once again returns to one of her favorite themes, "the capacity of material things to encumber the spirit" (1984, 129).

Interpretations and Criticisms

Those scholars who see this story as positive feel that hope is evident through characters, whose values grow out of "belief, desire, friendship, and shared memories" (Slote 1973, xxix). The life force Cather depicts in this tale is "inexorable," and human beings, despite their frailties and failings, are the only creatures capable of creating the things that last forever (Slote 1973, xxx). Cather depicts the few individuals who embrace these noble values, who are "deliberately out of step with the times," like old Doctor Engelhardt, as something like saints (Gerber 1975, 128). Giannone, too, finds the story somewhat uplifting and argues that in it Cather uses music, specifically vocal music, to make the point that life is as short and exquisite as a song (1968, 243).

Other critics consider the story to be "at once bitter and nostalgic" (Bradford 1955, 547). Stouck believes that the story's "nostalgia for the past and optimistic program for the future" gives it a "comfortable, even sentimental, surface which distracts the reader from the bleak vision of life underneath" (1975, 162). One of the bleakest visions of all is that of death not as "the completion of life, the final transcendence of earthly things, . . . nor [as] a purgatorial transition to a fuller life of the spirit," but as simply the "painful, ugly, and above all meaningless . . . measure of human existence"; although the story does depict a renaissance of both joy and sorrow, the dominant emphasis is on sorrow, "for the vignette at the end, of the pianist who has renounced life, brings us a glimpse again of the old Doctor's struggle at the death of his singer" (Stouck 1975, 162–63).

Arnold maintains that Doctor Engelhardt's suffering over Marguerite's death seems calculated to remind the reader of Christ's agony in the garden. Cather's reference to the doctor's treks to the hills beyond Mount Oliver is an unmistakable allusion to the Mount of Olives, and to "the three trees that grow in the Engelhardts' courtyard. Thus the loss of Marguerite . . . was a gain for the doctor as well as a loss, for through his suffering he was spiritually strengthened and ennobled" (1984, 128). Both the Engelhardts have certainly lost something dear to them, but at the same time both have lived a life "which has contained something worth spending everything for. Judged by this standard, the Engelhardts are rich indeed" (Arnold 1984, 128).

Works Cited

Arnold, Marilyn. 1984. *Willa Cather's Short Fiction*. Athens: Ohio University Press.

Bradford, Curtis. 1955. "Willa Cather's Uncollected Short Stories." *American Literature* 26:537–51.

Cather, Willa. 1973. "Double Birthday." In *Uncle Valentine and Other Stories: Willa Cather's Uncollected Short Fiction, 1915–1929*. Ed. Bernice Slote. Lincoln: University of Nebraska Press, 41–63

———. 1992. "Double Birthday." In *Cather: Stories, Poems, and Other Writings*. New York: Literary Classics of the United States, 250–75.

Faulkner, Virginia, ed. [1965] 1970. *Willa Cather's Collected Short Fiction, 1892–1912*. Lincoln: University of Nebraska Press. Reprint. Lincoln: University of Nebraska Press.

Gerber, Philip. 1975. *Willa Cather*. Boston: Twayne.

Giannone, Richard. 1968. *Music in Willa Cather's Fiction*. Lincoln: University of Nebraska Press.

Lee, Hermione. 1989. *Willa Cather: Double Lives*. New York: Pantheon.

Slote, Bernice. 1973. Introduction to *Uncle Valentine and Other Stories: Willa Cather's Uncollected Short Fiction, 1915–1929*, by Willa Cather. Lincoln: University of Nebraska Press.

Stouck, David. 1975. *Willa Cather's Imagination*. Lincoln: University of Nebraska Press.

Thurin, Erik Ingvar. 1990. *The Humanization of Willa Cather: Classicism in an American Classic*. Lund, Sweden: Lund University Press.

Woodress, James. 1987. *Willa Cather: A Literary Life*. Lincoln: University of Nebraska Press.

El Dorado: A Kansas Processional

Publication History

This story was first published in the June 1901 issue of *New England* magazine, n.s. (24:357–69) under the name Willa Sibert Cather (Faulkner 1970, 593). It was reprinted in 1965 by the University of Nebraska Press in *Willa Cather's Collected Short Fiction, 1892–1912*.

Circumstances of Composition, Sources, and Influences

According to Arnold, this story was probably written after Cather had accepted a position teaching English, Latin, and algebra at Pittsburgh's Central High School in March 1901. She had recently moved back to Pittsburgh from Washington, D.C., where she had been doing editing work. It was also during the spring of 1901 that she was invited to move into the home of the prominent and respected Pittsburgh family of Judge Samuel A. McClung, where she stayed until 1906 when she moved to New York. Cather had met Judge McClung's daughter, Isabelle, sometime during 1899, and the two women developed an intimate friendship that was to last until Isabelle's death in 1938. "El Dorado" is one of four stories that immediately precede *The Troll Garden* (1905), Cather's first collection of short stories (Arnold 1984, 37).

This story is largely a reflection of the overwhelming dismay Cather felt about the exploitation of the West by unscrupulous land developers. In Cather's opinion, the frontiersmen are admirable—even noble—and for their integrity they are made to suffer at the hands of money-grubbing land speculators (Bloom and Bloom 1962, 49). Her abhorrence of rampant materialism, which she sees as destroying the frontier, derives from firsthand observation. The land developers took no "personal pride in the development of the land. The region became . . . a debtor West. . . ." (Bloom and Bloom 1962, 48–49).

Bennett suggests that the character of Josiah Bywaters may have been based on one James Erickson, the grandfather of Cather's childhood friends in Red Cloud, Nebraska—Margie, Carrie, Mary, and Irene Miner. The Ericksons lived in Iowa, and "after Mrs. Erickson died, Mr. Erickson visited his daughter [and grandchildren] in Red Cloud and drifted eventually into Kansas to settle on the north branch of the Solomon River" (1961, 64).

Relationship to Other Cather Works

Bennett connects the character of Apollo Gump of "El Dorado" to the much more well-known Paul of "Paul's Case." Both had been theatre ushers in their youth, and both were social misfits. "Apollo Gump dies of snakebite when he is trying to dig up some relics of a happier time of his life. Paul jumps in front of a moving train because he cannot face life without money and prestige" (1982, 49). Pairing the story with "Behind the Singer Tower" (1912), Slote notes that both stories focus on those who "gain by corruption and the misuse of others," western land speculators in one story and New York builders in the other (1970, 9).

The unprincipled villain of the story reappears in several of Cather's novels. He is Wick Cutter of *My Ántonia* and Ivy Peters of *A Lost Lady* (Bloom and Bloom 1962, 49).

Interpretations and Criticisms

Most critics agree that this is not one of Cather's most memorable or important stories. Arnold calls it "overwritten" (1984, 38), and Woodress maintains that it "is told with heavy irony, with an O. Henry surprise ending, . . . but not much can be said for it. New England readers, however, may have been comforted to read about the horrors of life in Kansas and the misfortunes of gullible investors in western real estate" (1987, 149–50). Cather's early attempt to "fictionalize . . . the problem of the mortgage and its effects upon the victim and the holder" was not especially successful, and her handling of the subject results primarily in melodrama (Bloom and Bloom 1962, 65–66).

The critics were not the only people to find fault with this story. Slote explains that many of the inhabitants of Nebraska and Kansas were offended by Cather's bleak portrayal of the region. After the story appeared, the Lincoln *Courier* ran an article reprinted from the Kansas City *Journal* that described Kansans as enraged that someone who did not even seem to know much about the area would portray it so bleakly. The Kansans maintained the story was simply false—neither oak trees nor stunted corn is found in the Solomon Valley (1970, 12–13). However, because the author was a woman, "according to the chivalrous code of western Kansas, [she] cannot be killed or scalped" (quoted in Slote 1970, 13).

Works Cited

Arnold, Marilyn. 1984. *Willa Cather's Short Fiction*. Athens: Ohio University Press.

Bennett, Mildred R. 1961. *The World of Willa Cather*. Lincoln: University of Nebraska Press.

———. 1982. "Willa Cather's Bodies for Ghosts." *Western American Literature* 17:39–52.

Bloom, Edward A., and Lillian D. Bloom. 1962. *Willa Cather's Gift of Sympathy*. Carbondale: Southern Illinois University Press.

Cather, Willa. [1965] 1970. "El Dorado: A Kansas Recessional." In *Willa Cather's Collected Short Fiction, 1892–1912*. Ed. Virginia Faulkner. Lincoln: University of Nebraska Press, 323–31.

Faulkner, Virginia, ed. [1965] 1970. *Willa Cather's Collected Short Fiction, 1892–1912*. Lincoln: University of Nebraska Press. Reprint. Lincoln: University of Nebraska Press.

Slote, Bernice. 1970. "Willa Cather as a Regional Writer." *Kansas Quarterly* 2:7–15.

Woodress, James. 1987. *Willa Cather: A Literary Life*. Lincoln: University of Nebraska Press.

Eleanor's House

Publication History

This story was first published under the name Willa Sibert Cather in the October 1907 issue of *McClure's* (29:623–30) (Faulkner 596). It was reprinted in 1965 by the University of Nebraska Press in *Willa Cather's Collected Short Fiction, 1892–1912*.

Circumstances of Composition, Sources, and Influences

This story was the fourth one Cather published (the third to be published in *McClure's* magazine) after she moved to New York City from Pittsburgh and had taken a position on *McClure's* staff (Arnold 1984, 69).

Every critic who has commented on the story has mentioned the strong influence of Henry James on it. It has, in fact, been judged by several authorities to be perhaps Cather's *most* Jamesian story. All agree with Bennett that in "Eleanor's House" Cather truly "bows too humbly at the shrine of Henry James. . . ." (1970, xxxvii). The specific links to James are obvious: like so many of James's works, this story concerns Americans living in Europe. Cather's character Harriet Westfield is a typical Jamesian observer-narrator and strikingly similar to Mrs. Gereth in James's *The Spoils of Poynton*; the plots of both pieces are also alike. Furthermore, there are similarities between Harriet and Fanny Assingham of James's *The Golden Bowl* (Arnold 1984, 78).

O'Brien explains Cather's attraction to James during this period as part of the author's attempt to resolve "her own creative and psychic conflicts. She gravitated to a writer who possessed what she feared she lacked: the ability to shape powerful and disturbing feeling into art" (1987, 300). She was concerned that her writing was sometimes too emotional, too undisciplined, "fervent and florid" like so much women's writing, and she saw in James an artist whose "craftsmanship balanced her excesses" (1987, 300).

Thurin believes that besides its debt to James, the story also owes something to Poe's "Ligeia," which tells the story of a man who so mourns the loss of his first wife that she eventually returns to him by taking over the body of his second wife. In addition, the plot of "Eleanor's House" may be at least partially connected to Cather's own life. During her first trip to Europe in 1902, Cather and her friend Isabelle McClung had spent a pleasant week in the town of Lavandou on the Mediterranean, clearly the model for the fishing village near Hyères in this story. Many details of the village—even the mention of goat's milk and figs—come directly from the letters Cather wrote from Lavandou (1990, 147–49, 157n).

In Brown's view, although Cather certainly paid homage to James here, the "story is not authentic James: the renunciations are somewhat unreal, the conflicts a little sullen" (1964, 144). Eleanor's husband's grief passes too quickly. Furthermore, he is diminished rather than ennobled by pain, and "the elaborate Jamesian form has no real affinity with the simple sequence of feeling" (Brown 1964, 144).

Relationship to Other Cather Works

This story has been grouped with other Cather works solely on the basis of its indebtedness to Henry James, which places it especially in the company of "Flavia and Her Artists," "The Garden Lodge," "'A Death in the Desert,'" and "The Marriage of Phaedra" (all from *The Troll Garden*); the other 1907 stories—"The Namesake" and "The Profile"; and Cather's first novel, *Alexander's Bridge*.

Interpretations and Criticisms

Arnold maintains that the story is a kind of warning "against the mindless sacrifice of everything, especially a living human being, to a notion of the past that has little validity in the present" (1984, 78): one must be careful to view the past objectively and accurately because the past is capable of lying. The central fact of this story is that Harriet Westfield's worship of the past is folly. Cather allows the reader to trust Harriet so that when she is finally revealed as the jealous and reactionary person she is, the revelation hits the reader hard, and in the end "the reader is no less surprised than Harriet to discover that under Ethel's influence Forscythe has found himself, . . . and Harriet is buried in the nostalgia that had blurred her vision from the first"; another of Harriet's functions in the story is "to create the inescapable presence of Eleanor. . . . Harriet is her prophetess, . . . interpreting her will on numerous occasions" (Arnold 1984, 80). It is through the more reasonable responses of Robert Westfield, Harriet's husband, that we eventually come to understand that Harriet's observations about Eleanor or Eleanor's house are always unreliable. Once Harriet has been discredited, Cather's message becomes clear—an "appropriation of the past in order to escape painful reality [is] folly" (Arnold 1984, 81).

To O'Brien, the story examines one person's absorption by another in a marriage the same way that "The Willing Muse" examines one writer's absorption by another. One of the things that consistently disturbed Cather was any kind of "fusion that obliterated separate identities" (1987, 302). Harold Forscythe lost himself twice—once when he met Eleanor and again when she died. That the two people had become one is not something Cather viewed as positive or healthy, but sexual, romantic relationships are merely surface subjects in this story. The more important subject is Cather's "anxiety of influence and imitation. From this perspective, the absent presence is Henry James, whose powerful ghost dominates the story thematically and stylistically. 'Eleanor's House' . . . is also James' house of fiction" (O'Brien 1987, 303).

The story is framed by two classical images, according to Thurin. The first is "the blue ether of Olympus, the heaven of Greek mythology," and the second is the Mediterranean (1990, 148). Both images reinforce the notion that Harold and Eleanor were larger than life—perhaps superhuman—and unwilling to recognize the limitations of the flesh. After Eleanor's death and his remarriage, Harold sneaks back to Provence in memory of the time he and Eleanor were there. Eleanor was so attached to the place that she had vowed that they would return each year at grape-harvest time. "This Dionysian urge was thwarted . . . by her . . . death, but Harold feels going back there is a holy rite" (Thurin 1990, 148). In this way Ethel helps Harold return to the world of real human beings, but whether or not Cather saw this return of Harold's as a sign of maturity is unclear because "the attitude of the observer . . . makes the argument go two ways"—Harriet believes that Eleanor, not Ethel, brought Harold maturity and that he had "a temporary relapse into immature behavior after her . . . death" (Thurin 1990, 149). In no way does Harriet view Harold's and Eleanor's lifestyle as immature. Harriet's opinion takes on a good deal of credibility when we stop to consider that in 1907 Cather herself had "certainly not chosen to descend into the sphere of generation"; furthermore, Harold and Eleanor's love could certainly have been shared by two women: "Harold is male only in name" (1990, 149).

Works Cited

Arnold, Marilyn. 1984. *Willa Cather's Short Fiction*. Athens: Ohio University Press.

Bennett, Mildred. [1965] 1970. Introduction to *Willa Cather's Collected Short Fiction*. Ed. Virginia Faulkner. Lincoln: University of Nebraska Press. Reprint. Lincoln: University of Nebraska Press.

Brown, E. K. Completed by Leon Edel. [1953] 1964. *Willa Cather: A Critical Biography*. New York: Knopf.

Cather, Willa. [1965] 1970. "Eleanor's House." In *Willa Cather's Collected Short Fiction, 1892–1912*. Ed. Virginia Faulkner. Lincoln: University of Nebraska Press, 95–111.

Faulkner, Virginia, ed. [1965] 1970. *Willa Cather's Collected Short Fiction, 1892–1912*. Lincoln: University of Nebraska Press. Reprint. Lincoln: University of Nebraska Press.

O'Brien, Sharon. 1987. *Willa Cather: The Emerging Voice*. New York: Oxford University Press.

Thurin, Erik Ingvar. 1990. *The Humanization of Willa Cather: Classicism in an American Classic*. Lund, Sweden: Lund University Press.

The Elopement of Allen Poole

Publication History

This story was first published, unsigned, on April 15, 1893, in the University of Nebraska student journal the *Hesperian* (22:4–7) (Faulkner 1970, 590). It was reprinted in 1966 by the University of Nebraska Press in *The Kingdom of Art: Willa Cather's First Principles and Critical Statements, 1893–1896*, edited by Bernice Stote, and in 1970 by the same press in the revised edition of *Willa Cather's Collected Short Fiction, 1892–1912*. The story was identified too late to be included in the 1965 edition of the latter work (Woodress 1971, 102).

Circumstances of Composition, Sources, and Influences

Cather published this story while she was a sophomore at the University of Nebraska, apparently capable of writing "highly evocative prose at the age of nineteen" (Woodress 1971, 102). She spent the first nine years of her life in Virginia, and the story represents her first use of that state as a setting: "[S]he creates a richly nostalgic Shenandoah landscape ten years after leaving it, just as she later does the Nebraska prairie a decade following her move to Pittsburgh and New York" (1971, 102). Evidently Cather required both distance and time between herself and the people and places of her youth in order to work them into her fiction effectively

Relationship to Other Cather Works

Cather returns to Virginia as a setting in "A Night at Greenway Court" (1896), and finally in *Sapphira and the Slave Girl* (1940). Slote points out the similarities between the landscape of this piece and that of the novel. Cather evokes the same details of the Virginia mountains, woods, and fields in these two depictions (1966, 104).

Slote also notes numerous other correspondences between the two works: the scene containing reapers working in the valley in "Allen Poole" becomes the hay-cutting scene in *Sapphira*, and a graveyard with a stone wall appears in both "Allen Poole" and in *Sapphira*, as does a description of a bridge based on "the unique wooden footbridge, or suspension bridge, which crossed Back Creek near the Cather home" (1966, 104–105). Robinson notes a thread in the story that reappears several times in Cather's work—the notion that it is good to die young while life is yet full of joy, before age causes one to view life as mostly mundane and routine (1983, 46).

Slote points out other details that appear in "Allen Poole" and then reappear in later Cather works: the atmosphere and scents of the country and the "white mystery and tragedy of the moonlight night" are some examples (1966, 105). Further, Allen's impulse to sweep Nellie up into his arms prefigures the central episode of "On the Divide," and echoes Alexandra's dream of being lifted high and carried away in *O Pioneers!* (Slote 1966 105–106). In another recurring scene, Allen listens to the whippoorwill as he waits for Nellie and then begins whistling passionately, just as Nils in "The Bohemian Girl" waits in a field for Clara, where nature's night song is all around him (Slote 1966, 106).

According to O'Brien, this piece provides some of the earliest evidence of Cather's interest in the risks involved in "any engagement with the underground cavern of the erotic and the unconscious" (1987, 205). This underground cavern also includes a "submerged preoccupation with creativity," which is an obvious aspect of "The Elopement of Allen Poole" (1987, 204). Cather's concern with this subject reappears in "Coming, Aphrodite!" (1921) when Hedger relates the story of "The Forty Lovers of the Queen" to Eden Bower. There, "the metaphoric death and silence become literal for the explorer who engages with sexual and creative forces hidden in the cavern"; still later, in 1927, Cather uses the images again in *Death Comes for the Archbishop* (1987, 204).

Interpretations and Criticisms

Most critics dismiss this story as simply one of Cather's experiments in fiction from early in her apprenticeship period and as such unworthy of serious critical attention. In their opinion, the story is valuable only as evidence of the young writer's serious, but necessarily awkward, beginning efforts in her artistic development.

Only one Cather specialist, Sharon O'Brien, has advanced a thorough analysis of the story. In one of her essays, O'Brien points out that this story is useful primarily for the insights it provides into the author's own psychology : the motifs of "the child searching for a maternal figure, the association of erotic and maternal love, the dangers of passion—are [Cather's] own enduring preoccupations. . . . " (1982, 273). As is the case in nearly all Cather's early stories, "The Elopement of Allen Poole" illustrates Cather's ambivalence concerning all intimate, nurturing relationships. The person who succumbs to the desire for such nurturance pays a heavy price—at best, the loss of identity, at worst, as in this story, literal death (O'Brien 1982, 275). Here, the protagonist's love is a mother figure, a "little Madonna of the Hills," who literally "assumes the mother's role . . . [and] is alluring because she offers love and nurturance, but terrifying because she threatens loss of self; to regain the infant's preconscious oneness with the mother is to be obliterated, to die" (O'Brien 1982, 275). Readers of this story may reasonably ask whether Cather is not showing her own malice for "heterosexual passion and [for] her male rivals by killing off the male lover"; on the other hand, she may simply be "revealing her . . . discomfort with . . . erotic/emotional drives" (O'Brien 1982, 277).

In a later analysis of the story, O'Brien maintains that it is one of several that illustrate Cather's own experience of the conflict between self-disclosure and self-concealment as an artist (1987, 203). Although both can result in disaster, this story suggests that disclosure carries with it even more danger than concealment does. Allen's two secrets—that he is a moonshiner and secretly engaged—are both eventually discovered, a revelation that ends with his death (O'Brien 1987, 203).

That Cather ends with an allusion to *Hamlet* reveals both "the story's overt concern with sexuality and its covert concern with creativity"; although Allen cannot rightly be called an artist, he does have something of an artistic sensibility: he has committed to memory a variety of old tunes, which he is known to whistle. A significant fact is that, "after he breaks into a 'passion' of whistling on his way to meet Nell," he is killed: Allen has been found out in much the same way the writer is found out when she tells a story, and the death that results for Allen, "equated by Cather with silence, seems punishment for both his expression of desire and his distilling" (O'Brien 1987, 204).

Works Cited

Cather, Willa. 1966. "The Elopement of Allen Poole." In *The Kingdom of Art: Willa Cather's First Principles and Critical Statements, 1893–1896*. Ed. Bernice Slote. Lincoln: University of Nebraska Press, 437–41.

———. 1970. "The Elopement of Allen Poole." In *Willa Cather's Collected Short Fiction, 1892–1912*. Ed. Virginia Faulkner. Lincoln: University of Nebraska Press, 573–78.

Faulkner, Virginia, ed. [1965] 1970. *Willa Cather's Collected Short Fiction, 1892–1912*. Lincoln: University of Nebraska Press. Reprint. Lincoln: University of Nebraska Press.

O'Brien, Sharon. 1982. "Mothers, Daughters, and the 'Art Necessity': Willa Cather and the Creative Process." In *American Novelists Revisited: Essays in Feminist Criticism*. Ed. Fritz Fleischmann. Boston: G. K. Hall, 265–98.

———. 1987. *Willa Cather: The Emerging Voice*. New York: Oxford University Press.

Robinson, Phyllis C. 1983. *Willa: The Life of Willa Cather*. Garden City, NY: Doubleday.

Slote, Bernice, ed. 1966. *The Kingdom of Art*. Lincoln: University of Nebraska Press.

Woodress, James. 1971. "Willa Cather Seen Clear." *Papers on Language & Literature* 7:96–109.

The Enchanted Bluff

Publication History

This story was first published under the name Willa Sibert Cather in the April 1909 issue of *Harper's* (118:774–81) (Faulkner 596). It was reprinted in 1956 by Vintage Books in *Five Stories*; in 1965 by the University of Nebraska Press in *Willa Cather's Collected Short Fiction, 1892–1912*; and in 1992 by Literary Classics of the United States in *Cather: Stories, Poems, and Other Writings*, a volume in the Library of America series.

Circumstances of Composition, Sources, and Influences

Long before Cather ever visited the Southwest, the area had captured her imagination. In this story, she combines her fascination with that area and her memories of her Red Cloud childhood, specifically of the times she and her brothers camped on Far Island in the Republican River (Woodress 1987, 205). Cather and her brother Douglass had even talked about exploring the Southwest together, just as the boys in this story dream of a similar adventure (Bloom and Bloom 1962, 203).

In an October 1908 letter to Sarah Orne Jewett, Cather mentions that she is working on a story with a Western setting that she believes will please Jewett. According to Woodress, she probably enclosed a copy of the story with the letter, but there is no evidence that Jewett commented on it. The story did not please S. S. McClure, who pronounced it all "introduction" and refused to publish it in *McClure's* magazine, where Cather was employed at the time (Woodress 1970, 131). In the same letter to Jewett, Cather explains the Spanish influence felt in the West: "Spanish words enriched the English language, and . . . [t]here was something heady in the wind that blew up from Mexico" (Woodress 1970, 217).

In this story Cather allows her own childhood and her own interests to prevail, and she displays an awareness of the fact that to mature as an artist and find her own voice, she must write from her own experience, her own country. Nevertheless, she would not "mine her mother lode extensively" until after she wrote her first novel, *Alexander's Bridge* (1912), probably because her job as managing editor of *McClure's* absorbed so much of her time and was itself a ripe subject for her fiction (Woodress 1970, 143).

Cather had long been captivated by a legend that became one of the sources for this story as well as for *Death Comes for the Archbishop* (1927). The legend tells the tale of an Indian tribe whose home was at the top of Katzímo, a New Mexican mesa. While some of the tribesmen were farming the land at the foot of their mesa, a fierce storm blocked the only pathway to the top. The tribe was forced to move on to Acoma mesa, "where they established their now traditional home" (Bloom and Bloom 1962, 202).

Lee sees the influence of "Virgil's shepherds talking under the evening star" and of "modern pastoral models" for the story; the river at night is reminiscent of *The Adventures of Huckleberry Finn*, and "the sense of mystery and space is like Turgenev's 'Behzin Meadow'" (1989, 98). In Turgenev's story, a huntsman, lost in the country, spends the night with some boys at a campfire telling ghost stories: "their voices carry on the summer night like Cather's boys, and there is the same sense of a scene opening out and out into time and space" (1989, 99). Stouck agrees, saying that "The Enchanted Bluff" "follows the same structure and evokes the same mood" as the Turgenev story, the young boys stirred and animated by the "campfire and the moonlight and the future. In both her story and Turgenev's, an epilogue reveals that the dreams of boys invariably fade or are cut short by death" (1990, 5).

Relationship to Other Cather Works

This story was one of the first three Cather wrote after meeting Sarah Orne Jewett, and like the other two, "On the Gulls' Road" and "The Joy of Nelly Deane," it demonstrates Jewett's influence. One of the common themes in Jewett's fiction is "the alliance between creativity and friendship," and in each of these three Cather stories "human relationships stimulate self-expression" (O'Brien 1987, 365).

Gerber links this story to four Cather novels—*The Song of the Lark*, *The Professor's House*, *Death Comes for the Archbishop*, and *Shadows on the Rock*. In each work, but beginning with "The Enchanted Bluff," Cather uses "a much older civilization as a standard of measurement" (1975, 121). The story also marks Cather's first use of what the boys refer to as the big red rock that extends out of the sand about nine hundred feet. In her subsequent works the rock takes on new meanings: "For instance in *The Song of the Lark* (1915) the Rock's Utopianism is augmented by identification with esthetics. . . ."; in *The Professor's House* the Rock is even more prominent, "the main narrative being split in two for the insertion of 'Tom Outland's Story,' a tale of the Rock's discovery and loss. . . . Outland's story is 'The Enchanted Bluff' brought to reality" (1958, 152). *Death Comes for the Archbishop* reveals the rock's religious significance, and finally, in *Shadows on the Rock*, the rock becomes itself the novel's dominant figure. Because the rock remained fixed in Cather's imagination, taking on increased significance over time, it is certainly "one of the most thoroughly exploited symbols of modern fiction, climaxing [Cather's] rejection of twentieth-century life, which she saw as an agony of blatant commercialism and shallow artistic talents catering to Babbittry" (Gerber 1958, 153–55).

According to Robinson, the roots of this story can be traced back to Cather's much earlier story "The Way of the World," where this group of young boys was first introduced (1983, 159). Later, the story reappears as a chapter in *My Ántonia*, where we see "children listening and dreaming as a story is being told to them," in Jim Burden's relation of the tale of Coronado's search for the Seven Golden Cities (Welty 1984, 72). The story also shares its ending with that of *My Ántonia*. In both, the narrator looks back over twenty years "from the disillusioned perspective of adult life" (Stouck 1975, 44).

Cather used the technique of a story-within-a-story several times. The most obvious and perhaps best-known example is that of "Tom Outland's Story" in *The Professor's House*. In both "The Enchanted Bluff" and the novel, "the frame story . . . is set in the present day, and the story-within-a-story concerns an ancient tribe of Indians"; furthermore, "The Enchanted Bluff" may be said to contain the kernel of the theme that is finally fully developed in the novel (Chaliff 1978, 63–64, 67).

Ferguson is the only critic to link this tale with the better-known "Paul's Case" by finding a common theme: the frustrated ambition of a young boy. Despite the crucial difference in the desires of the two boys, the obstacle between them and their dreams is the same—"dull, prosaic life" (1970, 61).

Schneider points out that this story has much in common with all the other stories that display Cather's ambivalent feelings about the land itself. Along with "Lou, the Prophet" (1812), "The Clemency of the Court" (1893), "On the Divide" (1896), "Eric Hermannson's Soul" (1900), "A Wagner Matinée" (1904), and "The Bohemian Girl" (1912), this story reveals a "denigration and rejection" of the land, while at the same time displaying "appreciation and acceptance" (1967, 76). The reactions of various characters toward the land have more to do with the characters' personalities and class than with the land itself (1967, 77).

Brown connects this story directly to "The Treasure of Far Island," even referring to "The Enchanted Bluff" as a remolding of the earlier tale. Both stories are evidence of "the hold the memory of river and isle had upon Willa Cather's imagination as a place where her childhood was eternally enshrined." So too is the dedication to her brothers in the first edition of *April Twilights*, her volume of poetry, where "she remembered the 'Odysseys of summer mornings' and the 'starry wonder-tales of nights in April'" and "'Of the three who lay and planned at moonrise,/ On an island in a western river/ Of the conquest of the world together'" (quoted in Brown 1964,

40–41). The image of the river island is repeated again in Cather's first novel, *Alexander's Bridge*, when the title character spies a group of boys seated around a campfire beneath a railroad bridge, and wishes he could return to his own childhood, camping with boys on a Western river. Each time the image recurs in Cather's fiction, it "denotes a way of looking at the world when life is still untried and bespeaks only the excitement and wonder of the future" (Stouck 1975, 17–18).

Arnold groups this story with "The Namesake" and "Eleanor's House" as examples of Cather's tendency to pay homage to the importance of human ties, to one's own family, and to humanity in general (1984, 75). Woodress notes Cather's use of the moon in this story as a way of connecting it to some of her other works. Early on, Cather had made use of moon imagery in "Eric Hermannson's Soul," then again in "The Treasure of Far Island," *The Song of the Lark, A Lost Lady*, and *My Mortal Enemy* (1987, 220–21).

Interpretations and Criticisms

In Schneider's view, the river is a central symbol in this story. Its two opposing moods, one sunny, the other regretful, parallel the present and future of the boys around the campfire. Its dual moods also suggest Cather's own ambivalence toward the plains at this time in her career (1967, 87). Rosowski argues that duality is also expressed in other ways: the whooping crane that flies above the boys functions as a "sign that there is a southern land to which unfettered creatures can travel," and eventually both the sandbar and the enchanted bluff "become . . . symbol[s] of such freedom" (1986, 31). Such duality is often expressed in Cather's early essays: her characters start out with their feet firmly planted on the ground of reality, then soar above that ground briefly "to a spiritual, imaginative world," then descend abruptly back to earth, "but forever changed by their dream" (Rosowski 1986, 31).

Chaliff sees the story as a microcosm of everything Cather's work would eventually become. Her reliance on childhood memories and her use of "evocation, suggestion, and the creation of mood over direct statement and dramatic plot development" signal the beginning of the technique she would use in nearly all her later work (1978, 64–65). Edith Lewis, with whom Cather lived from 1913 until Cather's death in 1947, also notes the role of memory and evocation in the story: "It was as if she had here stopped trying to make a story, and had let it make itself, out of instinctive memories, deep-rooted, forgotten things" (1953, 70).

Arnold sees the story as a turning point in Cather's work because it represents the first time the author used a Nebraska setting "both tenderly and honestly"; many of her very early short stories paint unrelentingly harsh pictures of life on the prairie, whereas "The Treasure of Far Island," for example, presents it as unrealistically ideal (1984, 82). In this story, Cather has found the "middle ground" that would "inform her fiction for the rest of her life" (Arnold 1984, 82). Her awareness of the value of the past begins with this story and shapes much of her later fiction as well. Here the past is twofold: there is the narrator's own history and the vast human history of which everyone is a part. In some ways the story is "distinctly elegiac, . . . a tone that is enhanced by the juxtaposition of the present with personal past, and by the added perspective of two or three layers of ancient past"; Cather balances the downward movement of the death of one of the boys by mentioning Tip Smith's son, Bert, who keeps the dream of the Enchanted Bluff very much alive in his heart: the "continuity is always there, reaching backward and forward through time" (Arnold 1984, 83).

Stouck comments on Cather's manipulation of the imagery in the story. One image suggests another, which suggests another, and so on. The boys ponder Columbus steering his ship by the stars and Napoleon reading the stars for clues to his future. This same image is expanded as the moon rises like a full-sailed galleon, and the red moon then evokes the Aztecs' ritual of human sacrifice, which in turn brings to mind the story of Coronado, which leads the boys to contemplate those parts of the world they would most like to visit (1975, 44). The story is rooted in the pastoral and thus is "shaped by the fundamental paradox of pastoral art": the boys yearn to be done with childhood and get on with their journey, their plans, yet the reader always recognizes that "because this is a memory, . . . they are living in the most perfect time of their life" (Stouck 1975, 44).

Edward A. Bloom and Lillian D. Bloom argue that this story underscores Cather's belief that the only "really durable monument is the spirit," a notion Cather supports by fusing the past with the present (1962, 37). Positioning her characters "among the vestiges of a long silent order, [Cather] discovered a spiritual continuity whose aura conveyed intimations of immortality" (Bloom and Bloom 1962, 37).

As Wasserman argues, it is through the small talk of a group of boys that the story weighs the human condition. We come to realize that the human condition is not, as Wordsworth sensed, defined by the "serenity and reassurance [of] surrounding nature," but unstable, like the river on which the Sandtown boys camp" (1991, 16). The bluff, too, speaks of instability, having been "brought by a glacier, . . . its base . . . worn by wind and sand. Only the 'enchantment' survives—the 'romance' held in the human imagination and perpetuated by story, from Uncle Bill to Tip to Tip's son" (Wasserman 1991, 16). The bluff may be compared to the lighthouse of Virginia Woolf—"an ultimate destination promising fulfillment . . . never to be reached. Both . . . give meaning and direction across the gulfs of time, though what that meaning is must remain ineffable" because in fact the only meaning they have is bestowed on them by the human imagination and thus is anything but stable (Wasserman 1991, 17).

The human imagination is only one of the many elements that give shape to existence in the story, however. In Lee's opinion, others include the evening light that softens the rough surrounding; the river itself, which continually carves out new islands; the stars, which make their own diagrams on the sky; the flow of the river; and the glacial formation of the Bluff. The boys themselves are shape makers through their love of connections between things: Tip carries what he claims are relics from the Holy Land. The boys make fun of Percy's wondering whether the Spanish explorers came before or after the Mormons. Paradoxically, Cather suggests both predestination and free will here. The boys' futures seem to have been preordained, yet we are continually told that human beings are naturally inclined toward order and perseverance (Lee 1989, 100–101).

The theme Gerber sees as central to the story is vintage Cather: despite the boys' lofty aspirations, not one has reached his goal; "[e]ach has been seduced by life's paraphernalia." In fact one boy, who has grown up to become a stockbroker in a red touring car, embodies one of Cather's perennial themes, that the materialism of American culture crushes any possibility of an artistic sensibility developing (1975, 97).

O'Brien finds in the story indications that Cather was beginning to reject the masculine values she had once embraced wholeheartedly. The story is both pastoral and communal, set outside the vulgarity of American greed and consumerism. Although the boys' role models are the kinds of macho figures Cather once embraced as "models for the artist, . . . virile, Kiplingesque figures . . . both the content of the inset story of the Bluff and its method of narration contradict the image of the artist as a heroic, solitary conqueror": the story of the Bluff is passed on through an oral tradition in which the listeners participate in the story's creation (1987, 371). The sympathetic audience allows Tip to speak without embarrassment or hesitation. When some suggestion of competition and aggression creeps in—the boys' fixation on being the first to arrive, for example—it is an indication of the corrupting influence of the society on shore. Individual aspirations are negative: no single boy has the ability to act alone; each receives strength from the others (O'Brien 1987, 370–71). Unfortunately, "neither the communal nor the individualistic models of creative endeavor succeed. The Indian potters and cloth-makers are destroyed, . . . the boys do not climb the Bluff together, and yet no one climbs [it] separately" (O'Brien 1987, 371).

Works Cited

Arnold, Marilyn. 1984. *Willa Cather's Short Fiction*. Athens: Ohio University Press.

Bloom, Edward A., and Lillian D. Bloom. 1962. *Willa Cather's Gift of Sympathy*. Carbondale: Southern Illinois University Press.

Brown, E. K. Completed by Leon Edel. [1953] 1964. *Willa Cather: A Critical Biography*. New York: Knopf.

Cather, Willa. 1956. "The Enchanted Bluff." In *Five Stories*. New York: Vintage Books, 3–15.

———. [1965] 1970. "The Enchanted Bluff." In *Willa Cather's Collected Short Fiction, 1892–1912*. Ed. Virginia Faulkner. Lincoln: University of Nebraska Press, 69–77.

———. 1992. "The Enchanted Bluff." In *Cather: Stories, Poems, and Other Writings*. New York: Literary Classics of the United States, 64–73.

Chaliff, Cynthia. 1978. "The Art of Willa Cather's Craft." *Papers on Language & Literature* 14:61–73.

Faulkner, Virginia, ed. [1965] 1970. *Willa Cather's Collected Short Fiction, 1892–1912*. Lincoln: University of Nebraska Press. Reprint. Lincoln: University of Nebraska Press.

Ferguson, J. M., Jr. 1970. "'Vague Outlines': Willa Cather's Enchanted Bluffs." *Western Review* 7:61–64.

Gerber, Philip L. 1958. "Willa Cather and the Big Red Rock." *College English* 19:152–57.

———. 1975. *Willa Cather*. Boston: Twayne.

Lee, Hermione. 1989. *Willa Cather: Double Lives*. New York: Pantheon.

Lewis, Edith. 1953. *Willa Cather Living*. New York: Knopf.

O'Brien, Sharon. 1987. *Willa Cather: The Emerging Voice*. New York: Oxford University Press.

Robinson, Phyllis C. 1983. *Willa: The Life of Willa Cather*. Garden City, NY: Doubleday.

Rosowski, Susan J. 1986. *The Voyage Perilous: Willa Cather's Romanticism*. Lincoln: University of Nebraska Press.

Schneider, Sister Lucy. 1967. "Willa Cather's Early Stories in the Light of Her 'Land-Philosophy.'" *Midwest Quarterly* 9:75–94.

Stouck, David. 1975. *Willa Cather's Imagination*. Lincoln: University of Nebraska Press.

———. 1990. "Willa Cather and the Russians." In *Cather Studies*, vol. 1. Ed. Susan Rosowski. Lincoln: University of Nebraska Press, 1–20.

Wasserman, Loretta. 1991. *Willa Cather: A Study of the Short Fiction*. Boston: Twayne.

Welty, Eudora. 1984. "The House of Willa Cather." In *Critical Essays on Willa Cather*. Ed. John J. Murphy. Boston: G. K. Hall.

Woodress, James. 1970. *Willa Cather: Her Life and Art*. New York: Pegasus.

———. 1987. *Willa Cather: A Literary Life*. Lincoln: University of Nebraska Press.

Eric Hermannson's Soul

Publication History

This story was first published in the April 1900 issue of *Cosmopolitan* (28:633–44) under the name Willa Sibert Cather (Faulkner 1970, 592). It was reprinted in 1957 by Dodd, Mead in *Early Stories*. Mildred R. Bennett, who selected the stories for the Dodd, Mead edition, reports that "this story was translated into German by Eugene von Tempsky who labeled it a 'psychological masterpiece.' A request for translation rights was not usual at the time" (1957, 215). In 1965 the story was reprinted by the University of Nebraska Press in *Willa Cather's Collected Short Fiction, 1892–1912* and again in 1992 by Literary Classics of the United States in *Cather: Stories, Poems, and Other Writings*, a volume in the Library of America series.

Circumstances of Composition, Sources, and Influences

Written during Cather's last year of editing wire copy for the Pittsburgh *Leader*, "Eric Hermannson's Soul" was her most significant publication up to that time. Although she had previously published "On the Divide" (1896) in the *Overland Monthly*, that magazine was not nearly as prestigious as *Cosmopolitan* (Woodress 1970, 95).

The character of Eric Hermannson is a composite of the many Norsemen Cather knew in Nebraska. In fact, when she met the Norwegian explorer Fridjof Nansen in 1897, Cather realized immediately that there were hundreds of men like Nansen in Nebraska (Slote 1970, 10). In an article for the *Courier*, she wrote, "They are scattered all over those vast midland plains populated by the peasantry of Europe. I have passed some of my days among them" (*Courier*, December 18, 1897; quoted in Slote 1970, 10).

Bennett traces the story's windmill scene back to an incident in Cather's childhood. Cather and her brother Roscoe had climbed their uncle's windmill supposedly to see the moon rise, but once on top they became engrossed in watching a storm brewing on the horizon. They waited too long to begin their descent, and when they finally did, the wind was so strong that "Willa had to take off her outer skirts to get down, and in spite of Roscoe's help she blistered her hands clinging to the narrow ladder" (1961, 33).

Other incidents in the story that come from Cather's own experience include Margaret Elliot's trip west with her brother, which may be a description of some of the treks Cather and her brother Douglass made while he was working on the Burlington Railroad in Wyoming (Bennett 1957, 194). In the story, Cather actually mentions the town of Riverton, which was a real town on the Burlington line (Bennett 1957, 198).

Cather's interest in Daudet is well documented, and Bennett suggests that "in the delicacy of the feeling between Eric and Margaret," this story is at least reminiscent of "one of Daudet's 'Les Etoiles,' where a shepherd is secretly in love with his employer's daughter"; when a flood strands her at the shepherd's cabin, he keeps her safe all night, and tells her stories about the stars, especially about the shepherds' own special guardian star (1957, 215).

Relationship to Other Cather Works

Arnold groups this story with the many other Cather works, such as *O Pioneers!* that depict the Divide as an inhospitable home for European immigrants (1984, 20). In addition, the central place that the subject of art occupies in this story connects it to much of Cather's other work (Arnold 1984, 23).

Thurin points out that "Eric Hermannson's Soul" is similar to "The Resurrection" in that both stories deal "with a revival of the soul—of the whole human being—through the experience of erotic attraction and the life of the senses," and in both stories the male character is described as crude and clumsy, but each compensates for his clumsiness "through sheer, honest masculinity" (1990, 106).

One of the characters that effectively connects this story to other Cather works is Lena Hanson, the sensual but insubstantial woman Eric visits. Bennett refers to the many Lenas in the fiction as "ghosts that kept haunting Cather" (1982, 42). Lena appeared first as Canute's wife in "On the Divide," and later, in "Jack-A-Boy," she was the "Woman Nobody Called On." In "The Bohemian Girl," the character is Olena Yenson, and in that story she evolves toward what will become her final appearance—Lena Lingard of *My Ántonia* (Bennett 1982, 42–43).

Another character in this story who makes appearances in other works is Asa Skinner. There are echoes of the title character of "Lou, the Prophet" in Asa, although, as Bennett points out, Skinner is more suited to his environment than Lou is "and is therefore less pitiful, though less lovable. He is stupid but sincere. . . " (1957, 188). By the time a similar character, Brother Weldon, appears in *One of Ours*, he is both stupid and insincere. In Bennett's opinion these characters exemplify Cather's own difficulty with faith, which climaxes in *Death Comes for the Archbishop* and *Shadows on the Rock*. Her most tolerant portrait of a Protestant minister is that of Peter Kronberg in *The Song of the Lark*. But even he is dull and fairly inarticulate (1957, 188–89).

Margaret, too, is in many ways a typical Cather character. Arnold sees her as directly related to Bartley Alexander (*Alexander's Bridge*), Marie Shabata (*O Pioneers!*), Clara Vavrika ("The Bohemian Girl"), Thea Kronborg (*The Song of the Lark*), and Godfrey St. Peter (*The Professor's House*) (Arnold 1984, 22–23). Further, it is Margaret, not Eric, who most effectively foreshadows Cather's later characters, for "her brush with elementalism has stirred . . . her toward almost uncontrollable desires," just as many of Cather's later characters are often at the mercy of desires that are inexplicable to them (Arnold 1984, 25).

At one point in the story Cather mentions the habit that some wealthy Eastern gentlemen had of sending their sons to the West to toughen up on the plains. Wyllis Elliot was one young man who had been so sent. Bennett says that these youths were often called remittance men because their families mailed them money every month. Cather makes use of them in several Nebraska tales: Trevor and Brewster, the sheep raisers in *One of Ours*; the Boston-born rancher who takes advantage of Mary Dusak in *My Ántonia*; and even Frank Ellinger of *A Lost Lady*—all may be said to be based on these remittance men (1957, 193).

Interpretations and Criticisms

Most scholars agree that this story is important as one of the earliest examples of Cather's best work. It represents her first publication in a widely read national magazine and her first attempt to deal with the theme of the friction between East and West. Also, in this story she makes explicit for the first time the central conflict of her life—her deep desire for the cultural life of the East and her love of the untamed land of the West (Bennett 1970, xxxi). It is this conflict in Cather's own life that helps her create a long line of western characters who, like Cather herself, yearn for the refinement of the East, but who are unable to purge the West thoroughly from their blood (Arnold 1984, 21). The conflict is portrayed most effectively here by the contrast between Eric and Margaret's Eastern fiancé, who writes her a letter—"an affected parcel of drivel"—that arrives just after Eric "through brute strength and courage and love, saves Margaret from certain injury or even death. . . . Cather juxtaposes this insipid, self-conscious, sexless chatter against Eric's capacity for action and his vibrating, ingenuous avowal of love"; when Eric makes his unrefined, yet "rawly poetic speech," Cather is underscoring the "difference between an elemental feeling for language and a precious taste for the artificial frippery that sometimes passes for clever writing" (Arnold 1984, 21–22). Slote agrees that in this story the raw physicality of the West is presented as vastly superior to the cerebral sterility of the East (1970, 11).

Besides providing one important example of the East–West conflict, the letter from Margaret's fiancé also introduces another perennial Cather subject—art—and further exposes the conflict within Margaret herself (Arnold 1984, 22). In his description of the two paintings he has purchased—one depicting a pale maiden in a thoroughly placid setting and the other distinguished by a kind of flushed sensuality—Margaret's fiancé admits he prefers the pale maiden and that he purchased the other one because Margaret found it appealing. The implication here is that Margaret is repressing a potent and earthy sexuality beneath her civilized veneer, a passion that is now surfacing in her relationship with Eric (Arnold 1984, 22).

Another striking element of the story is Cather's handling of the "multiple use of incident and image and her careful control of rhetoric," the most obvious example of which is the wild horse scene (Arnold 1984, 23). It serves a much broader purpose than merely underscoring the difference between Eric and Margaret's fiancé—it emphasizes the agitation that Margaret's appearance has created in Eric, and the agitation that both Eric's raw masculinity and the wild prairie land have caused in Margaret (Arnold 1984, 23).

Arnold excuses Cather's occasional lapse into inflated language by pointing out that she was making conscious artistic choices. The language she uses during the four pivotal moments in the story—the wild horses incident, Eric's destruction of his violin as he surrenders to the Free-Gospellers, his consent to dance with Margaret, and the windmill scene—conveys exactly the emotion appropriate to each scene. In describing the final moment of climax, the windmill episode, "the once sarcastic narrator grows eloquent"; every element of the plot has moved the story relentlessly toward that scene (1984, 24). Once the final climax is past, Cather's rhetoric becomes subdued to match the feeling of deflation Eric feels as he returns to his daily routine of work after Margaret leaves for the East (Arnold 1984, 24).

Arnold's interpretation is that Eric plays out the old story of damnation and salvation but does not understand its message. He believes that for him the result of allowing his passion to run rampant will be the damnation of his soul, and, ironically, it is this belief in his own unpardonable sin that allows him to escape the clutches of Asa Skinner. His time with Margaret has prevented Eric from becoming a dour religious fanatic. Despite what Eric himself believes, the reader is left with the conviction that he has in fact saved his own soul, for Skinner's ravings no longer frighten him. In fact, he has become peaceful—even lighthearted—in Skinner's presence (1984, 24–25).

Schneider sees the Nebraska plains of the story as a metaphor for Margaret's desire to take risks. She wants to let herself go, a yearning symbolized by her attraction to running the horses on the level prairie. She often suggests that there is a great difference between the freedom she feels in this vast, open land and the trifling concerns of everyday life (1967, 82–83). Cather uses Eric to rouse Margaret to an awareness of what D. H. Lawrence might call "blood consciousness," and her fiancé—significantly nameless— becomes utterly vapid by comparison (Schneider 1967, 84–85). O'Brien's interpretation is similar in that she considers the landscape and the trip West as responsible for awakening the sensual in Margaret as Eric was (1987, 406).

Edward Bloom and Lillian Bloom find within the story one of Cather's early pronouncements on "esthetic apprehension": Cather believed that awareness of the esthetic comes in a sudden, jarring way, like a sudden, startling insight (1962, 155). Other scholars concentrate on the evidence the story provides of Cather's development as an artist. Woodress, for example, feels that the significance of the story lies in Cather's deft handling of her materials. She manipulates each small component skillfully and maintains a significant "measure of aesthetic distance," while treating the theme of East–West conflict (1970, 95–96). Robinson concedes that the story is "sometimes crude and the dialogue artificial," but its realistic portraits of both the country and the characters make it "almost a microcosm" of her later work; it also marks the first time Cather successfully deals with some of the themes that would dominate her later work—the suffering of the immigrants and the "eternal seduction of the land" (1983, 101).

According to Wasserman, "Eric Hermannson's Soul" is Cather's first truly polished story, all the more amazing in light of the fact that a love story about a refined city girl and a crude, macho Westerner was a common one by 1900. Cather saves her story from triteness by adding the story of Eric's conversion, which "adds a dimension to his avowals of which Margaret, in her sophistication, is scarcely aware"; Cather's rhetorical restraint in describing the shouting preacher, Asa Skinner, is also admirable (1991, 42).

Thurin's analysis of the story focuses exclusively on the classical references Cather includes, which are few in number but precisely placed. The Christian tradition is consistently characterized by "life-denying" forces that must be counteracted by the "pagan view of the world more in line with the natural tendencies of man. This view is stated by means of classical images reinforced by themes borrowed from Norse—partly Wagnerian—mythology"; Eric's conversion has been in effect a "kind of self-mutilation, . . . a spiritual suicide," while Margaret represents the corrective, life-embracing, pagan beauty, and it is her influence that allows Eric to regain his identity (1990, 106–107). Thurin goes on to argue that Cather associates Margaret with the gods bringing Eric his fate. Margaret herself compares her excitement at seeing the West to the childhood dream she shared with her brother of discovering the ruins of Troy. Later, the narrator tells us that in Margaret's company Eric felt awe like that of the Goths at the Roman Capitol. Furthermore, earlier in the story Margaret's gypsy blood is mentioned; "in her fiancé's letter she is wryly associated with tropical voluptuousness and African shores. The soul of a Cleopatra or Zenobia is slumbering within her beautiful frame," and despite the fact that Margaret runs away from Eric and the danger connected with her own passion, she has been the instrument of Eric's salvation precisely because she is not bound by the dictates of monotheistic religion (1990, 107–109).

Works Cited

Arnold, Marilyn. 1984. *Willa Cather's Short Fiction*. Athens: Ohio University Press.

Bennett, Mildred, ed. 1957. *Early Stories of Willa Cather*. New York: Dodd, Mead.

Bennett, Mildred R. 1961. *The World of Willa Cather*. Lincoln: University of Nebraska Press.

———. [1965] 1970. Introduction to *Willa Cather's Collected Short Fiction*. Ed. Virginia Faulkner. Lincoln: University of Nebraska Press. Reprint. Lincoln: University of Nebraska Press.

———. 1982. "Willa Cather's Bodies for Ghosts." *Western American Literature* 17:39–52.

Bloom, Edward A., and Lillian D. Bloom. 1962. *Willa Cather's Gift of Sympathy*. Carbondale: Southern Illinois University Press.

Cather, Willa. 1957. "Eric Hermannson's Soul." In *Early Stories*. Ed. Mildred Bennett. New York: Dodd, Mead, 187–215.

———. [1965] 1970. "Eric Hermannson's Soul." In *Willa Cather's Collected Short Fiction, 1892–1912*. Ed. Virginia Faulkner. Lincoln: University of Nebraska Press, 359–79.

———. 1992. "Eric Hermannson's Soul." In *Cather: Stories, Poems, and Other Writings*. New York: Literary Classics of the United States, 22–45.

Faulkner, Virginia, ed. [1965] 1970. *Willa Cather's Collected Short Fiction, 1892–1912*. Lincoln: University of Nebraska Press. Reprint. Lincoln: University of Nebraska Press.

O'Brien, Sharon. 1987. *Willa Cather: The Emerging Voice*. New York: Oxford University Press.

Robinson, Phyllis C. 1983. *Willa: The Life of Willa Cather*. Garden City, NY: Doubleday.

Schneider, Sister Lucy. 1967. "Willa Cather's Early Stories in the Light of Her 'Land-Philosophy.'" *Midwest Quarterly* 9:75–94.

Slote, Bernice. 1970. "Willa Cather as a Regional Writer." *Kansas Quarterly* 2:7–15.

Thurin, Erik Ingvar. 1990. *The Humanization of Willa Cather: Classicism in an American Classic*. Lund, Sweden: Lund University Press.

Wasserman, Loretta. 1991. *Willa Cather: A Study of the Short Fiction*. Boston: Twayne.

Woodress, James. 1970. *Willa Cather: Her Life and Art*. New York: Pegasus.

"The Fear That Walks by Noonday"

Publication History

This story won a $10 first-place prize from the University of Nebraska year-book, *Sombrero* (3:224–31), where it was first published in 1894 under the names Willa Cather and Dorothy Canfield (Faulkner 1970, 591). In 1931, thirty copies of the story were published as books by the Phoenix Book Shop of New York (Lathrop 1975, 118). It was reprinted in 1957 by Dodd, Mead in *Early Stories*, where the date of its first publication is incorrectly given as 1895; in 1965 it was again reprinted by the University of Nebraska Press in *Willa Cather's Collected Short Fiction, 1892–1912* (Lathrop 1975, 118).

Circumstances of Composition, Sources, and Influences

Albertini notes that for some reason Cather wrote two essays on football, in 1893 and 1894, in which she compares the game to an epic, complete with heroes and obstacles for them to overcome on their way to victory or defeat (Albertini 1986, 7, 9). The idea for this story was suggested to Cather by Dorothy Canfield after a football game they had both attended. When she met Willa after the game, Dorothy told her friend about her idea of the ghost of a football player who comes back to win a game for his old team. Willa evidently liked the idea and told Dorothy she intended to use it in a story (Bennett 1957, 45).

Bennett further reports that Dorothy forgot about her suggestion until she saw the story in print. When it was reprinted years later, Dorothy Canfield Fisher found it humorous, but Willa Cather was upset. When asked about the tale, Cather said, somewhat apologetically, that when she wrote it she admired no one more than Henry James. At another time she admitted that when she began writing she consciously imitated James (1957, 45). Evidently, Cather's reference to James's influence is intended as an explanation for having written this, her very first ghost story.

Relationship to Other Cather Works

Bennett sees the character of Horton as a standard Cather figure, perhaps an early version of Claude Wheeler in *One of Ours* (1922). Like Claude, Horton is too refined and sensitive for his surroundings, and he must cope with feelings of inferiority and envy toward Reggie, the same feelings Claude experienced for the Erlichs and for David Gerhardt in *One of Ours* (1957, 52). Albertini agrees that a connection exists between Horton and Claude Wheeler: Claude's football days at Temple College echo this much earlier story (1986, 13).

Arnold points out that Horton is an early example of the solitary misfits in Cather's later Nebraska stories. He was clumsy and ill at ease with both women and men, and he played football in an effort to give the impression that he belonged—at least with men (1984, 7).

This piece was Cather's first attempt to write about ghosts, a subject to which she returned in "The Affair at Grover Station" (1900) and in "Consequences" (1915), another fairly Jamesian tale (Arnold 1984, 7). Actually, in all three cases the presence of the ghosts suggests that Cather was, as she freely admitted, heavily influenced by James. However, at this point in her career, her handling of supernatural elements in her fiction was fairly inept (Woodress 1987, 83).

Interpretations and Criticisms

Very few critics have commented on this piece. Those who have consider it interesting either because it serves as evidence of James's influence on Cather's early work or because the subject was suggested to Cather by Dorothy Canfield (Faulkner 1970, 481). Arnold gives Cather credit for excellent descriptions of the game itself, which are almost on the level of a professional sportswriter (1984, 7).

Albertini contends that Cather placed the football player on a par with "the medieval knight on his quest and the classical hero in his prowess, but the Marathon team's attitude toward training, after months of rigid workouts, is not reminiscent of a Sir Gawain or an Achilles": team members smoke, they grumble about practice, they drink during the game, and although the players' undisciplined approach to training is not the cause of their defeat, in describing their indifference Cather does give the reader a hint that the team will eventually be destroyed (1986, 12).

Works Cited

Albertini, Virgil. 1986. "Willa Cather and Football: A Strange Duality." *Platte Valley Review* 14:7–18.

Arnold, Marilyn. 1984. *Willa Cather's Short Fiction*. Athens: Ohio University Press.

Bennett, Mildred, ed. 1957. *Early Stories of Willa Cather*. New York: Dodd, Mead.

Cather, Willa. 1957. "'The Fear That Walks by Noonday.'" In *Early Stories*. Ed. Mildred Bennett. New York: Dodd, Mead, 45–57.

———. [1965] 1970. "'The Fear That Walks by Noonday.'" In *Willa Cather's Collected Short Fiction, 1892–1912*. Ed. Virginia Faulkner. Lincoln: University of Nebraska Press, 505–14.

Faulkner, Virginia, ed. [1965] 1970. *Willa Cather's Collected Short Fiction, 1892–1912*. Lincoln: University of Nebraska Press. Reprint. Lincoln: University of Nebraska Press.

Lathrop, Joanna. 1975. *Willa Cather: A Checklist of Her Published Writing*. Lincoln: University of Nebraska Press.

Woodress, James. 1987. *Willa Cather: A Literary Life*. Lincoln: University of Nebraska Press.

Flavia and Her Artists

Publication History

This story was first published under the name Willa Sibert Cather in Cather's first collection of short stories, *The Troll Garden* (New York: McClure, Phillips, 1905, pp. 1–54) (Faulkner 1970, 595). In 1961 it reappeared in a Signet Classics paperback edition of the collection with modernized spelling and punctuation.

The story was reprinted in 1965 by the University of Nebraska Press in *Willa Cather's Collected Short Fiction, 1892–1912*; in 1983 by the same press in *The Troll Garden*, edited by James Woodress; and in 1987 by Literary Classics of the United States in *Cather: Early Novels and Stories*, a volume in the Library of America series.

Circumstances of Composition, Sources, and Influences

Like the rest of *The Troll Garden* stories, this one was written sometime between 1901 and 1903 while Cather was teaching high school and living with Isabelle McClung and her family in Pittsburgh. Isabelle had fitted up an attic study for her friend to use, and by all accounts Cather made very good use of it. (For a discussion of the enormous positive influence of Isabelle McClung on Cather's creativity see the "Circumstances of Composition, Sources, and Influences" section for the chapter "A Wagner Matinée.")

Virtually all Cather specialists agree that "Flavia and Her Artists" is one of the author's Jamesian stories. Rosowski expresses a prevailing opinion when she says that the characters of Imogen Willard and Jimmy Broadwood are typical "Jamesian observers" (1986, 23). Further, most critics believe one of the reasons Cather never reprinted the story is that she was somewhat embarrassed by her heavy and obvious reliance upon James's style once she realized that her best stories were those in which her own voice, not James's, prevailed. On the other hand, Woodress sees Cather's "attention to James's craftsmanship [as] important for her developing narrative skill" (1983, xix).

Rosowski and others argue that the character of Flavia is modeled after the mother of Cather's friend Dorothy Canfield Fisher. Fisher's mother, whose name was also Flavia, resembles the title character in some fairly remarkable ways (Rosowski 1985, 143–45). Madigan, too, outlines the connection in some detail. Flavia Canfield, it seems, was passionately devoted to art, was herself an amateur painter, and, like Flavia Hamilton, was proud of her connections to professional artists. When Cather describes Flavia Hamilton's rushing about to keep appointments with various artists, she is drawing heavily on Mrs. Canfield's real tendencies. In fact, Dorothy once had to leave her studies in Paris and go with her mother to see Valasquez paintings in Madrid (1990, 122–23). The similarity of the real woman to her fictional counterpart is simply too striking not to be noticed (Woodress 1987, 87)

Not only Mrs. Canfield, but Dorothy Canfield Fisher herself also seems to be a model for one of the characters: Imogen Willard is invited to one of Flavia's parties probably because her doctoral thesis from the Ecole des Chartes gives her a certain amount of prestige, and this part of the plot is almost certainly an allusion to Fisher's graduate work in France. Further,

Flavia's husband shares some similarities with Mr. Canfield, suggesting the possibility that Cather thought of Dorothy's father as "the husband of a foolish wife" (Madigan 1990, 123).

Madigan suggests that Cather's motive for painting such an unflattering portrait of the Canfield family might have been to retaliate for the Canfields' earlier interference in the publication of one of her other stories, "The Profile," whose protagonist was based on one of Dorothy's friends from her graduate school days at the Sorbonne—"there is evidence that ["Flavia and Her Artists"] was not originally so titled, for twice in a letter of March 29, 1903, Cather refers to a story in progress called 'Fulvia'"; Cather may have changed the name simply for revenge (1990, 122). (For a full discussion of the dispute between Cather and the Canfields over this story, see the "Circumstances of Composition, Sources, and Influences" section for the chapter "The Profile.") Regardless of the motive, the story represents what Woodress sees as a disturbing and long-standing pattern of lack of diplomacy and good judgment in Cather's use of the models she chose for her characters. While she was a student at the University of Nebraska, she destroyed her relationship with her best friend, Louise Pound, and her family by publishing a parody of Louise's brother Roscoe Pound in the student literary magazine, *Hesperian*. She also bluntly declared her aversion to one of her professors, consistently offended her classmates, and, sometime later, insulted her family and friends from Nebraska by publishing an unbecoming portrait of her Aunt Franc in "A Wagner Matinée." In 1916 H. L. Mencken refused to print her story "The Diamond Mine" for fear that a libel suit would be brought against him by Lillian Nordica, on whose career the story is based (1987, 86–87).

The Canfields were not the only sources for the characters in this story. Cather herself was apparently the model for Jemima ("Jimmy") Broadwood: both have big, robust laughs and masculine characteristics, and both worship art (Rosowski 1986, 23). In addition, "Cather must have observed archetypal Flavias in her years as music and drama critic in Pittsburgh when she attended soirées given by Pennsylvania matrons, wives of steel and coal moguls, who devoted themselves to lion-hunting" (Woodress 1983, xviii). Another possible source for the name of Flavia may have been the heroine in Anthony Hope's *The Prisoner of Zenda*, a book Cather adored and referred to often in her articles and reviews (Thurin 1990, 124).

Slote observes that with its many allusions to the Flavian emperors of Rome, the story reads almost like an allegory (1966, 96–97). Thurin expands a discussion of that atmosphere by commenting on the many classical allusions in the story: a bit of the Roman poet Juvenal, who satirized one of the Flavian emperors, may be seen in the character of M. Martel; further, in sweeping the parasitic artists out of the house, Flavia's husband closely resembles

Odysseus ridding his home of Penelope's suitors when he returns (1990, 124–25).

Relationship to Other Cather Works

As part of Cather's *The Troll Garden* collection, this story necessarily shares certain characteristics with at least some of the other stories in the book. The central theme of all seven stories concerns the nature of art, the artist's relation to life, and the effort to understand exactly where and how art fits in the world—Cather's own concerns at this time (Wasserman 1991, 21). Especially in "Flavia and Her Artists," "The Garden Lodge," and "The Marriage of Phaedra," Cather displays a somewhat ambivalent attitude toward artists, sympathizing with them, but at the same time portraying them as "the queer people they are and understand[ing] how much they can make members of the middle class suffer. She seems to feel that there is a natural, dog-and-cat antipathy between the two groups" (Bradford 1955, 543).

There is nearly universal agreement among critics that this story should be grouped with "'A Death in the Desert,'" "A Garden Lodge," and "The Marriage of Phaedra" in that all are Jamesian and that they foreshadow more Jamesian stories when Cather moved from Pittsburgh to New York to work for *McClure's* magazine. Those stories include "The Willing Muse," "The Profile," and "Eleanor's House."

Most Cather scholars also examine the story in relation to the epigraphs with which Cather introduces the book. (For a complete explanation of the thematic relationship of the *Troll Garden* stories to the epigraphs Cather chose for them, see the section "Relationship to Other Cather Works" for the chapters "'A Death in the Desert'" and "A Wagner Matinée.") In this respect, Arnold views the Hamilton home as the "seductive troll garden which lures artists, pseudoartists, and other people of arty or intellectual reputation" inside, where Flavia tempts them with luxury and decadent ease, and in return they "bestow the privilege and the prestige of their company upon their eager hostess" (1984, 46). Like "The Garden Lodge" and "The Marriage of Phaedra," this story depicts artists, or at least people with artistic sensibilities, at work among the wealthy, creating beauty (Brown 1964, 113–15).

Bennett notes that Flavia and Arthur Hamilton and Imogen Willard reappear later as Myra and Oswald Henshawe and Nellie Birdseye of *My Mortal Enemy*; the plot of this work is also occasionally reminiscent of "Flavia and Her Artists" (1982, 43). One of the few comparisons of this story to one outside *The Troll Garden* is drawn by Woodress when he notes that Cherry Beamish, a middle-aged female character from one of Cather's very late stories, "The Old Beauty," is a later version of Jimmy Broadwood (1987, 477).

Interpretations and Criticisms

In Arnold's view, "Flavia is both troll and forest child, both temptress and wide-eyed innocent. Ambitious, demanding, oblivious to her own blindness, she lives parasitically off the borrowed light of those whom she persuades to accept her sumptuous hospitality" (1984, 46–47). Flavia's own complexity indicates that the story is not so much about the place of the artist in society as it is about the friction between human beings—artists or not—whose actions arise out of a sincere concern for others, and those whose "exploitive instinct is destructive to both art and humanity, [isolating] human beings from their most salutary sources of sympathy." In this sense, only Arthur Hamilton is a truly admirable character (1984, 48). Wasserman's view is similar: although the story is largely unsuccessful, one of its most striking points is that the artist Flavia admires most commits "an act of the basest ingratitude, . . . and the man who counters the insult in a selfless effort to protect Flavia is . . . [her] businessman husband"; Cather's message seems to be that qualities necessary for excellence in art are not necessarily those that make for human excellence (1991, 27). If Cather had focused more on this element of irony, the story would have been more effective, according to Brown: "An ironic story might have been written about the chasm between the artist's devotion to beauty and what is sordid and trivial in the rest of his life" (1964, 116). Unfortunately, Cather never develops that aspect of the story; instead, at the very point when that theme "required definition and elaboration, in the rendering of Roux, it evaporates"—Cather never indicts Roux for anything more than his committing a breach of etiquette: when tact would require him to be silent, he is bluntly and inappropriately honest (1964, 116).

Rosowski also regards Arthur Hamilton as a positive character and Flavia as one of the maidens in Kingsley's epigraph to *The Troll Garden*: she is "a woman of neither taste nor talent, [who] has been bewitched by the glitter of success and . . . will bewitch others, . . . a grotesque imitation of wife, mother, and hostess" (1986, 23). Pers agrees, noting that Flavia thinks of her children as dolls, objects to be displayed—nothing more. Her icy indifference toward them translates into cruelty, whereas her husband's sincere affection for them enhances his image. He is simply a better person than she is (1975, 37).

In Sutherland's estimation, the story provides evidence that Cather would have been successful in writing "society novels" had she so chosen (1985, 135). Lee, on the other hand, sees this story as one of the weakest in the collection because of the artificiality resulting from Cather's imitation of James; it is simply a version of "one of James's literary house-parties (in 'The Death of the Lion,' for instance)" (1989, 74).

Thurin concurs with Lee's assessment of the story as weak, but for different reasons. He sees Cather's handling of the classical allusions in the story as inept and clumsy. Her reason for using them at all is that she wanted to portray Imogen and Jimmy as sophisticated. Before long, however, the two young women begin to make fun of their hostess behind her back, making Flavia the more sympathetic character. Furthermore, Imogen and Jimmy are so imprecise in their application of classical allusions in their attempt to disparage Flavia that their supposed urbanity and enviable education is brought into question. For example, "Jimmy's comparison of Flavia to the mother of the Gracchi" misses the mark, for "so far as we know, the widowed Cornelia did not bring her children up to be her 'intellectual companions'" (1990, 124–25). An even more inept use of a classical allusion occurs when Jimmy advises Imogen that if she sees any of Flavia's departed artists in town, she should say that she had "left Gaius Marius among the ruins of Carthage" (Cather 1987, 33). This is a reference Cather clearly borrowed from the ending of her earlier short story "The Way of the World," where the allusion to the Roman general was just as inappropriate as it is here. Thurin goes on to suggest that Cather had perhaps confused the story of Gaius Marius with one of Byron's *Don Juan* cantos: in describing British ladies with tarnished reputations, Byron says "Society, that china without flaw,/ (The Hypocrite!) will banish them like Marius,/ To sit amidst the ruins of their guilt:/ For Fame's a Carthage not so soon rebuilt"—lines that describe Flavia's situation closely (quoted in Thurin 1990, 124–26, 138n). Woodress assesses Imogen's and Jimmy's remarks quite differently, calling them "pleasing satiric barbs," effectively delivered in spite of the fact that Cather was generally inept at handling satire (1970, 112).

Works Cited

Arnold, Marilyn. 1984. *Willa Cather's Short Fiction*. Athens: Ohio University Press.

Bennett, Mildred R. 1982. "Willa Cather's Bodies for Ghosts." *Western American Literature* 17:39–52.

Bradford, Curtis. 1955. "Willa Cather's Uncollected Short Stories." *American Literature* 26:537–51.

Brown, E. K. Completed by Leon Edel. [1953] 1964. *Willa Cather: A Critical Biography*. New York: Knopf.

Cather, Willa. 1961. "Flavia and Her Artists." In *The Troll Garden*. New York: Signet Classics, 7–34.

———. [1965] 1970. "Flavia and Her Artists." In *Willa Cather's Collected Short Fiction, 1892–1912*. Ed. Virginia Faulkner. Lincoln: University of Nebraska Press, 359–79.

———. 1983. "Flavia and Her Artists." In *The Troll Garden*. Ed. James Woodress. Lincoln: University of Nebraska Press, 7–31.

———. 1987. "Flavia and Her Artists." In *Cather: Early Novels and Stories*. New York: Literary Classics of the United States, 7–33.

Faulkner, Virginia, ed. [1965] 1970. *Willa Cather's Collected Short Fiction, 1892–1912*. Lincoln: University of Nebraska Press. Reprint. Lincoln: University of Nebraska Press.

Lee, Hermione. 1989. *Willa Cather: Double Lives*. New York: Pantheon.

Madigan, Mark J. 1990. "Willa Cather and Dorothy Canfield Fisher: Rift, Reconciliation, and *One of Ours*." In *Cather Studies*, vol. 1. Ed. Susan J. Rosowski. Lincoln: University of Nebraska Press, 115–29.

Pers, Mona. 1975. *Willa Cather's Children*. Uppsala, Sweden: Almqvist & Wiksell International.

Rosowski, Susan J. 1985. "Prototypes for Willa Cather's 'Flavia and Her Artists': The Canfield Connection." *American Notes & Queries* 23:143–45.

———. 1986. *The Voyage Perilous: Willa Cather's Romanticism*. Lincoln: University of Nebraska Press.

Slote, Bernice, ed. 1966. *The Kingdom of Art*. Lincoln: University of Nebraska Press.

Sutherland, Donald. 1985. "Willa Cather: The Classic Voice." In *Willa Cather*. Ed. Harold Bloom. Garden City, NY: Chelsea House, 123–43.

Thurin, Erik Ingvar. 1990. *The Humanization of Willa Cather: Classicism in an American Classic*. Lund, Sweden: Lund University Press.

Wasserman, Loretta. 1991. *Willa Cather: A Study of the Short Fiction*. Boston: Twayne.

Woodress, James. 1970. *Willa Cather: Her Life and Art*. New York: Pegasus.

———. 1983. Introduction to *The Troll Garden*. Ed. James Woodress. Lincoln: University of Nebraska Press.

———. 1987. *Willa Cather: A Literary Life*. Lincoln: University of Nebraska Press.

The Garden Lodge

Publication History

This story was first published under the name Willa Sibert Cather in Cather's first collection of short stories, *The Troll Garden* (New York: McClure, Phillips, 1905, pp. 85–110) (Faulkner 1970, 595). It was reprinted in a 1961 Signet Classics paperback edition of the collection with modernized spelling and punctuation.

In 1965, the University of Nebraska Press included the story in *Willa Cather's Collected Short Fiction, 1892–1912*. The story appeared again in 1983, when the University of Nebraska Press published an edition of *The Troll Garden*, edited by James Woodress, and in 1987 in the Library of America edition of *Cather: Early Novels and Stories*.

Circumstances of Composition, Sources, and Influences

This story was written sometime between 1901 and 1903 while Cather was living with Isabelle McClung and her family in Pittsburgh, as were the rest of the stories Cather included in *The Troll Garden*. (For a discussion of the enormous positive influence of Isabelle McClung on Cather's creativity see the "Circumstances of Composition, Sources, and Influences" section for the chapter "A Wagner Matinée.")

Perhaps the most interesting explanation for the source of this story is offered by Thomas, who says that "The Garden Lodge" is "a contemporary reworking of Act I of [Wagner's] *Die Walküre*. . . . In Cather's version, Caroline plays Sieglinde, Howard a civilised Hunding, d'Esquerré is Siegmund and the lodge is Hunding's hut" (1990, 28). The translation from the Wagnerian setting of the *Volsung* legend to Cather's story with its "modern, bourgeois setting" results in "considerable ironic thrust" (Thomas 1990, 28). There is no passionate declaration of love in Cather's story, and Caroline becomes Sieglinde in a dream only. Nevertheless, the similarities between the two works are clear (Thomas 1990, 28).

According to Woodress, there is a strong possibility that the character of Caroline Noble is modeled on Ethel Litchfield, a Pittsburgh friend of Cather's, who chose marriage over a career as a concert pianist but maintained her ties with the music world by entertaining visiting musicians. She also sometimes joined members of the Pittsburgh Symphony to perform chamber music. Cather took great pleasure in her visits to the Litchfield home (1970, 88).

Cather's own opinions are clear in the story as well: the heroine's belief that succumbing to sexual attraction is one of the worst mistakes women can make seems to have come from Cather's own endeavor to keep sexual passion at bay (Wasserman 1991, 37).

Relationship to Other Cather Works

Nearly all Cather specialists group this story with the other *Troll Garden* stories, since like the others it is concerned with art and artists. Most also examine the story in relation to the epigraphs with which Cather introduces the book. (For a complete explanation of the thematic relationship of the *Troll Garden* stories to the epigraphs Cather chose for them, see the "Relationship to Other Cather Works" section for the chapters " 'A Death in the Desert' " and "A Wagner Matinée.") More specifically, however, the story shares elements with those stories in the collection that clearly reflect the heavy influence of Henry James—" 'A Death in the Desert,' " "Flavia and Her Artists," and "The Marriage of Phaedra."

Bradford sees precise parallels between this story and both "Flavia" and "The Marriage of Phaedra." All three stories reflect Cather's own ambivalence about pursuing art—despite her very real reverence for art, she was a practical woman who had to make a living (1955, 543–44). Even more detailed correlations with other stories are noted by Bennett, who points out that after Caroline Noble's mother eloped with her music teacher, she "lived on drudgery and dreams" in much the same way Aunt Georgiana lives on "drudgery and religion" after her marriage (1982, 49). "Paul's Case," too, presents a marriage entered into for the wrong reasons (Bennett 1982, 49).

Wasserman contrasts the story to "Paul's Case," which is the reverse situation; in "The Garden Lodge" a child is raised in a culturally and artistically rich environment. The story also resembles both "Paul's Case" and "A Wagner Matinée" in its insistence that art is essential for the human spirit; without it, "life dwindles into gray sameness" (1991, 26, 30).

Both Slote and O'Brien point out that both this story and "The Marriage of Phaedra" deal with a woman's connection to an absent artist (Slote 1966, 96; O'Brien 1987, 271). O'Brien gives a fuller explanation, however, and also connects the story to " 'A Death in the Desert' " and "The Sculptor's Funeral." In each case a man is seen as the supreme artist, and he is presented only through the reminiscences of his disciples. Cather's purpose in creating these absent artists is the same for each story: to admit the value of male artistic influence while at the same time disentangling herself from it. The dual purpose can be seen in these stories' portrayals of "gifted women whose creative power is suppressed or dissipated by social and psychological forces" (1987, 272). Especially in "The Garden Lodge," "'A Death in the Desert,'" and "A Wagner Matinée," Cather suggests that when women surrender to romantic love and become in every way dependent upon men, they soon "find themselves starving in a desert wasteland where . . . they decline, dwindle, and grow grey" (O'Brien 1987, 274). Their tragic mistake is not in their surrender to a sexual act, but in their attraction to "romantic love—that obsessive dream of fulfillment through another that absorbs women's imaginations so that they cannot act, create, or produce their own fruit" (O'Brien 1987, 274). O'Brien is also the only critic to link this story with the early "Eric Hermannson's Soul." In both stories "the male lover . . . both signifies and awakens the woman's passionate self" (1987, 115n).

The story is read by Van Ghent as a kind of foreshadowing of Cather's first novel, *Alexander's Bridge:* Alexander is, like Caroline Noble, carrying around an imprisoned self, but because Caroline's came to her in a dream, she was able to repress it. Alexander's diabolical caller, however, "had broken past the watches of the ego and could not be exorcised" (1985, 78).

Interpretations and Criticisms

For the few critics who concern themselves with this story, the major issue is how to interpret the dark night of the soul Caroline experiences in her garden lodge and the actions she takes afterwards. Woodress refers to this night as Caroline Noble's epiphany and suggests that it dramatizes the classic conflict of the nineteenth-century woman artist: the desire for both marriage and a career (1983, xxiii). Rosowski pronounces Caroline's subsequent actions positive, maintaining that Caroline saves herself by focusing on the human love in her life (1986, 25). Thurin sees Caroline as spineless in her acquiescence to defeat. Despite the fact that she claims the life she has chosen no longer satisfies her, she seems genuinely happy with it at the end of the story. Further, "the portraits of the father and the brother who 'tried' are clearly satirical," and Caroline herself realizes that her infatuation with d'Esquerré is shared by a great mob of ordinary, nondescript women (1990, 133). Her attraction to him indicates Caroline's immature desire to recapture her youth and compensate herself for the years she spent struggling financially for the sake of her family. Thus, Thurin also sees the ending in a positive light, for there is nothing to suggest that Caroline lost anything essential in herself by making the choice she did (1990, 133–34).

Arnold does not come down firmly on the side of either the positive or the negative in her judgment of the ending. Instead, she simply notes that the conflict presented in the story "is not between the sordid money-grubbing world and the heaven of pure art, but rather . . . between the practical and the imaginative impulses which can quicken inside anyone" (1984, 53).

Critical opinion concerning Cather's primary message in the story also varies. To Brown, it shows for the first time Cather's belief that working hard, not for art but simply for survival, eventually destroys the spirit and the personality (1964, 117). Woodress suggests that Cather is working with one of her most common themes—the notion that one must choose between art and romantic love. They simply cannot co-exist (1970, 116). To Wasserman, the central idea is that artistic aspiration is not always noble—after all, Caroline's father and brother are "deluded, egoistic misfits" (1991, 26). Arnold's view is similar: Cather is fully aware that "art itself can be a form of sorcery," easily capable of destroying lives (1984, 51). Far from guaranteeing its disciples any degree of prestige and fame, it is likely to leave them poor and ostracized by society (Arnold 1984, 51). Arnold also notes the irony in the story: it is the great artist who desires to experience Caroline's safe, practical life for a time, and Caroline who thirsts for the passion that comes with his life of art. The sad fact is that d'Esquerré's life is largely one of disappointment, despite his artistic success. Thus, "the garden of the imagination is enchanting chiefly to those outside it" (1984, 53). In Thurin's estimation, the story presents a balancing of two different ways of experiencing life. Reason, fortunately, is allowed to triumph over foolish, immature impulses and emotions (1990, 134).

Works Cited

Arnold, Marilyn. 1984. *Willa Cather's Short Fiction*. Athens: Ohio University Press.

Bennett, Mildred R. 1982. "Willa Cather's Bodies for Ghosts." *Western American Literature* 17:39–52.

Bradford, Curtis. 1955. "Willa Cather's Uncollected Short Stories." *American Literature* 26:537–51.

Brown, E. K. Completed by Leon Edel. [1953] 1964. *Willa Cather: A Critical Biography*. New York: Knopf.

Cather, Willa. 1961. "The Garden Lodge." In *The Troll Garden*. New York: Signet Classics, 51–63.

———. [1965] 1970. "The Garden Lodge." In *Willa Cather's Collected Short Fiction, 1892–1912*. Ed. Virginia Faulkner. Lincoln: University of Nebraska Press, 187–97.

———. 1983. "The Garden Lodge." In *The Troll Garden*. Ed. James Woodress. Lincoln: University of Nebraska Press, 46–56.

———. 1987. "The Garden Lodge." In *Cather: Early Novels and Stories*. New York: Literary Classics of the United States, 49–60.

Faulkner, Virginia, ed. [1965] 1970. *Willa Cather's Collected Short Fiction, 1892–1912*. Lincoln: University of Nebraska Press. Reprint. Lincoln: University of Nebraska Press.

O'Brien, Sharon. 1987. *Willa Cather: The Emerging Voice*. New York: Oxford University Press.

Rosowski, Susan J. 1986. *The Voyage Perilous: Willa Cather's Romanticism*. Lincoln: University of Nebraska Press.

Slote, Bernice, ed. 1966. *The Kingdom of Art*. Lincoln: University of Nebraska Press.

Thomas, Susie. 1990. *Willa Cather*. Savage, MD: Barnes & Noble.

Thurin, Erik Ingvar. 1990. *The Humanization of Willa Cather: Classicism in an American Classic*. Lund, Sweden: Lund University Press.

Van Ghent, Dorothy. 1985. "Willa Cather." In *Willa Cather*. Ed. Harold Bloom. Garden City, NY: Chelsea House.

Wasserman, Loretta. 1991. *Willa Cather: A Study of the Short Fiction*. Boston: Twayne.

Woodress, James. 1970. *Willa Cather: Her Life and Art*. New York: Pegasus.

———. 1983. Introduction to *The Troll Garden*. Ed. James Woodress. Lincoln: University of Nebraska Press.

A Gold Slipper

Publication History

This story was first published under the name Willa Sibert Cather in the January 1917 issue of *Harper's* (134:166–74); its next appearance was in Cather's second collection of short stories, *Youth and the Bright Medusa* (New York: Knopf, 1920, pp. 140–68) (Faulkner 1970, 597). (For a complete explanation of the evolution of Cather's association with Knopf, see the "Publication History" section for the chapter "Scandal.") The story reappeared in volume six of the thirteen-volume library edition of Cather's work, *The Novels and Stories of Willa Cather* (Boston: Houghton Mifflin, 1937–1941, pp. 141–72) (Faulkner 1970, 597).

In 1975, the story was reprinted by Vintage Books in a paperback edition of *Youth and the Bright Medusa*, and again in 1992 by Literary Classics of the United States in *Cather: Stories, Poems, and Other Writings*, a Library of America volume.

Circumstances of Composition, Sources, and Influences

Cather wrote this story during a visit to her family home in Red Cloud, Nebraska, in August 1916. Cather's dearest friend, Isabelle McClung, had married the violinist Jan Hambourg the previous April, and the loss was devastating to Cather. (For a discussion of the enormous positive influence of Isabelle McClung on Cather's creativity see the "Circumstances of Composition, Sources, and Influences" section for the chapter "A Wagner Matinée.") To try to compensate, Cather increased her social activity in New York; however, by June 1916, she tired of New York and abruptly decided to take an extended vacation in the West with stops in Denver, Taos, and Lander, Wyoming, where she visited her brother Roscoe. Woodress explains that by the time she arrived in Red Cloud in August, Cather was mapping out a new novel to be set in the Southwest, the title of which was probably *The Blue Mesa*. This draft was apparently the kernel of "Tom Outland's Story," which was eventually to form the middle section of *The Professor's House*, a novel that took her six more years to finish (1987, 281). Before beginning the novel of the Southwest in earnest, "she had to get opera singers out of her system" (Woodress 1987, 282). Woodress reports that the circumstances of Kitty Ayrshire's life closely resemble those of Mary Garden, a famous Scottish soprano, while Kitty's personality is reminiscent of that of another singer, Geraldine Ferrar. Although it is true that Cather was genuinely interested in opera singers, it is also true that she needed money, especially since World War I had brought a high rate of inflation, and the $450 she received for this story was welcome indeed (Woodress 1987, 281–83).

The setting of the story is based on Cather's years in Pittsburgh (1896–1906). By the time Cather arrived there in 1896, the city was—thanks to the steel industry—a place of great wealth; life was dominated by such entrepreneurs as Henry Clay Frick, Andrew Carnegie, Andrew Mellon, and George Westinghouse. In "A Gold Slipper," Marshall McKann is something of a composite of all these businessmen (Woodress 1987, 116).

Cather's deep admiration for Russian writers is also an important source for this story; in fact, she makes an obvious reference to Tolstoy when Kitty Ayrshire refers McKann to Tolstoy's *What is Art?* The allusion is significant because Tolstoy's view of art supported Cather's own. In fact, a reader will often find that ideas hinted at in Cather are fully developed in Tolstoy (Stouck 1990, 15).

Relationship to Other Cather Works

Cather included this story in her second collection of short fiction, *Youth and the Bright Medusa*, and it is bound together thematically with the other stories in that collection. (For a full discussion of the shared characteristics of the stories in *Youth and the Bright Medusa*, see the "Relationship to Other Cather Works" section for the chapter "The Diamond Mine.") "A Gold Slipper" has most in common with "Scandal," however, because the two stories share a protagonist, Kitty Ayrshire. Moreover, these two stories form a kind of trilogy, according to Arnold, because "Scandal" is a story-within-a-story. The first tale is "A Gold Slipper," the second is narrated by someone who visits Kitty at home, and the third is narrated by Kitty herself. The latter two tales are set within the frame story, "Scandal." All three resemble "The Diamond Mine" in that they are concerned with artists imperiled by people who are more interested in money or prestige than in art, and in each tale Kitty is in some way a victim of exploitation (1984, 109).

In terms of setting alone, the story is easily linked with others based on Pittsburgh—"Paul's Case," "Uncle Valentine," and "Double Birthday." Each emphasizes the rigid Calvinism and materialistic grasping of the business community, while simultaneously admitting that, because of wealthy businessmen like Frick, Mellon, Westinghouse, Heinz, and Carnegie, Pittsburgh possessed a strong cultural life, manifested in the Carnegie Arts Institute and Opera House, the Pittsburgh Symphony Orchestra, and the theatres (Lee 1989, 45–46).

Wasserman sees similarities between Kitty Ayrshire and Cressida Garnet of "The Diamond Mine," despite the fact that in many ways Kitty is a slighter character: "Where Cressida Garnet is magnificent and commanding, Kitty is flirtatious, her sexual charm a conscious part of her art" (1991, 34). Daiches, on the other hand, believes the story is similar to "The Sculptor's Funeral" in that both emphasize the contrast between the bourgeois and the artistic life. Kitty, however, is a much more effective advocate for art than is the lawyer in "A Sculptor's Funeral," probably because "her eloquence springs from a more fully realized personality than anything which springs from the wrath of the lawyer. . . " (1962, 153).

Interpretations and Criticisms

One reviewer calls this story a "delicious fling" (Field 1921, 74); another says it is an "American debate between body and soul, in which the soul is not yet wholly liberated but still feels as though heavy earth were strewn upon its wings" ("Short Story and Artifice" 1920, 353). Woodress considers the story "an entertaining tale that scores some neat points for open-mindedness, risk-taking, and willingness to try things new" (Woodress 1987, 283).

Certainly all Cather specialists agree that McKann represents the "body" side of the debate. He is one of those conventional, "money-minded, complacently respectable folk, devoted to mechanical things, or spiritual things mechanically apprehended"—the type of character Cather consistently denigrates in her work (Brown 1967, 74). McKann has "sought the Medusa of worldly success for itself alone and [has] figuratively and almost literally been turned to stone" (McFarland 1972, 36). To Giannone, McKann's "derision of the music he does not understand articulates a Babbittry which acts as foil for Kitty's moral awareness of art and self" (1968, 102–103). Ryder interprets McKann's rigidity as his shield against what he sees as the world's frivolity, an attitude that "surely reflects a growing sentiment among those men who [at the time] were engaged in the war to end all war" (1990, 168). Stouck, too, views McKann's hostility as the logical reaction for a man who believes that art—and all other things new and exciting—"subvert the perfect order of what is known and tried"; such subversion is exactly what appeals to Kitty. She leaves her gold slipper in McKann's berth as a challenge to his complacency (1975, 201).

Kitty Ayrshire herself also generates some critical comment. Giannone sees her as Cather's wittiest advocate for art. She knows her limits as an artist and is candid about them. At the same time, she appreciates whatever measure of talent she does have, and that strengthens her. Her respect for what she cannot have is also admirable (1968, 101–102).

Ryder says that Kitty possesses "Medusan fierceness," but is at the same time righteous and beautiful (1990, 168). McKann is like "Poseidon, who strove to possess these traits by dominating their possessors" (Ryder 1990, 168). Arnold is not so willing to condemn McKann out of hand while absolving Kitty of all faults. Although Kitty is perhaps less bigoted than McKann, she has her own assortment of prejudices. Her well-studied sarcastic replies to "anti-art reproaches" allow her to treat people with absolute scorn; the more she and McKann converse, the wider the gulf between them becomes until all hope for appeasement disappears (1984, 110–11). The "argument becomes a personal as well as a philosophical contest, and Kitty finally wins by throwing a punch after the bell" (1984, 111).

In the opinion of Edward A. Bloom and Lillian D. Bloom, one of the assertions Cather makes in this story is that the power to transfer inspiration and desire to the gifted can be effected only *by* the gifted. Furthermore, she believed a true artist must reject caution in all its forms: the faint-hearted are unable to survive the struggle necessary for artistic achievement. Cather herself did not tend toward caution, but she realized that the ability to throw

oneself into a project without fear must be coupled with generosity of spirit—the one simply could not exist without the other (Bloom and Bloom
1962, 131, 141, 144).

To Wasserman, Cather introduces another intriguing theme in this story—
the connection between the power of art and the power of sex. Cather clearly appreciates her protagonist's intelligence and elegance and enjoys plotting
McKann's defeat (1991, 36).

Works Cited

Arnold, Marilyn. 1984. *Willa Cather's Short Fiction*. Athens: Ohio University Press.

Bloom, Edward A., and Lillian D. Bloom. 1962. *Willa Cather's Gift of Sympathy*.
Carbondale: Southern Illinois University Press.

Brown, E. K. 1967. "Willa Cather." In *Willa Cather and Her Critics*. Ed. James
Schroeter. Ithaca, NY: Cornell University Press, 72–86.

Cather, Willa. 1975. "A Gold Slipper." In *Youth and the Bright Medusa*. New York:
Vintage Books, 141–66.

———. 1992. "A Gold Slipper." In *Cather: Stories, Poems, and Other Writings*. New
York: Literary Classics of the United States, 433–49.

Daiches, David. [1951] 1962. *Willa Cather: A Critical Introduction*. Ithaca, NY:
Cornell University Press; London: Oxford University Press. Reprint. New York:
Collier.

Faulkner, Virginia, ed. [1965] 1970. *Willa Cather's Collected Short Fiction, 1892–1912*.
Lincoln: University of Nebraska Press. Reprint. Lincoln: University of Nebraska
Press.

Field, Flo. 1921. "Willa Cather's *Youth and the Bright Medusa*." *Double Dealer*
1:73–74.

Giannone, Richard. 1968. *Music in Willa Cather's Fiction*. Lincoln: University of
Nebraska Press.

Lee, Hermione. 1989. *Willa Cather: Double Lives*. New York: Pantheon.

McFarland, Dorothy Tuck. 1972. *Willa Cather*. New York: Frederick Ungar.

Ryder, Mary Ruth. 1990. *Willa Cather and Classical Myth*. Lewiston, NY: Edwin Mellen
Press.

"Short Story and Artifice." 1920. *Nation*, 25 September, 352–53.

Stouck, David. 1975. *Willa Cather's Imagination*. Lincoln: University of Nebraska
Press.

———. 1990. "Willa Cather and the Russians." In *Cather Studies*, vol. 1. Ed. Susan
Rosowski. Lincoln: University of Nebraska Press, 1–20.

Wasserman, Loretta. 1991. *Willa Cather: A Study of the Short Fiction*. Boston: Twayne.

Woodress, James. 1987. *Willa Cather: A Literary Life*. Lincoln: University of Nebraska Press.

Her Boss

Publication History

This story was first published under the name Willa Cather in the October 1919 issue of *Smart Set* (90:95–108) (Faulkner 1970, 597). It was reprinted in 1973 by the University of Nebraska Press in *Uncle Valentine and Other Stories: Willa Cather's Uncollected Short Fiction, 1915–1929* and again in 1992 by Literary Classics of the United States in *Cather: Stories, Poems, and Other Writings*, a Library of America volume.

Circumstances of Composition, Sources, and Influences

This story was probably written around the time Cather was completing *My Ántonia*, perhaps early 1918. She was frantically trying to finish the novel in time for fall publication and was constantly troubled by money worries. She sent the story, then titled "Little Annie," along with "Ardessa" to *Century* via her literary agent, Paul Reynolds. (See the "Circumstances of Composition, Sources, and Influences" section for the chapter "Ardessa" for an explanation of the package mailed to the *Century* editor.) The editor decided that "Her Boss" was too sad a tale to be published during wartime; it did not appear until at least one year later (Woodress 1987, 286).

Relationship to Other Cather Works

Uncle Valentine and Other Stories contains five stories under the heading "New York Stories" and two under the heading "Pittsburgh Stories." As one of the "New York Stories," "Her Boss" is most often linked with the others under that heading—"Consequences," "The Bookkeeper's Wife," "Ardessa," and "Coming, Eden Bower." (For a discussion of the similarities between these stories, see the "Relationship to Other Cather Works" section for the chapter "Ardessa.")

This story is also more closely connected to *The Professor's House* than to any of Cather's other works. It foreshadows and illuminates the themes of the novel (Stouck 1973, 330). According to Ryder, one of these themes is "the ambivalent relationship between sisters, . . . opposite in both appearance and temperament (even their names—Roma and Florence—echo historical rivalry and antipathy)" (1990a, 44). These two sisters prefigure Godfrey St. Peter's daughters who, like Roma and Florence, are so full of themselves that they are incapable of comprehending their father's predicament (Ryder 1990b, 166).

Arnold notes that the protagonist in this story, Paul Wanning, shares some characteristics with Godfrey St. Peter of *The Professor's House*, and that Mr. Wanning's wife is an early version of Lillian St. Peter; both Wanning and St. Peter happily embrace the solitude that has been forced upon them when their families leave for summer vacation. Wanning appreciates the peace and contemplation he finds in his office in the same way that St. Peter enjoys his lazy indulgence in the old house or garden (1984, 103–105). Nevertheless, some differences between the two protagonists do exist: St. Peter, for example, has a much clearer understanding of his fractured family than Wanning does; further, "Her Boss" is less value-centered than *The Professor's House*, and Paul Wanning is "weak and indecisive, even comic, while St. Peter is strong and impressive" (Arnold 1984, 106). Also, Cather is careful to give us strong descriptions of St. Peter's family, but Mrs. Wanning and her children "fall into a rather undistinguished lump" (Arnold 1984, 106).

The story explores the theme of the older man who, somehow separated emotionally from a wife who does not understand him, turns for solace to a young person, either his memory of his own youthful self or another person. In this way it is connected not only to *The Professor's House*, but also to *Alexander's Bridge*, *My Ántonia*, "Uncle Valentine," *Lucy Gayheart*, and *Sapphira and the Slave Girl*; thus, "Her Boss" may be more important as an example of one of Cather's favorite themes than as a story in its own right (Slote 1973, xiv–xv).

Interpretations and Criticisms

Most critics have commented on the unrelenting sadness of this story. Woodress says it is "a melancholy commentary on what Mark Twain would have called 'the damned human race,'" noting that even the thoroughly unselfish Annie Wooley is treated mercilessly in the end (1987, 287).

Arnold feels that Annie functions as a contrast to people of the professional class. She possesses the definitively human traits the others lack, like the ability to face illness and death without shame. She can gracefully permit a man to die. In this story Cather once again indicts the material coldheartedness and arrogance she sees all around her, but she also accepts the fact that no one should be criticized for being unable to identify with another's death (1984, 104).

Ryder argues that Cather draws on the notorious luxury of ancient Rome in order to tell this tale of "humanitarianism gone awry" (1990b, 165). The description of Julia Wanning in her violet dressing gown arranging her hair certainly brings to mind "her ancient counterpart Julia, whom Ovid immortalized in the *Ars Amatoria*"; further, Roma and Florence Wanning's notion of love mirrors the Ovidian view of love—that "courtship is a game with rules to follow and short-cuts to wealth and status available to those willing to resort to conniving" (Ryder 1990b, 165–66). As a corrective to this decadence, according to Ryder, Cather has Wanning contemplate one of his friends who had fled to the freedom of the West, which for Cather often represents the last refuge from crass materialism and the deadening effects of modernization, forces that transformed men like Paul Wanning into moneygrubbers rather than a thoughtful and highly principled human being. In Cather's view, "the world was fast becoming a decadent Rome where essential humanity and nobility lay crushed beneath the onslaught of barbaric greed and homage to false art" (1990b, 165–66)

Works Cited

Arnold, Marilyn. 1984. *Willa Cather's Short Fiction*. Athens: Ohio University Press.

Cather, Willa. 1973. "Her Boss." In *Uncle Valentine and Other Stories: Willa Cather's Uncollected Short Fiction, 1915–1929*. Ed. Bernice Slote. Lincoln: University of Nebraska Press, 119–39.

———. 1992. "Her Boss." In *Cather: Stories, Poems, and Other Writings*. New York: Literary Classics of the United States, 185–208.

Faulkner, Virginia, ed. [1965] 1970. *Willa Cather's Collected Short Fiction, 1892–1912*. Lincoln: University of Nebraska Press. Reprint. Lincoln: University of Nebraska Press.

Ryder, Mary R. 1990a. "Loosing the Tie That Binds: Sisterhood in Cather." In *Willa Cather and the Family, Community and History: The BYU Symposium*. Ed. John J. Murphy. Provo, Utah: Brigham Young University, 41–47.

———. 1990b. *Willa Cather and Classical Myth*. Lewiston, NY: Edwin Mellen Press.

Slote, Bernice. 1973. Introduction to *Uncle Valentine and Other Stories: Willa Cather's Uncollected Short Fiction, 1915–1929*, by Willa Cather. Lincoln: University of Nebraska Press.

Stouck, David. 1973. Review of *Uncle Valentine and Other Stories*, by Willa Cather. *Southern Humanities Review* 9:329–30.

Woodress, James. 1987. *Willa Cather: A Literary Life*. Lincoln: University of Nebraska Press.

Jack-a-Boy

Publication History

This story was first published in the *Saturday Evening Post* on March 30, 1901 (173:4–5, 25)) under the name Willa Sibert Cather and reappeared in the Spring 1959 issue of *Prairie Schooner* (33:77–87) (Faulkner 1970, 593). Its next appearance was in the 1965 edition of *Willa Cather's Collected Short Fiction, 1892–1912*, published by the University of Nebraska Press. Hallmark Cards re-issued the story in 1974 under the title *Friend of My Springtime: A Classic Story of Friendship* with an introduction by Robert Aldace Wood; no mention of the original title was made (Lathrop 1975, 73).

Circumstances of Composition, Sources, and Influences

The story was probably written after April 1900, when Cather resigned from her job on the Pittsburgh *Leader*'s telegraph desk. She remained in Pittsburgh through the following summer and intended to move back to Lincoln in the late fall. In preparation for the move, she wrote to Will Owen Jones at the *Nebraska State Journal* in September, asking for a position on the paper. It is likely that by this time she had already sold "Jack-a-Boy" to the *Saturday Evening Post* (Woodress 1987, 147). Instead of moving back to Nebraska, however, Cather moved to Washington DC, where she worked as a translator for the U.S. Commission to the Paris Exposition of 1900. At the same time, she sent articles back to the *Journal* and to the *Index* of Pittsburgh Life, which had absorbed what was once the *Library* (Woodress 1987, 148). In March 1901, the same month "Jack-a-Boy" appeared in the *Saturday Evening Post*, Cather left Washington and returned to Pittsburgh, where she had been hired to teach at Central High School, probably as a replacement for a teacher who had become ill during the school year.

All of Cather's biographers and critics agree that this story is a tribute to the author's youngest brother, Jack, then eight years old. Cather had often taken care of him when he became seriously ill during the summer of 1893 (Bennett 1970, xxxv note). Woodress says that Cather and Jack were always especially close. She missed him terribly when they were separated and eventually sent him to Carnegie Tech for his education (1987, 149). According to Bennett, Cather often told her friends that "she would give anything just to look into his eyes for ten minutes" (1961, 38). O'Brien agrees that "Jack-a-Boy" was inspired by Cather's brother but explains that the story also grew out of the author's two other connections to brother-artists: the tie she assumed existed between herself and A. E. Housman even before she met him, and her actual friendship with Ethelbert Nevin, a musician whose family owned the Pittsburgh *Leader* (1987, 262).

Thurin suggests that Cather's reference in the story to the Borghese Gallery's marble children was probably "inspired by the early pages of a three-volume fictional work by Ouida, *The Story of Ariadne: A Dream*, which is mentioned repeatedly in [Cather's] early articles and reviews" (1990, 120n). For the analogy between Jack-a-Boy and Keats, "a Greekless Hellenist who also died a premature death, Cather seems to have drawn not only on the latter's own works but on some recently published biography—either Sidney Calvin's *Keats* . . . or W. M. Rossetti's *Keats*" (Thurin 1990, 120n).

Relationship to Other Cather Works

O'Brien groups this story with others Cather wrote from 1900 to 1903, all of which portray some sort of brother-sister relationship and explore the culture's narrow definition of masculine and feminine. The other stories in this group include "Eric Hermannson's Soul," "The Treasure of Far Island," and "The Professor's Commencement" (1987, 263).

According to Wasserman, the theme of the story—a gift of beauty to the world—reappears in the much later story "The Old Beauty," where the protagonist, Gabrielle Longstreet, earns her place in the Père-Lachaise cemetery alongside other artists. She had been true to her gift of beauty to the end and had renounced the life of the self (1991, 72). There are also some similarities between the characters of Gabrielle and Jack-a-Boy themselves. Both are said to have grey eyes, and both are consistently connected to flowers. Unlike Gabrielle, however, Jack-a-Boy "is a source of immediate moral harmony among the residents, and they explicitly recognize his unworldly quality" (Wasserman 1991, 72–73).

Bennett connects the character who is referred to as the "Woman Nobody Called On" to the several Lena characters that seemed to follow Cather throughout her career. Such a character appears as Canute's wife in "On the

Divide," as Lena Hanson in "Eric Hermannson's Soul," as Olena Yensen in "The Bohemian Girl," and as Lena Lingard of *My Ántonia* (1982, 42-43).

Interpretations and Criticisms–

Thurin discusses Cather's description of the Professor's affection for Jack-a-Boy as an instance of platonic pedagogical eros. The Professor thinks the boy resembles the young Keats and wants the chance to see him grow into adulthood. After the boy dies, the Professor admits that he had been joyfully anticipating teaching him Greek. But he always suspected that the child was too good to be true—that none of the adults would be able to hold on to him. Like Keats, he was too good for the world and would soon leave it (1990, 111).

When Keats is mentioned again in the story, "one glimpses the Platonic—and Romantic—notion that children are particularly apt to remember the heavenly sphere from which they have come"; here, however, the heaven referred to is that of Greek mythology (Thurin 1990, 111).

In Thurin's view, the lives of the three people Jack-a-Boy touches in this story—the Professor, Miss Harris, and the Woman Nobody Called On—are singularly empty before the child creates some meaning for them. The Professor, on whom Cather places the most emphasis, begins almost as a parody of an earnest scholar—all intellect and no heart—and is utterly transformed by the child. Through Jack-a-Boy, the "previously letter-bound scholar begins to rediscover the spirit of Greece" (1990, 110). The Professor seems to believe that the boy actually *is* the spirit, and when he "mourns the great poet or composer lost" when the boy dies, the narrator insists that *she* is not at all interested in what the boy might have become—that she loved the child as he was (Thurin 1990, 110–11). Nevertheless, the Professor argues effectively that the child was more spirit than human, and Miss Harris does at one point admit that the Professor is right, but not before she compares the child to Christ (Thurin 1990, 112). Arnold maintains that this comparison is acceptable but admits that "in a context of wood nymphs and Greek divinities frolicking in the fields of Arcady, such an allusion jangles the sensibilities" (1984, 38–39). What does recommend the story is its "poetic fluency" and the presence of the theme of human love and concern as remedies for loneliness (Arnold 1984, 39).

Thurin connects both Miss Harris's "insistent . . . invoking the name of Pan" and her image of Jack-a-Boy returning to Pan's dominion to Cather's "pantheistic account of the death of Ethelbert Nevin and other passages in [her] articles and reviews. It is as far removed as possible from the Christian idea of a transcendent God and a transcendent heaven" (1990, 112). The ending of the story especially, "where the gospel of aestheticism is compared and contrasted with that of Christ, . . . draws attention to the incompatibility of the main theme with Christian belief" (Thurin 1990, 112). As a tribute to him, Jack-a-Boy's three friends go maying, but instead of hanging the traditional bouquet on a door at dawn, they hang a basket of flowers on his grave at dusk. The boy loved this yearly festivity even more than Christmas, and since he knew the story of Narcissus, it is safe to say that the "pagan background of Northwestern Europe thus fuses with and reinforces the classical pagan themes as it does in 'Eric Hermannson's Soul'" (Thurin 1990, 113).

In a very different reading, Murphy argues that the story's theme is explicitly Christian: God often uses children as a means of grace for bringing people together. Such a preoccupation places Cather in the "tradition of Hawthorne and James in American literature and beyond them in the tradition of inspirational writing. . . " (1984, 13). The reason, the Professor argues, that Jack-a-Boy was the brief incarnation of one of the Greek immortals is that he is blind to anything beyond the pagan stories he studies. The narrator, too, is limited by her notion of romantic nature. It is only the Woman Nobody Calls On "who occasions the narrator's acceptance of the offered grace—the narrator's resolve to call on this ostracized woman—which reveals Jack-a-Boy's full significance" as a child of grace in the Christian sense (Murphy 1984, 14).

Some critics judge the story as reflecting unfavorably on the author. Arnold feels it is somewhat artificial in style, sentimental in its treatment of theme, and sentimental in its yearning for lost youth (1984, 43, 122). Woodress asserts that the story is a typical example of the sentimental *Saturday Evening Post* fare to which readers in 1900 were accustomed. Cather simply was not yet capable of using sentiment without sentimentality. In this area she was still suffering the "deleterious influence of [Ethelbert] Nevin, who had told her that as a child he had been taught never to be afraid of sentiment" (1987, 148). Robinson calls the story morbid and suggests that it illustrates Cather's belief in death as the only way to escape change (1983, 103). O'Brien maintains that "Jack-a-Boy," like "The Professor's Commencement," *seems* to venerate the tradition of the classics, but in fact it links "Greek and Latin literature with suffocation, decay, and death" (1987, 268). The story itself is stilted and sentimental, but it reveals Cather's evolving views of "gender, sexual identity, and artistic vocation" through her creation of a six-year-old boy who combines traditionally male and female characteristics, and so transcends gender classification (O'Brien 1987, 264).

Works Cited

Arnold, Marilyn. 1984. *Willa Cather's Short Fiction*. Athens: Ohio University Press.

Bennett, Mildred R. 1961. *The World of Willa Cather*. Lincoln: University of Nebraska Press.

———. [1965] 1970. Introduction to *Willa Cather's Collected Short Fiction*. Ed. Virginia Faulkner. Lincoln: University of Nebraska Press. Reprint. Lincoln: University of Nebraska Press.

———. 1982. "Willa Cather's Bodies for Ghosts." *Western American Literature* 17:39–52.

Cather, Willa. [1965] 1970. "Jack-a-Boy." In *Willa Cather's Collected Short Fiction, 1892-1912*. Ed. Virginia Faulkner. Lincoln: University of Nebraska Press, 311–22.

Faulkner, Virginia, ed. [1965] 1970. *Willa Cather's Collected Short Fiction, 1892–1912*. Lincoln: University of Nebraska Press. Reprint. Lincoln: University of Nebraska Press.

Lathrop, Joanna. 1975. *Willa Cather: A Checklist of Her Published Writing*. Lincoln: University of Nebraska Press.

Murphy, John. 1984. "Willa Cather's Children of Grace." *Willa Cather Pioneer Memorial Newsletter* 28:13–15.

O'Brien, Sharon. 1987. *Willa Cather: The Emerging Voice*. New York: Oxford University Press.

Robinson, Phyllis C. 1983. *Willa: The Life of Willa Cather*. Garden City, NY: Doubleday.

Thurin, Erik Ingvar. 1990. *The Humanization of Willa Cather: Classicism in an American Classic*. Lund, Sweden: Lund University Press.

Wasserman, Loretta. 1991. *Willa Cather: A Study of the Short Fiction*. Boston: Twayne.

Woodress, James. 1987. *Willa Cather: A Literary Life*. Lincoln: University of Nebraska Press.

The Joy of Nelly Deane

Publication History

This story was first published under the name Willa Sibert Cather in the October 1911 issue of *Century* (82:859–67) (Faulkner 1970, 596). It was reprinted in 1965 by the University of Nebraska Press in *Willa Cather's Collected Short Fiction, 1892–1912* and again in 1992 by Literary Classics of the United States in *Cather: Stories, Poems, and Other Writings*, a volume in the Library of America series.

Circumstances of Composition, Sources, and Influences

This was the first story Cather wrote after the death of her friend and mentor Sarah Orne Jewett in 1909; according to O'Brien, Jewett's death was also a strong inspiration for the story. Jewett had given Cather valuable advice about writing and was still very much alive in Cather's imagination (see the "Circumstances of Composition, Sources, and Influences" section for the chapter "On the Gulls' Road"). Part of Jewett's advice was that Cather's position as managing editor of *McClure's* magazine was robbing her of the time she needed to work seriously on her fiction; in O'Brien's opinion, at the time Cather wrote "The Joy of Nelly Deane" (which she originally entitled "Flower in the Grass"), she may have been taking this part of her mentor's admonition to heart. In a March 1911 letter to her friend Elizabeth Sergeant, Cather reports having visited Jewett's sister Mary at the Jewett family home in South Berwick, Maine, and feeling very anxious to make her living by writing fiction full time. As if Jewett were speaking to her from the grave, warning her that time was slipping away from her, Cather left her job at *McClure's* in late 1911 (1987, 373–74).

One source for the story is Cather's antagonism toward her own Baptist background, which she expresses clearly in some of her early letters to friends in Nebraska (Thurin 1990, 46, 154). The character of Nelly Deane was inspired by a young woman named Miss Gayhardt, whom Cather met shortly after her graduation from the University of Nebraska. One night the two women stayed up all night discussing literature (Bennett 1961, 217). It is significant that the story takes place around 1895 or 1896, the year Cather graduated from college and the year she met Miss Gayhardt (Stouck 1975, 215).

Petry argues that since Cather knew *Norse Stories* by Hamilton Wright Mabie, a probable source for the three wise old women in this story is Norse mythology, specifically, the Scandinavian Norns, who actually concoct a person's fate and mind the sacred well. Because they personify past, present, and future, they also represent the progression of time. In addition, the Norns are known for weaving and attending at births (1991, 124). Nelly Deane herself has a source in Norse mythology: "Her name echoes that of Idun, beautiful goddess of youth, who inspired the god of music . . . to sing . . . . Cather transfers the sweet voice to Nelly herself" (Petry 1991, 125). At one point in the story of Idun, she is taken forcibly from the gods' home by "the storm giant Thiassi with the collaboration of the malicious god Loki," an episode that parallels Nelly's abandonment by Guy Franklin and her subsequent marriage to Scott Spinny (Petry 1991, 125). Furthermore, "Loki is associated with steel, flint, and the recovery of Thor's hammer; Scott, his modern avatar, is a hardware merchant" (Petry 1991, 126). Idun's story ends when Ygdrasil, a tree nourished and kept forever green by the Norns, withers and dies and the sacred fountain dries up. Idun herself, like Nelly, then passes into the valley of death (Petry 1991, 126).

Relationship to Other Cather Works

All Cather critics agree that the character of Nelly Deane became Lucy Gayheart in the novel of the same name and that both characters are based on the Miss Gayhardt whom Cather met in 1896. Nelly's constricted, thwarted life and untimely death clearly foreshadow *Lucy Gayheart*. The novel suggests that Cather speculated on what Nelly's fate would have been had she left the small plains town for the big city, and perhaps taken a famous singer as a lover (Woodress 1987, 450). Other similarities between the two characters abound: both are the most vivacious young women in their communities, both are confined by Victorian notions of womanhood, both die because of the rigid natures of their male partners (Bennett 1982, 45–46). Bennett also links Nelly to Marie Tovesky of *O Pioneers!*—the phrases Cather uses to describe the women's eyes are very similar, as are the descriptions of their clothing and of the "unquenchable joy" in their personalities (1982, 46).

Arnold notes that other characters besides Nelly have their beginnings in this story: Jud Deane, for example, prefigures both Hillary Templeton of "Old Mrs. Harris" and James Ferguesson of "The Best Years"; Guy Franklin is an early version of Larry Donovan, "the railroad man who disappoints Ántonia" in *My Ántonia*; the sullen Scott Spinney represents a type of dispassionate character that reappears in several other Cather works (1984, 84–85). Nelly herself, although she most closely resembles Lucy Gayheart, is also quite similar to Thea Kronborg of *The Song of the Lark* and Claude Wheeler of *One of Ours*. All three characters revel in life and youth (Arnold 1984, 85). The related theme of youth as the best time of life—the most powerful and alive time—is also obvious here as it is in several novels and short stories, such as "Uncle Valentine," "Double Birthday," "Two Friends," "The Old Beauty," and "The Best Years" (Arnold 1984, 40).

Cather explores two of her most common themes in this story: one is the East–West conflict. The other is the role death plays as a merciful blessing in sparing from further disenchantment and loss a character who is full of enthusiasm but too sensitive to endure a world that systematically destroys the spirit and demands conformity to society's expectations (Arnold 1984, 85).

Thurin draws parallels between this story and "On the Gulls' Road." In both, "the image of a beautiful dead female is projected by an admiring narrator" who receives solace and inspiration through remembering her (1990, 152).

O'Brien argues that "The Joy of Nelly Deane" is a kind of reworking of the earlier "Tommy, the Unsentimental" (1896). In the latter story a strong woman is conspicuous in a small, conventional Nebraska town in much the same way Nelly is conspicuous. However, in the earlier work, the talented woman is clearly masculine—her closest friends are the town's distinguished older gentlemen, and the only people she cannot abide are the town's mindless, conventional women. Nelly Deane, on the other hand, is thoroughly feminine, as are her sympathetic friends. In fact, her only enemies are the domineering men in her life (1987, 376).

Interpretations and Criticisms

Thurin asserts that Nelly Deane is another of Cather's Aphrodite figures (see the "Interpretations and Criticisms" section for the chapter "On the Gulls' Road"), and Ryder associates her with Persephone (1990, 86–87). Murphy, on the other hand, views her in strictly Christian terms as one of Cather's characters who, like Jack-a-Boy, function to reveal God's grace. In the beginning of the story, Nelly is associated with the biblical Queen Esther, as Nelly has the part in the church performance of a cantata based on Queen Esther's life. Esther and Nelly are both sources of light, and in the same way that Esther saved her people from destruction, Nelly helps her people, especially the women, to overcome life's adversity. Nelly dispenses this light to everyone around her, including the "dear old matriarchs" who watched over her, but her special dispensation is to Margaret, the narrator, who equates Nelly's baptism and her marriage to Scott Spinny with death. Margaret does not come to see the light until ten years later when she returns to Riverbend and sees the two children Nelly left, an eight-year-old girl and a baby boy, the gray-haired matriarchs bent over him. It is at this point, Murphy asserts, that Margaret transcends her "feminist view, and the joy of Nelly Deane translates into the grace of the Holy Child and the glad tidings of Christ's redemption" (1984, 14).

Giannone agrees that the cantata, as well as the other music mentioned in the story, is thematically significant. Besides sharing the role of deliverer of her people, Queen Esther and Nelly Deane also "share in the suffering of their breed, Esther as a Jew and Nelly . . . as a sensitive among insensitives" (1968, 48). The hymn Nelly sings, "The Ninety and Nine," suggests that Nelly is not one of the ninety-nine sheep that are safe in the fold, but the stray whose inclination is to leave the herd (Giannone 1968, 48). Furthermore, although only a small part of the hymn's text is mentioned in the story, the rest of it is important: a "dialogue among the Shepherd, the ninety-nine, and a narrator," the hymn tells the listener that the one lost sheep is the cause and the justification of the shepherd's suffering (Giannone 1968, 48). Giannone sees the hymn as having a dual function—to present the perspective of the more sympathetic Baptist sewing circle ladies, who want Nelly to be a member of their church and social group, and to present Cather's view that Nelly is admirable because she is so *unlike* these women. The Baptists condescend to Nelly because they view her as a lost sheep. Cather turns that attitude around: the hundredth is the admirable one because her vitality challenges the notion that one must always choose the safe, conventional path. Giannone further argues that the two other hymns mentioned or alluded to in the story—"Washed in the Blood of the Lamb" and "There Is a Green Hill Far Away"—are significant. The first is associated in Margaret's mind with Nelly's baptism—to Margaret a symbolic death—and the hymn simply reinforces Margaret's impression of Nelly as "an innocent martyr to society's ways." The second is alluded to when Margaret thinks of the grave on a "green hill far away" (1968, 48–49). Margaret describes Nelly's grave in this way because she associates Nelly so closely with music, not because she thinks of her as being in a Baptist heaven somewhere. The implication is that death allows Nelly to escape the suffocation of Riverbend, or, as the Book of Esther puts it, "Our soul is escaped from the snare,/From the snare of fowlers . . . " (Giannone 1968, 49–50).

Arnold points out a typical Cather pattern in this story: an "extraordinary female character who is seen through the eyes of an admiring narrator . . . [who is] almost painfully conscious of her own deficiencies in verve and daring and charm" (1984, 84). In the case of this story, Margaret is clearly intended to be Nelly's foil. Arnold views the primary theme of the story as rebirth and restoration, illustrated through "images of baptism, which signify death, and images of birth, which signify new life after death and the restoration of things lost" (1984, 85). Margaret likens Nelly's religious baptism, which is prefigured by her twice falling through the ice, only to death until she returns to Riverbend after many years to discover "that baptism can go beyond burial, for the spirit of Nelly has been reborn in Nelly's two children," a recognition that takes place at the obviously appropriate time of Christmas (Arnold 1984, 86).

To O'Brien, the importance of the story lies at least partly in the fact that it represents the first time Cather seems to have acted on Jewett's advice, and also in the interest in women's power that Cather begins to display here. At the same time, O'Brien suggests, there is strong evidence in the story that Cather questioned whether or not such power could survive in a patriarchal society (1987, 373). Although the story harshly attacks romantic love, it balances that grim view with a description of deep and enduring love between women, despite distance between them or even death (O'Brien 1987, 373). O'Brien sees the three guardian matrons as "maternal powers" and "hometown Fates—the Clotho, Lachesis, and Atropos of the sewing circle"—who are nevertheless powerless to change Nelly's future from that decreed by the traditional woman's role (1987, 374). Margaret loves Nelly utterly, but she, too, realizes that their bond must be temporary, and that for Nelly marriage is almost certainly unavoidable. Perhaps Cather was remembering Jewett's advice to her concerning the earlier story "On the Gulls' Road": a woman could have loved Nelly in the same concerned way; certainly a woman could have loved her enough to want to help her escape such a life (O'Brien 1987, 374). Cather does seem to be trying to "cast aside the male mask" in this story, a step that she made less dangerous by describing Margaret's and Nelly's relationship as affectionate, but not passionate: Cather defuses the scene where Margaret and Nelly are in bed together by having Nelly reveal her love for Guy Franklin (O'Brien 1987, 374–75). Unfortunately, despite the story's theme of rebirth, the ending is far from positive. Nelly willingly submits, like countless women—both fictional and real—before and after her, to "a male-authored story," and she voluntarily allows herself to be seduced by romantic love, hoping that Guy Franklin will take her to Chicago, instead of setting out for Chicago on her own (O'Brien 1987, 375). The three kind old women, like Nelly herself, "accept the scripts that have already been written for women. . . . [M]ale authority is not, finally, to be defied, since the ladies will never question Christianity" (O'Brien 1987, 376). Nelly's three guardians "are loving but ineffective mother-goddesses, Cather suggests, because they accept God the Father as the sole Author of a woman's life story" (O'Brien 1987, 376).

The role of these three Baptist ladies has been discussed by several critics; most, but not all, see them as kindly. Ryder views them as "the Greek fates, the Moirai, whose functions were to determine each individual's portion in life." Although that association may "conjure up for the reader dark visions of impending doom and premature death," the three women also certainly appear to be benevolent, especially when one compares them to "the dark Fates of later literature, the blind Furies of Milton . . . or the cruel Fates of Landor's 'Orpheus and Eurydice'" (1990, 84–86). Cather seemed unperturbed that the three women are also associated with the Magi in the Christmas ending of the story, thus setting up a strange mix of Christian and pagan mythologies (Ryder 1990, 87). After all, both "support a belief in birth, death, and rebirth as a pattern of real life" (Ryder 1990, 88).

Rosowski, however, finds the three women positively sinister in their omnipresence, despite "the external trappings of female culture" presented through them (1984, 238). Rosowski sees Nelly's aspirations as thwarted at every turn by these three women. They consistently steer her toward conventional female roles—teaching, becoming active in the Baptist church, getting married, having children. The three women have themselves submitted so utterly to these roles that they can imagine nothing else for Nelly (1984, 238–39).

Works Cited

Arnold, Marilyn. 1984. *Willa Cather's Short Fiction*. Athens: Ohio University Press.

Bennett, Mildred R. 1961. *The World of Willa Cather*. Lincoln: University of Nebraska Press.

———. 1982. "Willa Cather's Bodies for Ghosts." *Western American Literature* 17:39–52.

Cather, Willa. [1965] 1970. "The Joy of Nelly Deane." In *Willa Cather's Collected Short Fiction, 1892–1912*. Ed. Virginia Faulkner. Lincoln: University of Nebraska Press, 55–68.

———. 1992. "The Joy of Nelly Deane." In *Cather: Stories, Poems, and Other Writings*. New York: Literary Classics of the United States, 74–88.

Faulkner, Virginia, ed. [1965] 1970. *Willa Cather's Collected Short Fiction, 1892–1912*. Lincoln: University of Nebraska Press. Reprint. Lincoln: University of Nebraska Press.

Giannone, Richard. 1968. *Music in Willa Cather's Fiction*. Lincoln: University of Nebraska Press.

Murphy, John. 1984. "Willa Cather's Children of Grace." *Willa Cather Pioneer Memorial Newsletter* 28:13–15.

O'Brien, Sharon. 1987. *Willa Cather: The Emerging Voice*. New York: Oxford University Press.

Petry, Alice Hall. 1991. [Untitled article]. In *Willa Cather: A Study of the Short Fiction*, by Loretta Wasserman. Boston: Twayne.

Rosowski, Susan J. 1984. "Willa Cather: Living History." *Women's Studies* 11:233–46.

Ryder, Mary Ruth. 1990. *Willa Cather and Classical Myth*. Lewiston, NY: Edwin Mellen Press.

Stouck, David. 1975. *Willa Cather's Imagination*. Lincoln: University of Nebraska Press.

Thurin, Erik Ingvar. 1990. *The Humanization of Willa Cather: Classicism in an American Classic*. Lund, Sweden: Lund University Press.

Woodress, James. 1987. *Willa Cather: A Literary Life*. Lincoln: University of Nebraska Press.

Lou, the Prophet

Publication History

This story was first published October 15, 1892, in the University of Nebraska student journal, the *Hesperian* (22:7–10), under the name W. Cather; in the spring of 1948, it was reprinted in *Prairie Schooner* (22:100–104) as part of "Willa Cather's Juvenilia," edited by James R. Shively (Faulkner 1970, 590; Lathrop 1975, 115). It was reprinted again in 1950 by the University of Nebraska Press in *Willa Cather's Campus Years* (46–53) (Lathrop 1975, 115), in 1957 by Dodd, Mead in *Early Stories*, and in 1965 by the University of Nebraska Press in *Willa Cather's Collected Short Fiction, 1892–1912*.

Circumstances of Composition, Sources, and Influences

Written while Cather was a student at the University of Nebraska, this story draws heavily on her experience of living on the Nebraska prairie. In this early period of her writing, Cather's memories of her immigrant neighbors, their struggles (and very often their defeats) were exceedingly strong. Like nearly all the Nebraska-based stories written from 1892 through 1912, "Lou, the Prophet" depicts the failings of the land and its inhabitants (Schneider 1967, 76). In a letter to Witter Bynner, one of Cather's associates at *McClure's* magazine, Cather reveals how preoccupied she was with the tragedies of her former neighbors in Nebraska. She tells Bynner that while she was in college, Nebraska farmers were utterly ruined by drought and economic depression and that several had gone insane or committed suicide (Cather 1905).

Despite the harsh view of Nebraska that this story presents, there is, as Woodress explains, a paradox about Cather's attitude; the stories and letters she wrote during this time contain contradictory material. In fact, much of her correspondence with friends suggests that she found the prairie spectacularly beautiful. For example, she once wrote to her friends the Gere sisters, inviting them to come from Lincoln and visit while "the country . . . was looking like a garden—green and beautiful beyond words, with cornfields like forests everywhere" (quoted in Woodress 1987, 78). In this as in the other early Nebraska stories, however, there is no hint of a garden-like, benevolent countryside. Instead, the fiction seems to be influenced more by Hamlin Garland, Cather's contemporary, whose works Cather had probably read.

Garland's 1891 collection of short stories, *Main-Travelled Roads*, were darkly pessimistic portrayals of Midwestern farmers. "It is tempting to speculate that Cather as a college freshman thought the proper tone for a story of farmers on the prairie should be Garland's" (Woodress 1987, 78).

Relationship to Other Cather Works

The figure of Lou in this story is the first version of a character that reappears in "On the Divide" (1896) and again in *O Pioneers!* (1913) (Bennett 1982, 40). He is a typical example Cather's development of a character over time. When he first appears, Lou is one of the weak, downtrodden folks who, because of nature's ferocity and the stubbornness of the unyielding land, "loses his grip on reality and believes that God is coming to destroy the earth" (Bennett 1982, 40).

When Lou appears later in "On the Divide," Mary Yensen, another character in the story, describes him as so hopelessly deranged that he should be locked up to ensure everyone else's safety. But by the time Lou becomes Crazy Ivar in *O Pioneers!* Cather has mellowed in her attitude about the land as destroyer of people. She views both the land and Crazy Ivar sympathetically, even reverently. Ivar is not dangerous; he is simply an eccentric old man who wants to protect nature and live in harmony with it. And Alexandra wants to prevent him from being committed to the state insane asylum because she believes that, although his behavior is unconventional, he is actually wiser than most people (Bennett 1982, 41–42).

Interpretations and Criticisms

In this and other early stories, many readers hear the voice of an author who is resentful of the systematic way the frontier destroys people (Bradford 1955, 538). Lou does not merely *go* insane; he is *driven* insane by surroundings that are depicted as almost conscious in their efforts to annihilate. Lou is especially susceptible to defeat because, unlike some of the immigrants to Nebraska, he is just sentimental and romantic enough to be somewhat affected by his relationship to the land. In other words, although he is not an artist, he has a touch of the artist's sensibility about him. After a dream about the drought, which was threatening to burn up his entire corn crop, Lou's mind gives way. As Schneider points out, "he then translates the immediate situation—his personal losses and the drought which threatens to destroy the crops—into teleological and apocalyptic terms" (1967, 78).

Lou, then, is the type of personality most easily conquered by frontier life. In an attempt to clarify his own relationship to the land, he imbues the land, the elements, and all events with a kind of relevance, in his case a cosmic significance. Indeed, the narrator says that "nature did not comfort him any, he knew nothing about nature, he had never seen her; he had only stared into a black plow furrow all his life. Before, he had only seen in the wide, green lands and the open blue the possibilities of earning his bread; now, he only saw in them a great world ready for the judgment, a funeral pyre ready for the torch" (Cather 1970, 537). Here, Cather implies that Lou's former self, the one who merely "stared into a black plow furrow," would have been much less easily destroyed than was his latter self, which was a version of the aesthete (Schneider 1967, 78). Such an implication does not bode well for the group of Danish boys whom Lou convinces "that the drought results from the sins of the world" and then leads in a "prayer for a thirsty land" (Schneider 1967, 78). They, too, are made to see the cosmic significance of events. When Lou dies, they interpret the death as his having been caught up into heaven by God. "But the majority of the people of the area—ordinary, hardworking people—are satisfied with the realistic conjecture that Lou drowned and disappeared into quicksand" (Schneider 1967, 79). These people, we are left to assume, are the only types able to survive the brutality of pioneer life.

Works Cited

Bennett, Mildred R. 1982. "Willa Cather's Bodies for Ghosts." *Western American Literature* 17:39–52.

Bradford, Curtis. 1955. "Willa Cather's Uncollected Short Stories." *American Literature* 26:537–51.

Cather, Willa. 1905. Letter to Witter Bynner, June 7. Houghton Library, Harvard University, Cambridge, MA.

———. 1957. "Lou, the Prophet. In *Early Stories*. Ed. Mildred Bennett. New York: Dodd, Mead, 9–17.

———. [1965] 1970. "Lou, the Prophet." In *Willa Cather's Collected Short Fiction, 1892–1912*. Ed. Virginia Faulkner. Lincoln: University of Nebraska Press, 535–40.

Faulkner, Virginia, ed. [1965] 1970. *Willa Cather's Collected Short Fiction, 1892–1912*. Lincoln: University of Nebraska Press. Reprint. Lincoln: University of Nebraska Press.

Lathrop, Joanna. 1975. *Willa Cather: A Checklist of Her Published Writing*. Lincoln: University of Nebraska Press.

Schneider, Sister Lucy. 1967. "Willa Cather's Early Stories in the Light of Her 'Land-Philosophy.'" *Midwest Quarterly* 9:75–94.

Woodress, James. 1987. *Willa Cather: A Literary Life*. Lincoln: University of Nebraska Press.

The Marriage of Phaedra

Publication History

This story was first published under the name Willa Sibert Cather in Cather's first collection of short stories, *The Troll Garden* (New York: McClure, Phillips, 1905, pp. 155–92) (Faulkner 1970, 595). It was reprinted in 1961 in a Signet Classics paperback edition of *The Troll Garden* with modernized spelling and punctuation. In 1965, the University of Nebraska Press included the 1905 version of the story in *Willa Cather's Collected Short Fiction, 1892–1912* (187–97). The same version appeared again in 1983, when the University of Nebraska Press published an edition of *The Troll Garden*, edited by James Woodress, and again in 1987 by Literary Classics of the United States in *Cather: Early Novels and Stories*, a volume in the Library of America series.

Circumstances of Composition, Sources, and Influences

Cather probably wrote this story in 1902, shortly after she and her friend Isabelle McClung returned from a European trip to the McClung family home in Pittsburgh, where Cather lived from 1901 to 1906 while teaching high school (Woodress 1983, xxiii). (For a discussion of the enormous positive influence of Isabelle McClung on Cather's creativity see the "Circumstances of Composition, Sources, and Influences" section for the chapter "A Wagner Matinée.") The story was probably included in a packet Cather sent to S. S. McClure in New York after her former editor at the *Nebraska State Journal* recommended her work to McClure's cousin. This packet eventually led to the publication of Cather's first collection of short stories, *The Troll Garden*, which McClure published in 1905. (A full explanation of McClure's role in the publication of these stories is given in the "Circumstances of Composition, Sources, and Influences" section for the chapter "The Sculptor's Funeral.")

Cather and Isabelle McClung left for their first trip to Europe in June 1902 and returned in late September of that same year. Cather had arranged to supplement her income while she was overseas by sending travel letters back to the *Nebraska State Journal*; the paper printed fourteen of these letters between July and October (Woodress 1987, 156). In one of them Cather gives an account of her visit to the Kensington studio of the pre-Raphaelite painter Sir Edward Burne-Jones. She describes the studio in detail and claims to have seen a painting called *The Passing of Venus* there; however, according to Thurin, since no information about such a painting is available, Cather may have had one or two of the artist's other paintings in mind—*Bath of Venus* or *Mirror of Venus* (1990, 138n). Whether or not Cather was mistaken about the title of the painting she saw there, the studio visit was a strong source for at least some aspects of the story. According to Kates, there was even an intelligent and garrulous man named James at the studio (1956, 66). Bennett agrees with this explanation of the source of the fictional James (1961, 163). Woodress, however, maintains that James was purely a Cather invention for the travel letter to the newspaper; he does agree, however, that the story's title came from Cather's visit to the studio (1983, xxiii).

Virtually all scholars who have commented on this story have mentioned its strong Jamesian flavor, some going so far as to assert that it is the most reminiscent of Henry James of any of the stories in *The Troll Garden*. O'Brien notes the Jamesian nature of both the studio setting and the artificial dialogue; further, "the central symbol is a painting, which as in [James's] *The Sacred Fount* is a 'cryptic index' both to the creative process and to a sexual and emotional relationship which is never adequately decoded" (1987, 277). Arnold mentions a connection to James's *The Outcry*, which also "centers around the possible sale of a famous painting" (1984, 69).

Lee contends that for this story Cather borrows the plot of an artist whose wife does not appreciate his work from James's story "The Author of 'Beltraffio,'" and that she relies on James's "The Figure in the Carpet" for the part of the plot that centers on the decisions made about the art work after the artist's death (1989, 75).

Relationship to Other Cather Works

Like all the other *Troll Garden* stories, this one explores the conflict between the ways of life represented by the trolls and forest children of the two epigraphs Cather chose for the collection (Woodress 1983, xxiii). (For a complete explanation of the thematic relationship of the *Troll Garden* stories to the epigraphs Cather chose for them, see the "Relationship to Other Cather Works" section for the chapters "'A Death in the Desert'" and "A Wagner Matinée.")

The idea of the painting being sold by someone who is interested in it only as a source of money anticipates Roddy Blake's selling the Indian relics he and Tom Outland discover in Cather's *The Professor's House* (Arnold 1984, 57). In a similar interpretation, Edward A. Bloom and Lillian D. Bloom assert that the artist is understood only by his servant, who opposes the sale of the painting, just as Professor St. Peter in *The Professor's House* resists "Outland's parasites" (1962, 126–27).

O'Brien sees a connection between this story and others, such as "'A Death in the Desert,'" "A Garden Lodge," and "The Sculptor's Funeral," that in some way explore the conflict between gender and vocation that was very much on Cather's mind. In each case, the male artist is absent. He is described only from memory, a strategy that allows Cather both "to convey the power of artistic influence" and at the same time free herself from her dependence on artistic forefathers (1987, 271). Cather's own awareness of her debt to her literary precursors is obvious in some of the titles she chose: she borrowed "'A Death in the Desert'" from a Browning poem "whose subject is also discipleship and legacy," and the titles "The Marriage of Phaedra" and "A Wagner Matinée" are also allusions to other works of art (O'Brien 1987, 278).

Both Woodress and Schroeter believe that the detestable art dealer in this story gives the piece a measure of anti-Semitism that may also be found in some of Cather's other work. For example, "Scandal" includes the brutal character of the Jewish millionaire Stein, and "The Diamond Mine" the offensive figure of Miletus Poppas; an early newspaper article describes a Jewish baby in a negative way, and Louis Marcellus of *The Professor's House* and "the villain in 'The Affair at Grover Station,' who looks Jewish but turns out to be oriental," may both be seen as growing out of Cather's anti-Semitism (Woodress 1987, 283). Schroeter adds "The Old Beauty" to the list, noting that the despicable banker who assaults the protagonist of the story is dark and foreign-looking. He is not identified as a Jew, but Cather describes him in much the same way she describes Stein in "Scandal" (Schroeter 1967, 367).

Bennett reads this story as one of six in *The Troll Garden* to portray women who either cause others to suffer or suffer themselves: the suffering women include Flavia in "Flavia and Her Artists," Harvey Merrick's mother in "The Sculptor's Funeral," and Lady Treffinger in "The Marriage of Phaedra." Those who cause pain for others are Katharine in "'A Death in the Desert,'" Caroline in "The Garden Lodge," and Aunt Georgiana in "A Wagner Matinée" (1970, xxxvi).

Interpretations and Criticisms

In Thurin's opinion, the loathing that Lady Treffinger expresses toward the paintings represents her feelings toward her husband as well. She is, perhaps, not so much jealous of his work as glad to be rid of *him*. However, the reader is never allowed to grasp the connection clearly because Cather's Jamesian technique gets in the way: although the story's point of view is for the most part MacMaster's, it does sometimes shift to James and even to Lady

Treffinger's sister. Unfortunately, these characters are not at all the kinds of observers Henry James created. Instead, they provide an unsteady focus that "results in obscurity rather than illumination" (1990, 128–29). Arnold agrees that the story is not really centered on MacMaster. In fact, there is no thoroughly reliable central figure (1984, 56). Wasserman attributes the lack of focus to Cather's introduction of a "number of psychological crosscurrents—so many that the reader wearies of following them" (1991, 27).

Thurin argues that the Treffingers can easily be related to *The Troll Garden*'s epigraph from Kingsley in that the painter may be seen as the "barbarian knocking at the door of the fairy palace of art . . . by breaking with the traditions of his class and becoming a painter"; on the other hand, Lady Treffinger may be the primary "barbarian or forest child" of the story—"she was dazzled by the brilliant Treffinger and yearned to be admitted to the fairy palace of art. But she is not flexible enough to cope with the situation that arises when he turns out to be a troll" (1990, 129). Arnold suggests only Treffinger for the role of forest child, if indeed there is a forest child in the story at all (1984, 56), and to Woodress, the barbarian is clearly the widow (1987, 179).

In O'Brien's opinion, the central issue raised by the story is one of literary influence. Cather is struggling here with the question of how an artist can learn to use her own voice while continuing to rely heavily on artists from the past. Perhaps the reason Cather made all the main characters male is that during the time the story was written, she viewed the literary tradition as purely male. In any case, MacMaster becomes engrossed by the dead artist so that he can pass on the artist's tradition (1987, 277–78). "After deciding to write his critical biography, like James he becomes the medium through which Treffinger speaks" (O'Brien 1987, 278). O'Brien argues that even the names Cather chooses—MacMaster and James—are weighted with significance. MacMaster may be a pun because he is as much a servant of the artist as is James. In selecting the name of the valet, Cather was probably making a deliberate reference to Henry James, perhaps "because she wished no longer to be serving James—all the while finding in the master-servant, artist-disciple relationship an analog to her own literary servitude, which she displays as well as comments on" (1987, 278).

Brown argues that Cather's own notions about art may be found in this story through a careful reading of Treffinger's path to greatness. Treffinger had to incorporate his own experience and knowledge of his craft into his final masterpiece. It is this ability to integrate personal experience and artistic skill that makes Treffinger a great artist (1964, 118–19).

To read this story simply as the chronicle of an artist trapped in a bad marriage is too easy, suggests Rosowski. Treffinger's wife can be cast in the role of victim as easily as the artist himself. He sacrificed everything—both his needs and his wife's—to the painting. In fact, Cather may be using the word *mas-*

terpiece ironically: art produced at this cost is more of a blight on, than a benefit to, humanity (1986, 26).

Works Cited

Arnold, Marilyn. 1984. *Willa Cather's Short Fiction.* Athens: Ohio University Press.

Bennett, Mildred R. 1961. *The World of Willa Cather.* Lincoln: University of Nebraska Press.

———. [1965] 1970. Introduction to *Willa Cather's Collected Short Fiction.* Ed. Virginia Faulkner. Lincoln: University of Nebraska Press. Reprint. Lincoln: University of Nebraska Press, xiii–xli.

Bloom, Edward A., and Lillian D. Bloom. 1962. *Willa Cather's Gift of Sympathy.* Carbondale: Southern Illinois University Press.

Brown, E. K. Completed by Leon Edel. [1953] 1964. *Willa Cather: A Critical Biography.* New York: Knopf.

Cather, Willa. 1961. "The Marriage of Phaedra." In *The Troll Garden.* New York: Signet Classics, 51–63.

———. [1965] 1970. "The Marriage of Phaedra." In *Willa Cather's Collected Short Fiction, 1892–1912.* Ed. Virginia Faulkner. Lincoln: University of Nebraska Press, 187–97.

———. 1983. "The Marriage of Phaedra." In *The Troll Garden.* Ed. James Woodress. Lincoln: University of Nebraska Press, 77–93.

———. 1987. "The Marriage of Phaedra." In *Cather: Early Novels and Stories.* New York: Literary Classics of the United States, 83–101.

Faulkner, Virginia, ed. [1965] 1970. *Willa Cather's Collected Short Fiction, 1892–1912.* Lincoln: University of Nebraska Press. Reprint. Lincoln: University of Nebraska Press.

Kates, George N. 1956. *Willa Cather in Europe.* New York: Knopf.

Lee, Hermione. 1989. *Willa Cather: Double Lives.* New York: Pantheon.

O'Brien, Sharon. 1987. *Willa Cather: The Emerging Voice.* New York: Oxford University Press.

Rosowski, Susan J. 1986. *The Voyage Perilous: Willa Cather's Romanticism.* Lincoln: University of Nebraska Press.

Schroeter, James. 1967. "Willa Cather and *The Professor's House.*" In *Willa Cather and Her Critics.* Ed. James Schroeter. Ithaca, NY: Cornell University Press, 363–81.

Thurin, Erik Ingvar. 1990. *The Humanization of Willa Cather: Classicism in an American Classic.* Lund, Sweden: Lund University Press.

Wasserman, Loretta. 1991. *Willa Cather: A Study of the Short Fiction.* Boston: Twayne.

Woodress, James. 1983. Introduction to *The Troll Garden.* Ed. James Woodress. Lincoln: University of Nebraska Press, xi–xxx.

———. 1987. *Willa Cather: A Literary Life.* Lincoln: University of Nebraska Press.

Nanette: An Aside

Publication History

This story was first published by the Lincoln *Courier* on July 31, 1897 (12:11–12), under the name Willa Cather; it reappeared a month later in *Home Monthly* (6:5–6) (Faulkner 1970, 592). In 1957 Dodd, Mead reprinted the story in *Early Stories*, where the date of publication is given incorrectly as August 1896; in 1965, it was republished by the University of Nebraska Press in *Willa Cather's Collected Short Fiction, 1892–1912*.

Circumstances of Composition, Sources, and Influences

"Nanette: An Aside" marks Cather's first use of an opera singer in her fiction (Woodress 1970, 82). This story and "The Prodigies" are the only two written during Cather's tenure at *Home Monthly* that concern music, a subject that would often occupy her in the future.

O'Brien explains that all of Cather's stories dealing with music grow out of her deep interest in that art. All her life, her most valued friendships were with musicians (1987, 170). Cather's longtime companion, Edith Lewis, comments that Cather reacted to music emotionally, rather than intellectually, and that music's ability to inspire her writing was tremendous (Lewis 1953, 47–48).

The many reviews of singers' performances Cather wrote during the 1890s attest to the awe in which she held opera singers, especially female singers, whose performances, as O'Brien notes, Cather often described in sweeping, emotional terms. One of the things Cather found especially compelling about women opera singers was that they were more self-sufficient than other artists—each had her own distinctive voice, which, unlike the woman writer, she did not have to develop while at the same time relying upon the models created by male artists (O'Brien 1987, 172).

In Bennett's opinion, at least one part of the story is based precisely on Cather's own life: it was around this time that Cather wrote one of her friends that she had no intention of marrying, and the reasons she outlined are strikingly similar to Madame's advice to Nanette—if she marries, she will have to give up many of the things most dear to her, not the least of which is her independence (Bennett 1957, 101).

Relationship to Other Cather Works

Cather reworks the material of this story into "A Singer's Romance" (1900). The singer in that story is, in turn, very similar to the fictionalized version of the Wagnerian soprano Lillian Nordica that Cather would later present in "The Diamond Mine" (Woodress 1987, 146). The most obvious and well-known fictional descendent of Tradutorri, however, is Thea Kronborg of *The Song of the Lark*.

O'Brien points out the parallels between this story and several others (see "The Burglar's Christmas," "The Clemency of the Court," "The Count of Crow's Nest," "A Son of the Celestial," and "A Tale of the White Pyramid," for example) that employ images of death, tombs, and repression. Here those images are used to describe creative power. The opera singer Tradutorri does not, like other singers, release her suffering on stage: instead she seals it within herself until it grows to the point where it must destroy her (1987, 201).

According to Bennett, this story shares with many other stories and novels Cather's conviction that one must choose between art and happiness (Bennett 1957, 99). Tradutorri's explanation to Nanette sums up Cather's own philosophy about art—a philosophy that emerges many more times in her fiction: "When I began life, between me and this lay everything dear in life—every love, every human hope. I have had to bury what lay between. It is the same thing florists do when they cut away all the buds that one flower may blossom with the strength of all" (Cather 1970, 410).

All of Cather's fictional artists are required to make exactly the same sacrifice if they are to achieve real artistry. Thea Kronberg chooses to pursue a career opportunity rather than attend her mother's funeral, and Clement Sebastian (*Lucy Gayheart*) seriously questions the toll he has paid in isolation in order to devote himself to art (Arnold 1984, 15).

Interpretations and Criticisms

This story has produced little critical comment. O'Brien maintains that part of the story's significance is its reflection of Cather's increasing respect for women artists and her growing realization that creativity is not necessarily linked to masculinity. The story also reveals Cather's interest in intimacies between women who are not united in any conventional sense. Most observers would see only Nanette's role as a maid, but the truth is that Nanette and Tradutorri are very much like daughter and mother (O'Brien 1987, 232). The story can also be read as evidence of Cather's increasing awareness of the writer's prerogative to give fictional women roles they rarely played in the real world, and of the power that prerogative could give her work (O'Brien 1987, 231).

Works Cited

Arnold, Marilyn. 1984. *Willa Cather's Short Fiction*. Athens: Ohio University Press.

Bennett, Mildred, ed. 1957. *Early Stories of Willa Cather*. New York: Dodd, Mead.

Cather, Willa. 1957. "Nanette: An Aside." In *Early Stories*. Ed. Mildred Bennett. New York: Dodd, Mead, 93–102.

———. [1965] 1970. "Nanette: An Aside." In *Willa Cather's Collected Short Fiction, 1892–1912*. Ed. Virginia Faulkner. Lincoln: University of Nebraska Press, 407–410.

Faulkner, Virginia, ed. [1965] 1970. *Willa Cather's Collected Short Fiction, 1892–1912*. Lincoln: University of Nebraska Press. Reprint. Lincoln: University of Nebraska Press.

Lewis, Edith. 1953. *Willa Cather Living*. New York: Knopf.

O'Brien, Sharon. 1987. *Willa Cather: The Emerging Voice*. New York: Oxford University Press.

Woodress, James. 1970. *Willa Cather: Her Life and Art*. New York: Pegasus.

———. 1987. *Willa Cather: A Literary Life*. Lincoln: University of Nebraska Press.

The Namesake

Publication History

This story was first published under the name Willa Sibert Cather in the March 1907 issue of *McClure's* (28:492–97) (Faulkner 1970, 596). It was reprinted in 1965 by the University of Nebraska Press in *Willa Cather's Collected Short Fiction, 1892–1912*, and in 1992 by Literary Classics of the United States in *Cather: Stories, Poems, and Other Writings*, a volume in the Library of America series.

Circumstances of Composition, Sources, and Influences

At the end of the school year in 1906, Cather resigned from her high school teaching position in Pittsburgh and moved to New York City, where she became a staff member of *McClure's* magazine. Her first New York residence was in an old building on Washington Square in Greenwich Village. According to her first biographer, E. K. Brown, the grimy New York accommodations were a sharp contrast to the opulence of Judge McClung's home, where she lived in Pittsburgh (1964, 133–34). (Cather had lived with her friend Isabelle McClung and her family in Pittsburgh from 1901 until 1906, when she moved to New York. For a discussion of the enormous positive influence of Isabelle McClung on Cather's creativity see the "Circumstances of Composition, Sources, and Influences" section for the chapter "A Wagner Matinée.") By all accounts, however, Cather was ecstatic to be living among artists.

The publisher of the magazine, S. S. McClure, had first become interested in Cather through a packet of work she sent him in 1903, which contained some, if not all, of the stories that McClure was to publish in 1905 as Cather's first collection of short stories, *The Troll Garden*. (A full explanation of McClure's role in the publication of these stories is given in the "Circumstances of Composition, Sources, and Influences" section for the chapter "The Sculptor's Funeral.") Although he knew Cather primarily as a creative writer, her position at *McClure's* had little to do with writing stories and poems. In fact, her first major assignment was to complete a manuscript entitled *Mary Baker G. Eddy: The Story of Her Life and History of Christian Science*, which had been begun by someone else and was in need of fact checking and polishing.

This project would not have been especially significant for a writer of Cather's stature had it not required that she stay for months at a time in Boston to research her subject. Cather's move to Boston put her in contact with people who would eventually become very important friends, the most significant of whom would be Sarah Orne Jewett (Brown 1964, 135, 138). The two women met for the first time in March 1908 at the home of Mrs. James T. Fields, the widow of a member of the renowned Ticknor and Fields publishing house. Mrs. Fields's house was a haven for famous writers: Charles Dickens had been a frequent visitor, and Thackeray wrote part of *Henry Esmond* there. Others who frequently dropped by included Longfellow, Lowell, Emerson, and Hawthorne; both Harriet Beecher Stowe and Henry James had dined there (Brown 1964, 136).

Although Jewett died only a year after her 1908 meeting with Cather, a letter of advice Jewett wrote to her much younger friend was the most important letter Cather ever received from anyone (Brown 1964, 140). In it Jewett urges Cather to find her own voice and cautions her not to allow her exhausting position at *McClure's* to undermine her artistic gifts. Jewett was somewhat dissatisfied with the stories Cather had written since joining *McClure's* staff because they did not show, in Jewett's opinion, enough evidence that their author had matured much from *The Troll Garden* period (1901–1903). She tells Cather, "You are older now than that book in general; you have been living and reading and knowing new types; but if you don't keep and guard and mature your force, and above all, have time and quiet to perfect your work, you will be writing things not much better than you did five years ago" (Fields 1911, 247–48). One may assume that Jewett was speaking of the first five stories Cather published after moving to New York, "The Namesake," "The Profile," "The Willing Muse," "Eleanor's House" (all 1907), and "On the Gulls' Road" (1908). All except "The Willing Muse" were published in *McClure's*.

For "The Namesake," the first of these stories to appear, Cather used the same title as that of one of the poems she had published in *Lippincott's* five years before in memory of her uncle William Boak, a Confederate soldier who had been killed in the Civil War (Brown 1964, 141). Like the poem, the short story "celebrates her male inheritance and develops parallels between her imagined bond with William Boak and the creative process. . . . Similarly, the adolescent [Cather's] male impersonation signified her search to inherit authority and power from the male line. . . " (O'Brien 1987, 109–110). (For a complete discussion of Cather's period of actual male impersonation, see the "Interpretations and Criticisms" section for the chapter "Paul's Case.") As O'Brien argues, in many ways "The Namesake" is "one of Cather's most autobiographical fictions" because she draws on her perceived bond with her uncle, whose middle name of Seibert she had claimed some years before, changing the spelling to Sibert in the process (1987, 330). "Connecting artistic self-discovery with a return from Europe to America," she at least makes a gesture toward ending her dependence on Henry James even while simultaneously deferring to him in the frame story (O'Brien 1987, 330). That she is not yet quite comfortable drawing on her own past in her fiction is clear: she distances herself from Lyon Hartwell by making him a Northern soldier from Pennsylvania, not a Confederate from Virginia like her uncle; nevertheless, all these maneuverings suggest the conflicts that Cather herself was experiencing at the time the story was written (O'Brien 1987, 330).

Relationship to Other Cather Works

Bennett and Arnold mention the obvious connection between Hartwell's young uncle in this story and Claude Wheeler in *One of Ours* (1922). Both die heroically during a war they thought just (Arnold 1984, 76; Bennett 1982, 49). Arnold further connects the story to the novel by noting that both soldiers are spared the disappointment that comes after the war. As she had done many times in the past, in this story Cather portrays war as hideous, not glorious, yet her admiration for the courageous young men who fight is obvious (1984, 76).

This story expresses some of the concerns that often appear in Cather's works. One example is the relationship between the home and the young person who goes in search of a better place. This issue is central to "The Namesake" as well as to the earlier story "A Sculptor's Funeral" (1905), the later novel *The Song of the Lark* (1915), and even to the much later "Two Friends" (1932). "The Sculptor's Funeral" is brutal enough to make readers yearn for some kind of escape from the suffocating town and family the author depicts, and Cather almost seems to be honoring that wish in "The Namesake" by portraying another sculptor who grew up away from his home (Wasserman 1990, 58–59). His coming home, however, and discovering his own artistic life by reconnecting with his past looks ahead to Thea Kronborg's similar discovery in *The Song of the Lark* (Arnold 1984, 77).

Another typical Cather preoccupation is the fate of the frontier after it has been conquered by the pioneers—when, as Bradford puts it, "the thin-blooded and the penny pinchers" take over and the rich cultural past of the immigrants is crushed by American materialism (1955, 539). This theme may be found in "The Namesake," "The Bohemian Girl" (1912), and the novel *One of Ours*, all of which may accurately be called stories of protest, unpolished but moving because they grow out of real experience (Bradford 1955, 539). In Arnold's view, this is the same thread that runs through "The Professor's Commencement," where it takes the form of the professor's regret that even as students sit in his classroom, the industrialism that will someday consume them is just outside the door, its noise filling the classroom. The same threat is described in both "The Namesake" and "Uncle Valentine" (1984, 42).

Bennett mentions the similarity between one of this story's emotional passages and corresponding passages in both *My Ántonia* and *O Pioneers!* At one point the narrator refers to the "feeling that artists know when we, rarely, achieve truth in our work; the feeling of union with some great force, of purpose and security" (Cather 1992, 62; quoted in Bennett 1970, xxxix). It is an emotion closely related to Jim Burden's insight in *My Ántonia* that true happiness comes only when a person becomes a part of something larger and better than himself. The same sentiment is heard again in *O Pioneers!* when Emil races, "wild with joy," to meet Maria Shabata: "His life poured itself out along the road before him as he rode to the Shabata farm" (quoted in Bennett 1970, xxxix).

Woodress groups the story with others that make use of Cather's memories of her early life in Virginia, including "The Elopement of Allen Poole" (1893), "A Night at Greenway Court" (1896), and "The Sentimentality of William Tavener" (1900). Although all these stories are apprentice work, they indicate that from the beginning of her career, Cather drew on the whole of her experience (1987, 29).

Thurin links the story to six others Cather wrote while she worked for *McClure's*, all of which "reflect her continued commitment to the classics as a writer of fiction": "The Willing Muse" (1907), "Eleanor's House" (1907), "On the Gulls' Road" (1908), "The Joy of Nelly Deane" (1911), and "The Bohemian Girl" (1912) (1990, 140). Thurin argues that they are also similar in that they depict the opposition between America and Europe, a very Jamesian concern—and one that did not seem to be declining in Cather's fiction at the time this story was written, with the exception perhaps of "The Bohemian Girl." Nevertheless, Thurin believes these stories reveal that Cather was trying new narrative strategies, "resorting more and more to the personal, symbolic-poetic way of writing fiction she is to use in her novels"; further, these stories evince "a strange disenchantment with actual life and a flight into the might-have-been" (1990, 140–41).

Interpretations and Criticisms

Although this story does not speak directly of family or community, it does suggest that an artist must embrace a specific place as his own if he is ever to understand his role *as* an artist (Wasserman 1990, 59). One's past is extremely valuable, perhaps even essential to unleashing creativity (Arnold 1984, 75).

Thurin places great emphasis on the references Cather makes to the *Aeneid* in this story: "Rome as Hartwell's birthplace; the idea of Empire taking its westward course (the theme-to-be of his art), and the 'Roman' man-hood incarnated by the boy he identifies with. . . . The vision of his heroic and patriotic namesake with his copy of the *Aeneid*" makes Hartwell feel con-nected to his fathers' land (1990, 140–42). He immediately experiences an intimate connection to the very earth itself, a kind of union with the "Earth-Mother," a union that is rather flawed by Cather's previous mention of the polluted environment—anyone connected to this particular land is unfortu-nate indeed (Thurin 1990, 141–42). Cather herself is brought into the story in spite of herself through a subtext that calls attention to itself and causes the reader to question the author's motives: "Hartwell, a bachelor, detests his father, . . . [and] since the person serving as an idealized father figure is real-ly a handsome young boy, there is a hint of the same-sex Platonic love which in the *Phaedrus* and the *Symposium* is said to inform all higher creative activ-ities" (Thurin 1990, 143). Cather's interest in "male love/friendship" is well established, but here there is "a special twist: the uncle is both the party whose youthful beauty inspires the older party with courage and the older man to whom the *ephebe* can look up as a role model" (1990, 143–44).

Brown sees this story as evidence that Cather was beginning to acknowl-edge the importance of her roots—both family and land—as the source of both her delight and artistic power. The artistry here is immature and unre-fined, however, and reads as though it had been written not by Henry James or Edith Wharton, but by someone who had been excessively influenced by their styles (1964, 142–43).

In a similar but more extensive interpretation, O'Brien sees Hartwell's return to America as Cather's expression of her own voice, free from James's influence. She was beginning to understand that "art has its source in American soil, American history, and American lives" (1987, 329). The creative process Cather envisioned always moved toward unity and away from frag-mentation, a process that is imaged in Hartwell's directing "his creative ener-gies to Civil War monuments, [transforming] the nation's historical experience of . . . conflict into a public representation of unity" (1987, 330). In this story, Cather is also moving away from connecting artistry with the masculine: even though on the surface the story "appears to equate the manly arts of war and sculpture, . . . on a deeper level it condemns masculine energies and relationships grounded in power rather than in reciprocity." This is shown by Cather's depiction of the female landscape being ruined by the masculine powers of "industry and technology. . ." (1987, 330–31). For Hartwell, peace is only available in the obviously feminine sanctuary of the garden. It is there that he has his epiphany, and Cather eventually reveals that he has women to thank for his new awareness. Several steps guide him to "a female creative inheritance": first, his purpose in returning to Pennsylvania is to play the traditional role of a woman in taking care of his elderly aunt; sec-ond, it is his uncle's mother, not father, who has preserved his trunk, which still smells of lavender and roses, thus preserving the absent mother's connection to the scene (1987, 331). His female relatives have been responsible for safeguarding the past, which eventually becomes his artistic inspiration. Finally, Hartwell gains his insight in the attic and garden, "feminine realms connected in Cather's life and fiction with dream, reverie, creativity, and maternal care" (see "Circumstances of Composition, Sources, and Influences" above) (1987, 331).

Works Cited

Arnold, Marilyn. 1984. *Willa Cather's Short Fiction*. Athens: Ohio University Press.

Bennett, Mildred. [1965] 1970. Introduction to *Willa Cather's Collected Short Fiction*. Ed. Virginia Faulkner. Lincoln: University of Nebraska Press. Reprint. Lincoln: University of Nebraska Press, xiii–xli.

———. 1982. "Willa Cather's Bodies for Ghosts." *Western American Literature* 17:39–52.

Bradford, Curtis. 1955. "Willa Cather's Uncollected Short Stories." *American Literature* 26:537–51.

Brown, E. K. Completed by Leon Edel. [1953] 1964. *Willa Cather: A Critical Biography*. New York: Knopf.

Cather, Willa. [1965] 1970. "The Namesake." In *Willa Cather's Collected Short Fiction, 1892–1912*. Ed. Virginia Faulkner. Lincoln: University of Nebraska Press, 137–46.

———. 1992. "The Namesake." In *Cather: Stories, Poems, and Other Writings*. New York: Literary Classics of the United States, 52–63.

Faulkner, Virginia, ed. [1965] 1970. *Willa Cather's Collected Short Fiction, 1892–1912*. Lincoln: University of Nebraska Press. Reprint. Lincoln: University of Nebraska Press.

Fields, Annie, ed. 1911. *Letters of Sarah Orne Jewett*. Boston: Houghton Mifflin.

O'Brien, Sharon. 1987. *Willa Cather: The Emerging Voice*. New York: Oxford University Press.

Thurin, Erik Ingvar. 1990. *The Humanization of Willa Cather: Classicism in an American Classic*. Lund, Sweden: Lund University Press.

Wasserman, Loretta. 1990. "Going Home: 'The Sculptor's Funeral,' 'The Namesake,' and 'Two Friends.'" In *Willa Cather and the Family, Community and History: The BYU Symposium*. Ed. John J. Murphy. Provo, Utah: Brigham Young University, 57–62.

Woodress, James. 1987. *Willa Cather: A Literary Life*. Lincoln: University of Nebraska Press.

Neighbour Rosicky

Publication History

This story, with the first word of the title spelled *Neighbor*, was first published serially under the name Willa Cather in the April and May 1930 issues of *Woman's Home Companion* (57:7–9, 52, 54, 57; 13–14, 92, 95–96) (Faulkner 1970, 598). Its next appearance was in Cather's third collection of short stories, *Obscure Destinies* (New York: Knopf, 1932, pp. 1–71); it also appeared in volume twelve of the thirteen-volume library edition of Cather's work, *The Novels and Stories of Willa Cather* (Boston: Houghton Mifflin, 1937–1941, pp. 5–62) (Faulkner 1970, 598).

The story was reprinted in two publications by Vintage Books: *Five Stories* in 1956, and in a paperback edition of *Obscure Destinies* in 1974. Its next appearance was in the 1992 Library of America edition, *Cather: Stories, Poems, and Other Writings*. The spelling *Neighbour* appears in all but the first printing of the story.

Circumstances of Composition, Sources, and Influences

According to her first biographer, E. K. Brown, Cather probably wrote this story early in 1928, when she was still emotionally fragile because of her father's death (1964, 275). Ryder, however, assumes the story was written after Cather's mother was stricken by a paralytic stroke in December of that year (1990, 266). In any case, the story is dated 1928 in the collection (Arnold 1984, 176n), the year that Woodress calls one of Cather's least productive (1970, 227).

Cather specialists generally agree that Anton Rosicky is modeled partly on the author's father, Charles Cather—Rosicky's heart ailment and the fatal heart attack that eventually kills him precisely mirror Charles Cather's illness and death—and partly on the husband of Annie Pavelka, Cather's Bohemian neighbor in Nebraska, who became the prototype for Ántonia in *My Ántonia* (Arnold 1984, 135). At least one incident in "Neighbour Rosicky" comes directly from a conversation Cather heard in the Pavelka home on one of her visits back to Nebraska, years after she had left the state. As Bennett reports the story, the Pavelkas were extremely proud of their children, and when neighboring farmers advised Mr. Pavelka to make more money by selling his cream, he refused, arguing "that roses in the cheeks of their children were more important than land or money in the bank" (1961, 50). When he died, Mr. Pavelka was buried in a small Bohemian cemetery close to his home—"the cemetery overlooking the cornfields and rich sloping pastures described in 'Neighbour Rosicky'" (1961, 50–51).

Rosowski notes that Cather's ideas about a stable family life are represented in the character of Anton Rosicky. Rosicky marries late in life and so has perhaps more patience than he would have had as a young man. Further, his relationship with his wife is based primarily on friendship, not romantic love. This description of a happy marriage is vintage Cather (Rosowski 1990, 76).

Relationship to Other Cather Works

Because Cather placed "Neighbour Rosicky" in her collection *Obscure Destinies*, the story has the strongest similarities to the other two stories in the book, "Old Mrs. Harris" and "Two Friends." All three tales fit neatly into the book's overall thematic design, and all were written during an especially difficult period in Cather's personal life. In March of 1928, her father died of a heart attack, and shortly after the funeral, her mother accompanied Cather's brother Douglass back to his home in California. Mrs. Cather intended only a temporary stay with her son before returning to Red Cloud, but shortly after her arrival in California, she suffered a paralytic stroke and had to be cared for in a nursing home. For two and a half years Cather exhausted herself traveling from one coast to another to be with her mother. All three *Obscure Destinies* stories indicate just how strong Cather's memories of her Nebraska life were at the time (Arnold 1984, 133). All three were begun at her mother's sickbed, and each is heavily "colored by a nostalgic longing for the irretrievable" (Ryder 1990, 266).

When her mother finally died in August 1931, Cather's "essential ties" to Red Cloud were broken (Arnold 1984, 133). In December of that year she returned to her hometown for the last time to spend Christmas with the rest of the family. The *Obscure Destinies* period, then, was a time when Cather was at an important turning point in her life and her writing. "*Obscure Destinies* is her pause, her private meditation" on her Nebraska experience (Arnold 1984, 133). In fact, with "Neighbour Rosicky," the earliest story in the collection, Cather returned to a Nebraska setting for the first time since the 1912 "The Bohemian Girl," eighteen years before (Arnold 1984, 176n). Danker explains this return in terms of Cather's increasing alienation from the society around her: shaken by the death of both her parents, she was challenging the validity of the beliefs she had once held so strongly; all three stories in the collection somehow concern the "passing of the certainties of youth" (1990, 24).

One aspect of this turning point was that Cather had finally stopped choosing artists or society's elite as subjects for her fiction and instead turned to the ordinary people she had known in her youth, as is suggested by the title of the book, an allusion to Gray's "Elegy Written in a Country Churchyard." The relevant lines of the poem are: "Let not Ambition mock their useful toil,/ Their homely joys, and destiny obscure;/ Nor grandeur hear with a disdainful smile/ The short and simple annals of the poor" (Gray 1972, 122–23). The value of fame and success is further questioned in the next stanza, where Gray asserts that the "paths of glory lead but to the grave" (Gray 1972, 124; Stouck 1975, 208). Each of the stories in this collection in some way bears witness to the truth of Gray's message. According to Daiches, Cather may have come to realize that artists choosing other artists as subjects is a bit incestuous, and this realization led to her abandonment of what had once been a common subject for her fiction (1962, 157).

Another theme from Gray's "Elegy" that contributes to the unity of the three stories in this collection is the idea that human destiny is played out under the moon, which has its source in the Aristotelian notion of the "superlunary sphere—the realm of eternity and immutability—and the sublunary sphere, the domain of mutability and mortal life" (Thurin 1990, 320). The latter sphere is much more prominent in these three stories than is the former; the focus in this collection is on "obscure, humble, and earth-bound lives," each of which comes to an end in the story without a subsequent emphasis on the afterlife in some other sphere (Thurin 1990, 320).

Giannone proposes another unifying element: each story explores the central fact of human existence—that people who might communicate with each other meet, part, and move on toward death alone, and it is death that gives meaning to the rest of their journey. In each story there is a gesture of intimacy of one kind or another and then a separation. This movement of coming together and pulling apart becomes emblematic of life. Furthermore, each story's center is occupied by an elderly character who represents something like the eye of the storm, or the solar system's sun, the stable, life-giving presence around which the others move (1968, 207, 209). Ryder interprets these conjunctions of individual lives as brief examples of Christian love: in the past, Cather had often depicted "the tragic consequences of the clash of . . . mythic powers symbolized by the planet Venus and the moon," but in the stories of this collection, there is no "violent clash of sensuality and sensibility," when the two powers meet (1990, 266–67). In "Two Friends," for example, Mr. Trueman and Mr. Dillon inform their young listener that she may only see Venus and the moon move into line once in her life. Thus, in "Neighbour Rosicky" the moment of understanding Rosicky and Polly share becomes one of those rare moments when two spirits meet, and in "Old Mrs. Harris" the moment of connection and fondness between Mrs. Rosen and Mrs. Harris helps determine Vickie Templeton's future (1990, 267–68).

Other elements the three stories have in common include the migration from East to West of all the principal characters, the treatment of Chicago as a kind of cultural model, and the narrator's assertion that the principal characters are highly literate and devotees of opera. In each case, too, a young woman is given either psychological or financial support by a kind older male who is in no way romantically involved with her (Mattern 1974, 1).

According to Lee, critics should take care not to make the three stories in this collection appear escapist or reassuring because in each case Cather sets up fragile negotiations—"between the solidity of the remembered figures, and their makeshift, transitory environments; between the feelings of childhood and the feelings of age; and between the eloquent simplicity of the narrative, and the difficulty of true speech" (1989, 311).

Virtually all critics agree that "Neighbour Rosicky" is in many ways as closely related to *My Ántonia* as it is to "Old Mrs. Harris" and "Two Friends." Woodress and others refer to the story as almost a sequel to the novel—that is, a return to Ántonia, her husband, and her family ten years after the novel ends (Woodress 1990, 25). Ántonia has become Mary: the mythic tale has become religious (Ryder 1990, 267). The entire story is often reminiscent of the novel with its "little Czech" hero and his wife dominating the plot (C. 1932, 246). Even Rosicky's physical description recalls Cather's prose in *My Ántonia* ("Three Stories . . . " 1932, 12).

One significant difference does exist between the two, however: Jim Burden, the male narrator of *My Ántonia*, is absent. Something of Burden lives on in Dr. Ed, but the doctor never threatens to become the focus of the story as Jim Burden sometimes does (Stouck 1984, 299). Another major difference, in the view of Rosowski, is that whereas in both *My Ántonia* and *O Pioneers!* Cather depicted characters who rose above their surroundings and transcended this world by turning life into art, in "Neighbour Rosicky" she suggests that life does not need to be transcended—it is acceptable as it is (Rosowski 1986, 189–90).

In addition to *My Ántonia*, Arnold groups this story with "On the Gulls' Road" and "Eleanor's House" in that all three tales analyze the principal characters' attitudes toward the past. Rosicky is the only one who refuses to pine for the past, and his is the attitude Cather clearly endorses (1984, 137). The story may also be linked to *Death Comes for the Archbishop*, for death comes *for* Rosicky and for Jean Latour in very similar ways. It is "neither a great calamity nor a final surrender to despair, but rather, a benign presence, anticipated and even graciously entertained" (1984, 137).

Rosowski pairs all the *Obscure Destinies* stories with *Shadows on the Rock*, which was written about the same time: all are about the loss either of loved places or people (1986, 190). And in all these works one sees Cather recognizing many parts of ordinary life as forms of art (Bohlke 1986, 42). Cather's development of the tension between Old World and New puts

"Neighbour Rosicky" in the company of not only the aforementioned novels, but also *One of Ours* and *The Professor's House*. Each of these works deals with cultivated Europeans who, though themselves damaged by the hard life of the New World, bequeath something like optimism to their children (Stegner 1987, 43).

Interpretations and Criticisms

Almost without exception, Cather scholars proclaim "Neighbour Rosicky" one of Cather's most memorable stories (Arnold 1984, 135). One reviewer, writing in the Manchester *Guardian*, asserts that the "delicacy and tenderness of the story . . . are perfect" (Moult 1932, 7). It "rarely fails to move even the most blasé reader" (Woodress 1987, 438). The story triumphs over sentimentality through its emphasis on "the relation of the action to its context in agricultural life" (Daiches 1962, 158). It is "a celebration of old-fashioned American agrarian values—immigrant hopefulness in the land of opportunity, self-help, honesty, pleasure in the everyday, domestic order, endurance, and a belief in land-ownership as better for the soul than urban wage-earning" (Lee 1989, 310). In Anton Rosicky, Cather has created "a fully developed, three-dimensional character" (Woodress 1987, 439). One of the few dissenting voices is that of Quennell, who calls the story sentimental and unimpressive (1932, 695).

Several authorities have commented on Cather's handling of the theme of unity through her ability to convey a sense of completeness by carefully balancing "past and present, . . . life and death" (Arnold 1984, 137). For example, one of the story's most significant settings, the small cemetery, is introduced early in the tale and becomes the place where the story ends, effectively bringing both the narrative and Rosicky's life to completion (Arnold 1984, 137). Mattern points out that there is something reminiscent of Whitman about the narrator's ability to see the grass in the graveyard as representing closure, beauty, and the cycle of life (1974, 1). Another technique Cather uses to achieve wholeness is that of "contrasting or pairing opposites: city and country, winter and summer, older generation and young, single life and married life, Bohemians and Americans" (Arnold 1984, 138). Further, the portrait of Rosicky and Mary's relationship is in itself the most perfect image of harmony Cather ever created. Rosicky himself, however, is the primary unifying force in the story, even touching the discord in the lives of his son and daughter-in-law (Arnold 1984, 140). It is Rosicky who calms and quiets those around him and thus is possessed of a unifying power that changes the world by bringing love into it, and he consistently mediates between the material and the spiritual, between life and death (Rosowski 1986, 191–92). According to Lewis, Cather uses this "coupling of opposition" less to achieve a sense of completion than to exhibit a peculiar "brand of aloneness" in her characters (1974, 3).

Leddy also focuses on Cather's narrative strategies in the story, but his remarks are confined to the difference between Doctor Ed Burleigh's view of life and the narrator's. The doctor's view of the family is somewhat unreliable because he focuses solely on the exemplary nature of the family and so is unable to see any potential for discord. The narrator, on the other hand, enjoys a much closer and more constant observation of the family and so is able to speak authoritatively. The reader, then, approaches Dr. Burleigh's observations skeptically. In the final paragraphs of the story, for instance, when the doctor stops his car at the graveyard where Rosicky is buried, he ponders his old friend's life and reaches a slightly faulty conclusion, which is based on insufficient information. The reader very likely comes to the same conclusion, but for very different reasons (1988, 142–44). Unlike Dr. Burleigh, the reader has seen everything clearly, including the family's troubles and the moment of emotional bonding shared by Polly and Rosicky, and therefore has a more accurate picture, but "to read the final sentence as a ringing affirmation is to ignore the disparity between the perspectives of observer and narrator" (1988, 144).

No reader of this story can fail to notice the intensity of Rosicky's passion for the land and for the values of those who work it. His hatred for the industrialized world is equally passionate. Cather emphasizes Rosicky's identification with the earth itself in several ways: his children have "natural good manners," his physical appearance is defined through the use of the earth tones, and he is often associated with images of farming the land (Piacentino 1979, 53). In a sense, Rosicky actually dies to save the land (Piacentino 1979, 54).

Schneider maintains that Rosicky is in many ways the land incarnate: Cather's "land-philosophy" included the belief that the land stands for all the positive characteristics extant in the world and represents a "blending of vitality and solidity, of the elemental and the traditional," pulling human beings toward reality, and allowing them to experience the fundamental forces from which both life and art spring (1968, 105–107). The land exemplifies a longing for the noblest goals and offers a glimpse of the transcendent, and in the character of Rosicky, Cather shows that the transcendence represented by the land is not actually separate from human beings, but in very real ways part of them (Schneider 1968, 108–110).

Rosicky's reverence for the land is also part of the pastoral tradition that Cather is consciously handling in this story. Cather found the pastoral idea— "retreat from the complexities of urban society to a secluded rural place such as a farm, field, garden, or orchard, where human life is returned to the simple essentials of the natural world of cyclical seasons"—particularly attractive at this time in her life (Danker 1990, 24). Danker argues that in "Neighbour Rosicky" the pastoral elements are especially obvious: for example, food is presented as having more significance than simply as something that sustains life. It is also a reward for labor, a connection to the Rosickys' Czech past, and the medium for establishing emotional bonds with family, friends, and animals. In a similar way, the country funeral is portrayed as an emotional event associated with human sympathy, while a city funeral is simply a business (1990, 24–25). These kinds of biases are typical of pastoral writing—real family life can be found only in the rural home and graveyard (Lee 1989, 317).

Andes maintains that Rosicky's attitudes and habits have more to do with his Bohemian heritage than with anything else. His optimism is an Old World trait that he brought with him to America, and he often uses "Old World strategies to solve New World problems, as Cather suggests when she asserts that one of Rosicky's Bohemian folk practices—the picnic on the day the family discovers the loss of the corn crop—brings good fortune to the family (1972, 63–64).

Ryder sees Christian overtones in the story. "Rosicky's life becomes expiatory, . . . not through heroic or mythic exploit but through Christian transcendence" (1990, 267). Thurin, in sharp disagreement, argues that in Rosicky's burial, he is not actually removed from the center of life and that the ancients buried their dead on a well-traveled road just outside a city so that the dead would not be lonely. The implication—that heaven is not some separate place, but right here on earth—is not Christian, but pagan, and the story ends with the idea that no otherworldly heaven waits for people. Further, at no point in the story is there any suggestion that Rosicky was interested in an afterlife. Instead, Cather depicts him as almost pagan in his freedom of behavior—an unconscious freedom that is in stark contrast to the behavior of the minister in the story, who is made uncomfortable by the sight of the naked Rosicky swimming in the horse tank with his children (1990, 321–22).

According to Wasserman, this story represents the only time in all of Cather's work that the author becomes, momentarily at least, patriotic. The mention of Independence Day allows Cather to bring her notion of the American dream into focus, and it turns out to be the same as "the original Jeffersonian American dream of the yeoman farmer, independent and virtuous" (1991, 55). Cather depicts Rosicky as completely indifferent to material wealth and deeply desirous that his sons gain, not money, but virtue and freedom; thus, she takes a fading American dream and reasserts "its oldest lineaments, . . . recreating an early America of the imagination" (1991, 55).

Works Cited

Andes, Cynthia J. 1972. "The Bohemian Folk Practice in 'Neighbour Rosicky.'" *Western American Literature* 7:63–64.

Arnold, Marilyn. 1984. *Willa Cather's Short Fiction*. Athens: Ohio University Press.

Bennett, Mildred R. 1961. *The World of Willa Cather*. Lincoln: University of Nebraska Press.

Bohlke, L. Brent, ed. 1986. *Willa Cather in Person*. Lincoln: University of Nebraska Press.

Brown, E. K. Completed by Leon Edel. [1953] 1964. *Willa Cather: A Critical Biography*. New York: Knopf.

C., A. 1932. Review of *Obscure Destinies*, by Willa Cather. *Catholic World* 136:246–47.

Cather, Willa. 1956. "Neighbour Rosicky." In *Five Stories*. New York: Vintage Books, 149–74.

———. 1974. "Neighbour Rosicky." In *Obscure Destinies*. New York: Vintage Books, 3–71.

———. 1992. "Neighbour Rosicky." In *Cather: Stories, Poems, and Other Writings*. New York: Literary Classics of the United States, 587–618.

Daiches, David. [1951] 1962. *Willa Cather: A Critical Introduction*. Ithaca, NY: Cornell University Press; London: Oxford University Press. Reprint. New York: Collier.

Danker, Kathleen A. 1990. "The Passing of a Golden Age in *Obscure Destinies*." *Willa Cather Pioneer Memorial Newsletter* 34:24–28.

Faulkner, Virginia, ed. [1965] 1970. *Willa Cather's Collected Short Fiction, 1892–1912*. Lincoln: University of Nebraska Press. Reprint. Lincoln: University of Nebraska Press.

Giannone, Richard. 1968. *Music in Willa Cather's Fiction*. Lincoln: University of Nebraska Press.

Gray, Thomas. 1972. "Elegy Written in a Country Churchyard." In *The Poems of Thomas Gray, William Collins, Oliver Goldsmith*. Ed. Roger Lonsdale. New York: Norton.

Leddy, Michael. 1988. "Observation and Narration in Willa Cather's *Obscure Destinies*." *Studies in American Fiction* 16:141–53.

Lee, Hermione. 1989. *Willa Cather: Double Lives*. New York: Pantheon.

Lewis, Jacquelynn S. 1974. "The Expression of Loneliness." *Willa Cather Pioneer Memorial Newsletter* 18:3.

Mattern, Claire. 1974. "The Themes That Bind." *Willa Cather Pioneer Memorial Newsletter* 18:1.

Moult, Thomas. 1932. "Miss Willa Cather." *Manchester Guardian*, December 16, 7.

Piacentino, Edward J. 1979. "The Agrarian Mode in Cather's 'Neighbour Rosicky.'" *Markham Review* 8:52–54.

Quennell, Peter. 1932. Review of *Obscure Destinies*, by Willa Cather. *New Statesman and Nation*, December 3, 694.

Rosowski, Susan J. 1986. *The Voyage Perilous: Willa Cather's Romanticism*. Lincoln: University of Nebraska Press.

———. 1990. "Willa Cather's Chosen Family: Fictional Formations and Transformations." In *Willa Cather and the Family, Community and History: The BYU Symposium*. Ed. John J. Murphy. Provo, Utah: Brigham Young University, 67–78.

Ryder, Mary Ruth. 1990. *Willa Cather and Classical Myth*. Lewiston, NY: Edwin Mellen Press.

Schneider, Sister Lucy. 1968. "'Land' Relevance in 'Neighbor Rosicky.'" *Kansas Quarterly* 1:105–110.

Stegner, Wallace. 1987. "Willa Cather, *My Ántonia*." In *Modern Critical Interpretations: Willa Cather's My Ántonia*. Ed. Harold Bloom. New York: Chelsea House, 41–49.

Stouck, David. 1975. *Willa Cather's Imagination*. Lincoln: University of Nebraska Press.

———. 1984. "Willa Cather's Last Four Books." In *Critical Essays on Willa Cather*. Ed. John J. Murphy. Boston: G. K. Hall, 290–304.

"Three Stories of the West." 1932. *Christian Science Monitor*, September 17, 12.

Thurin, Erik Ingvar. 1990. *The Humanization of Willa Cather: Classicism in an American Classic*. Lund, Sweden: Lund University Press.

Wasserman, Loretta. 1991. *Willa Cather: A Study of the Short Fiction*. Boston: Twayne.

Woodress, James. 1970. *Willa Cather: Her Life and Art*. New York: Pegasus.

———. 1987. *Willa Cather: A Literary Life*. Lincoln: University of Nebraska Press.

———. 1990. "A Dutiful Daughter: Willa Cather and Her Parents." In *Willa Cather and the Family, Community and History: The BYU Symposium*. Ed. John J. Murphy. Provo, Utah: Brigham Young University, 19–31.

A Night at Greenway Court

Publication History

This story was first published in June 1896 in *Nebraska Literary Magazine* (1:215–24) under the name Willa Cather; a revised version, signed Willa Sibert Cather, appeared in the *Library* (1:5–7) on April 21, 1900; the original version of the story was reprinted in 1950 by the University of Nebraska Press in *Willa Cather's Campus Years* (80–92) (Faulkner 1970, 591). In 1957, Dodd, Mead reprinted both versions in *Early Stories*; and in 1965, the University of Nebraska Press reprinted the original version in *Willa Cather's Collected Short Fiction, 1892–1912*.

Circumstances of Composition, Sources, and Influences

Slote establishes an important connection between this story and a Virginia writer popular during Cather's childhood. John Esten Cooke (1830–1886) wrote thirty-one novels and myriad periodical articles, mostly about the Civil War (1966, 41). Slote goes on to explain that Cather probably identified with Cooke because he was from the same part of Virginia as her family, and her early writing suggests that she was quite familiar with his work. While "A Night at Greenway Court" is not similar in plot to any of Cooke's fiction, its setting—Lord Fairfax's estate in Virginia—was one Cooke described both in his book *Fairfax* (1868) and in several magazine articles. Two of the magazine articles are especially significant. Both are entitled "Greenway Court," one published in an 1857 issue of *Putnam's*, and the other in an 1859 issue of the *Southern Literary Messenger* (1966, 41–42).

Woodress attributes "A Night at Greenway Court" more to Cather's interest in the English writer Anthony Hope than to Cooke's influence or her own recollections of Virginia (1970, 28). Indeed, Cather herself supports this claim in her early journalistic pieces. In a November 2, 1895, article, she asserts that "[w]e are growing too analytical ourselves, and we need young men like Rudyard Kipling and Anthony Hope, not because of the greatness of their talent, but because of the sincerity of their motive, because the atmosphere of their work is one in which men may love and work and fight and die like men" (quoted in Slote 1966, 232). In another article, she refers to Hope's romance *The Prisoner of Zenda* as "so realistic, so modern in tone and feeling that it made one see a new hope in fiction, made one dream for the moment that the world had not outgrown the possibilities of romance" (quoted in Slote 1966, 318–19). Romance did hold intense fascination for Cather, but as Slote makes clear, "she did not merely like the *stories* of romance; she believed in the central *principles* of Romanticism. . . . Her feeling about romance and realism relates primarily to the great value she gave to imagination" (Slote 1966, 64).

Bennett sees the influence of other authors Cather admired, especially Alexandre Dumas *père* and Henry James, who is most clearly felt in Cather's use of the damaged painting, of the expression "portrait of a lady," and of a character with a secret in his background (1957, 82–83). However, a bit of the plot owes something to Cather's own family history: "Jeremiah Smith, one of Willa's ancestors four generations back, had received land grants from Lord Fairfax, Baron of Cameron, dated September 30, 1762" (Bennett 1957, 77). Also, the narrator of the story was born in Frederick County, Virginia, as was Cather herself (Bennett 1957, 78).

Relationship to Other Cather Works

According to O'Brien, "A Night at Greenway Court" ends with "a silencing of the narrative impulse"—although the narrator uncovers Fairfax's secret concerning the painting of the lady, the damaged portrait itself "conceals her identity even while it betrays a mystery" (1987, 203). This silencing technique places this piece in company with "A Tale of the White Pyramid," *O Pioneers!* and *Death Comes for the Archbishop*, all of which have at least one episode of a silencing of the narrative impulse (1987, 203). Further, O'Brien argues, as in "On the Divide," "A Son of the Celestial," and "Peter," the presence of a knife is significant. Cather often used the knife to suggest both the power and danger of writing. In "A Night at Greenway" court, the danger is much more apparent—"the knife can mutilate and kill as well as create. We see this negative association in the serpent-headed knife the vicious Frenchman carries" (O'Brien 1987, 205).

Cather would later include clergymen in *Death Comes for the Archbishop* and *Shadows on the Rock*, although the clergyman in this story has little in common with the clergy in those novels; he is, however, as revolting as Brother Weldon in *One of Ours* (Bennett 1957, 81). When M. Maurepas tells the story of his adventures in the Deccan, Cather is employing the device of a story within a story, which she also uses in *My Ántonia*, *Death Comes for the Archbishop*, *Shadows on the Rock*, and many short stories (Bennett 1957, 87). Using a first-person male narrator is another strategy Cather would use again in the future, most strikingly in *My Ántonia* and *A Lost Lady* (Bennett 1957, 77). Finally, one passage from this story, "I have thrown a cup full of water in the air and seen it descend solid ice" (Cather [1965] 1970, 484), is remarkably similar to one from *Sapphira and the Slave Girl* where at one point Canada is described as being so cold that any water thrown into the air would fall to the ground as ice (Bennett 1957, 81).

Interpretations and Criticisms

Cather specialists have been more interested in discovering the sources for this piece and establishing connections between it and Cather's earlier and later work than they have in actually interpreting the story itself. In Brown's estimation the story is "only a routine cloak-and-sword piece written when Willa Cather was under the spell of *The Prisoner of Zenda*" (1964, 3–4).

Arnold argues that the tale is a good one for readers of popular fiction and is distinguished by the presence of many of "the standard elements of courtly intrigue—a mysterious lady, an oddly damaged portrait, a Frenchman who drinks and talks too much, a clergyman who takes more interest in a bowl of preserved cherries than in the soul's salvation, a viscount of questionable reputation, a near murder, and a duel at dawn" (Arnold 1984, 8).

Works Cited

Arnold, Marilyn. 1984. *Willa Cather's Short Fiction*. Athens: Ohio University Press.

Bennett, Mildred, ed. 1957. *Early Stories of Willa Cather*. New York: Dodd, Mead.

Brown, E. K. [1953] 1964. *Willa Cather: A Critical Biography*. New York: Knopf.

Cather, Willa. 1957. "A Night at Greenway Court." In *Early Stories*. Ed. Mildred Bennett. New York: Dodd, Mead, 77–91.

———. [1965] 1970. "A Night at Greenway Court." In *Willa Cather's Collected Short Fiction, 1892–1912*. Ed. Virginia Faulkner. Lincoln: University of Nebraska Press, 483–92.

Faulkner, Virginia, ed. [1965] 1970. *Willa Cather's Collected Short Fiction, 1892–1912*. Lincoln: University of Nebraska Press. Reprint. Lincoln: University of Nebraska Press.

O'Brien, Sharon. 1987. *Willa Cather: The Emerging Voice*. New York: Oxford University Press.

Slote, Bernice, ed. 1966. *The Kingdom of Art*. Lincoln: University of Nebraska Press.

Woodress, James. 1970. *Willa Cather: Her Life and Art*. New York: Pegasus.

The Old Beauty

Publication History

This story did not appear until 1948 in the posthumously published collection of short stories *The Old Beauty and Others*. According to Cather's longtime companion, Edith Lewis, Cather had sent the story to *Woman's Home Companion* in early 1937 at the request of the magazine's editor, Gertrude Lane. Upon receiving the story, Lane immediately agreed to publish it, but said that she was not as excited about it as she was about some of Cather's other work. Cather then asked Lane to send the story back, and she set it aside to publish later in a collection of short stories (1953, 180).

In 1976, the story was reprinted by Vintage Books in a paperback edition of the collection, and again in 1992 by Literary Classics of the United States in *Cather: Stories, Poems, and Other Writings*, a volume in the Library of America series.

Circumstances of Composition, Sources, and Influences

This story was written in late 1936. During most of the previous year, Cather had devoted much of her time to helping her old friend Isabelle McClung Hambourg, who was critically ill. (For a complete discussion of the importance of Cather's friendship with Isabelle McClung and its influence on her work, see the section "Circumstances of Composition, Sources, and Influences" for the chapter "A Wagner Matinée.") The Hambourgs, who had been living just outside Paris, returned to New York in March 1935 so that Isabelle could see specialists and undergo various treatments, and Cather spent as much time as possible at Isabelle's bedside. When the Hambourgs returned to France, Cather spent two months with them, returning to New York in November. It was the last time she ever saw her friend, who died three years later in Sorrento (Lewis 1953, 179). Some of this story's infatuation with the past, then, may be explained by the fact that it was written so soon after Cather had left her critically ill friend.

The setting of Aix-les-Bains is one Cather knew well. She had visited it in 1923, and in 1930 had lived in a hotel that resembled the Hôtel Splendide. It was there that she happened to meet Flaubert's niece, Mme. Franklin Grout, who by that time was an elderly woman. Wasserman suggests that this meeting may have given her the idea of treating living beyond one's time as a theme in her work (1991, 66). She did produce an essay about her encounter with Madame Grout, "A Chance Meeting," which she included in a collection entitled *Not Under Forty* that she was also putting together in 1936. The similarities between Madame Grout and Gabrielle Longstreet, however, are few and slight, the fictional character being in most ways very different from the vivacious Madame Grout (Wasserman 1991, 66).

As many critics have pointed out, Gabrielle Longstreet possesses some of Willa Cather's own characteristics—"nostalgia, a distaste for some aspects of the modern world, a tendency to resist change" (Arnold 1984a, 241). Specifically, as Woodress notes, Cather "had deplored Prohibition, the Jazz Age, the flapper, the relaxation of moral standards, the deterioration of taste, the scramble for money; she didn't like cubism, couldn't take Gertrude Stein or Ezra Pound seriously, [and] wouldn't go to see an O'Neill play" (1987, 476).

Wasserman argues that Gabrielle Longstreet's character may be drawn largely from the popular 1890s actress Lily Langtry, whose performances Cather had reviewed during her University of Nebraska days and whom Cather thought of as beautiful but devoid of talent (1988, 219). One of her early columns for the Pittsburgh *Leader* (December 26, 1897) begins with a story that Wasserman sees as the "Jamesian kernel" from which "The Old Beauty" eventually grew: "A little while ago a man who had once years ago saved Langtry's life was found dead. In his vest pocket was found Langtry's card, so worn that it was almost illegible. These are the materials for a story if you care to write it. Langtry is neither good nor great, but this poor devil probably went through life with the sublime conviction that he had saved an angel and an artist unaware" (quoted in Wasserman 1988, 219). It was not until forty years later that Cather transformed this kernel into the completed short story, which concerns the age-old problem of the relationship of beauty to virtue (Wasserman 1988, 219).

Aside from a reviewer's interest in Langtry, according to Wasserman, Cather may well have read the actress's autobiography, which provides even more parallels between Lily and Gabrielle: both were born on an island, could speak English and French, and were at one time married to English yachtsmen who took their young wives to family estates in northern England and then to London, where both women, real and fictional, gained renown for their beauty. Both women were divorced and remarried, both loved horses. Lily's hair style was known as the "Langtry knot" and Gabrielle's as the "mode Gabrielle." Finally, both kept pictures of former friends and admirers with them when they traveled. It seems the only aspect of Lily's life missing from Gabrielle's is the stage career of the former (1988, 220).

Relationship to Other Cather Works

This story is included in the posthumous collection *The Old Beauty and Others* along with two other stories, "Before Breakfast" and "The Best Years." As part of a collection, one would expect this story to resemble the others in the book more closely than it resembles other works. Since Cather did not arrange this collection herself, however, thematically the stories are not held together as tightly as are the stories in the three collections she did put together, *The Troll Garden*, *Youth and the Bright Medusa*, and *Obscure Destinies*. Nevertheless, some unity does exist in this published book. Dedmon, for example, notes that each story in the book is "written with the reserve and detachment which distinguished . . . Cather's writing from that personal identification with the author so characteristic of much modern fiction" (1948, sec. 10, p. 7). Thurin sees the three stories in the collection as variations on the theme of "the old beauty" (1990, 355). Arnold argues that the stories are held together by their emphasis on "adaptability and survival," each one the "product of many years of struggle between the will to face life straight on and the wish to escape from life and the painful changes brought inevitably by the passing of time" (1984a, 238). Although Cather's esteem for youth remains obvious in these stories, her respect for people's ability to withstand the shock of change is also evident, and she now values the qualities of endurance found in maturity. In this collection, Cather "seems to have concluded . . . that people could develop qualities of adaptability and endurance as an antidote against the changes that rob them of youth and beauty" (1984a, 239).

Arnold points out other works in which Cather exalts the concept of survival: in *A Lost Lady* Marian Forrester is admirable for her ability to withstand the strain caused by being trapped between two eras. In *The Professor's House*, too, the survivor is celebrated: Godfrey St. Peter chooses to follow the example of Augusta, thus facing the future with strength and perseverance. The earliest evidence of Cather's reverence for survivors, however, is in her story "The Way of the World," where Mary Eliza is the forerunner of Marian Forrester and Cather's other survivor characters (Arnold 1984a, 239). "The Old Beauty" has also been compared with *Alexander's Bridge*, *The Professor's House*, and *My Mortal Enemy*, the last containing the woman Gabrielle most resembles, Myra Henshawe. Cather's familiar theme of the double self can be found in all four works (Wasserman 1988, 222).

According to Schroeter, "The Old Beauty" is one more story in which Cather displays her anti-Semitism by creating a dark, foreign-looking villain who, although never identified as a Jew, is described as "repulsive," "vulgar," with a "clever way of pushing himself," "an immigrant who has made a lot of money," "belong[ing] to a country [Gabrielle] did not admire" (Cather 1976, 49–50, 56; Schroeter 1967, 367). (For a discussion of Cather's alleged anti-

Semitism, see the "Relationship to Other Cather Works" and the "Circumstances of Composition, Sources, and Influences" sections of the chapters "The Diamond Mine" and "Scandal.")

Interpretations and Criticisms

Several critics find this story, which "whispers the immemorial and useless regret of the present for the past," something of a step down for Cather (Reynolds 1948, 22). Unlike her best fiction, it does not involve the reader's emotions: since readers are not led to feel much for Gabrielle Longstreet, their primary emotion when she dies is relief (Woodress 1987, 476). Daiches finds the tale "preposterous, full of the most violent clichés and the most stagy situations," although he admits that the theme it attempts to explore—the nostalgia of people who feel uncomfortable in the world of the present—is a legitimate one (Daiches 1962, 169).

Although the story is undeniably sad, it never achieves the level of tragedy (Dedmon 1948, sec. 10, p. 7). Instead, it simply evokes nostalgia, and what results is a story in which the author only approaches one of the major themes of her late work—regret and facing the past honestly (Stouck 1975, 233). In Cather's hands, this lofty theme becomes "personal, nostalgic, and tensionless" and fails to achieve "a dramatic and moral significance" (Marshall 1948, 376). Stouck says that because most of the heavily symbolic actions in the story are never adequately illuminated, the story remains personal and idiosyncratic (1984, 62–63).

Most of the critical comment elicited by this story centers on a debate over just how closely the reader should associate Cather with Gabrielle Longstreet. Wasserman sees the conflation of Gabrielle's attitude toward the past with Cather's own to be extremely unfortunate. To the degree that she realizes she does not have a self to recover, Gabrielle is a tragic figure. Her remaining behind to look into the well at the monastery suggests that she is searching for understanding, and the scene resonates with meaning: "A form gazing into water suggests, inescapably, the myth of Narcissus and its network of meanings, reaching into depth psychology on the one hand (the undeveloped self), and on another . . . to the persistent image of the divided self of the artist—the desire for union with a transcendent self" (Wasserman 1988, 223). Although she was denied insight as she stood at the well, she may have received it as she neared death. Both Cherry and Seabury notice the regal appearance of her body, and the look of confession on her face: the word *confession*, with its "archaic overtones, points to public avowal, to self-definition and assertion, rather than to acknowledgment of guilt" (Wasserman 1988, 224). As she died, Gabrielle came to terms with who she was, and was proud of the way she had lived. Perhaps she deserves a place in the Père-

Lachaise cemetery in Paris alongside the other worthies. It is possible to read "The Old Beauty" as "Cather's belated apology to Lily Langtry" and also as Cather's "apologia for herself" (Wasserman 1988, 225). There is some suggestion in the story that the artist is more detached from the present than other people, and thus is apt to become "rigid, irrelevant, old fashioned" (Wasserman 1988, 225).

In Arnold's view, confusing Gabrielle and Cather is a major critical error because in fact Cather dislikes Gabrielle intensely (1984a, 239). Cather condemns Gabrielle for living in the past. Her attitude toward Gabrielle may be sympathetic, but it certainly is also mocking. The careful reader will see that Cather is attacking, not endorsing the "absurdly old-fashioned, . . . pettily superior" Longstreet and Seabury and their "stupidly intolerant" notions about youth and the modern world (1984b, 161). Further, none of the women Cather admired in life—Madame Grout, Mrs. Fields, Sarah Orne Jewett—resembles Lady Longstreet in any way. Cather, in fact, subscribes to Cherry's views and approach to life, specifically to the present: Cherry's optimistic view of life is meant to be a positive alternative to Lady Longstreet's dark brooding (Arnold 1984b, 162). McFarland agrees, declaring that although Gabrielle's mood dominates the story, Cherry's "cheerful presence suggests that it is not also Willa Cather's story and mood" (1972, 131).

Other Cather experts advance just the opposite interpretation. Responding specifically to Arnold's reading, Thurin says this story cannot "be saved, ideologically or artistically, by pretending that 'the old beauty' is not supposed to be taken entirely seriously, that the author's attitude to her is somewhat mocking" (1990, 358). Thurin is also the only authority to suggest that something besides the past preoccupies Gabrielle. By associating Gabrielle's youthful coldness with her being unawakened, Cather is suggesting that her major character "has always been not only indifferent but pained by the thought of sex." That suggestion is reinforced by Gabrielle's comparison of the dancing young couple to "reptiles coupling," her admission to Seabury that she is repulsed by the sight of young men and women "bathing naked," and the panic she displays when the dark, villainous banker makes a pass at her, a panic that seems excessive for a woman of her age and experience (1990, 363). The fact that her first husband demanded a divorce fairly soon after their marriage is also telling. Viewed in this light, Gabrielle's preference for older over younger men and her relationship with Cherry Beamish, a former actress who played boy parts exclusively, acquire added significance (Thurin 1990, 358, 363).

Daiches believes that the story mirrors Cather's disdain for much of the world around her, including the new literary and political movements. Her disillusionment turned into a "tawdry nostalgia which corrupted her art" (1962, 169–70). Bloom and Bloom maintain that Cather was forced to dwell on the past because looking to the future meant embracing a world Cather thought of as shallow, cheap, and petty. It also meant accepting her own old age and death (1962, 109). Cather's first biographer, E. K. Brown, excuses Cather, allowing that anyone who had written *My Ántonia* in her forties would likely write such stories as those in *The Old Beauty and Others* in her sixties (1964, 307).

Lee notes that Seabury is gradually forced to recognize that the past seems not to have been so wonderful after all when he remembers the night he prevented Gabrielle from being forced into exchanging sex for money (1989, 356). What is perhaps even more interesting is the fact that neither Cather nor Seabury pushes this realization to its logical end and considers the possibility that Marge and Jim, the postwar feminists, might have been spared that predicament (1989, 356).

Works Cited

Arnold, Marilyn. 1984a. "Cather's Last Three Stories: A Testament of Life and Endurance." *Great Plains Quarterly* 4:238–44.

———. 1984b. *Willa Cather's Short Fiction*. Athens: Ohio University Press.

Bloom, Edward A., and Lillian D. Bloom. 1962. *Willa Cather's Gift of Sympathy*. Carbondale: Southern Illinois University Press.

Brown, E. K. Completed by Leon Edel. [1953] 1964. *Willa Cather: A Critical Biography*. New York: Knopf.

Cather, Willa. 1948. "The Old Beauty." In *The Old Beauty and Others*. New York: Knopf, 3–72.

———. 1976. "The Old Beauty." In *The Old Beauty and Others*. New York: Vintage Books, 3–72.

———. 1992. "The Old Beauty." In *Cather: Stories, Poems, and Other Writings*. New York: Literary Classics of the United States, 695–727.

Daiches, David. [1951] 1962. *Willa Cather: A Critical Introduction*. Ithaca, NY: Cornell University Press; London: Oxford University Press. Reprint. New York: Collier.

Dedmon, Emmett. 1948. "Willa Cather's Last Three Stories." *Chicago Daily Sun Times*, September 19, sec. 10, p. 7.

Faulkner, Virginia, ed. [1965] 1970. *Willa Cather's Collected Short Fiction, 1892–1912*. Lincoln: University of Nebraska Press. Reprint. Lincoln: University of Nebraska Press.

Lee, Hermione. 1989. *Willa Cather: Double Lives*. New York: Pantheon.

Lewis, Edith. 1953. *Willa Cather Living*. New York: Knopf.

Marshall, Margaret. 1948. "Notes by the Way." *Nation*, October 2, 376.

McFarland, Dorothy Tuck. 1972. *Willa Cather*. New York: Frederick Ungar.

Reynolds, Horace. 1948. "A Bit of the Old Gleam." *Christian Science Monitor*, September 15, 22.

Schroeter, James. 1967. "Willa Cather and *The Professor's House*." In *Willa Cather and Her Critics*. Ed. James Schroeter. Ithaca, NY: Cornell University Press, 363–81.

Stouck, David. 1975. *Willa Cather's Imagination*. Lincoln: University of Nebraska Press.

————. 1984. "Willa Cather and the Impressionist Novel." In *Critical Essays on Willa Cather*. Ed. John J. Murphy. Boston: G. K. Hall, 48–66.

Thurin, Erik Ingvar. 1990. *The Humanization of Willa Cather: Classicism in an American Classic*. Lund, Sweden: Lund University Press.

Wasserman, Loretta. 1988. "Willa Cather's 'The Old Beauty' Reconsidered." *Studies in American Fiction* 16:217–27.

————. 1991. *Willa Cather: A Study of the Short Fiction*. Boston: Twayne.

Woodress, James. 1987. *Willa Cather: A Literary Life*. Lincoln: University of Nebraska Press.

Old Mrs. Harris

Publication History

This story was first published in Cather's third collection of short stories, *Obscure Destinies* (New York: Knopf, 1932, pp. 73–190); it was reprinted serially in the September–November 1932 issues of *Ladies' Home Journal* (49:3, 70, 72, 74, 76–77; 18, 85–87; 16, 84–85, 89), where it appeared under the title "Three Women" (Faulkner 1970, 598). Perhaps the editors thought this title would be more appealing to the magazine's readers (Woodress 1987, 441). The next appearance of the story was in volume twelve of the thirteen-volume library edition of Cather's work *The Novels and Stories of Willa Cather* (Boston: Houghton Mifflin, 1937–1941, pp. 63–158) (Faulkner 1970, 598). In 1974, the story reappeared when Vintage Books published a paperback edition of *Obscure Destinies* and again the 1992 Library of America edition, *Cather: Stories, Poems, and Other Writings*.

Circumstances of Composition, Sources, and Influences

According to Edith Lewis, Cather's companion for the last forty years of her life, this story was probably written in 1931 while Cather was staying in Pasadena, California, in order to be near her mother, who had suffered a stroke more than two years before. Cather had rented a cottage on the grounds of the sanatorium where her mother was a patient and spent as much time as possible writing there (1953, 157). (For a discussion of Mrs. Cather's illness and the effect it had on Willa, see the "Relationship to Other Cather Works" section for the chapter "Neighbour Rosicky" and "Circumstances of Composition, Sources, and Influences" for the chapter "Two Friends.")

Virtually every authority views this story as the most autobiographical piece Cather ever wrote. The Templeton house is nearly an exact duplicate of the Cather home in Red Cloud, Nebraska. Mrs. Harris is modeled on Cather's maternal grandmother, Rachel Seibert Boak; Victoria Templeton, on Cather's mother, Virginia ("Jennie") Boak Cather; Hillary Templeton, on Cather's father, Charles; Mahailey, on the Cather family's domestic servant, Marjorie; and Vickie, on Willa herself. Perhaps because she is a version of the author, Vickie receives the harshest treatment of any of the characters. Cather's merciless attack on Vickie for her indifference toward the elderly, so typical of young people, is perhaps the author's expression of regret over what she may have perceived as mistakes she made in her relationship with her own mother (Bennett 1961, 22). At least one critic feels that Cather can be found in all the characters, however, not just in Vickie (Stineback 1984, 390).

Even the Rosens have their prototypes in Cather's early life. They are versions of the Cathers' Jewish-German Red Cloud neighbors, Mr. and Mrs. Wiener, who first introduced Willa to German and French literary classics (Slote 1966, 38). Their home and habits were so refined compared to those of nearly everyone else in Red Cloud, that Willa thought of their house as a place to escape her uncultured neighbors—and even her own family (Lee 1989, 319).

Lee outlines some of the other events in the plot that are similar to those in Cather's life: Grandma Boak followed her daughter Jennie and her family to Nebraska from Virginia, not Tennessee, and she fell ill just when her granddaughter left for the university. As in the story, the money for Willa's education had to be borrowed, although in real life, Charles Cather borrowed it from a business associate. Despite these differences, however, the story reflects Cather's own life in about 1889. A Southern family must all live together in a small rented house in the West and adapt to the culture of the prairie (Lee 1989, 319).

Robinson points to one episode in "Old Mrs. Harris"—Mr. Templeton's departure on a business trip upon learning of his wife's most recent pregnancy—as evidence that Charles Cather, the prototype for Hillary Templeton, was "feckless," and that he, like his fictional counterpart, did his best to escape all unpleasantness and inconvenience (1983, 22). One of Willa Cather's nieces, Helen Cather Southwick, takes indignant exception to Robinson's inference: to call her grandfather feckless is simply untrue, she says. Furthermore, in Southwick's opinion, her Aunt Willa "deliberately made the character of Mr. Templeton very different from my grandfather's so that such an identification would not be assumed" (1985, 11).

Relationship to Other Cather Works

Because this story is one of three that Cather gathered into her third collection, *Obscure Destinies*, its closest links are to the other stories in that book, "Neighbour Rosicky" and "Two Friends." (For a complete discussion of the ways in which the stories in *Obscure Destinies* are held together thematically, as well as an explanation of the collection's title, see the "Relationship to Other Cather Works" section for the chapter "Neighbour Rosicky.")

Several scholars see Mrs. Harris as something of a female version of Anton Rosicky. Wasserman notes that, like Rosicky, Mrs. Harris guards the future and possesses great wisdom (1991, 57). Woodress points out that although both stories end with the death of the central characters, both celebrate life (1987, 444). In a letter to a friend written about the time of the composition of both stories, Cather said that "biologically speaking, life was rather a failure, but something rather nice happens in the mind as one grows older. A kind of golden light comes as a compensation for many losses," a truth that comes through in both "Neighbour Rosicky" and "Old Mrs. Harris" (Woodress 1987, 444). The title characters in both stories foresee the young recovering from their mistakes, and both help the young learn life's lessons (Arnold 1984, 150).

The story's similarity to Cather's 1925 essay on Katherine Mansfield ("Katherine Mansfield," in Cather's *Not Under Forty*, New York: Knopf, 1936, pp. 123–47) has been noted by several critics. Lee, for instance, sums up the similarity by saying that the Templetons act out "the drama which Cather describes in that essay between the group life and the individual self" (1989, 323).

O'Brien argues that Cather's drawing on her maternal relatives in this story places it in the company of both *My Ántonia* and *Sapphira and the Slave Girl*, and notes that, like several other Cather works, it uses the image of a matriarch who is sick or crippled to represent the restrictions on women's power in a male-dominated society (1987, 41). The female protagonists of *My Mortal Enemy* (Myra Henshawe) and *Sapphira and the Slave Girl* (Sapphira Colbert) are crippled during the last years of their lives; similarly, in

"Old Mrs. Harris," Victoria's illness and her infantile selfishness are results of her inability to control her own life (O'Brien 1987, 41). Lee also asserts that women's limitation or powerlessness is a dominant theme in this story: the plan of the house itself is emblematic of the confinement of generation after generation of women. Packing all the action into one summer also contributes to a sense of imprisonment or suffocation. Practically no scenes occur in the spacious outdoors, and even when one does, like the Methodist social, the women are trapped again, in a tent full of gossip (Lee 1989, 322).

Interpretations and Criticisms

A good many critics judge this story to be one of Cather's best. It is "flawless," full of tenderness but "without sentimentality"; each character is "clearly defined. The tone is light, the undertone tragic" ("Three Stories . . . " 1932, 12). To Stineback, the story's excellence is found in the "tension between the privacy of the family within the town of Skyline and the privacy of each individual within the family" (1984, 391). He goes on to argue that at times the privacy within the family becomes simply each member's self-absorption. Each individual is given his or her own space by the others, but Cather often lets one character enter the consciousness of another and thus changes the reader's focus. Victoria's appearance in section 1, for example, ends the reader's involvement with Mrs. Rosen's thoughts. In section 2, we enter Mrs. Harris's mind, but Mrs. Rosen's thoughts are the focus at the end of the section. This circle of interaction signifies Cather's intent to show "a system of relationships that turns in on itself when it cannot affect the world at large" (1984, 391–92).

Such a technique also creates an interesting manipulation of point of view. In fact, Cather's complex treatment of point of view in this story has often been noticed (Leddy 1988, 144). One way of highlighting the different points of view, according to Rosowski, is to focus on the answers provided to the question "What were families for, anyway?" asked in a caustic tone by Vickie (Cather 1974, 186; Rosowski 1990, 77). Mrs. Rosen answers it from an outsider's point of view; Mrs. Harris, Victoria, and Vickie each answer it from the particular point of view of her own generation. A strictly gender-based answer would be appropriate to explain Mr. Templeton's relationship with his wife and mother-in-law; whereas the family's migration requires "historical and sociological" interpretation (Rosowski 1990, 77).

Stouck's opinion of Cather's handling of point of view is that it allows her to portray each woman as sympathetic even though they do not understand one another. Initially the reader assumes that Mrs. Harris is the only character deserving of sympathy, but once inside Mrs. Harris's mind, we find that she is pleased with her role in her daughter's house and in no need of pity.

Mrs. Harris's point of view also softens the portrayal of her daughter provided by Mrs. Rosen, and it is further softened when we are allowed to see Victoria's despair when she learns she is pregnant again. Even Vickie's selfishness is tempered by the reader's recognition of the self-doubt she feels about going away to college, knowledge we gain mostly from Mrs. Harris (Stouck 1984, 292–94). In Rosowski's view, Cather's ever-changing point of view allows her to create a "rhythm between outside and inside, expectation and reality" and to present "intensely private lives of very different people" (1986, 196). The resulting contrasts inevitably produce irony. For example, an involuntarily childless woman is paired with one who is devastated by the knowledge that she is pregnant, the move West to secure a better life results in "reduced circumstances," within a large family the individuals are lonely, and new life is complemented by death (1986, 196–97).

Baker sees Mrs. Rosen as a Jamesian lens through which much of the story is viewed, even though Cather tells us from the outset that Mrs. Rosen's opinions do not embody the full and true story, as evidenced by her failure to see that there is nothing pitiful about Mrs. Harris's existence (1990, 35, 37). Arnold calls Mrs. Rosen the "controlling consciousness" of the story, for even when she is not in the scene, other characters adopt her views (1984, 141). Furthermore, despite her initial misperceptions and her continual puzzlement, Mrs. Rosen does eventually come to understand—and therefore the reader does also—that this family has "something of greater value than tidiness and strict democracy" (1984, 144–45). Ramonda assumes that Cather uses a shifting point of view to reveal the tensions that animate the story. Such a technique allows Cather to juxtapose "South and West, old and young, and the Rosen and the Templeton households" (1990, 176). Some critics, however, cling to the initial impressions established. Canby, for example, maintains that Mr. Templeton is shiftless; his wife, selfish and egotistical; and that they exploit "a poor old grandmother who believes that after forty the old should go to the kitchen and let youth have its way" (1984, 280). Another reviewer sees Mrs. Rosen to the end as "hurtful" and "offensive" (Quennell 1932, 695–96).

Several authorities have expressed the opinion that the strongest scene in the story is that of Mandy, the servant girl, washing Mrs. Harris's feet. Williams asserts that the scene proves the permanent greatness of Willa Cather and has a place in "immortal literature" (Williams 1932, 434). Stouck argues that the image of Mandy kneeling at Mrs. Harris's feet derives its power "from the Keatsian paradox that the servant's gesture of compassion is momentary but complete, while its artistic recreation must always be compensatory" (1984, 294). Baker ascribes Christian significance to the scene because of its similarity to Mary Magdalene's washing the feet of Jesus, and because it is part of a pattern of religious imagery in the story: after Victoria leaves the room to take care of the baby, Mrs. Rosen's attention is drawn to prints of "Hagar and

Ishmael in the Wilderness" and "The Light of the World" on the wall. Finally, Victoria appears nursing her baby, a figure of the Madonna and child. All these images contribute to the notion that the Templeton house is a refuge— a temple of love and acceptance (Baker 1990, 37).

Along this same line, Giannone argues that the whole story is an embodiment of Cather's idea that art and religion are one, even though such an idea is never explicitly stated. Cather draws on the Bible in this story in her portrayal of a soul's journey through life, in the depiction of which she uses Psalm 23: Grandmother Harris's death is the moment the psalmist describes as a walk through the valley of the shadow of death with God still there as guide. Mrs. Harris's Tennessee past is associated with the life of the shepherd tending a scattered flock. The psalmist looks back on a life guided by God and ahead to the eternal bliss. Likewise, the story's many images of a nurturing Mrs. Harris reflect the Lord—the good shepherd—within her: she becomes the God she worships (Giannone 1968, 1–5, 13). The allusion to the *Dies Irae* also points to a spiritual theme. Although neither Mrs. Rosen nor Vickie, who is translating the hymn from the Latin, understands its significance, Cather does: in this story the *Dies Irae* "underscores a deliverance from life for those who are approaching 'noble darkness'" (Giannone 1968, 212).

Lee agrees that the story presents a Christian message—"blessed are the poor in spirit; for theirs is the kingdom of Heaven," but that it is not explicit. Mrs. Harris has an unquestionably "meagre life to look back on from her deathbed. But the materials are transformed into dignified matters" (1989, 325). In a dissenting view, Thurin maintains that there is little concern on Mrs. Harris's part for an afterlife. She is interested solely in the members of her family, her major concern being that "her great effort"—making sure Vickie will be able to attend college—is successful (1990, 322). Grandma Harris's peace at the end of the story does not seem to come from thoughts of heaven, but from her acceptance of the truth that "everything that's alive has got to suffer" (Cather 1974, 141; McFarland 1972, 121). In addition, she has come to terms with the selfish young who do not yet recognize this truth (McFarland 1972, 121).

Another aspect of the story that has elicited much comment is Cather's handling of the conflict between the standards of Southern gentility and those of the bustling egalitarian West. Daiches says that Cather herself remains objective, allowing the situation in the story to explain itself through Mrs. Harris's interactions with her grandchildren, in which there is an element of the Southern clan (Daiches 1967, 92). To Ramonda, Mrs. Harris's values are shot through with the "Southern belle tradition," which prescribes a different role for each of the three phases of a woman's life: the first phase is youth, during which time a girl must be "carefree and foolish"; the second phase is motherhood, a role to which every other aspect of life must be sacrificed; finally, the woman comes to old age, when she should become a member of her daughter's or daughter-in-law's household and be seen but not heard, while yet managing all the domestic concerns so as to spare the younger members of the family any stress (1990, 178). In the context of these values, Grandma Harris's baking the cake that her daughter takes to the ice-cream social seems perfectly natural and right both to her and to her daughter (Arnold 1984, 146). It is no wonder, then, that Victoria is baffled by Mrs. Jackson's "cutting comments about now nice it would be if all of the women in town had someone confined in their kitchens to bake cakes for them" (Arnold 1984, 146). Victoria and her mother are out of place in their new environment, which in turn cannot comprehend the traditions that shape the Templeton household (Arnold 1984, 146). Consequently, Grandma Harris may be understood only in light of the old South: she finds her identity only in a group, and now her group is just her daughter and her family, rather than an extended family or larger community (Wasserman 1991, 57).

Ramonda sees hints, however, of the impending break with Southern customs in the story: the Southern belle tradition asked women to "suppress their individuality and assertiveness and to conform to an idealized role" (1990, 178). Furthermore, even though the women in this story are no longer required to meet the demands of plantation life, they live out the roles that life created; they cling to the old ways even as their new society presses them to give them up. Even the financial security that this system was supposed to procure for women is questionable in this story (Ramonda 1990, 178). The unreliable Hillary Templeton certainly does not offer much financial security. The women, therefore, must "struggle with inadequate resources to maintain their sense of propriety" (Ramonda 1990, 179). The clear implication by the story's end is that Grandma Harris's death represents a break with these Southern customs, and Victoria and Vickie will have to accept new responsibilities (Arnold 1984, 149).

Danker argues that the story's pastoral themes and imagery contribute heavily to its meaning. The Templeton family's move from South to West severed most of their connections with a pastoral life. Nevertheless, they have preserved some of their former ties to the land by transplanting their animals—a cat, a cow, and a horse—with them. The animals allow them to maintain links to their pastoral history. Mr. Templeton's riding into the country to visit the people who rent land from him may be seen as another gesture toward preserving the past (1990, 25). Despite their efforts, however, the family has lost a good deal—"the pastoral ideal has been weakened"—as indicated by the role food in the story: "No longer either a tie to the land (the Templeton's have no garden) or a source of social unity, food becomes both a sign and a cause of family and community disunity" (Danker 1990, 25–26). The family members do not take their meals together, and the friction between the Templetons and their neighbors often reveals itself in terms of food: Mrs. Rosen's gifts of sweets to Grandma Harris make Victoria jealous, and it is one of Mrs. Harris's cakes that elicits criticism of Victoria at the ice-cream social (1990, 26).

Most critics believe that the three women referred to by the title of the story as it appeared in *Ladies' Home Journal* are the grandmother, mother, and daughter. Ryder associates Vickie, the "brightest and strongest" of the women in the story, with Artemis; her mother, Victoria, with Aphrodite; and Grandma Harris with Athena (1990, 268). Mrs. Harris is also the only one of the three who is "blessed with the gift of self-forgetfulness." To the extent that Mrs. Harris represents Cather's maternal grandmother and Vickie, Cather herself, the author is suggesting that her own literary gift was passed to her matrilineally: in this story "grandmother and granddaughter love to read aloud to the Templeton children," and in one scene Vickie even takes over the task from her grandmother (O'Brien 1987, 27). Cather makes this literary inheritance more direct than it actually was in her own life: in the story, it is the grandmother who makes sure Vickie has the money to go to the University of Michigan; whereas in real life, it was Cather's father who borrowed the money that sent her to the university (O'Brien 1987, 27).

Works Cited

Arnold, Marilyn. 1984. *Willa Cather's Short Fiction*. Athens: Ohio University Press.

Baker, Bruce P. 1990. "'Old Mrs. Harris' and the Intergenerational Family." In *Willa Cather and the Family, Community and History: The BYU Symposium*. Ed. John J. Murphy. Provo, Utah: Brigham Young University, 33–40.

Bennett, Mildred R. 1961. *The World of Willa Cather*. Lincoln: University of Nebraska Press.

Canby, Henry Seidel. 1984. "The Last Four Books." In *Critical Essays on Willa Cather*. Ed. John J. Murphy. Boston: G. K. Hall, 280–82.

Cather, Willa. 1974. "Old Mrs. Harris." In *Obscure Destinies*. New York: Vintage Books, 75–190.

———. 1992. "Old Mrs. Harris." In *Cather: Stories, Poems, and Other Writings*. New York: Literary Classics of the United States, 619–72.

Daiches, David. 1967. "The Short Stories." In *Willa Cather and Her Critics*. Ed. James Schroeter. Ithaca, NY: Cornell University Press, 87–95.

Danker, Kathleen A. 1990. "The Passing of a Golden Age in *Obscure Destinies*." *Willa Cather Pioneer Memorial Newsletter* 34:24–28.

Faulkner, Virginia, ed. [1965] 1970. *Willa Cather's Collected Short Fiction, 1892–1912*. Lincoln: University of Nebraska Press. Reprint. Lincoln: University of Nebraska Press.

Giannone, Richard. 1968. *Music in Willa Cather's Fiction*. Lincoln: University of Nebraska Press.

Leddy, Michael. 1988. "Observation and Narration in Willa Cather's *Obscure Destinies*." *Studies in American Fiction* 16:141–53.

Lee, Hermione. 1989. *Willa Cather: Double Lives*. New York: Pantheon.

Lewis, Edith. 1953. *Willa Cather Living*. New York: Knopf.

McFarland, Dorothy Tuck. 1972. *Willa Cather*. New York: Frederick Ungar.

O'Brien, Sharon. 1987. *Willa Cather: The Emerging Voice*. New York: Oxford University Press.

Quennell, Peter. 1932. Review of *Obscure Destinies*, by Willa Cather. *New Statesman and Nation*, December 3, 694.

Robinson, Phyllis C. 1983. *Willa: The Life of Willa Cather*. Garden City, NY: Doubleday.

Ramonda, Karen Stevens. 1990. "Three in One Woman in 'Old Mrs. Harris.'" In *Willa Cather and the Family, Community and History: The BYU Symposium*. Ed. John J. Murphy. Provo, Utah: Brigham Young University, 175–81.

Rosowski, Susan J. 1986. *The Voyage Perilous: Willa Cather's Romanticism*. Lincoln: University of Nebraska Press.

———. 1990. "Willa Cather's Chosen Family: Fictional Formations and Transformations." In *Willa Cather and the Family, Community and History: The BYU Symposium*. Ed. John J. Murphy. Provo, Utah: Brigham Young University, 67–78.

Ryder, Mary Ruth. 1990. *Willa Cather and Classical Myth*. Lewiston, NY: Edwin Mellen Press.

Slote, Bernice, ed. 1966. *The Kingdom of Art*. Lincoln: University of Nebraska Press.

Southwick, Helen Cather. 1985. "Memories of Willa Cather in Red Cloud." *Willa Cather Pioneer Memorial Newsletter* 29:11–13.

Stineback, David. 1984. "The Case of Willa Cather." *Canadian Review of American Studies* 15:385–95.

Stouck, David. 1984. "Willa Cather's Last Four Books." In *Critical Essays on Willa Cather*. Ed. John J. Murphy. Boston: G. K. Hall, 290–304.

"Three Stories of the West." 1932. *Christian Science Monitor*, September 17, 12.

Thurin, Erik Ingvar. 1990. *The Humanization of Willa Cather: Classicism in an American Classic*. Lund, Sweden: Lund University Press.

Wasserman, Loretta. 1991. *Willa Cather: A Study of the Short Fiction*. Boston: Twayne.

Williams, Michael. 1932. "Willa Cather." *Commonweal*, August 31, 433–34.

Woodress, James. 1987. *Willa Cather: A Literary Life*. Lincoln: University of Nebraska Press.

On the Divide

Publication History

This story was first published in January 1896, in *Overland Monthly* (ser. 2, 27:65–74) under the name W. Cather (Faulkner 1970, 591). The story was Cather's first publication in a national magazine (Woodress 1970, 73). It was reprinted in 1957 by Dodd, Mead in *Early Stories*; in 1965 by the University of Nebraska Press in *Willa Cather's Collected Short Fiction, 1892–1912*, and in 1992 by Literary Classics of the United States in *Cather: Stories, Poems, and Other Writings*, a volume in the Library of America series.

Circumstances of Composition, Sources, and Influences

The story was probably written after Cather's graduation from the University of Nebraska in June 1895. During the following year, Cather divided her time nearly equally between Red Cloud and Lincoln and had taken a position as associate editor and dramatic critic at the Lincoln *Courier*, a weekly that covered the arts and society (Woodress 1970, 71). At the same time, she continued to write for the Lincoln *Journal*. Nevertheless, most scholars agree that the year following her graduation was one of uncertainty and anxiety about the future. While living in Red Cloud, Cather realized that she could not endure living there forever, even if she could sustain herself by writing fiction. In dating a letter written in January 1896, the same month "On the Divide" appeared in print, she referred to Red Cloud as "Siberia," both because of the weather and because of her sense of isolation there (Woodress 1970, 73). When she attended a Red Cloud dance that was considered by the locals a social event for the elite, she discovered to her dismay that "the boys were rowdy, seats were planks laid on chairs, and the sandwiches were served from a bushel basket" (Woodress 1970, 73). The frustration and dissatisfaction arising from situations like these may explain the grim view of life on the prairie presented in this story (Woodress 1983, xii).

According to Slote, Cather's newspaper articles of 1893–1896 reveal her intense interest in the "Roman–Barbarian conflict" as a symbol of the idea that highly civilized and refined cultures like Rome are always eventually destroyed—and in the process purified—by primitive, barbarous forces (1966, 93). Such destruction at the hands of strong, barbaric, but innocent outsiders is necessary to purge the corruption that invariably accompanies civilization: Cather's treatment of this theme reveals "a kind of delight in the barbarian, in savage strength and the dramatic movements of conquest and decay throughout history" (Slote 1966, 93–94). Indeed, in her November 2, 1895, *Courier* article, Cather asserts, "When the Roman world had corrupted the civilization it had made, enslaved the state it had freed, grown monstrous in its pleasures, . . . the barbarian races . . . brought down the snows of the Danube to cool the heated blood of the south, and the great hammer of Thor to crush the defiled altars of Aphrodite into dust" (reprinted in Slote 1966, 93–94). Slote reads "On the Divide" as an elaboration on this same theme: Canute Canuteson captures Lena just as his Viking ancestors captured the daughters of the decadent south of Europe centuries before. When civilization becomes overly refined or complicated, it eventually collapses and "the strong arm reaches out and takes by force what it cannot win by cunning" (Slote 1966, 94).

Relationship to Other Cather Works

The setting of this piece reappears in *O Pioneers!* and a section of *My Ántonia*. Bennett outlines the close similarities of all three of these Divide landscapes: the opening paragraph of "On the Divide" describes Rattlesnake Creek in terms that suggest it is not just a small stream, but a *failure* as a stream. Canute's cabin stands nearby, surrounded on three sides by the red prairie grass Cather often describes. In a corresponding way, a creek on the Bergson farm in *O Pioneers!* is described as another shiftless stream. We see the rust-red grass again in *My Ántonia* and in "Neighbour Rosicky" (1957, 59). Canute's "soliloquy" about his land on the first day of winter is reminiscent of Bergson's musing about his land in *O Pioneers!* (Bennett 1957, 61).

Bennett sees the central episode of "On the Divide," Canute sweeping Lena Yensen up and carrying her back to his cabin, as recurring in *O Pioneers!* when Alexandra feels as if someone is carrying her away physically (1957, 70–71). Slote finds an earlier version of this same scene in "The Elopement of Allen Poole," where Allen wants to pick Nelly up and carry her (1966, 105).

The description of the inside of Canute's shack may have its origins in the earlier story "The Clemency of the Court" (1893). In that story, Gerasim's chamber, like Canute's cabin, contains a huge plank bed and a few other rough furnishings (Bohlke 1974, 144n). Canute's carvings of demons and serpents also remind the reader of the crude wood-carvings of religious figures so often described in *Death Comes for the Archbishop* (Bennett 1957, 61).

The title character from another earlier story, "Lou, the Prophet," appears briefly in "On the Divide" as crazy Lou, for whom Mary Yensen mistakes

Canute. Lena, too, is frightened by what she thinks is crazy Lou's face at the window. Cather develops this same character fully as crazy Ivar in *O Pioneers!* (Bennett 1982, 40). However, according to Bennett, the strongest character connection between "On the Divide" and the rest of Cather's works is that between Lena Yensen and several later women characters. She is introduced for the first time in this piece; she then becomes Lena Hanson in "Eric Hermannson's Soul" (1900), a woman notorious all around the Divide. Next, she appears as Olena Yenson in "The Bohemian Girl," where she is no longer a disgrace, but a respectable young woman. The final version of the original Lena is in *My Ántonia*, where she becomes Lena Lingard, who still displays many of the qualities of her predecessors (Bennett 1970, xxxi–xxxii). To Bennett, the significance of the four versions of this character is that they allow the reader to see how Cather turned a flat character into a round one. The narrator of *My Ántonia* asserts that girls like Lena Lingard are the poetry of the world, but "such a statement about Lena Yensen [of 'On the Divide'] would sound like high-flown nonsense; that it seems right and true of Lena Lingard measures one aspect of Cather's accomplishment" (1970, xxxii).

Interpretations and Criticisms

In "On the Divide," Cather has abandoned the hostile, ironic voice she had used in "Peter" and "The Clemency of the Court" and instead creates a narrator who is an inhabitant of the country he describes (Arnold 1984, 5). However, this narrative shift does not result in a more sympathetic view of life on the Divide. In fact, one reviewer maintains that the story "is really one of the plains, and the characters of the people merely inevitable incidents of their surroundings" (Peattie 1896, 8).

Most critics agree that this story contains perhaps Cather's grimmest portrayal of life on the plains—darker even than the sections of *My Ántonia* that describe the Shimerdas' sufferings during their first winter on the prairie. Even Cather's spare style intensifies the "dry barrenness of the summers which are nearly as great a test of human endurance as the winters" (Arnold 1984, 4). The land is portrayed as utterly hostile, punishing relentlessly those who choose to dwell on it. Canute is no exception. Cather depicts his world as full of violence and Gothic terror (Slote 1970, 10). Cather's Nebraska neighbors were undoubtedly offended by her portrayal of Canute, but readers find it very difficult to refute her (Robinson 1983, 72–73).

Arnold sees Canute Canuteson as an "elemental man," but one who longs for human affection (1984, 5). His carvings of serpents and demons on the windowsills and his hanging snakeskins on the door suggest that until he discovered love, Canute "entertained a frightening conviction that the earth does indeed belong to the Devil" (1984, 5). To Bennett, the significance of the carvings is that they are attempts at expression by the inarticulate (1957, 61). O'Brien views Canute's carvings as more of a primitive artist's "imaginative self-expression"—the figures "reveal his inner demons and desires" (1987, 205). Further, Canute's use of the knife is significant in that Cather often uses the knife to symbolize writing and the power and dangers associated with it. Wood-carvers, of course, use the knife as an instrument of power and creation; Cather, however, realized that knives are used to wound as well as to sculpt (O'Brien 1987, 205).

The story provides clear evidence of Cather's adoption of male values in Lena's happy submission to Canute's barbaric advances and also the beginning of Cather's tendency to employ mythic symbolism, especially in the description of Lena's abduction, when she is carried off by a figure identified with the Vikings and the barbarians who sacked Rome (Woodress 1987, 106).

Works Cited

Arnold, Marilyn. 1984. *Willa Cather's Short Fiction*. Athens: Ohio University Press.

Bennett, Mildred, ed. 1957. *Early Stories of Willa Cather*. New York: Dodd, Mead.

Bennett, Mildred R. [1965] 1970. Introduction to *Willa Cather's Collected Short Fiction*. Ed. Virginia Faulkner. Lincoln: University of Nebraska Press. Reprint. Lincoln: University of Nebraska Press.

———. 1982. "Willa Cather's Bodies for Ghosts." *Western American Literature* 17:39–52.

Bohlke, L. Brent. 1974. "Beginnings: Willa Cather and 'The Clemency of the Court.'" *Prairie Schooner* 48:133–44.

Cather, Willa. 1957. "On the Divide." In *Early Stories*. Ed. Mildred Bennett. New York: Dodd, Mead, 59–75.

———. [1965] 1970. "On the Divide." In *Willa Cather's Collected Short Fiction, 1892–1912*. Ed. Virginia Faulkner. Lincoln: University of Nebraska Press, 493–504.

———. 1992. "On the Divide." In *Cather: Stories, Poems, and Other Writings*. New York: Literary Classics of the United States, 8–21.

Faulkner, Virginia, ed. [1965] 1970. *Willa Cather's Collected Short Fiction, 1892–1912*. Lincoln: University of Nebraska Press. Reprint. Lincoln: University of Nebraska Press.

O'Brien, Sharon. 1987. *Willa Cather: The Emerging Voice*. New York: Oxford University Press.

Peattie, Elia. 1896. "A Word with the Women." *Omaha World-Herald*, January 14, 8.

Robinson, Phyllis C. 1983. *Willa: The Life of Willa Cather*. Garden City, NY: Doubleday.

Slote, Bernice, ed. 1966. *The Kingdom of Art*. Lincoln: University of Nebraska Press.

Slote, Bernice. 1970. "Willa Cather as a Regional Writer." *Kansas Quarterly* 2:7–15.

Woodress, James. 1970. *Willa Cather: Her Life and Art*. New York: Pegasus.

———. 1983. Introduction to *The Troll Garden*. Ed. James Woodress. Lincoln: University of Nebraska Press.

———. 1987. *Willa Cather: A Literary Life*. Lincoln: University of Nebraska Press.

On the Gulls' Road

Publication History

This story was first published with the subtitle "The Ambassador's Story" under the name Willa Sibert Cather in the December 1908 issue of *McClure's* (32:145–52) (Faulkner 1970, 596). It was reprinted without the subtitle by the University of Nebraska Press in *Willa Cather's Collected Short Fiction, 1892–1912*.

Circumstances of Composition, Sources, and Influences

This story was the only piece of fiction Cather published in 1908. It appeared in *McClure's* magazine during the second year she worked on its staff. All critics agree that the story is heavily influenced by the style and subject matter of Henry James, particularly by his story "The Patagonia," which also involves a shipboard romance and a suicide, and "The Solution," whose characters include an American diplomat (Arnold 1984, 89). More Jamesian influence can be seen or felt in the story's foreign setting, in the dialogue, and most of all in a detached narrator reminiscent of so many of James's reflectors. The story's subtitle is clearly a reference to James's *The Ambassadors*: Cather's narrator has much in common with that novel's Lambert Strether (O'Brien 1987, 367).

Sarah Orne Jewett's work, which Cather greatly admired, also heavily influenced the story. It is especially similar to Jewett's "Martha's Lady," which tells of the endurance of a friendship between two women that survives despite their long separation and vast differences in temperament. Cather's story also describes a love that endures over time and separation, with the narrator taking the role of Martha: opening the box left to him by Alexandra, he is led to dream, to speak, to tell the story, thus, like the gifts in Jewett's stories, the contents of the box show the absent still present in memory and imagination (O'Brien 1987, 348, 368). It is possible that Cather modeled the character of Alexandra on Jewett herself, who was struggling with her final illness at the time this story was written (O'Brien 1987, 369).

"On the Gulls' Road" was the story that prompted the most important response to Cather's work that Jewett was ever to make. As Woodress explains, Jewett's initial pronouncement was that the story was very good— that it provided evidence that Cather was maturing as an artist in all the right directions. Jewett was bothered, however, by Cather's use of a male narrator, asserting that Cather should have either written the story in the third person or made the narrator a woman. Later, after reassessing her initial response to the story, Jewett wrote Cather a second letter admonishing her about the draining nature of the kind of work she was doing on the staff of *McClure's*. Jewett realized that the pressure of Cather's position on the staff of the magazine would prevent her from maturing as a writer of fiction. She advised Cather to draw on her Nebraska and Virginia roots as well as her experience as a journalist. Although Cather was deeply affected by these letters, she chose not to act on some of Jewett's advice: she continued on the staff of *McClure's* and continued to create male narrators (1987, 202–205).

Thurin believes another strong influence on this story was Cather's trip to Europe with her friend Isabelle McClung in 1902. The parts of the world central to the story are the very places Cather saw with Isabelle. Further, in Cather's mind Isabelle was linked with Aphrodite, the goddess of love who comes from the sea. Aphrodite is the story's central image. Alexandra is described as coming up out of a pale green gown, "regally white and gold," and this is very much a description of a statue of Aphrodite Cather had just seen in the Pompeii Museum (Cather 1970, 89; Thurin 1990, 150–51).

Relationship to Other Cather Works

Like many of Cather's stories, "On the Gulls' Road" suggests that special people, like those with great talent, die young. Alexandra Ebbling may be grouped with Katharine Gaylord of "'A Death in the Desert,'" Marguerite Thiesinger of "Double Birthday," Anne Aylward of *My Mortal Enemy*, Nelly Deane of "The Joy of Nelly Deane," Marie Shabata of *O Pioneers!*, Lucy Gayheart of *Lucy Gayheart*, Lesley Ferguesson of "The Best Years," Tom Outland of *The Professor's House*, and Claude Wheeler in *One of Ours*. Cather's implication seems to be that dying young is preferable to the misery of aging (Bennett 1982, 45).

Bennett points out a small but obvious detail that first appears in this story and recurs in several subsequent works—Lars Ebbling's turquoise ring. Turquoise is linked with love and death in three novels—first as the pieces of uncut turquoise Emil drops into Marie's lap in *O Pioneers!*, then as the turquoise memento Ray Kennedy shows to Thea Kronborg in *The Song of the Lark*, and finally as the two turquoise stones Tom Outland of *The Professor's House* gives his love. A fateful turquoise is also important in the Mexican tale Don Hedger tells Eden Bower in "Coming, Aphrodite!" (1970, xxxix–xl).

Cather's use of color is another connecting device, especially the color yellow, which she often links with sexuality or romance (Woodress 1987, 221). In *Alexander's Bridge* (1912), Cather's first novel, yellow or gold clothes, shoes, flowers, wine, candlelight, sunlight, clouds, and cityscapes are associated with love, and the same imagery is used to describe Alexandra Ebbling in "On the Gulls' Road" (Woodress 1987, 221).

The framework of the story—the eternal triangle—also connects it to other Cather works: "'A Death in the Desert,'" "The Bohemian Girl," *O Pioneers!*, and *A Lost Lady* (Woodress 1987, 222).

Rosowski places this story with others in which Cather fuses the romantic and the prosaic in an effort to describe a "visionary experience of breaking out of time and space" in a realistic narrative (1986, 11). In some stories, such as "'The Fear That Walks by Noonday'" and "The Affair at Grover Station," she places "otherworldly characters into ordinary reality"; in others, including "On the Gulls' Road," "The Treasure of Far Island," and "The Garden Lodge," she moves her characters "from ordinary settings to otherworldly ones" (Rosowski 1986, 11). In "The Treasure of Far Island," the central characters sail to the enchanted place of their childhood; in "The Garden Lodge," Caroline Noble is transported in a kind of trance to an alternate reality; and in "On the Gulls' Road" the narrator enters a different world by sailing to southern climes (Rosowski 1986, 11).

Thurin argues that Alexandra Ebbling is the first in a long line of Aphrodite figures in Cather's work: versions of the goddess reappear most prominently in Marie Shabata of *O Pioneers!* and the title character of *Lucy Gayheart*. Alexandra also prefigures Nelly Deane in "The Joy of Nelly Deane" in her Aphrodite-like physical appearance (1990, 150–51).

Interpretations and Criticisms

Bradford simply dismisses this story as "romantic bathos" (1955, 546). Arnold, on the other hand, argues that the story is perhaps a parody of sentimental fiction and drama—though an unconscious one. Cather's knowledge of this kind of fiction is well documented, and the story contains many of the conventions of popular romances: the vaguely villainous husband, the romantic hero and heroine caught in a doomed romance, the use of gloomy weather to reinforce the dire straits of the protagonists. The last paragraph of the story is perhaps the best evidence to support the notion that Cather was creating a parody. There the narrator is the stereotypical lover of romance, both in his early optimism and exuberance about love and in his later tears and dejection when love is gone. Nevertheless, the reader is never certain about Cather's intent in this story: in her early days of journalism she consistently preferred romance to realism, and there is no suggestion in Cather's letters to Jewett that she planned this story as a parody (Arnold 1984, 90–91, 97n).

O'Brien agrees that all the elements of popular romance are present in this story but maintains that it is more than simple sentiment: "The retrospective narrative allows the speaker to . . . return to—while keeping a safe distance from—a maternal/erotic presence who possesses the power to obliterate the self as well as to nourish it" (1987, 368). In this story the actual sea journey is a metaphor for the "child/artist's" psychological or "symbolic one: from the regressive desire for fusion and gratification (represented by the warm, sensuous waters of the Mediterranean), to the adult's separation from the mother (the chilly Atlantic, the sea of 'reality'), and finally to the artist's regaining of the lost connection through narrative (the storyteller's 'voyage' into the past)" (O'Brien 1987, 368).

Perhaps Jewett's criticism of Cather's use of a male narrator—her sense that a woman could have loved Alexandra just as effectively—grew out of Jewett's suspicion, whether conscious or not, that the narrator actually *was* a woman, despite Cather's intent that he be male (O'Brien 1987, 369). As O'Brien points out, Jewett, nearly twenty-five years Cather's senior, grew up before society began to view women's friendships and intimacies as unnatural; thus, unlike Cather, she was free to describe passionate female friendship, whereas Cather found she must camouflage the love the story depicts. The female images she includes—the box, hair, and seashells, for example—as well as Alexandra's association with Aphrodite, create a lesbian subtext: Cather linked Aphrodite with Sappho and Sappho's hymn to that goddess, and through her identification with Aphrodite, Alexandra is linked to the lesbian poet. Using a male narrator allows Cather to describe love between two women; thus, it seems to be an effort on Cather's part to describe the love that dares not speak its name (O'Brien 1987, 369). It is perhaps surprising that Cather was quite comfortable describing intimate friendships among men, but the same kinds of relationships between women, so important in her own life, are not found in her fiction, except between family members or women of widely different ages or stations (Robinson 1983, 158).

This story also contains a common Cather theme—the opposition of a life linked to the North Sea and the industrial world and another more graceful life associated with the Mediterranean. Cather believes it is the latter way of life we all yearn for yet are unable to realize fully, although we can occasionally return to it for a moment so that we are able to live more happily in the grimmer modern world (Thurin 1990, 152).

Works Cited

Arnold, Marilyn. 1984. *Willa Cather's Short Fiction*. Athens: Ohio University Press.

Bennett, Mildred. [1965] 1970. Introduction to *Willa Cather's Collected Short Fiction*. Ed. Virginia Faulkner. Lincoln: University of Nebraska Press. Reprint. Lincoln: University of Nebraska Press.

———. 1982. "Willa Cather's Bodies for Ghosts." *Western American Literature* 17:39–52.

Bradford, Curtis. 1955. "Willa Cather's Uncollected Short Stories." *American Literature* 26:537–51.

Cather, Willa. [1965] 1970. "On the Gulls' Road." In *Willa Cather's Collected Short Fiction, 1892–1912*. Ed. Virginia Faulkner. Lincoln: University of Nebraska Press, 79–94.

Faulkner, Virginia, ed. [1965] 1970. *Willa Cather's Collected Short Fiction, 1892–1912*. Lincoln: University of Nebraska Press. Reprint. Lincoln: University of Nebraska Press.

O'Brien, Sharon. 1987. *Willa Cather: The Emerging Voice*. New York: Oxford University Press.

Robinson, Phyllis C. 1983. *Willa: The Life of Willa Cather*. Garden City, NY: Doubleday.

Rosowski, Susan J. 1986. *The Voyage Perilous: Willa Cather's Romanticism*. Lincoln: University of Nebraska Press.

Thurin, Erik Ingvar. 1990. *The Humanization of Willa Cather: Classicism in an American Classic*. Lund, Sweden: Lund University Press.

Woodress, James. 1987. *Willa Cather: A Literary Life*. Lincoln: University of Nebraska Press.

Paul's Case

Publication History

This story was first published with the subtitle "A Study in Temperament" in Cather's first collection of short stories, *The Troll Garden* (New York: McClure, Phillips, 1905, pp. 211–53), under the name Willa Sibert Cather (Faulkner 1970, 595). A few weeks after the collection was published, the story appeared in the May 1905 issue of *McClure's* (25:74–83) with, according to Virginia Faulkner, many changes in spelling and punctuation and the deletion of two passages. Evidently Cather condensed some sections because of space constraints in the magazine; in any case, she restored the omitted passages in later reprintings (1970, 595).

A revision of the 1905 *Troll Garden* version appeared without the subtitle in Cather's second collection, *Youth and the Bright Medusa* (New York: Knopf, 1920, pp. 199–234); the fourth appearance of the story was in volume six of the thirteen-volume library edition of Cather's work *The Novels and Stories of Willa Cather* (Boston: Houghton Mifflin, 1937–1941, pp. 207–45), where the 1920 version was reprinted with eight substantive changes (Faulkner 1970, 595).

In 1956, Vintage Books reprinted the 1920 version in *Five Stories*, and in 1961, the 1905 version was published by Signet Classics in a paperback edition of *The Troll Garden* with modernized punctuation and spelling. In 1965, the University of Nebraska Press published the 1905 version in *Willa Cather's Collected Short Fiction, 1892–1912*, and in 1983 the same press published it again in *The Troll Garden*, edited by James Woodress. Its next two appearances were in two volumes of the Library of America series, published by Literary Classics of the United States: *Cather: Early Novels and Stories* (1987) and *Cather: Stories, Poems, and Other Writings* (1992). Both were the 1905 version of the story.

Circumstances of Composition, Sources, and Influences

Cather wrote this story sometime between 1901 and 1903, when all the *Troll Garden* stories were apparently written. At the time, Cather was teaching high school and living with Isabelle McClung and her family in Pittsburgh, where she stayed until 1906 (Woodress 1983, xxiii). (For a discussion of the enormous positive influence of Isabelle McClung on Cather's creativity see the "Circumstances of Composition, Sources, and Influences" section for the chapter "A Wagner Matinée.") The story was probably included in the packet Cather sent to S. S. McClure in New York in April 1903. (A full explanation of McClure's role in the publication of these stories is given in the "Circumstances of Composition, Sources, and Influences" section for the chapter "The Sculptor's Funeral.")

There are several possible sources for the story. The one mentioned by critics most often is Cather's own feelings "about New York and the old Waldorf-Astoria Hotel when she was teaching in Pittsburgh" (Woodress 1983, xix). Brown points out that before Cather moved in with the McClung family, she was living in drab Pittsburgh boardinghouses, working at *Home Monthly* magazine, and taking note of the split personality of the city: that such a smoky and ugly industrial city could also produce exquisitely beautiful things was a constant source of amazement to Cather. Two cultural events that consistently rejuvenated her spirit were Carnegie Hall's symphony performances, where, like Paul, she felt her spirit soar the moment the orchestra began to play, and the Pittsburgh stock company, which presented a different play every week and where Cather met Lizzie Hudson Collier, a leading actress of the day. For Cather the stage door into the actress's dressing room was the entrance to the world of romance. Many of Cather's recollections of these experiences went into "Paul's Case" (Brown 1964, 81–84).

In Lee's opinion, Cather saw the danger of being, like Paul, drawn to the world of art for bad reasons. Still, the allure of the performing arts was much the same for Cather as it was for Paul (1989, 49–50). Also, like Paul, Cather had visited the Schenley Hotel many times. According to Brown, her purpose was to interview certain visitors to Pittsburgh while she was working for the Pittsburgh *Leader*, but like Paul, she wanted to trade even the best of Pittsburgh scenes for more alluring New York vistas ([1953] 1964, 122). O'Brien states simply that in many ways "Paul is a male version of Willa Cather" (1987, 283). She shares with him a passion for the arts, a longing to escape the drab and ordinary, and a rejection of traditional gender roles, which Paul expresses by abandoning his father's Horatio Alger values (O'Brien 1987, 283).

Another of the story's sources in Cather's own life is her frequent trips to New York City while she was living in Pittsburgh. The first of these trips took place in February 1898, when she spent a week as drama critic for the New York *Sun* (Woodress 1987, 135). The New York Cather saw that February was probably translated into the winter scene into which Cather places Paul (Woodress 1970, 121).

Some authorities see additional sources for the story in things outside Cather's own life and predilections. For example, Woodress notes that while she was teaching high school in Pittsburgh, Cather had a student in one of her Latin classes who probably became the prototype of the title character in this story. The boy was nervous, always tried to make himself seem interesting, and often claimed to know the actors in the Pittsburgh stock company (1970, 118). One of the story's reviewers says that it is based on an actual incident that occurred in Pittsburgh while Cather lived there: two boys had stolen $2,000 from the company where they worked and had run away to Chicago, where they were found ten days later, having spent every penny. Since the stolen money was refunded by the boys' families, the firm agreed not to press charges. The story was widely reported by the Pittsburgh papers at the time (review of *The Troll Garden* 1905, 457).

Thurin maintains that Cather's love of classical echoes was a strong influence on this story. There are several references to Narcissus in much of Paul's behavior. His indulgence in his bath at the Waldorf, too, may reflect Cather's knowledge of the importance of bathing to the decadent ancient Romans: to mark the allusion, Cather shows Paul wrapping himself in a Roman blanket in his Waldorf bathroom. Paul also mentions his belief that he was "born to the purple," undoubtedly a reference to the imperial purple, which, in her early articles Cather often used to refer to the decline of Rome (1990, 134–35).

Summers considers Cather's contempt for Oscar Wilde and the Aesthetic movement in general to be an important influence on this story. Her early newspaper columns contain unmistakably malicious comments on Wilde that show that she not only rejected his ideas, but also found them psychologically threatening. In her scathing review of Wilde's *Lady Windermere's Fan*, for example, she blasts his philosophy as "contemptible" and "inane" and attacks his character Cecil Graham, who dresses much like Wilde himself—and like Paul (1990, 104–105). Summers goes on to suggest that at this very early, pre-*Troll Garden* stage in Cather's career she was still celebrating the kind of manly ideal represented by writers like Rudyard Kipling and thus was driven to reject what she saw as Wilde's subversion of that ideal as well as his celebration of the artificial and decadent. Much later, when Cather changed her ideas about the masculine aesthetic, she qualified her opinions about Wilde and the aesthetes, and "Paul's Case" reflects that change. Specifically, the inflexible reactions of Paul's teachers may mirror both the author's own extreme early opinions about Wilde and her later reconsiderations (1990, 107–111).

Relationship to Other Cather Works

Most critics attempt to place all the stories in *The Troll Garden*, including this one, within the framework of the epigraphs Cather chose for the collection. (For a complete explanation of the thematic relationship of the *Troll Garden* stories to the epigraphs Cather chose for them, see the "Relationship to

Other Cather Works" section for the chapters "'A Death in the Desert'" and "A Wagner Matinée.") However, most critics have more difficulty with this story than with the others in explaining how it conforms to the themes suggested by the epigraphs. Rosowski sees Paul as having been seduced and ruined by the trolls and goblins, actually losing his soul in the end (1986, 19–23). Brown does not actually discuss the placement of this story within the collection, but refers to it as "a fitting coda" for the book (1964, 114). Woodress groups the story with "Flavia and Her Artists" because both contain examples of characters beguiled by art. Paul is a "forest child destroyed by the forbidden fruit" (1987, 174). Arnold, too, sees Paul as "the hungry forest child who is utterly helpless before the luscious appeal of the garden" (1984, 61). The other stories in the collection illustrate how the pursuit of either art or money exacts a price, but in "Paul's Case" the two objects are fused: for Paul, art and money are one (Arnold 1984, 61).

In Wasserman's opinion, Paul may be compared with Clark in "A Wagner Matinée," a character who also escapes his dreary circumstances. Clark is saved not only by the music lessons he receives from his aunt but also by his memories of ploughing between long rows of green corn. Paul, on the other hand, can see nothing of beauty in his gray city of Pittsburgh (Wasserman 1990, 125). Wasserman goes on to suggest a connection between "Paul's Case" and "The Sculptor's Funeral." In that story, Steavens, the sculptor's friend, realizes just how incredibly narrow and dreary the sculptor's childhood was, and yet out of that very ugliness an artist was born. That these three stories from *The Troll Garden* are the ones that Cather chose to reprint when she collected her writings in the 1930s suggests that they exemplify Cather's own qualities and preoccupations (1990, 128).

Murphy suggests that this story is similar to Cather's novel *Lucy Gayheart* in that both portray young people toward whom the author is ambivalent and who are damaged by their environments as well as by their own weakness (1979, 26–27).

Both Petry and Summers assert that "Paul's Case" may be seen as a companion piece to "The Sculptor's Funeral": both have homosexual themes that are not explicitly stated. In the latter story, Cather depicts a society troubled by the sculptor's homosexuality than by his artistic sensibilities; in the former, she depicts the failure of the homosexual to resolve the problem of his relationship to society (Petry 1986, 108–109; Summers 1990, 108n).

Wasserman sees "Paul's Case" as an example of Cather's treatment of religion and religious feeling, noting that early in her career the author often shows religion to be stifling, whether it is the Presbyterianism of "Paul's Case" and "A Gold Slipper," the revivalism of "Eric Hermannson's Soul," or the Baptist church of "The Joy of Nelly Deane" (1991, 46). Lee adds "Uncle Valentine" to this list, asserting that each story depicts the unrelenting Calvinism and greed of the city (1989, 45).

To O'Brien, the fact that Paul uses music "to enter a solipsistic realm where he passively absorbs the sensations he craves" establishes connections between him and William of "The Burglar's Christmas" (1987, 284). Both Paul and William attain "idyllic space" through their thievery; Paul's pleasure trip, financed by stolen money, is Cather's attempt to show a regressive temperament like William's, not an artistic one (1987, 284–85). Despite these similarities in theme, however, Cather's narrative technique is much more mature in "Paul's Case": Cather here can both distance herself from her character and suggest some sympathy for his yearnings (1987, 284–85).

Interpretations and Criticisms

"Paul's Case" is without question Cather's most popular and most frequently anthologized story, although part of the reason for its standing is that it was the only story Cather would allow to be reprinted during the last years of her life. Regardless of the reasons, the story has elicited a good many critical responses, some of which have become standard, while others remain a bit more adventurous. Bloom and Bloom take a common approach: Cather was depicting, as she had so many times before in earlier stories and would again in later stories and novels, a young person with artistic sensibilities whose spirit is overwhelmed and eventually beaten by the prevalent American ethos—a crude, insensitive, unforgiving, relentlessly materialistic creed that demands mediocrity, that does not allow for specialness or even difference. In this story, Cather was attacking "national dullness" just as Sinclair Lewis did (Bloom and Bloom 1962, 86–87). Critics who adopt this reading believe that nurture, not nature, has absolute jurisdiction over human life. Church and state—represented by the pictures of Calvin and Washington over Paul's bed—had failed him (Wasserman 1991, 24).

Dissenting voices insistently point out that Paul is no artist—he is not, in fact, even special. He exaggerates the repugnance of Cordelia Street and creates and acts out his own escapist dreams. Those who hold this view maintain that Paul's own maladjustment, the arrested development of his emotional life, is responsible for his distorted view of his neighborhood, which, in reality, is merely an ordinary community (Wasserman 1991, 24). Paul is simply "half-crazy" and cannot be trusted to describe reliably either his neighborhood or the world of art (Arnold 1984, 43–445). His unhealthy imagination is excited only by the artificial and is unaroused by outside reality. Thus, instead of allowing him to see the good in his surroundings, his imagination destroys him (Pers 1975, 92). One writer even maintains that, based on a battery of tests he administered to the character, Paul can be diagnosed as a schizophrenic, and suggests that is why Cather referred to him as a case (Weigel 1958, 1). Carpenter combines both views; he sees Paul as a pathetic victim of a sort of determinism but at the same time culpable because he has "consumed himself morally and ethically by living a lie—one purchased through someone else's hard work" (1987, 591, 606).

Still, it is possible for us to exonerate Paul because, as Wasserman notes, we find extreme narcissists—like Falstaff—the embodiment of our own infantile desires. Paul, then, is simply another "Faust and Quixote" (1991, 25). Like Faust, he is drawn to the transcendent or "magical experience" that will transport him to a realm far above the mundane; like Quixote, he has the "fanatic heroism" necessary to battle to the end the onslaughts of the everyday world (Van Ghent 1985, 75).

Such widely disparate readings are, as Wasserman argues, evidence of Cather's success "in balancing the competing claims of the old arguments between nature and nurture, heredity and environment, freedom and determinism" (1991, 24). These tensions are what give the story its strength; further, it must be said that, at least for one day, Paul gets exactly what he wants and suffers no guilt. In the end, Paul recognizes no failure on his part—only that he failed to escape. In ending her story without ascribing remorse to Paul, Cather may have been ironically undercutting the moralists who predict torments of contrition for a boy like Paul (Wasserman 1991, 24–25). The story's major achievement, however, is in Paul's recognition that the final answer to everything in life comes down to money. Here romantic longing becomes a longing for the cash that can purchase the trappings of romance (Wasserman 1990, 128). In an early response to the story, a British reviewer asserts that Paul represents the majority of Americans, of whom the English have no clear conception (Williams 1920, 890).

O'Brien approaches this story as Cather's backward glance at an earlier version of herself: when she was fourteen, Cather decided to take on a masculine persona by "cropping her hair, donning boyish clothes, and naming herself 'William Cather, Jr. . . .'" (1987, 110). In so doing, Cather rejected the confining roles of the Victorian woman in favor of the freedom and power reserved for males in her culture. She remained within her male persona until the end of her second year at the University of Nebraska, believing that the great writers and thinkers of all kinds were exclusively male (O'Brien 1987, 110). It would be years before Cather came to recognize the existence of a legitimate female tradition in literature and other arts. Thus, in the character of Paul, Cather is describing her days as William Cather, "another imaginative, sensitive youth at odds with a repressive society" (O'Brien 1987, 282). At the same time, however, the author consistently holds herself apart from Paul, for "Paul's self-dissolution is not the artist's desire to create, but the child's regressive yearning to regain the preoedipal union with the mother" (O'Brien 1987, 283–84). For example, despite his professed love of music and culture, he never attends a musical performance in New York. In fact, he does nothing except sleep, eat, and drink. He spends his most memorable moments with the objects he has just acquired in the sitting room (O'Brien 1987, 283–84). Cather obviously feels both horror at and sympathy for her character and allows her readers to enter his melancholy world and even root for him as he escapes Pittsburgh (Lee 1989, 77).

From these more sweeping views of the story, we come to those scholars who focus on some more particular aspect of it. Many at least comment on Paul's homosexuality, whether they see it as latent or not. Larry Rubin and Claude Summers, however, concentrate exclusively on that element in the story. In Rubin's opinion, Cather's avoidance of a direct discussion of Paul's sexual nature is not surprising because the story was published during the heyday of Victorian repressiveness. Despite the absence of an explicit declaration of Paul's homosexuality, however, Cather provides plenty of clues in that direction: the description of his physical appearance consistently suggests a departure from the Victorian sexual norm; his fastidiousness suggests excessive femininity; he has exclusively male friendships; the tense parting from the Yale boy in New York, which Cather never explains, are all innuendo directed at the reader, as is the fact that Paul is apparently haunted by an unnamed fear. Finally, in another broad hint, Cather tells the reader that Paul is afraid that his father would someday wish that he had killed his son, the implication being that Paul had so disgraced him that such a wish on the part of the father is at least plausible (Rubin 1975, 127–31). To these clues, Summers adds the story's title, for at the time homosexuality was often discussed in medical or legal terms. Cather's very word choices, although they do not allude specifically to homosexuality, are certainly suggestive of it: words such as "*gay,* . . . *fairy, faggot, fagged, queen, loitering, tormented, unnatural, haunted, different, perverted, secret love,* and so on create a verbal ambience that subtly but persistently calls attention to the issue" (Summers 1990, 109). At the same time, however, Summers argues against the notion that Paul is simply the homosexual victim of a repressive society. Although it is true that society in this story is far from blameless, so is Paul. His lack of imagination exacerbates his failure to make his homosexuality part of his real life, and Cather intimates that this lack is partly due to his very aestheticism, which, in its rejection of society, succeeds in alienating him even further from society than his homosexuality does. What Paul needs is the ability to characterize his situation, including his relationship with his father, accurately—to take it seriously instead of trying to escape into art or entertainment. He would then be able to see that neither his father nor his neighborhood is as hideous as he envisions them (Summers 1990, 112–14). Summers goes on to say that in depicting the drabness of American middle-class life, Cather makes aestheticism attractive, but she also criticizes it as being unrealistic and naive in its absolute rejection of ordinary life. Middle-class American life may be dull, but the life of aestheticism is inflexible in its rejection of ordinary people. More important, Cather "implies that the solution to the homosexual dilemma in an unaccepting society lies in integration rather than separation and in self-acceptance rather than self-hatred" (Summers 1990, 117).

Briggs presents a reading of "Paul's Case" that shows how the story fits into the author's habit of creating a small, protected space that provides a panoramic view of the world. Cather herself had inhabited a small attic room in Red Cloud that looked out on a larger world. In her fiction she often provides similar spaces for her characters, havens where they can seek solace from the world outside. The room Paul creates is one such place. Unfortunately, the well-ordered and beautiful sanctuary Paul creates at the Waldorf cannot endure because it is built on theft and fantasy, not on truth (1990, 159–63).

Works Cited

Arnold, Marilyn. 1984. *Willa Cather's Short Fiction*. Athens: Ohio University Press.

Bloom, Edward A., and Lillian D. Bloom. 1962. *Willa Cather's Gift of Sympathy*. Carbondale: Southern Illinois University Press.

Briggs, Cynthia. 1990. "Insulated Isolation: WC's Room with a View." In *Cather Studies*, vol. 1. Ed. Susan Rosowski. Lincoln: University of Nebraska Press, 159–71.

Brown, E. K. Completed by Leon Edel. [1953] 1964. *Willa Cather: A Critical Biography*. New York: Knopf.

Carpenter, David A. 1987. "Why Willa Cather Revised 'Paul's Case': The Work in Art and Those Sunday Afternoons." *American Literature* 59:590–608.

Cather, Willa. 1956. "Paul's Case." In *Five Stories*. New York: Vintage Books, 149–74.

———. 1961. "Paul's Case." In *The Troll Garden*. New York: Signet Classics, 117–38.

———. [1965] 1970. "Paul's Case." In *Willa Cather's Collected Short Fiction, 1892–1912*. Ed. Virginia Faulkner. Lincoln: University of Nebraska Press, 243–61.

———. 1983. "Paul's Case." In *The Troll Garden*. Ed. James Woodress. Lincoln: University of Nebraska Press, 102–121.

———. 1987. "Paul's Case." In *Cather: Early Novels and Stories*. New York: Literary Classics of the United States, 111–31.

———. 1992. "Paul's Case." In *Cather: Stories, Poems, and Other Writings*. New York: Literary Classics of the United States, 468–88.

Faulkner, Virginia, ed. [1965] 1970. *Willa Cather's Collected Short Fiction, 1892–1912*. Lincoln: University of Nebraska Press. Reprint. Lincoln: University of Nebraska Press.

Lee, Hermione. 1989. *Willa Cather: Double Lives*. New York: Pantheon.

Murphy, John J. 1979. "'Lucy's Case': An Interpretation of *Lucy Gayheart*." *Markham Review* 9:26–29.

O'Brien, Sharon. 1987. *Willa Cather: The Emerging Voice*. New York: Oxford University Press.

Pers, Mona. 1975. *Willa Cather's Children*. Uppsala, Sweden: Almqvist & Wiksell International.

Petry, Alice Hall. 1986. "Harvey's Case: Notes on Cather's 'The Sculptor's Funeral.'" *South Dakota Review* 24: 108–11.

Review of *The Troll Garden*, by Willa Cather. 1905. *Bookman* 21:456–57.

Rosowski, Susan J. 1986. *The Voyage Perilous: Willa Cather's Romanticism*. Lincoln: University of Nebraska Press.

Rubin, Larry. 1975. "The Homosexual Motif in 'Paul's Case.'" *Studies in Short Fiction* 12:127–31.

Summers, Claude J. 1990. "'A Losing Game in the End': Aestheticism and Homosexuality in Cather's 'Paul's Case.'" *Modern Fiction Studies* 36:103–119.

Thurin, Erik Ingvar. 1990. *The Humanization of Willa Cather: Classicism in an American Classic*. Lund, Sweden: Lund University Press.

Van Ghent, Dorothy. 1985. "Willa Cather." In *Willa Cather*. Ed. Harold Bloom. Garden City, NY: Chelsea House, 71–85.

Wasserman, Loretta. 1990. "Is Cather's Paul a Case?" *Modern Fiction Studies* 36:121–29.

———. 1991. *Willa Cather: A Study of the Short Fiction*. Boston: Twayne.

Weigel, John A. 1958. "What Kind of Psychology for Students of Literature?" *CEA Critic* 20:1, 5.

Williams, Orlo. 1920. "Paul's Case." *Athenaeum*, 31 December, 890.

Woodress, James. 1970. *Willa Cather: Her Life and Art*. New York: Pegasus.

———. 1983. Introduction to *The Troll Garden*. Ed. James Woodress. Lincoln: University of Nebraska Press.

———. 1987. *Willa Cather: A Literary Life*. Lincoln: University of Nebraska Press.

Peter

Publication History

This story was first published on May 21, 1892, in a Boston weekly literary magazine called *The Mahogany Tree* (323–24) under the name Willa Cather (Faulkner 1970, 590). One of the founders of this magazine was Herbert Bates, a Harvard graduate who was also Cather's English instructor at the University of Nebraska (Kraus 1952, 493). The story, Cather's first published fiction, was slightly revised by Professor Bates and sent to the magazine without her knowledge (Bennett 1970, xxvii). On November 24, 1892, a slightly different version of the story was published in a University of Nebraska student journal, the *Hesperian* (22:10–12) with no attribution (Faulkner 1970, 590).

The story was reprinted with additional revisions under the title "Peter Sadelack, Father of Anton" on July 21, 1900, in the *Library* (1:5), where it was signed Willa Sibert Cather (Faulkner 1970, 590; Lathrop 1975, 5). In this version, Cather omitted the *thee*s and *thou*s she had used to suggest the speech patterns of her Czech characters, intensified the conflict between Peter and his son, and rewrote the opening (Woodress 1987, 77).

In 1950, the *Hesperian* version was included in *Willa Cather's Campus Years* (46–53), edited by James R. Shively and published by the University of Nebraska Press (Faulkner 1970, 590). The *Library* and *Hesperian* versions were reprinted in 1957 by Dodd, Mead in *Early Stories*, and the *Mahogany Tree* version in 1965 by the University of Nebraska Press in *Willa Cather's Collected Short Fiction, 1892–1912*. That version was again reprinted in 1992 by Literary Classics of the United States in *Cather: Stories, Poems, and Other Writings*, a volume in the Library of America series.

Circumstances of Composition, Sources, and Influences

Written soon after Cather entered the University of Nebraska, this story was sent off for publication by one of her professors, Herbert Bates. In later years Cather came to regret that she had been hurried into publishing by Professor Bates because it had delayed her shedding what she felt were bad writing habits; she later warned young writers not to publish too early. In spite of such regrets, however, Cather reveled in the degree of recognition that her writing brought her in Lincoln (Robinson 1983, 45). In E. K. Brown's opinion, Professor Bates's interest in Cather's work, even if it was "somewhat uncritical," was more a help than a hindrance (1964, 57).

According to O'Brien, at the time Cather wrote this story, she was preoccupied with characters who were overwhelmed and utterly defeated by forces beyond their control (1987, 207). Cather had moved with her family from Virginia to Webster County, Nebraska, at the age of nine. They settled on the Divide—the plateau between the Republican and Little Blue Rivers (Bennett 1970, xiv). Although later in her life she developed real affection for the area, the first strong impression Cather had of the prairie was that it was a harsh, crushing, even life-denying place to be. The memories of this side of prairie life were especially strong during the 1890s, a time of droughts, crop failures, and economic depression (O'Brien 1987, 207).

As she became acquainted with her many immigrant neighbors, she heard the various stories of their homelands and of their lives on the Divide. One of the first of these stories was about a Mr. Francis Sadilek, who had committed suicide in Webster County two years before the Cather family moved there (Bohlke 1974, 135). The account of the suicide given by Mr. Sadilek's daughter, Annie Pavelka (who later became the model for Ántonia Shimerda in Cather's *My Ántonia*), differs somewhat from Cather's fictionalized version of it in "Peter": there is no suggestion that the real Mr. Sadilek was inordinately fond of alcohol, nor is there any suggestion of a conflict with his son. Also, although Cather makes Peter's motivation for killing himself perfectly clear, his daughter's account gives little hint of why the real Mr. Sadilek committed suicide (Baker 1990–91, 40–41). Bennett reports that Cather was so affected by the story that she said later she would have to write about that if she wrote about anything (Bennett 1982, 40).

Relationship to Other Cather Works

Cather reuses the character of Peter in a slightly revised version of the 1892 story called "Peter Sadelack, Father of Anton" (1900) (Bennett 1982, 39). As Bennett reports, the 1892 story, entitled simply "Peter," portrays the title character as a dissolute, worn-out character, whose strained relationship with his son creates the tension in the story. The son, Antone, cares only about profit and forces his father to work on Sunday in freezing weather instead of allowing him to go to church. The central conflict in the story arises from the son's intention to sell his father's violin, the embodiment of the old man's dreams and ambitions. The son cares nothing for his father's artistic temperament and is concerned only with eking a profit out of the resistant prairie land. When his father destroys his own violin and then kills himself—despite his awareness that his son will not pay for a funeral mass—Antone sells the bow in town before the funeral is conducted. Further, the old man has to be buried in a packing box instead of a coffin because his body was frozen in a bent-over position. The second version of the story is essentially the same as the first, except for the deletion of references to the cold and to cutting wood on Sunday (Bennett 1982, 39–40).

Nearly twenty years after the publication of "Peter Sadelack, Father of Anton," Cather reworked the same suicide incident in *My Ántonia*, where it becomes the account of Mr. Shimerda's death. A comparison of the two incidents reveals how much Cather's attitude toward the prairie had changed over the intervening twenty years (Bradford 1955, 541). Ántonia's father is neither a drunkard nor a sluggard. Instead he is portrayed as a sensitive man who has become aged prematurely and is unequal to a harsh, disordered life (Bennett 1982, 40). He is fastidious about his personal appearance—even his suicide is neat: "He layed down on that bunk-bed, close to the ox stall, where he always slept. When we found him, everything was decent . . . except what he couldn't nowise foresee. His coat was hung on a peg, and his boots was under the bed. He'd took off that silk neckcloth he always wore, and folded it smooth and stuck his pin through it. He turned back his shirt at the neck and rolled up his sleeves. . . . He layed over on his side and put the end of the barrel in his mouth, then he drew up one foot and felt for the trigger" (Cather 1987, 776). To Bradford, this account suggests a much more sympathetic attitude on Cather's part than does the earlier one. In addition, in the *My Ántonia* version of the story, even the son—whose name has become Ambrosch—is treated fairly kindly. This son, Ambrosch, pays for funeral masses for his father (1955, 541).

The themes presented in this story are reiterated in many of Cather's later works: sensitive old people who cannot adjust to life on the prairie occur repeatedly in both her short stories and novels, as does the conflict between ways of life in the Old and New Worlds, and the tension between the old and the young (Daiches 1962, 4). The conflict over values seen first in this story reappears in much of Cather's fiction: the level-headed, "practical businessman farmer" reappears as Nat Wheeler in *One of Ours* and, in a thoroughly negative version, as Ivy Peters in *A Lost Lady*; the confrontation of the materialistic and the sensitive reappears in *The Professor's House* (Woodress 1987, 77–78).

Interpretations and Criticism

Few critics have commented at length on "Peter," the assumption being that it is important only as an example from Cather's apprenticeship period that can be used to analyze her early style and themes and compare them with her later, mature handling of them.

One of the themes Cather became well known for—the transcendent power of art—has its first appearance here. In the last paragraph of the story, Antone takes his father's fiddlebow to town in order "to exchange the instrument of music and art for money. And yet, if the bow is sold, it will no doubt 'live on' to help some violinist create music once again" (Baker 1990–91, 41). Ultimately art, not materialism, is victorious.

In addition to its usefulness to the study of Cather's development as a writer, O'Brien sees "Peter" as one of Cather's attempts at social realism, an interest that contrasts with the other stories and essays Cather wrote during her college years, which show her reverence for both romance and force (O'Brien 1987, 207). The undergraduate Cather was more interested in the power of nature to overwhelm and ultimately destroy than she was in the awe that nature could inspire. Robinson feels the story is a striking example of Cather at her most bitterly ironic (1983, 46).

One of the themes explored in "Peter" is the conflict between the values of "Presbyteria" and those of "Bohemia" (O'Brien 1987, 225). Cather did not explicitly articulate this conflict until the late 1890s when she was living in Pittsburgh editing the new women's magazine *Home Monthly*. In one of the journalistic pieces she sent back to the Lincoln *Journal*, Cather, as quoted in O'Brien, describes Pittsburgh as "divided into two parts. Presbyteria and Bohemia, and the former is the larger and the more influential kingdom of the two" (1987, 225). "Presbyteria" and "Bohemia" were the terms Cather used to signify the two sides of the conflict. Presbyteria was "the fusion of religious and commercial values that ruled the city, the mutually reinforcing Protestant ethic and spirit of capitalism that denigrated emotion and art" (O'Brien 1987, 225). Bohemia was simply the opposite of Presbyteria; it included "art and artists who worshipped truth and beauty with aesthetic and emotional fervor rather than mercantile piety [and] opposed conventional values and bourgeois morality. . ." (O'Brien 1987, 225). "Peter" illustrates just such a conflict, with the title character representing the artistic values that are eventually crushed by the marketplace values of greed and profit.

Works Cited

Bennett, Mildred R. [1965] 1970. Introduction to *Willa Cather: Collected Short Fiction, 1892–1912*, by Willa Cather. Ed. Virginia Faulkner. Lincoln: University of Nebraska Press.

———. 1982. "Willa Cather's Bodies for Ghosts." *Western American Literature* 17:39–52. Reprint. Lincoln: University of Nebraska Press.

Baker, Bruce P. 1990–91. "Willa Cather's 'Peter': From Anecdote to Narrative." *Willa Cather Pioneer Memorial Newsletter* 34:40–41.

Bohlke, L. Brent. 1974. "Beginnings: Willa Cather and 'The Clemency of the Court.'" *Prairie Schooner* 48:133–44.

Bradford, Curtis. 1955. "Willa Cather's Uncollected Short Stories." *American Literature* 26:537–51.

Brown, E. K. [1953] 1964. *Willa Cather: A Critical Biography*. New York: Knopf.

Cather, Willa. 1957. "Peter." In *Early Stories*. Ed. Mildred Bennett. New York: Dodd, Mead, 1–8.

———. [1965] 1970. "Peter." In *Willa Cather's Collected Short Fiction, 1892–1912*. Ed. Virginia Faulkner. Lincoln: University of Nebraska Press, 541–43.

———. 1987. *My Ántonia*. In *Cather: Early Novels and Stories*. New York: Literary Classics of the United States, 707–937.

———. 1992. "Peter." In *Cather: Stories, Poems, and Other Writings*. New York: Literary Classics of the United States, 5–7.

Daiches, David. [1951] 1962. *Willa Cather: A Critical Introduction*. Ithaca, NY: Cornell University Press; London: Oxford University Press. Reprint. New York: Collier.

Faulkner, Virginia, ed. [1965] 1970. *Willa Cather's Collected Short Fiction, 1892–1912*. Lincoln: University of Nebraska Press. Reprint. Lincoln: University of Nebraska Press.

Kraus, Joe W. 1952. "Willa Cather's First Published Story." *American Literature* 23:493–94.

Lathrop, Joanna. 1975. *Willa Cather: A Checklist of Her Published Writing*. Lincoln: University of Nebraska Press.

O'Brien, Sharon. 1987. *Willa Cather: The Emerging Voice*. New York: Oxford University Press.

Robinson, Phyllis C. 1983. *Willa: The Life of Willa Cather*. Garden City, NY: Doubleday.

Woodress, James. 1987. *Willa Cather: A Literary Life*. Lincoln: University of Nebraska Press.

The Princess Baladina—Her Adventure

Publication History

This story was first published under the pseudonym Charles Douglass in the August 1896 issue of *Home Monthly* (6:20–21) along with "Tommy, the Unsentimental." The latter story, however, appeared under Cather's own name (Faulkner 1970, 591). "Princess Baladina" has been reprinted only once, by the University of Nebraska Press in *Willa Cather's Collected Short Fiction, 1892–1912* in 1965.

Circumstances of Composition, Sources, and Influences

This story appeared in the August 1896 issue of *Home Monthly*, an issue Cather was forced to put together by herself after the editor, Charles Axtell, left on vacation; thus, it is safe to say that Cather was desperate for material simply to fill pages (Woodress 1970, 81–82). (See the "Publication History" section for the chapter "Tommy, the Unsentimental.")

The pseudonym Charles Douglass combines the names of Cather's father (Charles) and her brother Douglass (Arnold 1984, 32n). According to Woodress, Cather often invented fairy tales similar to this one to entertain her brothers and sisters at home (Woodress 1970, 82). Bennett speculates that Cather may have written—or at least told—the story before she moved to Pittsburgh (Bennett 1970, xxviii).

Relationship to Other Cather Works

This story is similar to the other children's story Cather wrote while she was on the staff of *Home Monthly* in Pittsburgh, "The Strategy of the Were-Wolf Dog." It proves that she could throw herself into the sort of "home-and-fire-side" material she claimed to disdain (O'Brien 1987, 230).

Interpretations and Criticisms

Most Cather specialists do not mention this story at all, and those who do generally agree with Woodress that it is simply magazine filler that can be safely ignored (Woodress 1970, 81–82). Bennett does not discuss the story, but does assert that it has "charm and humor" (Bennett 1970, xxviii).

O'Brien argues that the story is of at least slight importance in that it reveals one of Cather's own conflicts: in both her *Home Monthly* children's stories, "Cather undermines the protagonists' urge for escape" by having them face the unpleasant reality that the world away from home is not as exciting as they thought; it is, in fact, worse in many ways than life at home (1987, 230). Although the "return of a wandering child is a formula in children's fiction . . . Cather's continued use of the pattern suggests" her own mixed feelings about moving to Pittsburgh (O'Brien 1987, 231).

Works Cited

Arnold, Marilyn. 1984. *Willa Cather's Short Fiction*. Athens: Ohio University Press.

Bennett, Mildred R. [1965] 1970. Introduction to *Willa Cather's Collected Short Fiction*. Ed. Virginia Faulkner. Lincoln: University of Nebraska Press. Reprint. Lincoln: University of Nebraska Press.

Cather, Willa. [1965] 1970. "The Princess Baladina—Her Adventure." In *Willa Cather's Collected Short Fiction, 1892–1912*. Ed. Virginia Faulkner. Lincoln: University of Nebraska Press, 567–72.

Faulkner, Virginia, ed. [1965] 1970. *Willa Cather's Collected Short Fiction, 1892–1912*. Lincoln: University of Nebraska Press. Reprint. Lincoln: University of Nebraska Press.

O'Brien, Sharon. 1987. *Willa Cather: The Emerging Voice*. New York: Oxford University Press.

Woodress, James. 1970. *Willa Cather: Her Life and Art*. New York: Pegasus.

The Prodigies

Publication History

This story was first published in the July 1897 issue of *Home Monthly* (6:9–11) under the name Willa Cather; on July 10 and 17 of that same month it was reprinted in two parts by the Lincoln *Courier* (12:4–5; 8–9), the first of Cather's stories to be published by the *Courier* (Faulkner 1970, 592). It was reprinted in 1957 by Dodd, Mead in *Early Stories*, and in 1965 by the University of Nebraska Press in *Willa Cather's Collected Short Fiction, 1892–1912*.

Circumstances of Composition, Sources, and Influences

Written while Cather was on the staff of *Home Monthly* magazine in Pittsburgh, this story is one of the first to feature a fascination with art (Woodress 1983, xii). In some ways the piece may be said to be an imitation of Henry James, not only because its subject is art, but also because it contains a "devouring woman" very similar to those so often found in James's work; the story's ending is very like that of James's "The Story of a Year" (Bennett 1957, 169, 185).

Bennett identifies several ways in which the story reflects Cather's own beliefs and mirrors actual events in her life. Like Harriet in the story, Cather felt that for youth, all was possible: she was at this point trying desperately to put off growing older—even altering her birth date three times to gain another year of youth. The narrator's description of Mackenzie as unromantic but of strong character—and her assertion that such a man is the safest kind to marry—may have a connection to 1897 letter Cather wrote to a friend about a young doctor who was evidently interested in marrying her. In the same letter, she also insisted that the fact that she had no intense feelings about him was not important, though it is not clear whether or not she ever seriously considered accepting a proposal (Bennett 1957, 171–72).

Perhaps the most obvious of Cather's convictions is the idea expressed in the narrator's assertion that Mrs. Mackenzie "knew well enough that if the cruelly exacting life of art is not wholly denied a woman, it is offered to her at a terrible price" (Cather 1970, 413). Cather repeated this belief often, and, according to Bennett, it was a conviction that prevented her from seeing how much happiness she in fact possessed (Bennett 1957, 172).

Arnold, on the other hand, maintains that the story reflects a different Cather sentiment—that the price art exacts is excessive, and that to choose art is to reject human society (Arnold 1984, 15). Arnold finds that several of Cather's newspaper articles written in the mid-1890s support this view. In an 1895 *Courier* column, Cather reports that she has been delighted by the performances of the ten- and twelve-year-old Dovey sisters (the likely sources for the children in "The Prodigies") (Arnold 1984, 32n). In a column about pianist Josef Hofmann written a short time later, however, Cather clarifies her position. She declares that it is Hofmann's great fortune that he has ceased to be a prodigy. She says, as quoted in Arnold, "As long as he was a prodigy he could never be an artist, indeed not a musician even. There have been certain great men . . . who have been able to live down the fact that they were once prodigies, but they had to be great indeed to do it"; Cather felt that child performers were somehow unnatural (Arnold 1984, 32–33n).

Relationship to Other Cather Works

Woodress places this story with "The Count of Crow's Nest" and "Nanette: An Aside," both written during the same period, as the first indications of Cather's preoccupation with art as a subject for fiction. As such, the stories foreshadow the central themes of *The Troll Garden*, Cather's first collection of short fiction (Woodress 1983, xii). O'Brien groups "The Prodigies" with "A Resurrection" and "Nanette: An Aside" in that all three are early examples of her turn from male protagonists to ever more complex female protagonists (1987, 231). The story also shares with "A Resurrection" the "bad mother/good mother opposition" that was an obvious interest of Cather's (O'Brien 1987, 231). The unhappy marriage in the story also serves as a link to other Cather works. It is just one of many such marriages Cather would eventually portray (Woodress 1987, 122).

Bennett connects Mr. Mackenzie to Victoria Templeton of "Old Mrs. Harris" by noting the "harmless perversity" the former displays by not answering his wife when, early in the story, she asks if the carriage had arrived, knowing full well that it had. This same perversity—by this time truly vicious—is seen in Myra of *My Mortal Enemy* (1957, 170).

Interpretations and Criticisms

Cather scholars have made very few interpretive comments about this story, most having confined themselves to the sources of the plot itself. Arnold suggests that what is the most pathetic about the story is that the two young children have been used to indulge their mother's vanity, yet the inclusion of the devouring, destructive mother also allows Cather to use the contrasts and juxtapositions that became the hallmark of her work. She places in the story two other children, whose mother envies the exploited children's success. Harriet Mackenzie apparently wishes she had the chance to destroy her children in the same way Kate Massey is destroying hers. Fortunately, Harriet's children are completely devoid of talent (1984, 16).

Works Cited

Arnold, Marilyn. 1984. *Willa Cather's Short Fiction*. Athens: Ohio University Press.

Bennett, Mildred, ed. 1957. *Early Stories of Willa Cather*. New York: Dodd, Mead.

Cather, Willa. 1957. "The Prodigies." In *Early Stories*. Ed. Mildred Bennett. New York: Dodd, Mead, 25–32.

———. [1965] 1970. "The Prodigies." In *Willa Cather's Collected Short Fiction, 1892–1912*. Ed. Virginia Faulkner. Lincoln: University of Nebraska Press, 411–23.

Faulkner, Virginia, ed. [1965] 1970. *Willa Cather's Collected Short Fiction, 1892–1912*. Lincoln: University of Nebraska Press. Reprint. Lincoln: University of Nebraska Press.

O'Brien, Sharon. 1987. *Willa Cather: The Emerging Voice*. New York: Oxford University Press.

Woodress, James. 1983. Introduction to *The Troll Garden*. Ed. James Woodress. Lincoln: University of Nebraska Press.

———. 1987. *Willa Cather: A Literary Life*. Lincoln: University of Nebraska Press.

The Professor's Commencement

Publication History

This story was first published in the June 1902 issue of *New England* magazine, n.s. (26:481–88) under the name Sibert Cather (Faulkner 1970, 593). It was reprinted in 1965 by the University of Nebraska Press in *Willa Cather's Collected Short Fiction, 1892–1912*.

Circumstances of Composition, Sources, and Influences

Cather wrote this story while she was teaching at Pittsburgh's Central High School, a position she occupied from 1901 to 1903; she then moved to Allegheny High School, where she remained until 1906. The high school described in "The Professor's Commencement" is clearly Central High (Slote 1970, 11). According to Woodress, the school itself was a depressing place, very close to Union Station. Its whole impression was one of grayness, dirt, and ugliness, which was aggravated by the noise and smoke from the trains. Cather's classroom was at the top of three dingy flights of stairs. The real school is thus nearly identical to the observations that the story's narrator makes about the fictional place (1987, 152).

Relationship to Other Cather Works

Professor Emerson Graves, Cather's first portrait of a teacher, anticipates the characters of Lucius Wilson (*Alexander's Bridge*), Gaston Cleric (*My Ántonia*), and Godfrey St. Peter (*The Professor's House*) (Bradford 1955, 546). Arnold notes that Emerson Graves, like Godfrey St. Peter after him, wonders what he has done of value in a life of teaching, and only one of his many students comes to mind. For St. Peter that student is Tom Outland; Professor Graves feels certain that his students will succumb to the crass materialism that infects America. Tom Outland would probably have shared the same fate, "but Cather rushes him off to war where, like Claude Wheeler in *One of Ours*, he is killed before the brightness of his youth can be tarnished" (Arnold 1984, 42).

Slote establishes further connections between this story and other Cather works by pointing out that by characterizing the students in this story as "practical, provident, unimaginative, and mercenary at sixteen" (Cather 1970, 287), the author is describing "what might be the people of 'The Sculptor's Funeral' in their youth" (1970, 11).

Gerber draws thematic parallels between "The Professor's Commencement" and *Sapphira and the Slave Girl*, a novel Cather published forty years later. In both, Cather was concerned with heroic figures who value principle more than self, society more than family (1975, 132).

Because it contains one of the many Cather characters who believe that youth is the only truly wonderful time of life, this story may be grouped with "The Treasure of Far Island," "The Joy of Nelly Deane," "Uncle Valentine," "Double Birthday," "Two Friends," "The Old Beauty," and "The Best Years" (Arnold 1984, 40–41).

Interpretations and Criticisms

Many critics agree that Cather's main theme in this story is the human duty to appreciate beauty and the ways in which industrial society interferes with that calling. Professor Graves is one of Cather's heroes because he triumphs in spirit rather than in action. He is superior to his colleagues in that they appear to be interested only in the literal level of things, whereas Graves is interested in their spirit and beauty. This difference is symbolized by Graves's inability to recite the passage from Macaulay. The literal holds little attraction for him (Thurin 1990, 113).

O'Brien disagrees with this explanation of Graves's failure of memory, interpreting it instead as a sign of "a loss of energy [that] may owe something to the professor's somewhat servile approach to the classics: he regards them as texts to be memorized," and it is this worshipful attitude that prevents him from speaking anything but memorized text (1987, 268). O'Brien does agree with Thurin, however, on the subject of the worship of beauty: Graves fights materialism by championing art and literature (1987, 264). Gerber sees Professor Graves as "an early-day ecologist" and describes him as a sort of Horatius who holds the bridge in the battle to defend culture while waiting for a new generation to take up the struggle (1975, 96).

Hall suggests that the story is framed by "sex, art, and betrayal" (1988, 144). Graves is closely associated with his library, which holds the great love of his life—his books—and in comparing that room to both a boudoir and an artist's studio, Cather hints that this love is almost sexual. Later, we see the professor *caressing* a book. His devotion to literature, then, is almost unnatural, and his eventual collapse indicates Cather's disapproval of such adoration (Hall 1988, 144–45).

Thurin discusses the significance of Cather's surrounding the character of Professor Graves with classical allusions: he thinks of the high school where he teaches as "a Pharos" (Cather 1970, 286); as a college student he took the pledge of Tennyson's "Ulysses"; Cather creates an analogy between him and Horatius Cocles of Macaulay's lay. Finally, the several references to the Trojan wars animate the story: age and weakness are described with a reference to Priam, and the beauty that gives life meaning . . . to Helen (1990, 114).

Cather's characterization of Professor Graves as somewhat effeminate is also significant. According to Thurin, his delicate hands, his sister's masculine manner, and his admission that he has a woman's heart all underscore his female nature. Although on the one hand he is portrayed throughout the story as having a "martial spirit," on the other, he is represented as never having been truly virile. He is precisely a blend of the martial and the effeminate and as such indicates that Cather at that time had no objection to androgyny in men who appreciate beauty (1990, 115). Here, as elsewhere, Cather separates the love of beauty from heterosexual love. But in Thurin's view "Cather comes dangerously close to celebrating devitalization and emasculation in elaborating these themes" (Thurin 1990, 115).

Works Cited

Arnold, Marilyn. 1984. *Willa Cather's Short Fiction*. Athens: Ohio University Press.

Bradford, Curtis. 1955. "Willa Cather's Uncollected Short Stories." *American Literature* 26:537–51.

Cather, Willa. [1965] 1970. "The Professor's Commencement." In *Willa Cather's Collected Short Fiction, 1892–1912*. Ed. Virginia Faulkner. Lincoln: University of Nebraska Press, 283–91.

Faulkner, Virginia, ed. [1965] 1970. *Willa Cather's Collected Short Fiction, 1892–1912*. Lincoln: University of Nebraska Press. Reprint. Lincoln: University of Nebraska Press.

Gerber, Philip. 1975. *Willa Cather*. Boston: Twayne.

Hall, Joan Wylie. 1988. "Treacherous Texts: The Perils of Allusion in Cather's Early Stories." *Colby Library Quarterly* 24:142–50.

O'Brien, Sharon. 1987. *Willa Cather: The Emerging Voice*. New York: Oxford University Press.

Slote, Bernice. 1970. "Willa Cather as a Regional Writer." *Kansas Quarterly* 2:7–15.

Thurin, Erik Ingvar. 1990. *The Humanization of Willa Cather: Classicism in an American Classic*. Lund, Sweden: Lund University Press.

Woodress, James. 1987. *Willa Cather: A Literary Life*. Lincoln: University of Nebraska Press.

The Profile

Publication History

This story was first published under the name Willa Sibert Cather in the June 1, 1907, issue of *McClure's* (29:135–40); it was reprinted in 1965 by the University of Nebraska Press in *Willa Cather's Collected Short Fiction, 1892–1912*.

Circumstances of Composition, Sources, and Influences

This story was the second one published in *McClure's* magazine after Cather had moved to New York City from Pittsburgh and taken a position on the magazine's staff (Arnold 1984, 69). Although the date of composition is not certain, Cather probably wrote the story in 1904, since it was under consideration for inclusion in *The Troll Garden* (1905).

Madigan explains that one obvious source for the story was an incident that occurred in 1902 while Cather and her friend Isabelle McClung were traveling in Europe with Dorothy Canfield, who at that time was doing doctoral work at the Sorbonne. Cather's friendship with Canfield had begun at the University of Nebraska, where they once collaborated on a story that was subsequently published by the university's literary magazine. (See the "Circumstances of Composition, Sources, and Influences" section for the chapter "'The Fear That Walks by Noonday.'") While they were in Paris, Cather was introduced to one of Canfield's friends, a fellow graduate student named Evelyn Osborne, who dressed lavishly and had a conspicuous scar on her face. Two years later, in December 1904, Canfield read "The Profile" for the first time and was convinced that the central character was a thinly disguised version of her friend Evelyn. Canfield then wrote to Cather, begging her not to publish the story; she was convinced it would destroy Evelyn's already limited self-esteem. Cather's response was that the story would be included as planned in her first collection, *The Troll Garden*, because the volume would be too slight without it. The dispute over the story then moved to S. S. McClure's office in New York. There, in a strained meeting, Cather and Canfield argued in the presence of McClure's editors, Cather insisting the story be published despite the suggestion that seeing the story in print might push Osborne to suicide. In the end, the story was withdrawn from *The Troll*

Garden. However, the rift between the two old friends lasted for some sixteen years, until 1921, when Cather wrote to Canfield, apologizing and urging a reconciliation (Madigan 1990, 116–23).

O'Brien suggests that another possible source was Cather's own mother, Virginia. Besides the shared first names, Virginia Cather and Virginia Gilbert have similar characteristics: each is strong-willed, interested in clothes, and concerned with her appearance. Another similarity may be the mother's disappointment with a daughter who is not as pretty as she had hoped (1987, 50). Virginia Gilbert is by no means an exact duplicate of Cather's mother, however. Cather simply draws on the "psychological and emotional dynamics of the mother–daughter relationship . . ." (O'Brien 1987, 58n).

The strong influence of Nathaniel Hawthorne is suggested by the similarities between this story and Hawthorne's "The Birthmark." Like Hawthorne, Cather uses a physical defect to signify "a hidden psychological or emotional reality" (O'Brien 1987, 50). In fact, the two stories are so similar that Witter Bynner, who was on the staff of *McClure's* when the story was published, recalled the title of Cather's story as "The Birthmark" years later (Woodress 1987, 191).

Relationship to Other Cather Works

This story is one of many that reveal Cather's aversion to and fear of any physical defect. Bennett argues that Cather was obsessed by a fear of mutilation. Some form of disfigurement is included in many of her stories and novels, among them "The Bohemian Girl," in which Eric rips his hand open on a cornsheller; "The Namesake," where Lyon loses his arm in battle; and "Behind the Singer Tower," where an opera singer's hand is severed cleanly at the wrist. Even in Cather's very early works, images of mutilation abound: in "The Clemency of the Court" (1893), Serge is bound by his arms until they are no longer of any use to him, and, in *Sapphira and the Slave Girl*, Aunt Jezebel names a little black child's hand as the only thing she has an appetite for (1970, xxxviii). O'Brien notes that although some sort of mutilation occurs consistently in Cather's fiction, the most dramatic example of that pattern is in *Shadows on the Rock*, where almost all the secondary characters are marked by some deformity (1987, 89).

O'Brien also suggests that "The Profile" may be grouped with the others of the same period ("The Willing Muse," "Eleanor's House," and "The Namesake") in which Cather relies heavily upon Henry James's style and character types. These stories reflect the interests that Cather still shared with James—"the nature of the artist, the mysteries of the creative process, the ambiguous connection between art and life, the conflict between fealty to art and the desire for popular success" (1987, 299).

Interpretations and Criticisms

Rosowski sees "The Profile" as a minor turning point in the way Cather handles one of her common themes. Her tendency had been to present the grotesque as external to human lives, something to be exorcised or suffered. In this story, however, she fuses the beautiful and the ugly, the joyful and the painful, suggesting that love can reconcile the opposites. These ideas would reappear in the novels, most notably in *Death Comes for the Archbishop* (1986, 212).

According to O'Brien, the story may be read on two levels: on one, it is a tale of mother–daughter conflict. On another, the story explores "the relationship between art and life by examining similarity and difference, representation and reality" (1987, 303). O'Brien also sees Dunlap's role as an artist as questionable because, although he seems simply to represent what he sees, his painting of his future wife's profile is subtly misleading. In fact, Dunlap is not an artist at all, but merely a copyist. When his future wife suggests that he paint only her profile, she in effect herself becomes the artist and creates the illusion that Dunlap merely copies (1987, 303). O'Brien concludes that Cather was actually commenting on her own artistic process here: "Because in writing the story Cather had allowed [Henry] James to be the model, through Dunlap she . . . undermines her own process of composition and representation" (1987, 304).

Arnold's reading compares Dunlap with Hawthorne's Aylmer in "The Birthmark." Both characters have a mad fixation on their wives' single blemish. Dunlap is in fact himself to blame for much of what he sees as a sad change in his wife's nature. Because of his grisly fascination with misery, he chooses his wife less in spite of her scar than because of it. He indulges his ego by viewing himself as a kind of all-powerful hero who can transform his wife into a perfect specimen in both their eyes. The truth is that pity may be the only emotion Dunlap can feel. Virginia's leaving him is admirable, then, because it allows her to exist as a person, rather than as a scar to be pitied. Instead of learning from his experience, Dunlap once again enters into a marriage more out of pity than out of love (1984, 70–72).

Thurin sees the opening description of *Circe's Swine* as central to the story's meaning. One "old conservative painter" denounces the painting on the grounds that the human body "as Nature has evolved it, is sanctified by her purpose; in any natural function or attitude decent and comely. But lop away so much as a finger, and you have wounded the creature beyond reparation" (Cather 1970, 125; Thurin 1990, 144). Thurin goes on to argue that Dunlop's embarrassed response comes from the fact that he has been married twice to women with disfiguring scars. Cather continues to refer to the Circe story by mentioning various animals. Dunlap is even compared to "a man who knows that some reptile has housed itself and hatched its young in his cellar, and who never cautiously puts his foot out of his bed without the dread of touching its coils" (Cather 1970, 131; Thurin 1990, 145). When Dunlap finally refers directly to his wife's scar, "she pointed him steadily to the door, her eyes as hard as shell, and bright and small, like the sleepless eyes of reptiles" (Cather 1970, 134). In Thurin's view this mention of reptiles may be seen as a divergence from *Circe's Swine*, since no reptiles are depicted in it, a deviation that suggests Cather has another myth in mind—the story of Keats's "Lamia," in which a bride turns out to be a serpent. The allusion is connected to the monstrousness of both central characters and to each's failure to see the other's true nature (Thurin 1990, 145–46).

Bradford's assessment of the story places the focus and the blame squarely on Dunlap. The story's message, like that of "'A Death in the Desert,'" is that immense talent consumes whoever possesses it and damages those around it: art is dangerous (1955, 544).

In a diametrically opposite reading, Pers suggests that the focus and the blame should be exclusively on Virginia, mostly because of her coldness toward her child. She reads "The Profile" as a Jamesian horror story, where the pivotal figure is the passive child (1975, 37).

Works Cited

Arnold, Marilyn. 1984. *Willa Cather's Short Fiction*. Athens: Ohio University Press.

Bennett, Mildred R. [1965] 1970. Introduction to *Willa Cather's Collected Short Fiction*. Ed. Virginia Faulkner. Lincoln: University of Nebraska Press. Reprint. Lincoln: University of Nebraska Press.

Bradford, Curtis. 1955. "Willa Cather's Uncollected Short Stories." *American Literature* 26:537–51.

Cather, Willa. [1965] 1970. "The Profile." In *Willa Cather's Collected Short Fiction, 1892–1912*. Ed. Virginia Faulkner. Lincoln: University of Nebraska Press, 125–35.

Faulkner, Virginia, ed. [1965] 1970. *Willa Cather's Collected Short Fiction, 1892–1912*. Lincoln: University of Nebraska Press. Reprint. Lincoln: University of Nebraska Press.

Madigan, Mark J. 1990. "Willa Cather and Dorothy Canfield Fisher: Rift, Reconciliation, and *One of Ours*." In *Cather Studies*, vol. 1. Ed. Susan J. Rosowski. Lincoln: University of Nebraska Press, 115–29.

O'Brien, Sharon. 1987. *Willa Cather: The Emerging Voice*. New York: Oxford University Press.

Pers, Mona. 1975. *Willa Cather's Children*. Uppsala, Sweden: Almqvist & Wiksell International.

Rosowski, Susan J. 1986. *The Voyage Perilous: Willa Cather's Romanticism*. Lincoln: University of Nebraska Press.

Thurin, Erik Ingvar. 1990. *The Humanization of Willa Cather: Classicism in an American Classic*. Lund, Sweden: Lund University Press.

Woodress, James. 1987. *Willa Cather: A Literary Life*. Lincoln: University of Nebraska Press.

A Resurrection

Publication History

This story was first published in the April 1897 issue of *Home Monthly* (6:4–8) under the name Willa Cather (Faulkner 1970, 592). It was reprinted in 1957 by Dodd, Mead in *Early Stories*, and in 1965 by the University of Nebraska Press in *Willa Cather's Collected Short Fiction, 1892–1912*.

Circumstances of Composition, Sources, and Influences

By the summer of 1894, Cather had been making her living as a journalist for some months (Robinson 1983, 65). One of her articles was based on a trip she, her brother Roscoe, and her friends Mariel Gere and Grace Broady took to Brownsville, Nebraska, the oldest city in the state, on the occasion of the town's fortieth birthday. The article, which appeared in the *Nebraska State Journal* on August 12, 1894, painted a very grim picture of the town. Despite being the first settlement in the Territory, it faced a bleak future because the Missouri River had silted up, the Union Pacific Railroad had chosen a route through Omaha, and the state had built a new city at Lincoln for a state capital (Woodress 1987, 97). According to Mariel Gere, in fact, Cather was interested only in the town's decay and even posed some of the photographs to make conditions seem grimmer than they were (Bennett 1957, 147). Gere was evidently very uncomfortable about insulting the locals and was especially troubled by one incident, in which Cather had Mariel take a picture of the inside of the town's chapel after Cather had first dragged all the kneeling benches to one end of the sanctuary (Arnold 1984, 31). The piece that resulted from this trip was Cather's first extended feature article (Woodress 1970, 68).

Three years later, Cather reworked the article into "A Resurrection." Far from making amends to the people of Brownsville, who were immensely offended by the first account, the story's appearance in *Home Monthly* only exacerbated the situation (Robinson 1983, 66).

The Brownsville trip had such a strong effect on Cather that she returned to the subject for a third time in "The Hottest Day I Ever Spent," an article published in the *Library* in 1900 (Arnold 1984, 31n). In this version, the intense heat—115° in the shade and 135° in the sun—is the dominant feature. She repeated a good deal of the original material, but created two fictional characters, Japanese and Swedish newspapermen, to enliven the account (Woodress 1987, 97–98).

Bennett believes Miss Margie's intense love for the child Bobbie is probably based on Cather's own love for her youngest brother, Jack. The story was published after Cather had moved to Pittsburgh and was intensely homesick for her little brother (Bennett 1957, 153).

Relationship to Other Cather Works

Arnold notes that this piece is one of many in which Cather contrasts a strong woman and a weak man (1984, 10). Bennett locates it within the rather large category of Cather stories and novels in which a character dies by drowning, as Martin Dempster's wife does in this story: Lou in "Lou, the Prophet"; Serge's mother in "The Clemency of the Court"; Eric Hermannson's father in "Eric Hermannson's Soul"; Ned and Shorty in "The Treasure of Far Island"; Cressida Garnet in "The Diamond Mine"; the queen's paramours in "Coming, Aphrodite!"; the tramp in *The Song of the Lark*; and Sebastian, Mockford, and Lucy in *Lucy Gayheart* all drown (Bennett 1982, 51).

Slote views the disintegrating town of Brownsville in this story as a precursor of the decaying Western town in *A Lost Lady* (1970, 12). Bennett identifies several descriptions of the countryside in this story that reappear in Cather's later works. The smell of burning grass in the spring, for example, is mentioned in *My Ántonia*; wagon trains heading to Cherry Creek are referred to in *Death Comes for the Archbishop*; and the Indian's wish to be buried high on a bluff in a sitting position so he can watch the river steamers below him recalls the place of Myra Henshawe's death in *My Mortal Enemy* (1957, 153–55).

Cather portrays the "river rats" as people who move in and deface the land by cutting down the stately oak trees for firewood and who ruin the terraces by planting potatoes. The description is reminiscent of other scenes depicting the despoiling of nature: Lucy Gayheart suffers when an orchard is to be destroyed, and the despicable Ivy Peters drains a swamp and mutilates a woodpecker in *A Lost Lady* (Bennett 1957, 156).

According to Bennett, some of the characters also resemble those in other Cather stories and novels. Aimee, for example, Martin's French wife, resembles 'Toinette Gaux, little Jacques's mother in *Shadows on the Rock*. Martin himself can be grouped with characters like Eric Hermannson of "Eric Hermannson's Soul" and Canute Canuteson of "On the Divide." Later versions of Martin include Emil Bergson of *O Pioneers!* and Claude Wheeler of *One of Ours*. Although the latter have more education, they share Martin's frustrations (Bennett 1957, 159–60).

Interpretations and Criticisms

Arnold dismisses the piece as essentially sentimental (1984, 10). Thurin and O'Brien see it as somewhat more significant and give it more analysis. Thurin's reading of the story focuses on the predominately Greek classical references he finds. The opening scene, in which two women are decorating a Protestant church for Easter, and the title of the story itself, would seem obvious allusions to Christ's resurrection. Cather was, after all, writing for *Home Monthly*, whose readers were for the most part conservative, traditional, and Christian (Thurin 1990, 101). But as Thurin goes on to explain, however, instead of catering to Protestants, Cather proceeds to taunt her audience a bit: Mrs. Skimmons is presented as rigid and petty like the rest of the world in which Margie is trapped. Furthermore, except for Miss Pearson's reference to what she has "starved and . . . crucified" in herself, the imagery is pagan rather than Christian (Cather 1970, 428–29; Thurin 1990, 101–102). She substitutes a river for Christ as the story's central symbol of the life-force, and like classical river gods, this river is sometimes cruel to people; yet the resolution of the relationship between Dempster and the woman he loves is balanced by the rising of the river in the spring. Human actions are put in the context of nature, not of any divine plan (Thurin 1990, 101). Cather's comparison of Brownsville to Pompeii—a Pompeii buried in debt—is a classical allusion that reinforces the notion that Marjorie Pearson is one of many exquisite things buried in obscurity like the art works lost in the lava (Thurin 1990, 101–102).

Later, Cather's narrator asserts that those who devote themselves faithfully to the river , "not for gain but from inclination," are given in return "a simpleness of life and freshness of feeling and receptiveness of mind not to be found among the money changers of the market place. . . . It gives . . . something of that intimate sympathy with inanimate nature that is the base of all poetry, something of that which the high-faced rocks of the gleaming Sicilian shore gave Theocritus" (Cather 1970, 433). Here, according to Thurin, Cather is attempting to signal her readers that they are reading a pastoral. Dempster is presented as being in almost perfect harmony with nature so that the Dionysian rhapsody at the end of the story, in which he "compares his—and

Marjorie's—situation to that of the swollen river painfully but ecstatically digging a new channel," comes as no surprise (1990, 102).

O'Brien sees the story as a reflection of Cather's "emotional preoccupations" at the time—the "good mother/bad mother opposition," and the story's attack on the restrictions of women's roles (1987, 231). In some way Margie is the standard Victorian angel in the house, but Cather diverges sharply from this tradition when she portrays Margie as allowing herself to experience intense passion and emotion (1987, 231).

Works Cited

Arnold, Marilyn. 1984. *Willa Cather's Short Fiction*. Athens: Ohio University Press.

Bennett, Mildred, ed. 1957. *Early Stories of Willa Cather*. New York: Dodd, Mead.

Bennett, Mildred R. 1982. "Willa Cather's Bodies for Ghosts." *Western American Literature* 17:39–52.

Cather, Willa. 1957. "A Resurrection." In *Early Stories*. Ed. Mildred Bennett. New York: Dodd, Mead, 147–67.

———. [1965] 1970. "A Resurrection." In *Willa Cather's Collected Short Fiction, 1892–1912*. Ed. Virginia Faulkner. Lincoln: University of Nebraska Press, 425–39.

Faulkner, Virginia, ed. [1965] 1970. *Willa Cather's Collected Short Fiction, 1892–1912*. Lincoln: University of Nebraska Press. Reprint. Lincoln: University of Nebraska Press.

O'Brien, Sharon. 1987. *Willa Cather: The Emerging Voice*. New York: Oxford University Press.

Robinson, Phyllis C. 1983. *Willa: The Life of Willa Cather*. Garden City, NY: Doubleday.

Slote, Bernice. 1970. "Willa Cather as a Regional Writer." *Kansas Quarterly* 2:7–15.

Thurin, Erik Ingvar. 1990. *The Humanization of Willa Cather: Classicism in an American Classic*. Lund, Sweden: Lund University Press.

Woodress, James. 1970. *Willa Cather: Her Life and Art*. New York: Pegasus.

———. 1987. *Willa Cather: A Literary Life*. Lincoln: University of Nebraska Press.

Scandal

Publication History

This story was first published under the name Willa Sibert Cather in the August 1919 issue of *Century* (98:433–45) (Faulkner 1970, 597). Later, Cather included it in her second collection of short stories, *Youth and the Bright Medusa* (New York: Knopf, 1920, pp. 140–68), her first publication with Alfred A. Knopf. Robinson reports that Cather had been following Knopf's career since 1916, when she saw the publisher's edition of *Green Mansions* for the first time. The volume was very attractive, and since a book's appearance was extremely important to Cather, she began to think of Knopf as a desirable publisher for her. In fact, one of the reasons she was less than happy with Houghton Mifflin, which had published her first four novels, was that she disliked the design and illustrations they had given her work. Furthermore, the fact that Knopf himself was a great music lover, as was Cather, convinced her that his company would be the perfect publisher for her future work. Thus, in 1920, Cather walked into Knopf's New York office and asked him to be her publisher (Robinson 1983, 218–19). After Cather had committed herself to Knopf, her stories were suddenly sought after by magazine publishers. H. L. Mencken reported that George Jean Nathan, his partner at *Smart Set*, was full of envy while reading the story in *Century* (Gerber 1975, 154). This kind of high praise for "Scandal" would have come as a shock to Cather's literary agent, Paul Reynolds, who had received fifteen rejections of the story before *Century* agreed to publish it (Woodress 1987, 282).

The story reappeared in volume six of the thirteen-volume library edition of Cather's work, *The Novels and Stories of Willa Cather* (Boston: Houghton Mifflin, 1937–1941, pp. 173–205) (Faulkner 1970, 597). In 1975, it was reprinted by Vintage Books in a paperback edition of *Youth and the Bright Medusa*, and again in 1992 by Literary Classics of the United States in *Cather: Stories, Poems, and Other Writings*, a volume in the Library of America series.

Circumstances of Composition, Sources, and Influences

Cather wrote both this story and "A Gold Slipper" while on a trip to the West in 1916. Specifically, Cather wrote "Scandal" in Denver, where she stopped briefly in June (Woodress 1987, 282). (For a complete description of Cather's trip to the West, see the "Circumstances of Composition, Sources, and Influences" section for the chapter "A Gold Slipper.") That all three stories were written in 1916, the year after she published *The Song of the Lark*, suggests that Cather wanted to continue writing about singers as she had in the novel (Stouck 1975, 204n).

Like "The Diamond Mine," this story was written a few months after the marriage of Cather's dearest friend, Isabelle McClung, to violinist Jan Hambourg, while Cather was still smarting from what she felt was Isabelle's abandonment of her. Several critics attribute the negative portraits of Miletus Poppas ("The Diamond Mine") and Siegmund Stein ("Scandal") to these hurt feelings. As Woodress explains, Hambourg, who was of Russian-Jewish-English descent, has a good deal in common with Poppas: he was a violinist, his brother a cellist, and his father a music teacher in Toronto. Cather was very likely venting some resentment of Jan Hambourg in her portraits of Poppas and Stein, though Stein is too exaggerated to bear much resemblance to any real figure (1970, 189).

Relationship to Other Cather Works

Cather included this story in her second collection of short fiction, *Youth and the Bright Medusa*, and it is bound together thematically with the other stories in that volume. (For a full discussion of the shared characteristics of the stories in *Youth and the Bright Medusa*, see the "Relationship to Other Cather Works" section for the chapter "The Diamond Mine.") However, since this story actually shares a protagonist with "A Gold Slipper," it is clearly more closely tied to that story than to the others. Arnold regards Kitty as more of a victim in this story than she is in "A Gold Slipper" because in the latter story she can defend herself against an antagonist for whom she is a fair match. The Kitty of "Scandal," however, is merely a victim of people who use her to serve their own interests. Here, Kitty has no chance to defend herself or fight back (1984, 111).

This story also has much in common with "The Diamond Mine" and "A Gold Slipper" in that all three stories provide evidence of just how strong a hold opera singers had on Cather's imagination. Whenever she was between novels, she tended to write short stories about them (Brown 1964, 210). Further, each of the three stories describes the sufferings of those who devote themselves to art (Gerber 1975, 99).

Unfortunately, "The Diamond Mine" and "Scandal" also share what many authorities view as anti-Semitic portraits of Jewish characters, and Siegmund Stein is the more offensive portrait of the two (Robinson 1983, 207).

Interpretations and Criticisms

Few scholars have commented at length on this story, most dismissing it as uninteresting at best and unpleasant at worst (Woodress 1987, 282). Generally, this critical aversion to the story may be attributed to what is often perceived as Cather's anti-Semitic portrayal of Siegmund Stein. McFarland points out that Stein's name is German for "stone," and that the character himself represents materialism. Stein is this story's Medusa figure. There is a subtle implication in the story that some relationship exists between Stein's exploitation of Kitty and the loss of her voice. He turns her, artistically, into a silent stone (McFarland 1972, 37).

Giannone suggests that the title of the story refers to the "perishability of genius," and that the real scandal is the lamentable fact that beautiful voices cannot last (1968, 103).

Arnold believes Stein represents that part of society that is "inimical to art"—that uses art to disguise the hideousness of its crass commercialism (1984, 112). Cather's message in this story is that empty displays of art by the commercial consign art to the category of decor and rob the artist of spiritual and moral authority. Kitty Ayrshire, then, becomes a metaphor for legitimate art. Both have become simply commodities—serviceable, but not truly valuable in the way art should be (Arnold 1984, 112).

Works Cited

Arnold, Marilyn. 1984. *Willa Cather's Short Fiction*. Athens: Ohio University Press.

Brown, E. K. Completed by Leon Edel. [1953] 1964. *Willa Cather: A Critical Biography*. New York: Knopf.

Cather, Willa. 1975. "Scandal. In *Youth and the Bright Medusa*. New York: Vintage Books, 123–48.

———. 1992. "Scandal." In *Cather: Stories, Poems, and Other Writings*. New York: Literary Classics of the United States, 450–67.

Faulkner, Virginia, ed. [1965] 1970. *Willa Cather's Collected Short Fiction, 1892–1912*. Lincoln: University of Nebraska Press. Reprint. Lincoln: University of Nebraska Press.

Gerber, Philip. 1975. *Willa Cather*. Boston: Twayne.

Giannone, Richard. 1968. *Music in Willa Cather's Fiction*. Lincoln: University of Nebraska Press.

McFarland, Dorothy Tuck. 1972. *Willa Cather*. New York: Frederick Ungar.

Robinson, Phyllis C. 1983. *Willa: The Life of Willa Cather*. Garden City, NY: Doubleday.

Stouck, David. 1975. *Willa Cather's Imagination*. Lincoln: University of Nebraska Press.

Woodress, James. 1970. *Willa Cather: Her Life and Art*. New York: Pegasus.

———1987. *Willa Cather: A Literary Life*. Lincoln: University of Nebraska Press.

The Sculptor's Funeral

Publication History

This story was first published under the name Willa Sibert Cather in the January 1905 issue of *McClure's* (26:329–36) (Faulkner 1970, 594). According to Robinson, the story did not appear in that magazine without some controversy within the *McClure's* offices. Apparently Witter Bynner, one of *McClure's* editors, had been asked by the publisher himself to excise a good many words from the story. Cather was not informed of this decision, and when McClure finally told her, he blamed everything on Bynner. Cather was so enraged that her relationship with Bynner was permanently damaged (Robinson 1983, 135–36).

The next appearance of the story, with some minor changes in word order and spelling, was in Cather's first collection of short stories, *The Troll Garden* (New York: McClure, Phillips, 1905, pp. 55–84) (Faulkner 1970, 595). Fifteen years later, Cather made more revisions in the story and included it in her second collection, *Youth and the Bright Medusa* (New York: Knopf, 1920, pp. 248–72), where it was extensively revised. It contained three large cuts and more than 200 smaller ones, including changes in wording, spelling, capitalization, and punctuation (Faulkner 1970, 594).

The fourth printing of the story, with twenty substantive changes from the 1920 version, was in volume six of the thirteen-volume library edition of Cather's work, *The Novels and Stories of Willa Cather* (Boston: Houghton Mifflin, 1937–1941, pp. 263–89). The 1905 version was reprinted in 1961 with modernized spelling and punctuation by Signet Classics in a paperback edition of *The Troll Garden*.

In 1965 the University of Nebraska Press reprinted the 1905 version in *Willa Cather's Collected Short Fiction, 1892–1912*, and again in 1983 in *The Troll Garden*, edited by James Woodress. Literary Classics of the United

States included it in *Cather: Early Novels and Stories* (1987) and in *Cather: Stories, Poems, and Other Writings* (1992), two volumes in the Library of America series.

Circumstances of Composition, Sources, and Influences

Cather was teaching high school in Pittsburgh and living with Isabelle McClung and her family when she wrote this story in 1903. (For a discussion of the enormous positive influence of Isabelle McClung on Cather's creativity see the "Circumstances of Composition, Sources, and Influences" section for the chapter "A Wagner Matinée.") During that same year, Will Jones, Cather's former editor on the *Nebraska State Journal*, recommended Cather to H. H. McClure of the McClure Newspaper syndicate, who in turn recommended her to his cousin Sam S. McClure of *McClure's* magazine. In April 1903, Cather sent several of her stories to *McClure's* in a packet that almost certainly contained five or six of the stories that eventually became *The Troll Garden*, Cather's first collection. Two of them had already been published— "'A Death in the Desert'" in the January 1904 issue of *Scribner's*, and "A Wagner Matinée" in the February 1904 issue of *Everybody's* magazine. It is possible that "Flavia and Her Artists," "The Garden Lodge," and "The Marriage of Phaedra" were in the package as well, but it is certain that both "The Sculptor's Funeral" and "Paul's Case" were included (Woodress 1983, xv–xvi). Cather had sent her fiction to *McClure's* before, but had received only rejection letters. This time, however, S. S. McClure responded to her work by inviting her to his New York office. She met with him on May 1, 1903, an interview that changed Cather's life forever. He informed her that he would publish a collection of her stories and that he wanted exclusive rights to her work from that time on (Woodress 1983, xiv–xv).

McClure claimed that he would publish the best of her stories in his magazine and place the rest of them for her in other periodicals. Then, after each story had appeared in a journal, he would publish the collection in book form. What actually happened, however, was that three of the stories eventually included in *The Troll Garden* ("Flavia and Her Artists," "The Garden Lodge," and "The Marriage of Phaedra") never appeared in a periodical, either *McClure's* magazine or anything else, before they appeared in *The Troll Garden*. Furthermore, McClure waited until two years after his interview with Cather before publishing the collection, supposedly because he was waiting for all the stories to appear first in his magazine; in the end, however, the book actually appeared some weeks before "The Sculptor's Funeral" came out in *McClure's* (Woodress 1983, xv–xvi).

In many ways, "The Sculptor's Funeral" may be said to have grown out of Cather's own concerns. In Arnold's opinion, in this story "Cather is writing from the heart about things that are so terribly true for her that the whole force of her personality and her belief resonates through the lines" (1984, 48). Her admiration for what she sees as the genuine artist and his or her complete renunciation of all interests but art is obvious. In fact, "the coffin of the sculptor is in some sense a monument to those values" (Arnold 1984, 49).

Bennett reports that the plot of the story is based on an actual incident that occurred, not in Kansas or Nebraska as many readers understandably assume, but in Pittsburgh at about the time of Cather's move to that city in 1896. A year later, she recounted the event in one of the columns she was still contributing to the Lincoln *Courier* under the title "The Passing Show" (Bennett 1959, 71). She tells the story of an artist named Charles Stanley Reinhart whose body was brought back to his hometown of Pittsburgh to be buried: "A number of artists and literary men and several great editors came down from New York with his body, but his death was not even known in Pittsburgh. . . . I never knew how entirely one must live and die alone until that day when they brought Stanley Reinhart home"; the most typical reaction to his death, one Cather claimed to have heard repeatedly, was, "Reinhart dead? Oh yes; his brother is a fellow of some means I guess. Stanley never amounted to much" (quoted in Bennett 1959, 71). These people appreciated only the practical features of life and felt artistic pursuits to be a waste of time.

That Cather detested this attitude is a commonplace. Edward A. Bloom and Lillian D. Bloom believe this story emerges primarily from the revulsion Cather felt toward the Midwest's reverence for the practical and its refusal to accept the artist, even in his own hometown. Doubtless this reaction came from Cather's own recent flight from the prairie to the refinement and culture of Eastern cities and to European culture. In any case, it is a reaction that mellowed considerably in later years (1962, 11). Brown agrees with this assessment: the source of this story is Cather's feeling that she was an outsider, too different from the people in Red Cloud to be appreciated by them (1964, 119). Lee suggests that Cather's "ferocious, unforgiving satire on mid-Western philistinism" may also be "an angry elegy for [Ethelbert] Nevin," her composer friend who died at a young age (1989, 75). (For a discussion of the Nevin-Cather friendship see the "Circumstances of Composition, Sources, and Influences" section for the chapter "'A Death in the Desert.'")

Although he takes a slightly different approach, Gerber also maintains that the source of this story is Cather's own experience. However, he considers the story a projection of Cather's primary conflict at the time: the desire to be an artist and the need to make a living at the same time (1975, 44–45).

Although the idea for a story about an artist who is brought back after his death to a town that appreciates only practicality and financial success came from the Reinhart incident in Pittsburgh, the train that carries the body home and the depot where it finally arrives come straight out of Cather's youthful experiences in Nebraska. Mountford reports that by the time Cather and her family moved there from Virginia in 1883, Red Cloud was a crossroads on the Burlington and Missouri Railroad line from Kansas City to Denver. A hotel and a restaurant stood near the depot, and Cather spent many hours there with her brothers and sisters to watch the commotion of passenger trains arriving and departing. These scenes appear constantly in her work, and it is, indeed, this very depot where the artist's body arrives (1965, 2).

Cary mentions an 1888 tale by Sarah Orne Jewett as another possible source for Cather's story. Although Cather had not yet met Jewett in 1903, it is probable that she had read Jewett's story "Miss Tempy's Watchers." Jewett handles her subject much more deftly than Cather does, and the stories reach very different resolutions. Nevertheless, the two stories emerge from the same situation: the effect of a corpse in a coffin upon the people who view it (Cary 1973, 172).

Finally, although the earlier work of writers like E. W. Howe and Hamlin Garland may not be actual sources for this story, "The Sculptor's Funeral" is reminiscent of the work of those authors in that "it exposes the philistinism of the prairie town." Like their work, Cather's story may be placed under the literary category of "revolt from the village" (Woodress 1970, 112).

Relationship to Other Cather Works

Because this story is included in Cather's first collection, *The Troll Garden* (1905), its strongest ties are to the other stories in that book. In "A Sculptor's Funeral" the people who wait for Merrick's body to arrive are merely more examples of the goblins mentioned in the Christina Rossetti poem from which Cather took one of the two epigraphs for the book. (For a complete explanation of the thematic relationship of the *Troll Garden* stories to the epigraphs Cather chose for them, see the "Relationship to Other Cather Works" section for the chapters "'A Death in the Desert'" and "A Wagner Matinée.")

Several critics have mentioned the relationship between this story and one of Cather's early discarded poems, "The Night Express." In fact, Robinson suggests that "The Sculptor's Funeral" may be seen as a kind of revised version of a scene in that poem (1983, 124). Woodress quotes the lines from the poem that describe almost exactly the opening scene of the story: "From out the mist-clad meadows, along the river shore,/The night express-train whistles with eye of fire before/ . . . . While lads who used to loiter with wistful steps and slow/Await to-night a comrade who comes, but will not go" (1971, 101).

Gerber finds the story most closely related to "Paul's Case" and "A Wagner Matinée" in that all three embody Cather's major fears about her life: that she does not have enough talent to succeed as a writer, that the security of family and a steady income may seduce her away from her art, and that her youth will slip away from her before she accomplishes anything of value (1975, 45). Bennett groups the story with those two as well, but also adds "'A Death in the Desert'" because for all three stories Cather used her own material, whereas the others in *The Troll Garden* show her imitating other writers, especially Henry James (Bennett 1970, xxxvi).

Woodress pairs "A Sculptor's Funeral" with "A Wagner Matinée" because both stories center on characters whom the West destroys and because "A Wagner Matinée," in which a Nebraskan is brought back to the East, balances the situation of "The Sculptor's Funeral," in which the artist is brought back to the West (1987, 176). Differing slightly from Woodress, Wasserman points out that although the two stories do have a great deal in common, the West Cather depicts in "The Sculptor's Funeral" is very different from the earlier West—that is, it had fallen victim to "second- and third-generation money-grubbers, fixated on deal-making and gossip. . . . In contrast, the West of 'A Wagner Matinée' is the harsh, backbreaking world of the first homesteaders" (1991, 29).

Jones mentions the similarity in theme of "The Sculptor's Funeral" and "Coming, Aphrodite!": both stories glorify youth and art while at the same time castigating American domesticity and the provincial mentality of the small town, a theme Cather returns to in "Coming, Aphrodite!" where it is handled much more gracefully and subtly because Cather had matured greatly as a writer by the time she wrote it (1967, 237).

Rosowski establishes more far-reaching correlations when she suggests that this story is one of many that represent Cather's "need to project beyond the ending of the conventional script of pioneer possibilities and from there to evaluate the way the script has been ordered" (1990, 70). One of the ways she fulfills that need is to position the point of view "past the End—after the crops have failed, the settlers have abandoned the boom town, or the artist has died" (Rosowski 1990, 70). From that point of view, the unrealistically optimistic attitudes of the pioneers appear childishly romantic. In "A Sculptor's Funeral," "Peter," "Lou, the Prophet," "On the Divide," and "A Wagner Matinée," Cather describes the characters' increasing awareness of the "dark unintelligibility of their lives" (Rosowski 1990, 70).

Interpretations and Criticisms

Cather had already been severely chastised once for her harsh portrayal of Nebraska life in "A Wagner Matinée," and the Kansas setting of this story may have been Cather's attempt to avoid a second scolding. Unfortunately, the setting evidently was not enough of a disguise, and the story's appearance once again brought the author under attack by her Nebraska readers, who were mightily offended by what they saw as an unfairly negative portrayal of their home (O'Brien 1987, 287n).

The vast majority of critics admire the story. Sarah Orne Jewett, for example, ranked it number one in *The Troll Garden*, and many more recent critics praise it as at least one of the two best, citing "Paul's Case" as deserving of special consideration as well. In a review for the *Bookman* in 1908, Ford says the story is a prime example of Cather's talent for capturing a character—or a whole life—in a single well-drawn moment (1908, 152). Bennett proclaims the tale a masterpiece—among the most scathing attacks on provincial smugness ever written (1961, 198). To Arnold, the story merits special recognition as a hallmark of American fiction (1984, 43). In a more tempered, yet still glowing assessment, Woodress calls the story one of the best examples of Cather's early work (1983, xxii).

Perhaps the most notable detractor is Richard Cary, who finds little to recommend this story. He believes Jewett was merely being kind to a beginning writer when she praised it. Cather's portrayal of the conflict between art and commercialism dissolves into melodrama, he says, and all too often the author herself intrudes between the reader and the action (1973, 171–73). She fails to conjure much reader sympathy for Merrick, for his "escape to art is not persuasive; his return a questionable fulfillment. In death, he degrades and divides" (1973, 173). Cary does give Cather credit for at least making an effort to improve the story before its subsequent reprintings by excising many purple passages. Nevertheless, the story remains "a victory of observation over insight" (1973, 176).

A good deal of consensus among Cather specialists may be found in their opinions about the story's theme. Most agree that in Jim Laird's speech, Cather articulates clearly the tension between materialism and the artistic sensibility (Arnold 1984, 49). Arnold, who views Laird as the central character, relates the story to one of the epigraphs with which Cather introduces *The Troll Garden*. Laird realizes that he yielded to the trolls' seduction while Harvey did not, and his powerful verbal indictment of the other townspeople results from his own self-loathing (1984, 49). The primary conflict, then, is between "Jim's better nature and the self that prospers by serving scoundrels." The return of Merrick's body may be said to represent the return of Jim's own scruples, which are subsequently buried with the sculptor (Arnold 1984, 50). Without Jim Laird, the reader would remain unaware of the contrast between the integrity of the artist and the crassness and ignorance of everyone else in town (Ford 1908, 153).

Jones views Laird's tongue-lashing of his neighbors as an early example of the kind of thing that Sinclair Lewis would write seventeen years later in *Main Street* (1967, 236). O'Brien believes Laird's primary role is that of

Cather's spokesperson, arguing that although Laird is unquestionably expressing Cather's own anger at "small-town Nebraska, big-city Presbyteria, and America's Philistine society," Cather creates a speech for him that makes sense for her character in terms of both his psychology and his dialect (1987, 306). His speech patterns and his use of rhetorical questions fit a provincial lawyer perfectly; however, Cather chooses to end the story not with Laird's invective, since the community has silenced him as effectively as death has silenced the sculptor, but with the narrator's matter-of-factly relation of the manner of Laird's death (O'Brien 1987, 306). In Zabel's view, as important as Jim Laird is to the story in his own right, one of Cather's main purposes is to define the character of the artist. Inasmuch as they conspire to destroy the artist, homespun, small-town values are reprehensible (1985, 43–44).

Edward A. Bloom and Lillian D. Bloom assert that Cather's belief that creative genius results more from nature than from nurture diminishes the importance of the artist's physical environment. Nevertheless, the artist's surroundings are often, as in this story, portrayed as an obstacle—the refusal of Merrick's family and society to understand him jeopardized his talent. Merrick, like all artists, had to struggle against the forces at work to defeat him, and his face bears the marks of the struggle (1962, 126, 137).

Wasserman argues that in many ways Merrick's mother may be viewed as the most important example of the forces conspiring against art. Through Merrick's disciple, Steavens, we learn that Merrick's mother is even more responsible for his unhappiness than is the town in general—that "desert of newness and ugliness and sordidness"—and that the scars she caused may be seen not only in Merrick's life and in the evidence of resistance and struggle in his dead face, but also in his art (1991, 28). For example, Steavens recalls the bas-relief Merrick had made after a visit home and finally understands that it is "a sentimentalized vision" of Merrick's mother, not a realistic depiction of her (Wasserman 1991, 28). Wasserman goes on to suggest that perhaps "through the butterfly, an ancient symbol for the soul, Merrick may have been protesting the soul-destroying effect of early rejection and ignorance" (1991, 29). Arnold's view of Merrick's mother is that "she is like an exposed nerve someone has stepped on, Jim's nerve," and that she, like everyone else in the story, is merely played off against the main character, Jim Laird, providing yet another example of the vulgar life to which he has surrendered himself (1984, 50).

The importance of Steavens himself is mentioned by a couple of critics. Rosowski calls him "a Jamesian observer" who is essentially responsible for describing the repulsive life Merrick was forced to live in his youth (1986, 24). Petry suggests that, because there is some suggestion in the story that Merrick was a homosexual, some of the animosity that made Merrick's life so difficult was a result of the townspeople's homophobia (1986, 108–11).

Works Cited

Arnold, Marilyn. 1984. *Willa Cather's Short Fiction*. Athens: Ohio University Press.

Bennett, Mildred R. 1959. "Willa Cather in Pittsburgh." *Prairie Schooner* 33:64–76.

———. 1961. *The World of Willa Cather*. Lincoln: University of Nebraska Press.

———. [1965] 1970. Introduction to *Willa Cather's Collected Short Fiction*. Ed. Virginia Faulkner. Lincoln: University of Nebraska Press. Reprint. Lincoln: University of Nebraska Press.

Bloom, Edward A., and Lillian D. Bloom. 1962. *Willa Cather's Gift of Sympathy*. Carbondale: Southern Illinois University Press.

Brown, E. K. Completed by Leon Edel. [1953] 1964. *Willa Cather: A Critical Biography*. New York: Knopf.

Cary, Richard. 1973. "The Sculptor and the Spinster: Jewett's 'Influence' on Cather." *Colby Library Quarterly* 10:168–78.

Cather, Willa. 1961. "The Sculptor's Funeral." In *The Troll Garden*. New York: Signet Classics, 35–49.

———. [1965] 1970. "The Sculptor's Funeral." In *Willa Cather's Collected Short Fiction, 1892–1912*. Ed. Virginia Faulkner. Lincoln: University of Nebraska Press, 235–47.

———. 1983. "The Sculptor's Funeral." In *The Troll Garden*. Ed. James Woodress. Lincoln: University of Nebraska Press, 32–45..

———. 1987. "The Sculptor's Funeral." In *Cather: Early Novels and Stories*. New York: Literary Classics of the United States, 34–48.

———. 1992. "The Sculptor's Funeral." In *Cather: Stories, Poems, and Other Writings*. New York: Literary Classics of the United States, 497–511.

Faulkner, Virginia, ed. [1965] 1970. *Willa Cather's Collected Short Fiction, 1892–1912*. Lincoln: University of Nebraska Press. Reprint. Lincoln: University of Nebraska Press.

Ford, Mary K. 1908. "Some Recent Women Short-Story Writers." *Bookman* 27:152–53.

Gerber, Philip. 1975. *Willa Cather*. Boston: Twayne.

Jones, Howard Mumford. 1967. "Excerpt from *The Bright Medusa*." In *Willa Cather and Her Critics*. Ed. James Schroeter. Ithaca, NY: Cornell University Press.

Lee, Hermione. 1989. *Willa Cather: Double Lives*. New York: Pantheon.

Mountford, Miriam. 1965. "Places Made Famous by Willa Cather." *Willa Cather Pioneer Memorial and Educational Foundation* 9:1–2.

O'Brien, Sharon. 1987. *Willa Cather: The Emerging Voice*. New York: Oxfrod University Press.

Petry, Alice Hall. 1986. "Harvey's Case: Notes on Cather's 'The Sculptor's Funeral.'" *South Dakota Review* 24: 108–11.

Robinson, Phyllis C. 1983. *Willa: The Life of Willa Cather*. Garden City, NY: Doubleday.

Rosowski, Susan J. 1986. *The Voyage Perilous: Willa Cather's Romanticism*. Lincoln: University of Nebraska Press.

———. 1990. "Willa Cather's Subverted Endings and Gendered Time." In *Cather Studies*, vol. 1. Ed. Susan J. Rosowski. Lincoln: University of Nebraska Press, 68–88.

Wasserman, Loretta. 1991. *Willa Cather: A Study of the Short Fiction*. Boston: Twayne.

Woodress, James. 1970. *Willa Cather: Her Life and Art*. New York: Pegasus.

———. 1971. "Willa Cather Seen Clear." *Papers on Language & Literature* 7:96–109.

———. 1983. Introduction to *The Troll Garden*. Ed. James Woodress. Lincoln: University of Nebraska Press.

———. 1987. *Willa Cather: A Literary Life*. Lincoln: University of Nebraska Press.

Zabel, Morton D. 1985. "Willa Cather: The Tone of Time." In *Willa Cather*. Ed. Harold Bloom. Garden City, NY: Chelsea House, 41–49.

The Sentimentality of William Tavener

Publication History

This story was first published in the *Library* on May 12, 1900 (1:13–14), under the name Willa Sibert Cather (Faulkner 1970, 593). It was reprinted in 1957 by Dodd, Mead in *Early Stories*, in 1965 by the University of Nebraska Press in *Willa Cather's Collected Short Fiction, 1892–1912*, and in 1992 by Literary Classics of the United States in *Cather: Stories, Poems, and Other Writings*, a volume in the Library of America series.

Circumstances of Composition, Sources, and Influences

At the time Cather wrote this story in Pittsburgh, she was focusing nearly all her energy on writing material for a short-lived periodical called the *Library*. In its brief run, the *Library* carried about twenty-four of Cather's pieces, including articles, poems, and stories (Brown 1964, 91).

The countryside setting and names of places and people in this story—including the name Tavener—come directly from Cather's childhood in Winchester, Virginia (Bennett 1957, 231). However, the suggestion for Hester, William Tavener's strong-willed, commanding wife, probably came from Cather's reading of and admiration for Henry James's fiction (Bennett 1957, 231).

Woodress suggests that the story probably originated in one of Cather's parents' or grandparents' memories of a circus they once had attended long before Cather was born (1970, 28). According to O'Brien, the source of the actual story is less important than the fact that Cather drew on her Virginia childhood and family history, thus beginning an artistic exploration of her personal and family memories of both Virginia and Nebraska. Cather's memories evoke this story just as William's and Hester's memories evoke their shared stories (O'Brien 1987, 270, 286n).

O'Brien also maintains that the story foreshadows Cather's later novels about Nebraska in that it features the undramatic lives of ordinary people, but it also reveals the clear influence of Sarah Orne Jewett's work. Cather did not meet Jewett in person until several years later, but she had read Jewett's *The Country of the Pointed Firs*, which almost certainly gave Cather the courage to use her own rural experience in her fiction (1987, 269–70).

Relationship to Other Cather Works

Romney, Back Creek, the character of Tap, and the figure of a domineering woman at her worst reappear in Cather's novel *Sapphira and the Slave Girl* (1940), where Pewtown is spelled Peughtown (Bennett 1957, 231).

Arnold notes that the characters in this story have much in common with the Burdens of *My Ántonia*. The story may also be read as something of a companion piece to "Eric Hermannson's Soul," in that it presents another perspective of life on the Divide. Cather would employ much the same tone she uses in this story in *My Ántonia*, "Neighbor Rosicky," and *Death Comes for the Archbishop* (1984, 29).

Interpretations and Criticisms

Most Cather scholars do not mention this story at all, presumably because they feel, as Woodress does, that although the story gives evidence that in her early career Cather incorporated the whole scope of her experience into her fiction, it is nevertheless apprentice-level material (1987, 29). Brown goes even further, saying the story suggests that Cather had not matured much as a writer during her first Pittsburgh years, despite the fact that she was beginning to have some success placing her work in various periodicals (1964, 92).

Only Arnold and O'Brien devote any amount of discussion to the story. Arnold praises the story and argues that it shows Cather's increasing ability to judge how much or how little to say and to define a character or a relationship (Arnold 1984, 28, 37). According to O'Brien, the story is one of Cather's finest, especially in its description of the resurfaced intimacy between the husband and wife. Furthermore, although the story has its roots in her own life, Cather remains sufficiently detached to avoid burdening it with her own unresolved concerns. This story even reverses the pattern of some of her earlier work in that here a mother finds her attachment to her husband and children increased, rather than diminished. Cather seems to have discovered examples of women's creativity in her own past, as is reflected in the verbal power she gives the women characters—William is simply silent, while Hester is articulate (1987, 269–70).

Works Cited

Arnold, Marilyn. 1984. *Willa Cather's Short Fiction*. Athens: Ohio University Press.

Bennett, Mildred, ed. 1957. *Early Stories of Willa Cather*. New York: Dodd, Mead.

Brown, E. K. Completed by Leon Edel. [1953] 1964. *Willa Cather: A Critical Biography*. New York: Knopf.

Cather, Willa. 1957. "The Sentimentality of William Tavener." In *Early Stories*. Ed. Mildred Bennett. New York: Dodd, Mead, 231–37.

———. [1965] 1970. "The Sentimentality of William Tavener." In *Willa Cather's Collected Short Fiction, 1892–1912*. Ed. Virginia Faulkner. Lincoln: University of Nebraska Press, 253–57.

———. 1992. "The Sentimentality of William Tavener." In *Cather: Stories, Poems, and Other Writings*. New York: Literary Classics of the United States, 46–51.

Faulkner, Virginia, ed. [1965] 1970. *Willa Cather's Collected Short Fiction, 1892–1912*. Lincoln: University of Nebraska Press. Reprint. Lincoln: University of Nebraska Press.

O'Brien, Sharon. 1987. *Willa Cather: The Emerging Voice*. New York: Oxford University Press.

Woodress, James. 1970. *Willa Cather: Her Life and Art*. New York: Pegasus.

———. 1987. *Willa Cather: A Literary Life*. Lincoln: University of Nebraska Press.

A Singer's Romance

Publication History

This story was first published in the *Library* on July 28, 1900 (1:15–16) under the name Willa Sibert Cather (Faulkner 1970, 593). It was reprinted in 1957 by Dodd, Mead in *Early Stories*, and in 1965 by the University of Nebraska Press in *Willa Cather's Collected Short Fiction, 1892–1912*.

Circumstances of Composition, Sources, and Influences

This is one of several Cather stories that center on musicians and opera singers. Edith Lewis, with whom Cather lived during the last forty years of her life, even asserts that musical forms influenced Cather's prose style (1953, 47–48).

   Cather's fascination with and admiration for opera singers is obvious in her early journalistic pieces. In an article she wrote for the *Nebraska State Journal* in 1894, she says, "Singing is idealized speech, and, in order to preserve the proportion and harmony between words and action, the acting which accompanies it must be ideal. A singer is on the stage before her audience less than an actress is, and she must do more when she is there. She must do in one gesture what the actress of spoken words does in many. . . . The stage is the kingdom of the emotions and the imagination. Literature, painting and even music are all more or less stilted by pedantry and technique, but on the stage skill counts for nothing" (quoted in Slote 1966, 217).

Relationship to Other Cather Works

Woodress notes that musicians are central to two of Cather's novels, (*The Song of the Lark* and *Lucy Gayheart*), and several short stories besides this one ("Nanette: An Aside," "A Wagner Matinée," "'A Death in the Desert,'" "The Garden Lodge," "The Diamond Mine," "A Gold Slipper," and "Uncle Valentine," among others). Although "A Singer's Romance" shares its subject with many other works, it is most closely related to "Nanette: An Aside." In fact, "A Singer's Romance" is essentially a revision of "Nanette," in which the point of view is the singer's instead of her attendant's. The singer in this story foreshadows Cather's fictional portrait of the real singer, Nordica, in "The Diamond Mine," which was published sixteen years later (1987, 146). (See the "Circumstances of Composition, Sources, and Influences" section for the chapter "The Diamond Mine.")

Unlike "Nanette," this story does not contain specific pronouncements about performing artists, and although the plot of "A Singer's Romance" is very close to that of "Nanette," there is one very important difference—the singer in "A Singer's Romance" is not a genius, while Tradutorri in "Nanette" certainly is (Arnold 1984, 16). Bennett agrees and maintains that this difference makes "A Singer's Romance" much more tragic a tale than the earlier story—since the artist is not a great one, the blow of realizing that she is old and unattractive falls still harder (1957, 257). In both stories, however, as well as in *The Song of the Lark*, Cather declares her belief that artistic accomplishment may only be realized if everything else—including human relationships—is sacrificed to it (Bennett 1970, xxix).

Interpretations and Criticisms

Some critics point to this story as an example of Cather's celebration of youth (Bloom and Bloom 1962, 110). O'Brien speculates that this story, as well as the others with music as their central theme, provides evidence that Cather was attracted to music because it was an art without words—or at least without words in English (1987, 171). Because in her youth Cather had gradually become aware that society viewed her intimate relationships with other women as unnatural, the absence of a text was a convenience and a pleasure because it allowed her to "project 'unnatural' passions directly into the aesthetic experience. In music nothing is named and so everything can be imagined by the listener who is less constrained by the text than [is] the reader" (1987, 171). It is not surprising, then, that she would frequently choose female opera singers as protagonists in her fiction.

Works Cited

Arnold, Marilyn. 1984. *Willa Cather's Short Fiction*. Athens: Ohio University Press.

Bennett, Mildred R., ed. 1957. *Early Stories of Willa Cather*. New York: Dodd, Mead.

Bennett, Mildred R. [1965] 1970. Introduction to *Willa Cather's Collected Short Fiction*. Ed. Virginia Faulkner. Lincoln: University of Nebraska Press. Reprint. Lincoln: University of Nebraska Press.

Bloom, Edward A., and Lillian D. Bloom. 1962. *Willa Cather's Gift of Sympathy*. Carbondale: Southern Illinois University Press.

Cather, Willa. 1957. "A Singer's Romance." In *Early Stories*. Ed. Mildred Bennett. New York: Dodd, Mead, 257–63.

———. [1965] 1970. "A Singer's Romance." In *Willa Cather's Collected Short Fiction, 1892–1912*. Ed. Virginia Faulkner. Lincoln: University of Nebraska Press, 333–38.

Faulkner, Virginia, ed. [1965] 1970. *Willa Cather's Collected Short Fiction, 1892–1912*. Lincoln: University of Nebraska Press. Reprint. Lincoln: University of Nebraska Press.

Lewis, Edith. 1953. *Willa Cather Living*. New York: Knopf.

O'Brien, Sharon. 1987. *Willa Cather: The Emerging Voice*. New York: Oxford University Press.

Slote, Bernice, ed. 1966. *The Kingdom of Art*. Lincoln: University of Nebraska Press.

Woodress, James. 1987. *Willa Cather: A Literary Life*. Lincoln: University of Nebraska Press.

A Son of the Celestial

Publication History

This story, subtitled "A Character," was first published on January 15, 1893, in the University of Nebraska student journal, the *Hesperian* (22:7–10), under the name W. Cather and was reprinted in 1950 by the University of Nebraska Press in *Willa Cather's Campus Years*, edited by James R. Shively (61–68) (Faulkner 1970, 590; Lathrop 1975, 117). In 1957 it was reprinted by Dodd, Mead in *Early Stories*, and in 1965 by the University of Nebraska Press in *Willa Cather's Collected Short Fiction, 1892–1912*.

Circumstances of Composition, Sources and Influences

This piece is one of the seven stories Cather wrote as an undergraduate at the University of Nebraska in Lincoln. Like "A Tale of the White Pyramid" and "A Night at Greenway Court," the story's setting is based more on Cather's reading than on her own experience (O'Brien 1987, 195). Arnold reports that at the time this story was published in the *Hesperian*, Cather was an associate editor of that magazine and a well-known campus figure. She was also contributing newspaper columns to the Lincoln *Journal*, some of which exhibit her fascination with oriental culture (1984, 6).

Thurin says that the story reflects Cather's interest in the classics: Cather includes references to *Hamlet*, Michelangelo, and Plato; furthermore, the story's last sentence is taken from one of Horace's poems, in which the poet "answers his friend Maecenas, who has expressed a fear that the poet might die before him and thus leave him bereaved" (1990, 96).

Relationship to Other Cather Works

As Bennett notes, this story represents Cather's first use of a professor in her work: Here Ponter, who was once a professor of Sanskrit, seems an intellectual out of place in a materialistic society. The next appearance of a professor is the Greek scholar in "Jack-A-Boy." Then comes Emerson Graves of "The Professor's Commencement," who, like Ponter, decorates his study with objects that show his interest in the East, and, like the Professor in "Jack-A-Boy," is laboring at an unfinished book. Cather's most famous professor, of course, is Professor St. Peter of *The Professor's House* (1982, 47–48).

In one sense, the ironic narrator of "A Son of the Celestial" can be said to grow out of the journalistic pieces Cather was also writing in early 1893, when this story appeared in the *Hesperian* (Arnold 1984, 6). She was fairly ruthless in her reviews of theatre performances in Lincoln. One of her fellow journalists characterized Cather the critic as "fearless, [with] the ability to see things as they really are" (Slote 1966, 17). Many others, however, felt that she offered condemnation more often than praise. The theatre people themselves reacted bitterly to some of Cather's comments in the *Journal*—and not without reason (Slote 1966, 17). The same angry voice that attacks poor performances in the theatre and the state penal system in "The Clemency of the Court" is heard clearly in "A Son of the Celestial," where Cather targets the sometimes dry scholarship of academe (Arnold 1984, 6).

The images and symbols found in this piece recur in other stories and also in some novels. One such symbol is the knife, which in both "A Son of the Celestial" and "On the Divide" is used as an artist's tool and represents, according to O'Brien, "the power and the danger Cather associated with the act of writing" (1987, 205). In these instances the knife is a positive power, but it can also be dangerous and mutilating, as it is in the hands of the Frenchman in "A Night at Greenway Court." Perhaps the most well-known instance of the knife as a weapon of death and mutilation occurs in Cather's novel *A Lost Lady*, where Ivy Peters slits the eyes of a woodpecker simply to watch the bird fly blindly and frantically into trees (O'Brien 1987, 205). Bennett, too, recognizes Cather's "preoccupation with disfigurement—especially of the hand" (Bennett 1970, xxxviii).

Interpretations and Criticisms

Thurin suggests that the classical references in the story indicate Cather's intense interest in male friendship, an interest that could be a reflection of her own desire for female friendship (1990, 96). Also, the similarity of the names—Cather and Ponter, Pound and Yung—suggests that Ponter's frustration may actually be the author's own frustration over her turbulent but intimate friendship with Louise Pound, whom Cather met while both women were students at the University of Nebraska (Thurin 1990, 104n).

Most critics, however, view this piece as one of Cather's derivative stories of the exotic, written, as Cather herself told an interviewer, during her early days when she was given to overwritten flowery prose (Hockett 1966, 450). Woodress suggests that Cather may have been criticizing some of her own teachers; in any case, the story is of little importance, and Cather's experiments in exoticism here and in "Tale of the White Pyramid" were an artistic dead end (1987, 79).

Works Cited

Arnold, Marilyn. 1984. *Willa Cather's Short Fiction*. Athens: Ohio University Press.

Bennett, Mildred R. [1965] 1970. Introduction to *Willa Cather's Collected Short Fiction*. Ed. Virginia Faulkner. Lincoln: University of Nebraska Press. Reprint. Lincoln: University of Nebraska Press.

———. 1982. "Willa Cather's Bodies for Ghosts." *Western American Literature* 17:39–52.

Faulkner, Virginia, ed. [1965] 1970. *Willa Cather's Collected Short Fiction, 1892–1912*. Lincoln: University of Nebraska Press. Reprint. Lincoln: University of Nebraska Press.

Cather, Willa. 1957. "A Son of the Celestial." In *Early Stories*. Ed. Mildred Bennett. New York: Dodd, Mead, 25–32.

———. [1965] 1970. "A Son of the Celestial." In *Willa Cather's Collected Short Fiction, 1892–1912*. Ed. Virginia Faulkner. Lincoln: University of Nebraska Press, 523–28.

Faulkner, Virginia, ed. [1965] 1970. *Willa Cather's Collected Short Fiction, 1892–1912*. Lincoln: University of Nebraska Press. Reprint. Lincoln: University of Nebraska Press.

Hockett, Ethel M. 1966. "The Vision of a Successful Fiction Writer." In *The Kingdom of Art*. Ed. Bernice Slote. Lincoln: University of Nebraska Press.

Lathrop, Joanna. 1975. *Willa Cather: A Checklist of Her Published Writing*. Lincoln: University of Nebraska Press.

O'Brien, Sharon. 1987. *Willa Cather: The Emerging Voice*. New York: Oxford University Press.

Slote, Bernice, ed. 1966. *The Kingdom of Art*. Lincoln: University of Nebraska Press.

Thurin, Erik Ingvar. 1990. *The Humanization of Willa Cather: Classicism in an American Classic*. Lund, Sweden: Lund University Press.

Woodress, James. 1987. *Willa Cather: A Literary Life*. Lincoln: University of Nebraska Press.

The Strategy of the Were-Wolf Dog

Publication History

This story was signed Willa Cather and first published in *Home Monthly* (6:13–14, 24) in December 1896 along with "The Burglar's Christmas," which was printed under the pseudonym Elizabeth L. Seymour (Faulkner 1970, 592). The story was reprinted in 1965 by the University of Nebraska Press in *Willa Cather's Collected Short Fiction, 1892–1912*.

Circumstances of Composition, Sources, and Influences

Bennett explains that this story grew out of the oral tales Cather invented and told to her younger siblings at home. Cather's sister Elsie told Bennett that she recalled hearing stories very like this one when she was a child, many of which featured a great white bear (Bennett 1973, 4). Woodress says that the story is similar to "Rudolph, the Red-Nose Reindeer" (1987, 121).

Relationship to Other Cather Works

Like some other stories written during this period, this one was probably used primarily to fill up space in *Home Monthly* (Woodress 1970, 82).

Interpretations and Criticisms

In O'Brien's opinion, "Cather undermines the protagonists' urge for escape, independence, and adventure" by having them escape from Santa's house only to drown in the freezing sea (1987, 230–31). (See also the "Interpretations and Criticisms" section for the chapter "The Princess Baladina—Her Adventure.") Cather signed her own name to the story, indicating that she was pleased with the quality of the writing (Woodress 1987, 121).

Arnold calls the piece "one of those 'how will Santa ever deliver the toys now?' stories so popular with children at Christmastime"(1984, 12). The idea that the frozen North is magical is not original, nor is the plot of the story, but Cather's descriptions and the "stylistic ease" with which she tells the tale are splendid (Arnold 1984, 12).

Works Cited

Arnold, Marilyn. 1984. *Willa Cather's Short Fiction*. Athens: Ohio University Press.

Bennett, Mildred. 1973. "A Note on the White Bear Stories." *WC Pioneer Memorial Newsletter* 7:4.

Benson, Peter. 1981. "Willa Cather at *Home Monthly*." *Biography* 4:227–48.

———. [1965] 1970. "The Strategy of the Were-Wolf Dog." In *Willa Cather's Collected Short Fiction, 1892–1912*. Ed. Virginia Faulkner. Lincoln: University of Nebraska Press.

Faulkner, Virginia, ed. [1965] 1970. *Willa Cather's Collected Short Fiction, 1892–1912*. Lincoln: University of Nebraska Press. Reprint. Lincoln: University of Nebraska Press.

O'Brien, Sharon. 1987. *Willa Cather: The Emerging Voice*. New York: Oxford University Press.

Woodress, James. 1970. *Willa Cather: Her Life and Art*. New York: Pegasus.

———. 1987. *Willa Cather: A Literary Life*. Lincoln: University of Nebraska Press.

A Tale of the White Pyramid

Publication History

This story was first published on December 22, 1892, in the University of Nebraska student journal, the *Hesperian* (22:8–11), under the name W. Cather (Faulkner 1970, 590). It was reprinted in 1950 by the University of Nebraska Press in *Willa Cather's Campus Years* (54–60), in 1957 by Dodd, Mead in *Early Stories*, and in 1965 by the University of Nebraska Press in *Willa Cather's Collected Short Fiction, 1892–1912*.

Circumstances of Composition, Sources and Influences

This piece is one of seven stories written while Cather was a student at the University of Nebraska in Lincoln, three of which, like this one, do not have settings based on Cather's own experience. According to O'Brien, the idea for the story and its setting in ancient Egypt seems to have grown out of Cather's reading of Shakespeare, Daudet, and Gautier at the university (1987, 198). Thurin disagrees, arguing that the story "is written in biblical language . . . and is set in the Egypt of the early pyramid-building pharaohs," not in the later Egypt that O'Brien describes (Thurin 1990, 95).

In addition, Cather was doubtless influenced by both Henry James's and Edith Wharton's use of architectural metaphors to discuss the craft of fiction (O'Brien 1987, 200).

Relationship to Other Cather Works

Woodress sees Cather's use of first-person narration for the first time as the only interesting thing about the story (1987, 79). Although she returns to it in later stories, she does not quite master it until it appears in *My Ántonia*, "where she uses the preface to create an author separate from Jim Burden" (O'Brien 1987, 199).

Many of the recurrent themes in Cather's later fiction appear for the first time in "A Tale of the White Pyramid." It was the first story in which she attempts to describe her own fictional method and the first in which "she reveals artistic anxieties and ambitions in stories ostensibly concerned with the building" of a variety of structures (O'Brien 1987, 200). *Alexander's Bridge* and "Behind the Singer Tower" reveal the same theme and use the same technique in exploring it (O'Brien 1987, 200).

The imagery of "entombment, repression, and death" in "White Pyramid" reappears often (O'Brien 1987, 201). O'Brien maintains that the coffins that appear in "Peter," the cell in "The Clemency of the Court," the bedrooms in "The Burglar's Christmas" and "'A Death in the Desert,'" and the hotel room in "Paul's Case" are all examples of this "imagery of enclosure, signifying silence, repression, and death" (1987, 201).

This imagery begins to change slightly in the later fiction, where "the intermediate metaphor of the box is featured" (O'Brien 1987, 201). The box image functions a bit differently from the tomb imagery only because a box is not absolutely sealed; it can be opened. A significant point is that "the box is a female symbol suggesting both Pandora's box of sexuality and the container of unexpressed but potential creativity" (O'Brien 1987, 201). Boxes weighted with symbolic significance appear in "A Son of the Celestial," "The Count of Crow's Nest," "The Burglar's Christmas," "El Dorado: A Kansas Recessional," "The Treasure of Far Island," "The Namesake," and "On the Gulls' Road" (O'Brien 1987, 201).

O'Brien further explains that as Cather moves into the novels, the metaphor of enclosures is transformed again. "In *The Song of the Lark* the drawer where Thea hides the secret of creativity until she is ready to release it" is one example; more are to be found in *O, Pioneers!* and the novels that follow it, where "the boxes and drawers are transformed into enclosed yet continually open spaces which . . . are without a lid" (1987, 202).

O'Brien traces clear correlations between the ending of "A Tale of the White Pyramid" and those of both "A Night at Greenway Court" and *Death Comes for the Archbishop*. All three end with a "silencing of the narrative impulse," a significance O'Brien sees as connected directly to Cather herself: "if Cather could not find a way to tell tales from the underground, the art of 'concealment' would become one of silence, and thus no art at all" (1987, 203).

Interpretations and Criticisms

O'Brien is the only authority who has afforded "A Tale of the White Pyramid" more than a cursory reading. In fact, most scholars do not even mention the story, and the few who do view it as a thoroughly inconsequential piece except as a kind of narrative experiment necessary to the evolution of Cather's voice and style. Arnold, for example, considers the story "exotically appealing," but "trifling" (1984, 6). Robinson sees it as interesting primarily "for containing one of Willa's early poems" (1983, 46). Woodress maintains that both it and "A Son of the Celestial" can simply be "dismissed as experiments that led nowhere" (1970, 60).

Like the other critics, O'Brien admits that the story is "slight" and seriously flawed as a work of art—derivative and artificial: after all, "what did a girl from Nebraska know about pyramids and pharaohs?" (O'Brien 1987, 199–200). Nevertheless, O'Brien contends that if the piece is read in the light of one of Cather's statements from "The Novel Demeuble," her essay on the craft of fiction, "the story becomes more interesting and its place in Cather's work less anomalous" (1987, 201). In that essay, Cather insists that the presence of something that is suggested, but not named explicitly, is what makes a work truly art.

Taking Cather at her word, O'Brien asserts that the final comment of the story's narrator "suggests an equation between the story he tells and the pyramid" (1987, 199). He is constrained from telling some secret—is gagged in much the same way the pyramid is sealed. Cather implies that the reason he must keep silent is that his secret is the "homosexual relationship between the king and his builder. The only possible referent in the story for 'the sin of the king' is his unpopular relationship with the stranger to whom no other man can compare 'for beauty of face or form'" (1987, 199). That Cather should choose the word *sin* is significant. She probably meant it to refer to the one sin that neither she nor her narrator could name. The author and narrator are telling a "story of concealment and repression in which the creative is intertwined with the sexual" (1987, 199). Sealing the tomb with the rock is the central "act of concealment," and it is associated closely with the narrator's refusal to solve the mystery that is somehow connected to sex. Since the narrator is the sole teller of the tale, "his closing and enclosure of the story" are hers as well (1987, 200).

The story, then, embodies one of Cather's central conflicts—whether to disclose or conceal "the inner, the secret, and the passionate." If she discloses it, she risks censure, but, if she conceals it "she may find herself silenced and her creativity as concealed—or, perhaps, as dead—as the body in the tomb" (O'Brien 1987, 200).

Works Cited

Arnold, Marilyn. 1984. *Willa Cather's Short Fiction*. Athens: Ohio University Press.

Cather, Willa. 1957. "A Tale of the White Pyramid." In *Early Stories*. Ed. Mildred Bennett. New York: Dodd, Mead, 19–24.

———. [1965] 1970. "A Tale of the White Pyramid." In *Willa Cather's Collected Short Fiction, 1892–1912*. Ed. Virginia Faulkner. Lincoln: University of Nebraska Press, 529–33.

Faulkner, Virginia, ed. [1965] 1970. *Willa Cather's Collected Short Fiction, 1892–1912*. Lincoln: University of Nebraska Press. Reprint. Lincoln: University of Nebraska Press.

O'Brien, Sharon. 1987. *Willa Cather: The Emerging Voice*. New York: Oxford University Press.

Robinson, Phyllis C. 1983. *Willa: The Life of Willa Cather*. Garden City, NY: Doubleday.

Thurin, Erik Ingvar. 1990. *The Humanization of Willa Cather: Classicism in an American Classic*. Lund, Sweden: Lund University Press.

Woodress, James. 1987. *Willa Cather: A Literary Life*. Lincoln: University of Nebraska Press.

Tommy, the Unsentimental

Publication History

This story was first published in August 1896 in *Home Monthly* (6:6–7) under the name Willa Cather, one of two Cather stories to appear in this issue of the magazine; the other, "The Princess Baladina—Her Adventure," was published under the pseudonym Charles Douglass (Faulkner 1970, 591). Cather had been hired as assistant editor to Charles Axtell a short time before and had moved to Pittsburgh to begin her new job on the staff of *Home Monthly*. However, shortly after she arrived, Mr. Axtell went on vacation, leaving Cather to put together the entire August issue, the first issue since Axtell, Orr, and Company had bought the magazine and changed its name from *Ladies' Journal* (Woodress 1970, 76–77). The story was reprinted in 1957 by Dodd, Mead in *Early Stories*, and in 1965 by the University of Nebraska Press in *Willa Cather's Collected Short Fiction, 1892–1912*.

Circumstances of Composition, Sources, and Influences

According to Robinson, Cather wrote this story while she was still in Nebraska, just before moving to Pittsburgh (Robinson 1983, 77). The tale shows a softening in Cather's attitude toward the prairie. Bennett, on the other hand, maintains that the story was written after Cather had been in

Pittsburgh a month (1957, 107). If so, the change in her attitude toward Nebraska may be the result of comparisons between the "clogged skies of Pittsburgh" and the open horizons of the prairie (Slote 1970, 10). Clearly, the character Tommy has great affection for her hometown, especially as she compares it to the Eastern city where she attends school. Bennett sees Cather's attitude as one that may be more accurately described as ambivalent than as outright affectionate—"the love and hate, the blessing and the curse of Nebraska that was to follow her throughout her life" (1957, 107).

Many critics have discussed Cather's rejection of the Victorian notion of femininity and womanhood, generally agreeing that Cather strongly identified with men because she despised the confining roles women were expected to fill. Because the women of nineteenth-century America were required to be delicate, sentimental, or weak—and consequently to write fiction of the same type—Cather insisted upon defining herself in opposition to such culturally prescribed postures (Bennett 1970, xxviii). "Tommy, the Unsentimental," then, contains a fair amount of autobiography, and the setting, Southdown, represents the first time Cather had used her hometown of Red Cloud in fiction (Bennett 1970, xxviii). There is a good deal of Cather herself in the character of Tommy: "Tommy" is a masculine nickname for Theodosia, the character's real name; Willa Cather was baptized "Wilella," but changed it when she was an adolescent to the more masculine version we know her by today (O'Brien 1987, 13). Further, her caustic description of the women of Southdown mirrors the author's own opinion of the bland lives conventional women led: Southdown women are for the most part uninterested "in anything but babies and salads" (Cather 1970, 474; O'Brien 1987, 120). We have no reason to believe that Red Cloud's notions about womanhood were any different from those of the larger culture. Articles in the local newspapers reveal a very conventional view of women: ambitious, independent girls are criticized, whereas submissive, domestic girls are held up for admiration (O'Brien 1987, 98–99).

Despite her disdain for the nineteenth-century cult of domesticity and the fragile women it produced, Cather always appreciated conventional feminine beauty. According to O'Brien, in one of Cather's articles for the Lincoln *Journal* "she lavishly praised the portraits she discovered at a local art exhibit—aesthetic constructions of idealized femininity" (1984, 581). The portrait that most impressed her was of a cultured and refined woman with a slender waist and firm flesh—exactly the kind of woman Cather often created in art: "her fiction's lost ladies—Marian Forrester, Myra Henshawe, Sapphira Colbert" (O'Brien 1984, 581). In "Tommy, the Unsentimental" the character of Miss Jessica is probably part of this tradition. O'Brien argues that the physical beauty of these women probably owes a good deal to Louise Pound, the beautiful and elegant daughter of a distinguished Lincoln family, whom Cather met at the University of Nebraska. Pound and Cather developed an

intensely emotional attachment; the relationship was one of the most important in Cather's life. Pound's "college photograph reveals a delicate-featured
young woman with long red hair gracefully swept up in a bun, wearing a
dress with fashionable leg-of-mutton sleeves and a gold necklace," much the
same in appearance as many of Cather's conventionally beautiful characters
(O'Brien 1984, 581).

Woodress notes that the story may have grown out of Cather's need to
react against what she felt was the disgusting "sentimental pabulum that she
found in the *Home Monthly*'s inventory when she arrived to edit the magazine" (1970, 83). O'Brien suggests a similar motive: "Despite her assurances
to [her college friend] Mariel Gere that she could control her antipathy to the
magazine's domestic content, she seems to have wanted to declare herself
under the cover of fiction, to tell the truth but tell it slant." This inference
seems credible, especially when one takes into account that this piece was
the only Cather contribution to the first issue of the magazine to which she
signed her real name; the other two (the short story "The Princess
Baladina—Her Adventure" and "My Little Boy," a poem) were pseudonymous
(O'Brien 1987, 229–30).

Relationship to Other Cather Works

This piece is significant largely because it represents the first time Cather
expressed her ambivalence toward Nebraska (Baker 1968, 22). The stories in
The Troll Garden, Cather's first collection, certainly reveal a similar ambivalence, as do her novels *O Pioneers!* and *My Ántonia*.

Bennett points out that like Cather herself, the protagonist in this story
had a close relationship with the "town's elder statesmen, two of whom
would sit for a memorable portrait in 'Two Friends' (1932)" (1970, xxviii). In
fact, modified versions of many of the characters in this piece reappear in
Cather's later work. As has already been noted, Jessica may be thought of as
an early version of Cather's lost ladies—Marian Forrester (*A Lost Lady*), Myra
Henshawe (*My Mortal Enemy*), Sapphira Colbert (*Sapphira and the Slave
Girl*). Jay Ellington Harper is very similar to Victor Morse in *One of Ours*:
"Victor had been a bank clerk in Crystal Lake, Iowa, and had little to com-
mend him except that he was, like Jay, likable" (Bennett 1957, 104).

Bennett considers the relationship between Tommy and the older businessmen of the town a typical Cather portrait. These men had been something of a mother to her, giving her advice on subjects most men feel
uncomfortable discussing. Cather often portrays solid male–female relationships as the "father–daughter or older man–young girl" variety: Lucy
Gayheart and Sebastian (*Lucy Gayheart*), Thea Kronborg and Dr. Archie
(*The Song of the Lark*), Alexandra and Ivar (*O Pioneers!*), and Anton Rosicky

and his daughter-in-law ("Neighbour Rosicky") are some obvious examples (1957, 106).

Interpretations and Criticisms

Most Cather scholars agree that this story is primarily intended as a scathing attack on the suffocating and restricting Victorian ideal of womanhood that the magazine in which it was published, *Home Monthly*, seemed to uphold. In O'Brien's view, not only does the author create a protagonist who is a woman, but one who is traditionally masculine in most ways. Then "Cather goes even further by substituting a male plot for a female one" (1987, 229). Tommy's initial attraction to Jay Ellington Harper suggests that the story will follow a conventional romantic plot: boy meets girl, and after several misunderstandings and reconciliations, they finally marry. But Cather does the unexpected and turns the story into the "masculine . . . adventure story . . . with a female hero as Tommy mounts her bicycle and sets off to save Harper from financial ruin" (O'Brien 1987, 229). Brown argues that Cather's plot is successful and that the story is her best up to that time and until nine years later, when "The Sculptor's Funeral" appeared (1964, 80).

Robinson suggests that, although the plot is simple on its surface, very little effort is required to see it as "one in which a clever girl is attracted to a clinging maiden, introduces her to a man of her acquaintance and loses her to him" (1983, 78). Cather was probably aware that such a reading was a possibility and perhaps "took a wicked satisfaction" from it (Robinson 1983, 78). The Old Boys of the story assert that affection between a rebellious girl and another girl is a very bad sign—an assertion Robinson sees as significant: "Exactly what they meant by this observation is never quite established but it remains as explicit a statement of Willa's own susceptibility as anything she ever wrote and serves as the purest example of her self-awareness of the duality of her nature" (Robinson 1983, 78–79).

O'Brien observes that Cather had thoroughly "internalized the male aesthetic," and in her early days as a writer was not pleased to be a woman. Because the female writers of sentimental fiction were not acceptable models to Cather, she admired male artists almost exclusively. "Women writers were limited, male writers were universal; to escape female limitations, a woman had to write like a man" (O'Brien 1982, 271). Cather's male identification explains her frequent use of male protagonists and narrators in several of her early stories. In "Tommy," of course, the protagonist is a woman; nevertheless, the story is clear evidence of Cather's preference for male characteristics. Tommy is "blunt, intelligent, [and] resourceful, qualities that seem to grow naturally from the 'unfeminine'" (O'Brien 1982, 273). Miss Jessica, on the other hand is "shrinking, delicate, [and] childlike"; in other words, she is feminine in the extreme, and therefore "useless and ridiculous, Cather's caricature of Victorian America's ideal woman. . . . The human qualities she admired she still considered male" (O'Brien 1982, 273).

Works Cited

Baker, Bruce Paul. 1968. "Nebraska Regionalism in Selected Works of Willa Cather." *Western American Literature* 3:19–35.

Bennett, Mildred R., ed. 1957. *Early Stories of Willa Cather*. New York: Dodd, Mead.

Bennett, Mildred R. [1965] 1970. Introduction to *Willa Cather's Collected Short Fiction*. Ed. Virginia Faulkner. Lincoln: University of Nebraska Press. Reprint. Lincoln: University of Nebraska Press.

Brown, E. K. [1953] 1964. *Willa Cather: A Critical Biography*. New York: Knopf.

Cather, Willa. 1957. "Tommy, the Unsentimental." In *Early Stories*. Ed. Mildred Bennett. New York: Dodd, Mead, 103–113.

———. [1965] 1970. "Tommy, the Unsentimental." In *Willa Cather's Collected Short Fiction, 1892–1912*. Ed. Virginia Faulkner. Lincoln: University of Nebraska Press.

Faulkner, Virginia, ed. [1965] 1970. *Willa Cather's Collected Short Fiction, 1892–1912*. Lincoln: University of Nebraska Press. Reprint. Lincoln: University of Nebraska Press.

O'Brien, Sharon. 1982. "Mothers, Daughters, and the 'Art Necessity': Willa Cather and the Creative Process." In *American Novelists Revisited: Essays in Feminist Criticism*. Ed. Fritz Fleischmann. Boston: G. K. Hall.

———. 1984. "'The Thing Not Named': Willa Cather as a Lesbian Writer." *Signs: Journal of Women in Culture and Society* 9:576–99.

———. 1987. *Willa Cather: The Emerging Voice*. New York: Oxford University Press.

Robinson, Phyllis C. 1983. *Willa: The Life of Willa Cather*. Garden City, NY: Doubleday.

Slote, Bernice. 1970. "Willa Cather as a Regional Writer." *Kansas Quarterly* 2:7–15.

Woodress, James. 1970. *Willa Cather: Her Life and Art*. New York: Pegasus.

The Treasure of Far Island

Publication History

This story was first published in the October 1902 issue of *New England* magazine, n.s. (27:234–49) under the name Willa Sibert Cather (Faulkner 1970, 594). It was reprinted in the Winter 1964/65 issue of *Prairie Schooner* (38:323–43) (Lathrop 1975, 79), and in the 1965 University of Nebraska Press volume *Willa Cather's Collected Short Fiction, 1892–1912*.

Circumstances of Composition, Sources, and Influences

Cather probably wrote this story while she was living with the McClung family and teaching at Pittsburgh's Central High School. Isabelle McClung had asked Cather to move in with her and her family in the spring of 1901 after Cather had returned to Pittsburgh from Washington, D.C., where she had worked briefly. The years Cather spent with the McClungs, 1901–1906, were immensely important in her development as a writer, for they provided exactly what she needed to flourish—"an ordered protected life in comfortable— even luxurious—surroundings" (O'Brien 1987, 235). Cather preferred to think of the artist as a loner, but she herself always "needed to be rooted in a warm, familiar domestic space in order to write" (O'Brien 1987, 235).

According to Woodress, the main source for the story is Cather's memory of the wonderful times when she and her friends, including her brothers Roscoe and Douglass, played on a sandbar in the Republican River, not far from the Cather home in Red Cloud, Nebraska. The children spent many hours on their island, playing Long John Silver and Jim Hawkins, characters from *Treasure Island*. Often they built fires and actually spent the night on the beach. The island was perfect for exploring, with its "thousands of yellow-green willows and cottonwood seedlings, brilliantly green even in the hottest summer weather," and kept an important place in Cather's memory (Woodress 1987, 59). It was a place where Cather and her playmates could let their imaginations have free rein. There they created dramas and acted scenes from adventure novels (O'Brien 1987, 84).

Most Cather authorities point out that the first name of the story's protagonist is also Cather's brother's name. Douglass Burnham's return to his hometown as a star was something Cather probably dreamed about doing herself (Bradford 1955, 539–40).

Relationship to Other Cather Works

Bennett notes that the boys of "The Treasure of Far Island"—Douglass Burnham, Rhinehold Birkner, Temp, and Shorty Thompson—had also appeared in Cather's 1898 story "The Way of the World." Their names in the earlier story are a bit different: Speckle Burnham, Jimmie Templeton, Shorty Thompson, and Reinholt Birkner. Pagie's tobacco tags in "The Treasure of Far Island" reappear in "The Enchanted Bluff" as Tip's cigarette cards and tin tobacco tags (Bennett 1982, 48).

Campfire scenes, as Bennett goes on to explain, recur in Cather's fiction as well: "The Enchanted Bluff" follows a similar group of boys, who swear allegiance to the river's spirit. The protagonist of Cather's first novel, *Alexander's Bridge*, has a nostalgic episode when he sees some boys around a campfire, and recalls his own camping days. Another group of boys, one of whom is named Rheinhold Blum, "appears in the picnic in *A Lost Lady*. . . . Blum is the development of the two previous characters with a similar first name" (Bennett 1982, 48). The same type of scene appears in Cather's 1903 poem that she dedicated to her brothers and included in her volume of poetry *April Twilights* (1903). The poem "recalls their 'vanished kingdom' and fixes the image of the children 'who lay and planned at moonrise,/ On an island in a western river,/ Of the conquest of the world together'" (quoted in Bennett 1970, xxxiii).

Woodress mentions the moon imagery in this story, noting that Cather relied heavily on the same imagery in "Eric Hermannson's Soul," "The Enchanted Bluff," and later in *The Song of the Lark*, *A Lost Lady*, and *My Mortal Enemy* (1987, 220–21). A predominance of moon imagery is perhaps not surprising, since in this story Cather is more interested in the woman's attractions than in the man's (Thurin 1990, 117). Thurin, too, connects "The Treasure of Far Island" to "Eric Hermannson's Soul" but also to "A Resurrection" in terms of the central theme shared by all three—"the mutual attraction of man and woman—with only a touch of the idea of a Transcendentalist quest for beauty which looms so large in the tales involving . . . professors" (1990, 115).

According to Arnold, in both setting and subject this story anticipates Cather's later work, especially *My Ántonia* and *Lucy Gayheart*, and like so much of Cather's fiction, it reveals youth as the perfect time of life. Such a love of youth is also obvious in "The Joy of Nelly Deane," "Uncle Valentine," "Double Birthday," "Two Friends," "The Old Beauty," and "The Best Years" (1984, 39–40). Margie's charge that Douglass had lost their childhood for them by growing up and becoming worldly-wise is reminiscent of an earlier story, "The Way of the World," where the author describes "the calamity wrought in the child world by a sellout to a materialistic ethic. 'The Treasure of Far Island' reverses the tragedy of 'The Way of the World,' recouping the loss and returning its characters to freedom and light and childlike sharing" (1984, 40).

The character of the lawyer in this story, whose inability to adjust to the small town drives him to alcoholism, is described by Bloom and Bloom as "the pathetic victim of an intractable order in which refinement must be stamped out as uselessly weak" (1962, 58). This description links this character to Cather's sculptor in "The Sculptor's Funeral," whose tragedy was that he thirsted for something of quality in a place where the vulgar and materialistic reigned supreme (Bloom and Bloom 1962, 58–59).

Rosowski groups the story with others in which Cather presents "an extraordinary, usually visionary experience . . . by inserting otherworldly characters"—they may be ghosts or simply very special human beings—"into ordinary reality or by moving characters from ordinary settings to otherworldly ones" (1986, 11). One tactic or the other is employed in "'The Fear That Walks by Noonday,'" "The Affair at Grover Station," "The Garden Lodge," "On the Gulls' Road," "Jack-a-Boy," "Eric Hermannson's Soul," "A Wagner Matinée," and "A Resurrection" (Rosowski 1986, 11).

Nearly all Cather specialists mention the story most directly related to this one—"The Enchanted Bluff" (1909). The consensus of opinion is that "The Enchanted Bluff" may be viewed as a reworking of "The Treasure of Far Island," and that the later story is the better of the two. Wasserman says, for example, that the earlier story is encumbered "with a grown-up love affair and many allusions to *Treasure Island*. To compare the two is to see what Cather meant by throwing out the furniture," an expression she uses in her well-known essay "The Novel Demeuble," where "she argues for an austere selectivity of detail, for 'unfurnishing' the social-historical surroundings and even the moods and emotions of characters" (1991, 13, 17).

Robinson, too, refers to "The Enchanted Bluff" as a reworking of "The Treasure of Far Island" and imagines that Cather "winced in later years at the false and sentimental ending" of the latter, especially in light of the fact that the reworking produced "a flawless tale" (1983, 159).

Interpretations and Criticisms

Many Cather experts feel that despite the "charm of childhood fantasy [that] warms the heart in this day of stark reality," this story is too sentimental a tale to be considered an important artistic achievement (Schweider 1965, F-11). Rosowski agrees and points to Cather's self-conscious and artificial use of symbols. Cather "tended to give objects significance, then to position them in the [story] as reminders rather than sources of meaning" (1986, 12–13). Arnold contends that the story is one of "excesses," that the characters' world is "shot through with celestial fire and furbished with romantic profusion. . . . The self-imposed curbs and low-keyed restraint that distinguish Cather's later work are absent . . ." (1984, 39). Woodress considers the story "mawkish and uncontrolled," although he gives Cather credit for drawing on her early memories (1987, 156).

Hall gives Cather a bit more credit than most other critics do. Although there is no denying that there are some excesses in the story, most of the overblown rhetoric belongs to the character of Douglass Burnham. Margie is provided to "undercut [his] self-conscious oratory. . . . [Her] analysis of his literary fantasies as arrested development and her fear that Burnham's proposal of love in terms of the Edenic myth is 'only a new play' (Cather 1970, 281) invest the story with a distrust of the derivative eloquence" that so many of Cather's critics find disturbing (1988, 142–43).

The story's allusions themselves are the subjects of Thurin's study, in which he notes that some, but not all, are classical: there are "references to texts like *Romeo and Juliet*, *The Tempest*, Keats' 'May Day Ode,' Emerson's 'The Poet,' Daudet's *Kings in Exile*, *Treasure Island*, *Arabian Nights*, and Genesis" (1990, 116). Greek mythology, however, is predominant, especially when the childhoods of Douglass and Margie are described. Among the Roman references is Douglass's recollection that "reciting 'Regulus to the Carthaginians' was one of his old 'stunts.' Regulus was of course also an empire builder. So were the Roman generals whose triumphs are alluded to again and again—triumphs in which Margie apparently played the role of the conquered" (Cather 1970, 268; Thurin 1990, 116).

Thurin feels that Cather cannot seem to decide which classical references to associate with Margie. Douglass thinks of her as something of a goddess, but not always the *same* goddess. In the sense that she seems to have waited patiently for Douglass's return, she is not a goddess at all, but rather Penelope waiting for Ulysses (1990, 116). In any case, what may be most significant about this confusing portrayal of Margie is that it indicates "the first sign of the hesitation or tension between two different conceptions of womanhood so often glimpsed in Cather's later fiction" (Thurin 1990, 117).

Although it is difficult to see Douglass as virile and masculine, Cather does to a certain extent attribute to him some of those traditional characteristics, according to Thurin: he seems to enjoy being the aggressor, the pursuer, and the dominant intellect. Despite Margie's lively intellect, he persists in seeing her "chiefly as a sex object. . . . Their ancient search for pirate gold is resumed not only as an attempt to relive their childhood games in imagination, but in terms of the idea that Margie is the buried treasure and Douglass the pirate chief determined to lay his hands on it" (Thurin 1990, 117–18). Thurin is one of several critics to pronounce the story "artificial" largely because "it contains too many literary references; there is not enough room for reality to seep in" (1990, 118).

Some positive critical comments do exist, however. Among them is O'Brien's opinion that the story is important for its strong portrayal of a typical Cather view of "childhood as a period of freedom and unselfconscious wholeness when sisters were both equal to and indistinguishable from their brothers" (1987, 111). Once they become adults and begin to embrace conventional sex roles, they "enter the fallen world . . . and repress the part of the self then assigned to the other gender," a view made explicit in the story by Cather's association of the "treacherous landscape" with "puberty and sexual" fears (O'Brien 1987, 112). In her youth Margie never required protection or support from the boys; as an adult, however, she has become somewhat fragile, and Douglass finds the change attractive (1987, 112).

Agreeing that the story is "overladen with intrusive references to male writers—Stevenson, Emerson, Shakespeare, Homer, Housman"—O'Brien maintains that Cather's use of them "demonstrates the woman writer's need to declare herself a descendant of the male literary tradition to which she fears she does not belong" (1987, 151).

Bloom and Bloom feel the story provides important information about Cather's developing theory of genius. Genius, Cather was coming to believe, was neither the result of environment nor heredity, but instead had a "divine or miraculous origin." She refers to it as "one of the 'dark things' ordered by a 'dread Providence'" (Cather 1970, 267; Bloom and Bloom 1962, 124).

Works Cited

Arnold, Marilyn. 1984. *Willa Cather's Short Fiction*. Athens: Ohio University Press.

Bennett, Mildred R. [1965] 1970. Introduction to *Willa Cather's Collected Short Fiction*. Ed. Virginia Faulkner. Lincoln: University of Nebraska Press. Reprint. Lincoln: University of Nebraska Press.

———. 1982. "Willa Cather's Bodies for Ghosts." *Western American Literature* 17:39–52.

Bloom, Edward A., and Lillian D. Bloom. 1962. *Willa Cather's Gift of Sympathy*. Carbondale: Southern Illinois University Press.

Bradford, Curtis. 1955. "Willa Cather's Uncollected Short Stories." *American Literature* 26:537–51.

Cather, Willa. [1965] 1970. "The Treasure of Far Island." In *Willa Cather's Collected Short Fiction, 1892–1912*. Ed. Virginia Faulkner. Lincoln: University of Nebraska Press.

Faulkner, Virginia, ed. [1965] 1970. *Willa Cather's Collected Short Fiction, 1892–1912*. Lincoln: University of Nebraska Press. Reprint. Lincoln: University of Nebraska Press.

Hall, Joan Wylie. 1988. "Treacherous Texts: The Perils of Allusion in Cather's Early Stories." *Colby Library Quarterly* 24:142–50.

Lathrop, Joanna. 1975. *Willa Cather: A Checklist of Her Published Writing*. Lincoln: University of Nebraska Press.

O'Brien, Sharon. 1987. *Willa Cather: The Emerging Voice*. New York: Oxford University Press.

Robinson, Phyllis C. 1983. *Willa: The Life of Willa Cather*. Garden City, NY: Doubleday.

Rosowski, Susan J. 1986. *The Voyage Perilous: Willa Cather's Romanticism*. Lincoln: University of Nebraska Press.

Schweider, Nancy. 1965. "Stirrings of Growing Talent Captured in Early Stories." *Sunday Journal and Star*, September 5, F-11.

Thurin, Erik Ingvar. 1990. *The Humanization of Willa Cather: Classicism in an American Classic*. Lund, Sweden: Lund University Press.

Wasserman, Loretta. 1991. *Willa Cather: A Study of the Short Fiction*. Boston: Twayne.

Woodress, James. 1987. *Willa Cather: A Literary Life*. Lincoln: University of Nebraska Press.

Two Friends

Publication History

This story was first published under the name Willa Cather in the July 1932 issue of *Woman's Home Companion* (59:7–9, 54–56) (Faulkner 1970, 598). Cather included the story in her third collection, *Obscure Destinies* (New York: Knopf, 1932, pp. 191–230), and it reappeared in volume twelve of the thirteen-volume library edition of Cather's work, *The Novels and Stories of Willa Cather* (Boston: Houghton Mifflin, 1937–1941, pp. 159–91) (Faulkner 1970, 598). The story was reprinted in 1974 by Vintage Books in a paperback edition of *Obscure Destinies*, and again in 1992 by Literary Classics of the United States in *Cather: Stories, Poems, and Other Writings*, a volume in the Library of America series.

Circumstances of Composition, Sources, and Influences

This story was written during the months Cather spent at the bedside of her mother, who had suffered a paralytic stroke shortly after Cather's father's death in 1928; her mother was confined to a nursing home in Pasadena, California, until her death in 1931. Woodress maintains that during this time, Cather's thoughts continually strayed back to her childhood in Nebraska, when both her parents were healthy and the family was all together (1970, 240). Arnold believes the story was probably written in 1931 and that Cather's preoccupation with things lost at this time is completely natural: her mother was dying and her father's death was still fresh in her mind. She "must have sensed that things would never be the same again, that she was losing Nebraska, except as a memory" (Arnold 1984, 152–53). Brown notes that the time of composition was during the period between Cather's completion of *Shadows on the Rock* and that novel's appearance in 1931 (1964, 291).

The two men in the story are modeled on two of Cather's childhood acquaintances. Mr. Dillon is drawn from the father of Carrie Miner, one of Cather's childhood playmates in Red Cloud, and Mr. Trueman from a Red Cloud stock dealer named William N. Richardson (Woodress 1987, 445). After the story appeared in print, Cather even wrote to her friend Carrie Miner, hoping that Carrie did not find offensive Cather's use of Mr. Miner as a model for Mr. Dillon (Wasserman 1991, 59). The red brick building outside which the two friends sit and talk is actually the Miner brothers' store, where Cather and the Miner children had often gathered (Bennett 1961, 44, 66). Besides these specific prototypes, however, Dillon and Trueman serve as Cather's tribute to all the "heroic men, daring planners, and bold executors"—that is, to all the true pioneers Cather had known during her young life (Bloom and Bloom 1962, 112–13). The two men may also be Cather's "spokesmen for the depression years," appearing as they did during the nation's economic collapse (Geismar 1967, 188). Wasserman maintains that Mr. Dillon is a much less admirable man than Mr. Trueman, even though he is more aware of "precise commercial values"; only Trueman is represented as "magnanimous," "large-souled," and "heroic" (1991, 62).

Wasserman suggests that the portrayal of the deep friendship between the two men may have come from Cather's recollection of Aristotle's or Cicero's ideas on friendship, and she was perhaps experimenting to see how their ideas would work in a small western American town (1991, 60). Thurin has a similar insight—that "the concept of male friendship in 'Two Friends' bears a striking resemblance to the ideal relationship sketched by Cicero in *Laelius de amicitia*" (1990, 326). Making such a connection even more probable is the fact that Cather associates the two men with Rome: the way they are described moving through the town is "just the way one would imagine two

Roman patricians like Scipio and Laelius" comporting themselves (Thurin 1990, 327).

Murphy argues that Cather must have had Whitman's poem "Out of the Cradle Endlessly Rocking" in mind while writing this story. In both works the adult writer remembers a scene from childhood that is charged with meaning. In the case of the persona in Whitman's poem, the recollection is of two mockingbirds, whose love for each other inspired him in much the same way Cather's narrator was impressed by the two men's friendship: "The crisis point in both works is when the satisfactory equilibrium of love—romantic love or friendship love—is disturbed. Whitman's female bird flies out to sea, never to return" and the friendship between the two men in Cather's tale dissolves in a quarrel (1987, 39–40).

Relationship to Other Cather Works

Because this story is one of three that Cather gathered into her third collection, *Obscure Destinies*, its closest links are to the other stories in that book, "Neighbour Rosicky" and "Old Mrs. Harris." (For a complete discussion of the ways in which the stories in *Obscure Destinies* are held together thematically, as well as an explanation of the collection's title, see the "Relationship to Other Cather Works" section for the chapter "Neighbour Rosicky.") In some ways, however, "Two Friends" diverges from the other two stories, especially, according to Leddy, in terms of the narrator's role. As in the other two tales, "observation is a central concern," but in this story there is more distance between the narrator and the observed; the narrator is always "on the periphery of things, passing through Dillon's store in the winter and passing by in other seasons" (1988, 149). Wasserman notes that the opening of the story is in striking contrast to the openings of the other two, where the reader is thrust suddenly into the midst of some personal worry (Wasserman 1991, 60). In Thurin's view, all three stories downplay the importance of religion: years after the two men's friendship has disintegrated, "it is still associated with the idea that man lives and dies under the moon" (1990, 327). In a diametrically opposed point of view, Ryder argues that this story "shows by negation the importance of the Christian values of understanding, tolerance, and forgiveness" (1990, 268).

Cather specialists have not missed the connections this story has to Cather's works outside *Obscure Destinies*. Rosowski, for example, notes that through the device of recalling from a distance in time something that once seemed an unshakable truth, Cather questions what she calls the "Romantics' faith." In facing the possibility that "truth can be distorted and lost, Cather anticipated the dark romanticism of her final novels" (1986, 203–204).

Arnold finds links between this story and "Coming, Aphrodite!" In both stories, Cather formalizes emotion, a technique that makes the earlier story "somewhat cold and remote," while in "Two Friends" she is able to keep more distance from her characters without "sacrificing warmth and humanness" (1984, 178n). Wasserman points out that Cather's use of the "night sky as a manifest for lurking questions" also occurs in "The Enchanted Bluff" and "Before Breakfast" (1991, 61). Thurin asserts that Dillon's Roman nose and Trueman's ring, with its onyx Roman soldier, are clear classical references. These details connect the story to other Cather works in which she alludes to Rome while describing male friendships. For example, Godfrey St. Peter and Tom Outland read Latin poetry together in *The Professor's House*, "A Son of the Celestial," contains a quotation from one of Horace's odes on his friendship with Maecenas, and an early Cather essay on Shakespeare describes the friendship of Caesar and Mark Antony (Thurin 1990, 326).

Interpretations and Criticisms

Most critics agree that the friendship represented in this story is meant to give "solidity and meaning to the little town" and to the life of the narrator (Canby 1984, 281), for whom the relationship between the two men is extremely important, "not only for the solidity it represents, but because the two men, in their talk and deportment, explain and enlarge her world" (Wasserman 1991, 60). Without the friendship, the narrator's life is listless and dull—almost unreal. In Danker's view, there is a good deal of the insubstantial in the story in spite of the early description of the friendship, however. Even the narrator is a "lost and ghostly child," whose sex remains indeterminate. If we assume she is a girl, it is only because playing jacks is traditionally a girl's pastime (1990, 27). But Lee notes the boyishness of the narrator, who is reminiscent of Jim Burden in *My Ántonia* (1989, 311). At least one reviewer insists that not everything about the story is ghostly and unreal, that there is something solid about the scene itself, "at once a sculptural quality and a poetry . . ." (C. 1932, 246–47).

Arnold argues that the mood and the oral quality of the story are deliberate: the story is "an artistic production, carefully constructed and managed to produce rather formal feelings about certain kinds of change and loss" (1984, 152). The dissolution of the friendship between the two men jolted the narrator into an "upheaval of almost cosmic significance" (1984, 154–55), and all the images the narrator associated with the friendship—the sidewalk, store, moonlight, and dusty road—have been transmuted into "symbols of aching memory and reminders of loss" (1984, 156). The exact loss for the narrator is "a picture of equilibrium, a memory of harmony. She is left with the uneasiness of seeking a retreat that no longer exists" (Rosowski 1986, 203).

Trueman tells the readers what their attitude toward change should be—that is, acceptance of change as an inevitable part of life (Wasserman 1991, 63).

Leddy argues that the narrator is somewhat unreliable because of her necessarily limited perspective of Mr. Dillon and Mr. Trueman: she only sees them in the evenings at the store, and some of her information comes from other people. What is more, much of the communication between the two men is in the form of silent gestures and signs, and although she learns a good deal from these nonverbal or semiverbal communications, she inevitably misses a good deal and is forced to guess and draw fairly uncertain conclusions. For example, the reader would like to think that in the end Mr. Trueman remembers with fondness his friendship with Mr. Dillon as he sits in his San Francisco office and watches the Bay, but we are given no certainty that he does (1988, 150–51). With this last story in *Obscure Destinies*, then, "Cather . . . ends her trilogy in obscurity; with unanswered and unanswerable questions; with lives that are incomplete, isolated, and puzzling; with a narrator who is, literally and figuratively, in the dark" (1988, 152).

Although the narrator may have some problems reporting reliably because of the conversational habits of Mr. Dillon and Mr. Trueman, it is nevertheless their language that initially draws the narrator to them. As Arnold puts it, "It is as if Cather were saying, I may have lost the Nebraska of childhood, but I have retained the Nebraska of memory and art. In Nebraska were the beginnings of art, the first conscious sensitivities to the rhythms of language" (1984, 157). In fact, the precision of the two men's language sets them apart from others. They have achieved "linguistic harmony"—a harmony that is unfortunately "broken in on by another language" (Lee 1989, 314). As Lee explains, one of the things that repulses Trueman about his friend's immersion in populism is the language associated with it. The narrator, too, hears changes in Dillon's voice as he becomes more political; it becomes false. It is the intrusion of this artificial diction that ruins the friendship (1989, 314). In many ways, according to Arnold, the story is less about friendship and change than it is about language itself. Language is capable both of destroying and of unifying. It initially draws the three characters together, but in the end is the cause of their separation. Perhaps most significant, "it was language that enabled the narrator to order her emotions and deal with the loss" (Arnold 1984, 158).

Works Cited

Arnold, Marilyn. 1984. *Willa Cather's Short Fiction*. Athens: Ohio University Press.

Bennett, Mildred R. 1961. *The World of Willa Cather*. Lincoln: University of Nebraska Press.

Bloom, Edward A., and Lillian D. Bloom. 1962. *Willa Cather's Gift of Sympathy.* Carbondale: Southern Illinois University Press.

Brown, E. K. Completed by Leon Edel. [1953] 1964. *Willa Cather: A Critical Biography.* New York: Knopf.

C., A. 1932. Review of *Obscure Destinies*, by Willa Cather. *Catholic World* 136:246–47.

Canby, Henry Seidel. 1984. "The Last Four Books." In *Critical Essays on Willa Cather.* Ed. John J. Murphy. Boston: G. K. Hall.

Cather, Willa. 1974."Two Friends." In *Obscure Destinies.* New York: Vintage Books, 193–230.

———. 1992. "Two Friends." In *Cather: Stories, Poems, and Other Writings.* New York: Literary Classics of the United States, 673–90.

Danker, Kathleen A. 1990. "The Passing of a Golden Age in *Obscure Destinies.*" *Willa Cather Pioneer Memorial Newsletter* 34:24–28.

Faulkner, Virginia, ed. [1965] 1970. *Willa Cather's Collected Short Fiction, 1892–1912.* Lincoln: University of Nebraska Press. Reprint. Lincoln: University of Nebraska Press.

Geismar, Maxwell. 1967. "Willa Cather: Lady in the Wilderness." In *Willa Cather and Her Critics.* Ed. James Schroeter. Ithaca, NY: Cornell University Press.

Leddy, Michael. 1988. "Observation and Narration in Willa Cather's *Obscure Destinies.*" *Studies in American Fiction* 16:141–53.

Lee, Hermione. 1989. *Willa Cather: Double Lives.* New York: Pantheon.

Murphy, John J. 1987. "Cather's 'Two Friends' as a Western 'Out of the Cradle.'" *Willa Cather Pioneer Memorial Newsletter* 31:39–41.

Rosowski, Susan J. 1986. *The Voyage Perilous: Willa Cather's Romanticism.* Lincoln: University of Nebraska Press.

Ryder, Mary Ruth. 1990. *Willa Cather and Classical Myth.* Lewiston, NY: Edwin Mellen Press.

Thurin, Erik Ingvar. 1990. *The Humanization of Willa Cather: Classicism in an American Classic.* Lund, Sweden: Lund University Press.

Wasserman, Loretta. 1991. *Willa Cather: A Study of the Short Fiction.* Boston: Twayne.

Woodress, James. 1970. *Willa Cather: Her Life and Art.* New York: Pegasus.

———. 1987. *Willa Cather: A Literary Life.* Lincoln: University of Nebraska Press.

Uncle Valentine

Publication History

This story was first published serially under the name Willa Cather in the February and March 1925 issues of *Woman's Home Companion* (52:7–9, 86, 89–90; 15–16, 75–76, 79–80) (Faulkner 1970, 598). It was reprinted in 1973 by the University of Nebraska Press in *Uncle Valentine and Other Stories: Willa Cather's Uncollected Short Fiction, 1915–1929*, and in 1992 by Literary Classics of the United States in *Cather: Stories, Poems, and Other Writings*, a volume in the Library of America series.

Circumstances of Composition, Sources, and Influences

In the fall of 1924, Cather was hard at work trying to complete her novel *The Professor's House*. Nevertheless, she traveled to Red Cloud to spend Christmas with her parents that year. She probably wrote this story and placed it in *Woman's Home Companion* before leaving New York (Woodress 1987, 359). "Uncle Valentine" was the first short story Cather had published in five years, during which time she had been absorbed in the writing of three novels, *One of Ours* (1922), *A Lost Lady* (1923), and *The Professor's House* (1925) (Arnold 1984, 119). For Cather, the years 1922–1926 were extraordinarily productive. In addition to the appearance of three novels and a short story, she also published an essay on Katherine Mansfield in Knopf's *Borzoi 25*; a preface to *The Best Stories of Sarah Orne Jewett*; and introductions to *The Wagnerian Romances* by Gertrude Hall, Defoe's *Fortunate Mistress*, and volume 9 of *The Works of Stephen Crane* (Robinson 1983, 242).

In "Uncle Valentine," for the first time in years, Cather drew on her memories of her life in Pittsburgh, where she lived from 1896 until 1906, and especially on her friendship with the musician Ethelbert Nevin, whose family owned the Pittsburgh *Leader*, where Cather was employed for three years. (For a discussion of Cather's friendship with Nevin, see the "Circumstances of Composition, Sources, and Influences" section for the chapter "'A Death in the Desert.'" More information about Cather's Pittsburgh years is provided in the "Circumstances of Composition, Sources, and Influences" section for the chapter "A Wagner Matinée.") Most Cather experts agree that Nevin was the prototype for Valentine Ramsey, but Miller points out that the resemblance is not as close as is generally assumed. Unlike Ramsey, Nevin was not at all the "selfish and self-indulgent" character who is capable of hurting the people close to him (1990, 135–36). Slote, too, notes the difference between Nevin and Ramsey: Valentine Ramsay's life and psychological makeup are more like Stephen Crane's than like Ethelbert Nevin's (1973, xxiv). Robinson sees another divergence between the real and fictional characters in Cather's portrayal of Valentine Ramsey's marriage to a crude, greedy woman. Cather considered Anne Paul Nevin, Ethelbert's wife, to be the perfect mate for him; Cather's portrait of Valentine's wife as a very different type was simply appropriate for her story. Mrs. Nevin is much more likely the model for Charlotte Waterford, "who was said to resemble her, and whose sensitivity and kindliness are counterpoints to the rapacity of Mrs. Ramsay" (Robinson 1983, 94).

As Robinson explains, Nevin lived in Sewickly, a suburb of Pittsburgh, on an estate called Vineacre. His next-door neighbors, Mr. and Mrs. John Slack, were also friends of Cather, and she was often a guest at their musical parties. Cather very likely borrowed this setting of the two houses for "Uncle Valentine." In fact, it was quite probably at the Slacks' home that she met Ethelbert Nevin for the first time. One Christmas Nevin himself took Cather shopping, an episode that reappears in the story when Valentine Ramsey and Charlotte Waterford go Christmas shopping together (1983, 94). In Woodress's opinion, the character of Charlotte is modeled on Mrs. Slack, not Mrs. Nevin. He further notes that there actually was a girls' chorus that had its Sunday rehearsals with Nevin, just as in the story (Woodress 1987, 360).

The importance of place to Cather also figures largely in this story. Slote explains that throughout her writing career, Cather was able to write in certain places and absolutely not in others. She was successful in the McClung house in Pittsburgh (see the "Circumstances of Composition, Sources, and Influences" section for the chapter "A Wagner Matinée"), in her New York Bank Street apartment, and at the Shattuck Inn in Jaffrey, New Hampshire. In general, however, she "could not work in special studies created by and hovered over by her friends and family" (Slote 1973, xxv). Thus, the importance of Greenacre and Fox Hill to Valentine Ramsey comes from Cather's own understanding of the significance of place for an artist.

Relationship to Other Cather Works

One of the themes this story explores is that of a troubled marriage, a subject Cather returned to repeatedly in her work. Miller argues that the narrative technique she employs is similar to that of *A Lost Lady* and *My Mortal Enemy*: like Niel Herbert and Nellie Birdseye, Marjorie has only a dim understanding of the behavior of the adults close to her. And because of this limited insight, readers are required to take whatever information Marjorie can give, then fill in the blanks themselves (Miller 1990, 133–34). Also, in this story, as in *O Pioneers!* and *My Ántonia*, Cather tells her story chronologically (Arnold 1984, 121).

Cather had previously explored the artist's requirement of certain places in which to create in *The Professor's House*: Godfrey St. Peter is absolutely unable to work outside his house. Leaving his home and garden is like stepping out of his body. This same necessity is expressed in "Uncle Valentine" (Slote 1973, xxiv–xxv). Woodress points out that Ramsey's affinity for the land and woods around his childhood home is like that of Alexandra or Ántonia for their land (1987, 360–61). Another theme that connects this story to *The Professor's House*, as well as to other works, is that of "America's will to plunder its own body and ravage its beauty" (Slote 1973, xxvi). As Cather had said many times before, it is "exploitive materialism that scores lives and destroys landscapes"; she says it again here as she does in "three novels of the same period," *One of Ours*, *A Lost Lady*, and *The Professor's House* (Arnold 1984, 124).

Several characters in this story are familiar Cather types. Arnold sees similarities between Charlotte and Mrs. Harling in *My Ántonia*, for example, and between Louise Ireland and Thea Kronborg (*The Song of the Lark*), Lucy Gayheart (*Lucy Gayheart*), and Marian Forrester (*A Lost Lady*) (1984, 122). The role of Roland is reminiscent of the ghost in "Consequences." Roland comes to symbolize what Valentine will become in the future. Like Kier Cavenaugh in "Consequences," Valentine is horrified by what he could become; when he flees to Europe, he is trying to escape his own future as he sees it in Roland (Arnold 1984, 125).

Interpretations and Criticisms

The story contains several images from composer Richard Wagner's work, but the most significant one comes in the form of an allusion to Wagner's *Ring* and occurs while Valentine and his friends walk through the countryside: "Suddenly, in the low cut between the hills across the river, we saw a luminousness, throbbing and phosphorescent, a ghostly brightness with mists streaming about it and enfolding it, struggling to quench it. We knew it was the moon, but we could see no form, no solid image; it was a flowing, surging, liquid gleaming; now stronger, now softer. 'The Rhinegold!' murmured Valentine and Aunt Charlotte in one breath" (Cather 1973, 25). As Woodress notes, this reference to the Rhinegold "foreshadows [Valentine's and Charlotte's] own twilight of the gods. As possession of the ring made from the Rhinegold causes the conflict and downfall in Wagner's *Ring* cycle, so does money destroy the happiness of the characters in this story" (1987, 361). The intrusion of crass materialism destroys Valentine's spiritual connection to the land in a way that borders on the blasphemous; suddenly his world belongs only to those with money and power, not to those who have a spiritual connection to it (Slote 1973, xxiv). Miller disagrees somewhat with this interpretation: although it will certainly be destroyed by industrial expansion, "Greenacre carries within it the seeds of its own self-destruction. It is a world populated by women, children, and elderly alcoholics who isolate themselves on a hill and vainly try to ignore the passage of time" (Miller 1990, 137).

Slote cautions readers against reading the story as a version of Wagner's *Ring* cycle because "Cather's technique was never to follow a myth or allegory thoroughly and consistently. She wished rather to touch lightly and pass on, letting the suggestions develop as the course of individual imaginations might take them" (1973, xxvi). On the other hand, there are close parallels between the two works. Thomas notes that the land is corrupted by the Oglethorpes just as the Rhinegold is corrupted by Alberich in Wagner's work: the Ramsays live solely on inherited wealth, which is not enough to allow them to outbid the Oglethorpes, just as in Wagner's *Ring* Wotan and the gods decline into weakness and cannot pay for Valhalla. Furthermore, Wagner himself left his wife, "took whatever money he could get his hands on, abused his friends and bent the social order to accommodate his will" (1990, 50–1). Thomas goes on to assert that Valentine in many ways emulates Wagner, but he simply does not have Wagner's drive or talent. Cather seems to prefer Valentine to Wagner at this stage of her life, even though at one time she had "relished the spectacle of Wagner trampling on everyone and extolled him as the archetypal artist" (Thomas 1990, 51). This story, however, may be viewed as evidence of how much Cather had changed over time: "She became less exigent in her demands; an unassuming man composing a few beautiful songs was then something to be treasured. 'Uncle Valentine' is a mature and sensitive presentation of the artist, a gentle and moving account of defeat. . . ." (Thomas 1990, 52).

According to Arnold, with Charlotte's and Valentine's simultaneous recognition of the view's resemblance to the Rhinegold, Cather is also making a point about human attachments—that the deepest human bonds are those that spring from an ability to be moved by beauty. Janet Oglethorpe has no such ability, and therefore she is not admirable, as Charlotte and Louise Ireland are. Janet Oglethorpe serves as a symbol of the real threat to the beautiful—"a world run by machines and money" (1984, 122–23). Miller's view is that despite their mutual aesthetic appreciation of the beautiful, Charlotte and Valentine have a flawed relationship. It does not "sustain Valentine when his ex-wife invades the territory he perceives as his own" (1990, 136).

Another theme that runs through the story, according to Arnold, is that of individual freedom. Marjorie especially learns about the freedom to be oneself from Valentine, who, she realizes, is despised by "city people" simply because he did not follow their rigid Calvinist rules, insisting instead upon personal liberty. One of the most persistent symbols of this freedom in the story is that of the window. Unfortunately this personal liberty, so necessary to someone with artistic sensibility, has a negative side—ultimately each individual is alone in the world. More than anything else in the story, Roland represents the anguish of that essential aloneness (1984, 124–25).

Although most critics regard Valentine as a fairly admirable character, Miller's reading represents a dissenting view. He sees Valentine as something of a self-serving, shady character, whose treatment of women is inexcusable, as is obvious in his language: Valentine describes his former wife as "beefy" (Cather 1973, 13) and sees Louise Ireland as "the sacrifice" (Cather 1973, 14) that allowed him to free himself from his marriage (Miller 1990, 134–35). Miller also points out that Valentine is willing to give up Charlotte if she becomes an obstacle to his fulfilling his own needs. In his account of his marriage to Janet Oglethorpe and his dalliance with Louise Ireland, he justifies his own behavior. Moreover, there is plenty of evidence in the story to suggest that he has seduced or is trying to seduce Charlotte: for example, Charlotte blushes when her husband mentions innocence and when he remarks on how rosy she appears when Valentine is present (1990, 134–35). Even Valentine's success as an artist is suspect—his support and nurture come from someone else's family, which he has usurped (Miller 1990, 134–35). He has rid himself of all the responsibilities and constraints that come with having a family of one's own, and so is able to enjoy "several months wandering through a pastoral landscape in the company of a surrogate wife and children who make no demands upon him" (Miller 1990, 137). The difficult choice for the reader, then, is not the one between "the gross materialism of a Janet Oglethorpe and the sensitive cultivation of a Charlotte Waterford," but between "the freedom for self-expression and the responsibility one owes to other people. Valentine Ramsay equivocates when faced with this choice" (Miller 1990, 137).

Works Cited

Arnold, Marilyn. 1984. *Willa Cather's Short Fiction*. Athens: Ohio University Press.

Cather, Willa. 1973. "Uncle Valentine." In *Uncle Valentine and Other Stories: Willa Cather's Uncollected Short Fiction, 1915–1929*. Ed. Bernice Slote. Lincoln: University of Nebraska Press, 3–38.

———. 1992. "Uncle Valentine." In *Cather: Stories, Poems, and Other Writings*. New York: Literary Classics of the United States, 209–49.

Faulkner, Virginia, ed. [1965] 1970. *Willa Cather's Collected Short Fiction, 1892–1912*. Lincoln: University of Nebraska Press. Reprint. Lincoln: University of Nebraska Press.

Miller, Robert K. 1990. "What Margie Knew." In *Willa Cather and the Family, Community and History: The BYU Symposium*. Ed. John J. Murphy. Provo, Utah: Brigham Young University.

Robinson, Phyllis C. 1983. *Willa: The Life of Willa Cather*. Garden City, NY: Doubleday.

Slote, Bernice. 1973. Introduction to *Uncle Valentine and Other Stories: Willa Cather's Uncollected Short Fiction, 1915–1929*, by Willa Cather. Lincoln: University of Nebraska Press.

Thomas, Susie. 1990. *Willa Cather*. Savage, MD: Barnes & Noble.

Woodress, James. 1987. *Willa Cather: A Literary Life*. Lincoln: University of Nebraska Press.

A Wagner Matinée

Publication History

This story was first published in the February 1904 issue of *Everybody's* magazine (10:325–28) (Faulkner 1970, 594). In 1905, Cather included it in her first collection of short stories, *The Troll Garden* (New York: McClure, Phillips, pp. 193–210) with "important additions as well as three major cuts and many minor ones, [including] alterations in wording, spelling, capitalization, and punctuation" (Faulkner 1970, 594]. The third version of the story appeared in Cather's second collection, *Youth and the Bright Medusa* (New York: Knopf, 1920. pp. 235–47), containing "thirty-five substantive changes, including paragraph cuts, from the 1905 version" (Faulkner 1970, 594). This version was reprinted in *Book of Modern Short Stories*, edited by Dorothy Brewster (New York: Macmillan, 1929, pp. 228–35) (Lathrop 1975, 85). The fourth appearance of the story was in volume six of the thirteen-volume library edition of Cather's work, *The Novels and Stories of Willa Cather* (Boston: Houghton Mifflin, 1937–1941, pp. 263–89), published with fourteen substantive changes from the 1920 version (Faulkner 1970, 595).

When the story first appeared in *Everybody's* magazine, its portrayal of Nebraska's harsh and uncultured life resulted in a good many hurt feelings on the part of Cather's Nebraska friends and family. For example, her old friend Will Jones, editor of the *Nebraska State Journal*, reprimanded Cather in his editorial column of February 26, 1904: "If the writers of fiction who use western Nebraska as material would look up now and then and not keep their eyes and noses in the cattle yards, they might be more agreeable company" (quoted in Bennett 1961, 254n). Woodress explains that even though she defended the story vehemently, Cather was affected by the deluge of criticism, and in the subsequent reprintings of the story she softened the harshness of the aunt's portrait considerably: in the *Troll Garden* version (1905) the changes are minor, but even there Cather omitted some description of the aunt. In 1920, however, she made extensive revisions in order to portray the aunt less harshly. In fact, she cut a whole paragraph describing the aunt. In the final version (1937) she softened the portrait even more (Woodress 1970, 117). Most Cather scholars agree that this increasingly softer portrait reflects Cather's own increasingly charitable feelings toward Nebraska.

The story was reprinted in 1961 by Signet Classics in a paperback edition of *The Troll Garden* with modernized spelling and punctuation. The 1905 version of the story was reprinted in 1965 by the University of Nebraska in *Willa Cather's Collected Short Fiction, 1892–1912*. This same version was reprinted in 1983 by the University of Nebraska Press in an edition of *The Troll Garden*, edited by James Woodress, in 1987 by Literary Classics of the United States in *Cather: Early Novels and Stories*, and again in 1992 by the same press in *Cather: Stories, Poems, and Other Writings*. The last two volumes are part of the Library of America series.

Circumstances of Composition, Sources, and Influences

Cather wrote this story sometime between 1901 and 1903, the two-year span during which all the *Troll Garden* stories apparently were written (Woodress 1983, xiv). At this time Cather was living with Isabelle McClung and her family in Pittsburgh and teaching high school. By this time, however, she had moved from Central High School, where she had begun her teaching career (see the "Circumstances of Composition, Sources, and Influences" section for the chapter "The Treasure of Far Island"), to a post at Allegheny High School, where she earned a higher salary and taught in more pleasant surroundings (Robinson 1983, 123).

The years she lived with the McClungs (1901–1906) were very productive for Cather. According to O'Brien, Cather's living circumstances and her intimate relationship with Isabelle allowed her to refine her craft and produce more work. The McClung family, and Isabelle in particular, provided a balance in Cather's "conflicting needs for autonomy and connection. . . . Isabelle acknowledged her friend's separate existence and wanted to enhance her creativity, offering her a third-floor study" where Cather could escape into the world of the imagination—a world Isabelle respected and wanted to promote (1987, 237). Cather the artist loved the space Isabelle had created for her—which reminded her of the attic bedroom she had occupied in her childhood home in Red Cloud, Nebraska (1987, 238).

The strongest and most obvious sources of this story are Cather's own experiences on the Divide and those of her aunt by marriage, Frances Cather, or Aunt Franc, as Cather called her. Bennett explains that the episode where Georgiana and her husband measure off their land by tying a handkerchief to a wagon wheel comes directly from a family story about the actual home-steading experience of Cather's Uncle George and Aunt Frances Cather: when he moved to Nebraska with his wife, George Cather "hired a man with team and wagon, measured the circumference of one of the back wheels, tied a rag on the rim so they could more easily count the revolutions and started across the prairie. . . . His wife sat in the back of the wagon, counted revolutions, and computed mileage," and when their calculations reached a certain number of miles, they knew they had arrived at their homestead (1961, 12).

Aunt Franc was from Boston and had graduated from Mount Holyoke Female Seminary. Bennett explains that her move to Nebraska with her hus-band left her lonely, and because she longed for the world of art and culture she had left behind, she became active in what were called "literaries"—cul-tural events hosted by different families on the Divide. Cather once remarked that these events were her aunt's way of providing manna in the wilderness. In addition, she led choral groups, and tutored and read to groups of chil-dren. After her five children were born, she left them with Grandmother Cather and paid a visit back East to soak up some of the culture she had left behind, a trip that becomes the central event in "A Wagner Matinée" (Bennett 1961, 14). Cather reportedly also once described her aunt as ugly, smart, and eccentric, a description that matches the narrator's memory of his aunt in this story (Robinson 1983, 124).

The unrelieved bleakness of Cather's portrayal of the Divide in this story also owes something to Cather's own memories of her move from Virginia to Nebraska when she was nine years old. Georgiana's farmhouse is based on Cather's own grandparents' farmhouse, and her anguish over leaving the refinement of the East reflects Cather's own experience of cultural depriva-tion in Nebraska (O'Brien 1987, 281). Gerber considers the story a reflection of Cather's own fears: that she will, like Georgiana, eventually have to face returning to the frontier after an excursion into the world of culture in the East, and that the life of culture has perhaps passed her by while she has spent her time in more mundane pursuits (1975, 45).

Relationship to Other Cather Works

Because Cather included this story in *The Troll Garden*, most critics compare it to other stories in the collection. Some hold that the stories divide themselves into two categories: "those with Eastern settings, which reflect Cather's apprenticeship to Henry James, . . . and those with Western or Nebraska settings in which Cather looks back to early stories like 'Peter' and 'Lou, the Prophet' and ahead to *O Pioneers!* and *My Ántonia*" (O'Brien 1987, 280). Using this division, "A Wagner Matinée" would obviously be placed in the latter category. However, O'Brien finds a more valuable division to be "that between stories in which Cather seems to be speaking in another's voice—whether that of Henry James, Edith Wharton, or of genteel magazine fiction of the day—and those in which she seems to be finding her own cadences" (1987, 280). This story would have to be placed in the group where Cather is learning to use her own voice, as would two other stories— "The Sculptor's Funeral" and "Paul's Case." All three stories reflect Cather's growing tendency to rely on personal experiences or observations rather than on other writers' work (O'Brien 1987, 280).

E. K. Brown categorizes the stories strictly on the basis of the two epigraphs Cather chose for the collection. (For a complete explanation of the stories in *The Troll Garden* based on the epigraphs Cather chose for them, see the "Relationship to Other Cather Works" section for the chapter "'A Death in the Desert.'") In Brown's system, *The Troll Garden* elaborates two themes—the artist and the forces consistently at work to undermine or destroy the artist—both of which are contained in the epigraphs. The goblins of Rossetti's poem are the foes of the artist, and the trolls of the Kingsley quotation are the artists themselves (1964, 113–15).

"A Wagner Matinée" is a kind of "Sculptor's Funeral" in reverse—the farm wife goes back to the East in one, and the artist is brought back to the West in the other. Moreover, "A Wagner Matinée" conforms to "the overall design of *The Troll Garden* by making the narrator's Aunt Georgiana a former musician who has been denied for more than thirty years any possibility of entering the garden" (Woodress 1983, xxii).

Arnold connects this story to the later *My Ántonia* in that Georgiana is for Clark what Ántonia was to be for Jim Burden, "heroic and wonderful, if not mythic," who, despite a hard life on the plains, keeps a certain amount of refinement, "with which she unconsciously and continually blessed his life" (1984, 59). The story also anticipates *My Ántonia* in that the narrator is a young man (Woodress 1983, xxii).

Interpretations and Criticisms

Many of Cather's stories explore the predicament of the person of refined sensibilities who finds himself or herself in an inhospitable environment, but this story is perhaps the one that explores that theme most vividly. In the last paragraph of the story, according to Baker, Cather describes the grim scene to which Georgiana must return—the "unpainted house," the "black pond," the "crookbacked ash seedlings," and the "gaunt, molting turkeys picking up refuse about the kitchen door"—to show just how much the artistic spirit must suffer in Nebraska (Cather 1970, 242; Baker 1987, 15–17). It is a world of defeat—a portrayal that reveals how disgusted Cather had been with Nebraskan small-town life (Bloom 1985, 9, 20). In addition, according to Gerber, Cather positions her descriptions of the world of culture and the world of the plains so that one world comments on the other. The prairie, where, "as in a treadmill, one might walk from daybreak to dusk without perceiving a shadow of change," is placed against the outlines of the orchestra itself: "the beloved shapes of the instruments, the patches of yellow light thrown by the green shaded lamps on the smooth, varnished bellies of the 'cellos and the bass viols in the rear, the restless, wind-tossed forest of fiddle necks and bows" (Cather 1970, 239; Gerber 1975, 72). Gerber argues that Georgiana is utterly exiled in Nebraska. Although she lacked sufficient talent to succeed as a concert pianist, she did have enough to build a solid career as a piano teacher, but even that small joy is sacrificed for a Nebraska homestead, and the realization of what she has renounced is like a death summons (1975, 72). According to Edward A. Bloom and Lillian D. Bloom, such a strong attack on Nebraska was inevitable because at the time she wrote the story, Cather was too close to her subject to treat it with the "esthetic mellowness" that would later allow her to give a more complex portrait of life on the plains (1962, 8).

Giannone points out that Georgiana's struggle to preserve her music in the hard sterility of the plains was actually a war between the noble and base in human beings, the base being victorious (1968, 42). When Georgiana arrives at the concert hall in Boston, the reader is allowed to see her struggle played out through the music—that is, "in the leading motifs of the overture to *Tannhäuser*, . . . in which Wagner sets the symbolic struggle between the sacred and the profane in man. Willa Cather incorporates in her narrative Wagner's opposing motifs of man's higher and lower yearnings and gives them special fictive immediacy and significance of her own" (Giannone 1968, 42–43).

To Schneider, Cather's intention in this story is clear: to attack the kind of life in Nebraska that she sees as fully responsible for draining the sensitivity and artistry out of any soul who happens to possess them. The narrator describes the house as "naked," and words like "pitted" and "gullied" underscore the ugliness of the area. The ash trees are "dwarf ash seedlings where the dishcloths were always hung to dry" (Cather 1970, 242; Schneider 1967, 86). Whereas in her later work Cather often used "the circle as a symbol of fulfillment and completion," here flat Nebraska landscape means just the opposite—the Nebraska land may go on forever, "but there is no indication that there is a promising horizon beyond whose curve the fulfillment of aspiration . . . lies" (Schneider 1967, 86).

Thurin, too, views the story as a study in unrelieved grimness. Aunt Georgiana is utterly defeated. Her only contribution—helping "to open up the prairie and make it safe for civilization," as well as bearing and raising six children—are the kinds of triumphs Cather praises in some of her later fiction, but in this story they are not even slightly redemptive (1990, 132). The symbol of Georgiana's battered wedding ring could suggest that Cather is reiterating here one of her common themes—that marriage is incompatible with art, but a more precise interpretation is that Georgiana's "tragedy is not so much that she fell in love, . . . but that she ended up in Nebraska" (Thomas 1990, 26).

Even the exhausting and dissipating frontier life is not entirely responsible for Georgiana's defeat, however. Cather's belief that her provincial Protestant background was antilife *and* antiart is also obvious in this story's negative references to religion, such as the "sardonic suggestion that a submissive female piety was part of Aunt Georgiana's problem" (Thurin 1990, 131–32).

Not all critics agree that the message of "A Wagner Matinée" is unrelentingly negative. Jensen, for example, does not see Georgiana's artistic spirit as destroyed. In fact, Cather's message seems to be quite the opposite: Georgiana's "weeping response to the music reflects an inner grace that thirty years of deprivation could not destroy," and the real values in life are thus shown to be indestructible (1983, 133).

This resurrection, seen by Jensen as the triumph of the artistic spirit, is seen by Gale as the result of Georgiana's rediscovery of her past: Cather shows that life can be full only when the individual is connected to his or her past. Whether one's past is the world of art and music or the world of prairie and homesteading makes little difference; the important event is the return to one's roots (1958, 211).

Rosowski reads the story as an account of the narrator's own awakening. "As Aunt Georgiana moves from unconsciousness to consciousness, Clark moves from cold objectivity to empathy" (1986, 27). As Rosowski goes on to explain, his first encounter with his aunt in Boston elicits from him only cruel comments about her appearance, and he does not realize the unfairness of his assessment until the two of them enter the concert hall. Then he begins to identify with her as he sees the music affect her in much the same way it affected him when he first arrived in the city. Throughout the concert, Clark continues to move toward complete empathy with his aunt, and when the concert is over and Georgiana cries that she does not want to return home, Clark says he understands. His final "joining with his aunt in experiencing the pain of that desolation, provides the compassion that is the only stay against it" (1986, 27–28). Arnold agrees, maintaining that Clark's progression toward maturity, as evidenced by his ability to understand his aunt, makes the story as much about love and appreciation as about a merciless frontier that destroys the soul (1984, 58).

Wasserman's reading of the story is also fairly positive. Although many of the images of the West are undeniably desolate, some of them connect the two worlds presented in the story. Citing the same examples as Gerber (discussed above) concerning the fusion of descriptions of the Nebraska landscape and those of the orchestra landscape, Wasserman comes to quite the opposite of Gerber's conclusion: "Here Cather hints, just hints, that there is a link between the austere beauty of the plains and the designs of musical form"; in the process, Clark has come to realize that his aunt "has borne her fate stoically, even heroically," and he discovers a new respect for her (1991, 30).

In O'Brien's view, the story may also be seen as evidence of Cather's sympathy for and understanding of women who choose love over art. She herself was in some ways tempted by that choice. Her own intimate attachments to women posed a threat to her independence and allowed her to understand the conflict all women artists experienced (1987, 169). One world is chosen, the other rejected: in "A Wagner Matinée" a woman's "two worlds pause in equipoise as the concert ends. . . . Appropriately, Cather leaves the story at the door of the concert hall, with the return to Nebraska as inevitable as the winter prairie wind; . . . but for the moment [Georgiana] is caught hopelessly between the two worlds that have shaped her life" (Arnold 1984, 60). It is a dilemma Cather treats with compassion, not with impatience or belligerence (Arnold 1984, 60).

Works Cited

Arnold, Marilyn. 1984. *Willa Cather's Short Fiction*. Athens: Ohio University Press.

Baker, Bruce. 1987. "Nebraska's Cultural Desert: Willa Cather's Early Short Stories." *Midamerica* 14:12–17.

Bennett, Mildred R. 1961. *The World of Willa Cather*. Lincoln: University of Nebraska Press.

Bloom, Edward A., and Lillian D. Bloom. 1962. *Willa Cather's Gift of Sympathy*. Carbondale: Southern Illinois University Press.

Bloom, Harold, ed. 1985. *Willa Cather*. New York: Chelsea House.

Brown, E. K. Completed by Leon Edel. [1953] 1964. *Willa Cather: A Critical Biography*. New York: Knopf.

Cather, Willa. 1961. "A Wagner Matinée." In *The Troll Garden*. New York: Signet Classics, 7–34.

———. [1965] 1970. "A Wagner Matinée." In *Willa Cather's Collected Short Fiction, 1892–1912*. Ed. Virginia Faulkner. Lincoln: University of Nebraska Press, 235–47.

———. 1983. "A Wagner Matinée." In *The Troll Garden*. Ed. James Woodress. Lincoln: University of Nebraska Press, 94–101.

———. 1987. "A Wagner Matinée." In *Cather: Early Novels and Stories*. New York: Literary Classics of the United States, 102–110.

———. 1992. "A Wagner Matinée." In *Cather: Stories, Poems, and Other Writings*. New York: Literary Classics of the United States, 489–96.

Faulkner, Virginia, ed. [1965] 1970. *Willa Cather's Collected Short Fiction, 1892–1912*. Lincoln: University of Nebraska Press. Reprint. Lincoln: University of Nebraska Press.

Gale, Robert L. 1958. "Willa Cather and the Past." *Studi Americani* 4:209–222.

Gerber, Philip. 1975. *Willa Cather*. Boston: Twayne.

Giannone, Richard. 1968. *Music in Willa Cather's Fiction*. Lincoln: University of Nebraska Press.

Jensen, Marvin D. 1983. "An Application of Bibliotherapy: Search for Meaning in the Writings of Willa Cather." *Journal of Communication Therapy* 2:131–35.

Lathrop, Joanna. 1975. *Willa Cather: A Checklist of Her Published Writing*. Lincoln: University of Nebraska Press.

O'Brien, Sharon. 1987. *Willa Cather: The Emerging Voice*. New York: Oxford University Press.

Robinson, Phyllis C. 1983. *Willa: The Life of Willa Cather*. Garden City, NY: Doubleday.

Rosowski, Susan J. 1986. *The Voyage Perilous: Willa Cather's Romanticism*. Lincoln: University of Nebraska Press.

Schneider, Sister Lucy. 1967. "Willa Cather's Early Stories in the Light of Her 'Land-Philosophy.'" *Midwest Quarterly* 9:75–94.

Thomas, Susie. 1990. *Willa Cather*. Savage, MD: Barnes & Noble.

Thurin, Erik Ingvar. 1990. *The Humanization of Willa Cather: Classicism in an American Classic*. Lund, Sweden: Lund University Press.

Wasserman, Loretta. 1991. *Willa Cather: A Study of the Short Fiction*. Boston: Twayne.

Woodress, James. 1970. *Willa Cather: Her Life and Art*. New York: Pegasus.

———. 1983. Introduction to *The Troll Garden*. Ed. James Woodress. Lincoln: University of Nebraska Press.

The Way of the World

Publication History

This story was first published in the April 1898 issue of *Home Monthly* (6:10–11) under the name Willa Cather and was reprinted on August 19, 1899, by the Lincoln *Courier* (14:9–10) (Faulkner 1970, 592). In 1965 it was reprinted by the University of Nebraska Press in *Willa Cather's Collected Short Fiction, 1892–1912*.

Circumstances of Composition, Sources, and Influences

The story was written after Cather had resigned from her editing job at *Home Monthly* and had begun working for the Pittsburgh *Leader* as a wire copy editor. She had been contributing drama reviews to the *Leader* since 1896, holding down her job at *Home Monthly* at the same time. Even after her resignation, she continued to write two monthly columns for that magazine.

According to both Woodress and O'Brien, "The Way of the World" is a reworking of one of Cather's childhood experiences. When she was growing up in Red Cloud, Nebraska, Cather and several of her friends constructed a small play town, using empty boxes and crates as buildings. Cather appointed herself mayor, banker, and newspaper editor—all traditionally male roles—of the town, called Sandy Point, of which Speckleville was the fictional version. Since by this time in her young life Cather was already thoroughly disgusted with the behavior expected of girls, the typically female jobs in Sandy Point, such as running a candy store or millinery shop, were assigned to her more conventional girlfriends. She wanted the more powerful and interesting roles, all of which—both in play and real life—were reserved for men. In fact, at this time Cather's dream was to become a surgeon, and one of the people she most admired was Dr. McKeeby, her own family doctor, who had been elected mayor of Red Cloud shortly before Cather and her friends erected Sandy Point (Woodress 1987, 55–57; O'Brien 1987, 87). Thus, in some ways, Cather herself is the basis for both Speckle and Eliza. Robinson says there is a good deal of Cather in Speckle's domineering ways and also in Mary Eliza's peculiar ability to govern in a boys' town (Robinson 1983, 31).

Governing and dominating Sandy Point was natural for the young Cather, not only because she was, as was obvious to the whole town, a tomboy and a maverick in nearly every way, but also because she was enthralled by stage productions of all kinds; it takes no great stretch of the imagination to envision a play town as a set on a stage. After the opera house opened in Red Cloud in 1885, plays and operas were staged there regularly by itinerant theatre companies. Cather and her friends pleaded with their parents to be allowed to attend these performances every night. For Cather in particular, these stage productions meant an opportunity to transcend her own reality, including the restrictions of Victorian womanhood (Woodress 1987, 55; O'Brien 1987, 86–87).

The idea for Cather's crate-and-box town—and thus, indirectly at least, for the story itself—may have come from a small political scandal in the local Red Cloud government that caused a sensation in the town when Cather was thirteen years old. According to Woodress, it occurred after Dr. McKeeby was elected mayor and Cather's father, Charles Cather, was elected an alderman. The scandal involved a quarrel between a committee—of which both Cather's father and Dr. McKeeby were members—and the county treasurer, whom the committee was investigating for misappropriation of funds. The ongoing battle between the committee and the treasurer was recorded by the local newspaper, and such a "spectacle of grass-roots politicking, which young Cather observed firsthand, may have inspired the children in the neighborhood to enact a juvenile version of local government" (1987, 57). Woodress also suggests that the story very likely owes a bit to Mark Twain's *Tom Sawyer* (1987, 57).

Relationship to Other Cather Works

One of Cather's favorite childhood places was a sandy island in the Republican River, where she spent a great deal of time fishing and camping with her friends (Bennett 1970, xxxii). The island itself appears in several of her stories and in her novels centered in the Southwest. Bennett sees "The Way of the World" as "a kind of prologue to the cycle of scenes and episodes linked by the island associations [because] it introduces a band of children— Speckle Burnham, Jimmy Templeton, Reinholt Birkner, and others—who will reappear under these and other names as adolescents and adults in nearly a dozen novels and stories" (1970, xxxii). Speckle, for example, becomes Douglass Burnham in "The Treasure of Far Island" (1902), and all of them are found again in "The Enchanted Bluff" (1909). Their names are changed, but they are all from Sandtown, a name reminiscent of Sandy Point (Bennett 1970, xxxiii).

Interpretations and Criticisms

Nearly all Cather authorities at least mention the significance of the comparison of Mary Eliza's actions in the story to Eve's part in the creation story of Genesis. Woodress believes the association indicates Cather's distrust of women (Woodress 1987, 57). In Arnold's opinion, it is the narrator who effectively and ironically retells the Eden story as a grandfather would to his grandsons, ostensibly warning them about women's ways, but actually teasing them without their knowledge (1984, 18). As he tells his story, the narrator seems to accept the traditional male interpretation of the Genesis story: woman is the nemesis of man. In the end, however, he shows clearly that he accepts no such thing. Men and women are equally guilty of ruining their Eden by turning it into a marketplace (Arnold 1984, 19).

Thurin disagrees with Arnold's assessment, insisting the story is too slight to convey a theme as lofty as the loss of childhood innocence. Instead, the theme is, in one sense, sex as disastrous. Furthermore, the significance of the Garden of Eden in general should be downplayed because it is not the primary image of the story—the city of Rome is: Cather connects Speckleville to "that old mud-walled town in Latium that was also founded by a boy" (Cather 1970, 398; Thurin 1990, 98). Cather's next classical allusion requires her to skip about a thousand years of Roman history so that she can say that Eliza "made herself sole imperatrix of Speckleville"; she then returns to republican times, when she speaks of Eliza's defection: "It was as though Coriolanus, when he deserted Rome for the camp of the Volscians, had asked the Conscript Fathers to call on him and bring their families!" (Cather 1970, 403; Thurin 1990, 98). Finally, Speckle is left sitting alone in his town "as Caius Marius once sat among the ruins of Carthage" (Cather 1970, 404). All of these classical allusions are both affected and, especially in the case of Cather's reference to Marius, somewhat inaccurate (Thurin 1990, 98).

Works Cited

Arnold, Marilyn. 1984. *Willa Cather's Short Fiction*. Athens: Ohio University Press.

Bennett, Mildred R. [1965] 1970. Introduction to *Willa Cather's Collected Short Fiction*. Ed. Virginia Faulkner. Lincoln: University of Nebraska Press. Reprint. Lincoln: University of Nebraska Press.

Cather, Willa. [1965] 1970. "The Way of the World." In *Willa Cather's Collected Short Fiction, 1892–1912*. Ed. Virginia Faulkner. Lincoln: University of Nebraska Press, 395–404.

Faulkner, Virginia, ed. [1965] 1970. *Willa Cather's Collected Short Fiction, 1892–1912*. Lincoln: University of Nebraska Press. Reprint. Lincoln: University of Nebraska Press.

O'Brien, Sharon. 1987. *Willa Cather: The Emerging Voice*. New York: Oxford University Press.

Robinson, Phyllis C. 1983. *Willa: The Life of Willa Cather*. Garden City, NY: Doubleday.

Thurin, Erik Ingvar. 1990. *The Humanization of Willa Cather: Classicism in an American Classic*. Lund, Sweden: Lund University Press.

Woodress, James. 1987. *Willa Cather: A Literary Life*. Lincoln: University of Nebraska Press.

The Westbound Train

Publication History

This story was first published in the Lincoln *Courier* on September 30, 1899 (14:3–5), under the name Willa Cather (Faulkner 1970, 592). It was reprinted in 1965 by the University of Nebraska Press in *Willa Cather's Collected Short Fiction, 1892–1912*.

Circumstances of Composition, Sources, and Influences

Cather wrote this story while she was working for the Pittsburgh *Leader*. It and "The Way of the World" are the only two stories she produced during her tenure at that newspaper (1897–1900). Bennett says that newspaper work was a monotonous grind for Cather, much as magazine work had been (1970, xxi). Little else is known about Cather's three *Leader* years, except that she was still contributing two columns to other publications. One, "Old Books and New," she sent to *Home Monthly*, where she had worked as an editor until 1897; the other, "The Passing Show," she sent back to the Lincoln *Journal* (later the *Courier*) (O'Brien 1987, 232). Bennett implies that the chaotic and pressured life Cather was living at this time left her little time for fiction writing (1970, xxi).

Relationship to Other Cather Works

No scholars have devoted any serious attention to this story. It is not clearly connected to any of Cather's other published fiction. Many critics have, however, discussed Cather's intense interest in drama (see the "Circumstances of Composition, Sources, and Influences" section for the chapter "The Way of the World"). Arnold connects this story only to "the two juvenile dialogues" written during Cather's years as a student in Lincoln, "A Sentimental Thanksgiving Dinner: In Five Courses," which appeared in the *Hesperian* on November 24, 1892, and "Daily Dialogues; Or, Cloak Room Conversation as Overheard by the Tired Listener," an attack on fraternities, which appeared in the same publication on February 15, 1893 (1984, 20, 35).

Interpretations and Criticisms

Arnold is the only Cather specialist to mention this story in more than a passing way, and she judges it "a trifling little dramatic sketch" not nearly as cleverly devised as "The Way of the World," the other story Cather wrote during this period (1984, 20). It is "either a deliberate farce or an unsuccessful comic psychological venture which brings a woman into an unnerving confrontation with her presumptuous and snooty alter ego" (1984, 20).

Works Cited

Arnold, Marilyn. 1984. *Willa Cather's Short Fiction*. Athens: Ohio University Press.

Bennett, Mildred. [1965] 1970. Introduction to *Willa Cather's Collected Short Fiction*. Ed. Virginia Faulkner. Lincoln: University of Nebraska Press. Reprint. Lincoln: University of Nebraska Press.

Cather, Willa. [1965] 1970. "The Westbound Train." In *Willa Cather's Collected Short Fiction, 1892–1912*. Ed. Virginia Faulkner. Lincoln: University of Nebraska Press.

Faulkner, Virginia, ed. [1965] 1970. *Willa Cather's Collected Short Fiction, 1892–1912*. Lincoln: University of Nebraska Press. Reprint. Lincoln: University of Nebraska Press.

O'Brien, Sharon. 1987. *Willa Cather: The Emerging Voice*. New York: Oxford University Press.

The Willing Muse

Publication History

This story was first published under the name Willa Sibert Cather in the August 1907 issue of *Century* (74:550–57) (Faulkner 1970, 596)and was reprinted in 1965 by the University of Nebraska Press in *Willa Cather's Collected Short Fiction, 1892–1912*.

Circumstances of Composition, Sources, and Influences

This story was the third Cather published after moving to New York City from Pittsburgh to take a position on *McClure's* magazine. It was probably written in 1907, the same year it was published (Faulkner 1970, 596).

Woodress notes this story's similarity to Henry James's "The Next Time," in which the character of Jane Highmore corresponds closely to Bertha Gray. Kenneth Gray could be a combination of two James characters—Paul Overt in "The Lesson of the Master" and Ray Limbert in "The Next Time" (1970, 125).

O'Brien also sees Henry James as one source of the story's subject matter, in particular ". . . a parasitic, vampirelike relationship in which one partner thrives at the other's expense. This was also one of James' recurring interests, having just received its fullest treatment in *The Sacred Fount*" (1987, 294). Of even more significance, in O'Brien's opinion, are the sources for this story to be found in Cather's own life. Symbiotic relationships were of great personal interest to Cather; she simply shared that interest with James rather than borrowing it from him (1987, 294). Furthermore, Cather herself may be thought of as the prototype of Kenneth Gray—he is a disciple of her religion of art "in a sheltered Midwestern Parnassus" (O'Brien 1987, 294). Like Cather, he had a long apprenticeship period and his acquaintances expected him to produce great books long before he finally did so at age thirty-five. Also like Cather, he fears a waning of his creativity (O'Brien 1987, 294). In sapping his energy, Bertha represents "all the people and the tasks absorbing Cather's energy and taking over her identity, all the writers for whom she was playing the muse's helping role" in her position as editor at *McClure's* magazine (O'Brien 1987, 295). S. S. McClure himself was benefiting from Cather's energy, but considering her loyalty to him, quitting her job would have been tantamount to abandonment. Kenneth Gray's escape to China, then, may be Cather's way of portraying her own "inability to imagine a satisfactory resolution both to the character's dilemma and to her own conflict between her commitment to *McClure's* and to her writing" (O'Brien 1987, 295). This interpretation is questioned by Thurin, who wonders if Cather had been at *McClure's* long enough at this time to have such strong feelings (1990, 157n).

Cather seems to have taken her title from one of James's novels, *The Tragic Muse*, according to Arnold, and two of the characters in that novel, Nick Dorimer and Miriam Rooth, "are prototypes for Kenneth Gray and Bertha Torrence. . . . Gray's art is private and self-absorbing like Dorimer's, and Bertha's is social like Miriam's" (1984, 72). The relationship between Kenneth and Bertha is anticipated in James's *The Sacred Fount*. Much like Mrs. Brissendon in that novel, Bertha seems to be getting younger and more vital, while her husband becomes rapidly older and weaker. The women seem to sap the life out of their husbands (Arnold 1984, 72).

Relationship to Other Cather Works

In its imitation of Henry James, all Cather's critics agree that this story may be grouped with her other Jamesian work, especially "Flavia and Her Artists"; "The Garden Lodge"; "'A Death in the Desert,'" "The Marriage of Phaedra" (all from *The Troll Garden*); the other 1907 stories "The Namesake," "The Profile," and "Eleanor's House"; and her first novel, *Alexander's Bridge*.

Gerber links the story specifically with Cather's third novel, *The Song of the Lark*. The interweaving of the commercial and the aesthetic prefigures the eventual belief espoused by Thea Kronborg in that novel—that in order to love the good passionately, one must hate the bad just as intensely (Cather 1970; Gerber 1975, 96–97).

Interpretations and Criticisms

O'Brien views Gray's departure at the end of this story as significant for its abruptness and unbelievability. It can, however, be at least partially explained: "Bertha's absorption of his will and energy was too subtle a phenomenon to be described, and since he partially conspired in the process, he couldn't be 'churlish' and confront her" (1987, 295). It may also be seen as the author's own "desire to escape James' confining architecture and invisible presence" (O'Brien 1987, 303).

Arnold suggests that the story may be a variation on one of Cather's favorite themes: art and marriage don't mix. In this case, however, there is a slight twist in that the marriage represented is between two types of talent—

one cheap, the other authentic; but a marriage between the two is just as doomed as one between an artist and a nonartist. Bertha, of course, produces false art, but, it is perhaps surprising to note, Cather does not destroy her: after all, Bertha is not a bad writer. Furthermore, as a young journalist, Cather respected energetic emotional performers and even maintained that the technically perfect artists often lacked depth of feeling (1984, 73–74). Bradford does not see any such sympathy in the author's view of Bertha. He sees her as Cather's "study of the 'kitsch' artist, the purveyor of daydreams. Bertha Torrence writes as though she were pedaling a sewing machine," and Cather describes her "with delightful acidity" (1955, 544).

Gerber sees another of Cather's favorite themes, the destruction of American life by rampant commercialism, in this story when Kenneth Gray returns to his hometown of Olympia, Ohio, which has been utterly destroyed by the pollution and visual ugliness of industrialism. The description of the Ohio town is almost certainly based on Cather's memory of Pittsburgh, where she lived from 1896 to 1906 (Gerber 1975, 97). In Cather's view, "contemporary mechanization . . . has disturbed the peace and serenity . . . [and] helped destroy the incipient fineness of the second-generation pioneers even as it depersonalized them" (Bloom and Bloom 1962, 91). It is a cancer that is striking all over the country. She describes the problem metaphorically in this story when she identifies modern life with a six-day bicycle race: "mechanization. . . induces a purposeless, self-perpetuating, never-ending speed" (Bloom and Bloom 1962, 91). Gray's retreat at the end of the story, then, may be read not only as his escape from his wife, but as an escape from the "materialistic encroachments upon his sanctuary, in this case a small college town" (Bloom and Bloom 1962, 108).

Thurin identifies the muse of the title as the primary classical image, but notes the existence of secondary ones as well. Cather's juxtaposition of the European name Gray with a name like Olympia, his hometown, functions "to symbolize . . . a situation diametrically opposed to the feverish commercial pressures encountered by writers in New York City. . . . Although Olympia is not to be confused with Mount Olympus, Cather's choice of name certainly has something to do with her hero's refusal to descend into the market place" (1990, 146). As Thurin goes on to explain, Cather's use of classical imagery in this story is pointedly ironic: the story "stands on its head the relationship between a female muse and a male poet as pictured from Homer on. On the other hand, it respects the ancient and archetypal view of woman as the receiver of the male *influxus*," making the story of little use to someone looking for evidence that Cather was a feminist (1990, 147).

Works Cited

Arnold, Marilyn. 1984. *Willa Cather's Short Fiction*. Athens: Ohio University Press.

Bloom, Edward A., and Lillian D. Bloom. 1962. *Willa Cather's Gift of Sympathy*. Carbondale: Southern Illinois University Press.

Bradford, Curtis. 1955. "Willa Cather's Uncollected Short Stories." *American Literature* 26:537–51.

Cather, Willa. [1965] 1970. "The Willing Muse." In *Willa Cather's Collected Short Fiction, 1892–1912*. Ed. Virginia Faulkner. Lincoln: University of Nebraska Press, 113–23.

Faulkner, Virginia, ed. [1965] 1970. *Willa Cather's Collected Short Fiction, 1892–1912*. Lincoln: University of Nebraska Press. Reprint. Lincoln: University of Nebraska Press.

Gerber, Philip. 1975. *Willa Cather*. Boston: Twayne.

O'Brien, Sharon. 1987. *Willa Cather: The Emerging Voice*. New York: Oxford University Press.

Thurin, Erik Ingvar. 1990. *The Humanization of Willa Cather: Classicism in an American Classic*. Lund, Sweden: Lund University Press.

Woodress, James. 1970. *Willa Cather: Her Life and Art*. New York: Pegasus.

Index of Cather's Works

General Index

Nordica, Lillian, 67, 68, 103, 140, 229
Norris, Frank, 49

O'Brien, Sharon, xiv, 2, 6, 11, 12, 13–14,
  15, 23, 27, 30, 31, 34, 35–36, 39, 40,
  51, 52, 53, 60, 62, 63, 64, 80, 81,
  84–85, 87, 91, 97, 109, 110, 121,
  123, 125, 126, 128–29, 135, 136,
  137, 139–40, 141, 143, 144, 146,
  158, 168–69, 173, 178, 179–80, 182,
  185, 188, 189–90, 194, 196, 198,
  199, 201, 204, 207, 208, 212, 213,
  222–23, 226, 227, 229, 230, 231,
  234, 235–36, 237, 239, 240, 241,
  242, 243, 247, 260, 261, 262, 265,
  267, 268, 270, 272, 273
  Willa Cather: The Emerging Voice,
  xiv
Odysseus (*Odyssey*), 104
Oehlschlaeger, Fritz, 46, 47
Osborne, Evelyn, 206
Ouida, 121
  Story of Ariadne: A Dream, The,
  121
Overland Monthly, 49, 93, 175
Ovid, 119
  Ars Amatoria, 119

Pan, 24
Paris, xvi
"Passing Show, The" (newspaper col-
  umn), 219, 270
Pavelka, Annie, 148, 194
Peattie, Elia, 177
Penelope (*Odyssey*), 246
Pers, Mona, 105, 188, 209
Persephone, 127
Petry, Alice Hall, 39, 42, 43, 125–26, 187,
  223
Piacentino, Edward J., 153
Pittsburgh, xvi, 20
Plato, 146, 231
  Phaedrus, 146
  Symposium, 146
Poe, Edgar Allan, 45
  "Ligeia," 80
  "William Wilson," 45
Pound, Louise, 38, 103, 232, 239–40
Pound, Roscoe, 103
Prairie Schooner, 32, 120, 131, 243
Proserpine, 18

Pseudonyms
  Douglass, Charles, 198, 238
  Nicklemann, Henry, 55
  Seymour, Elizabeth L., 29, 233
Putnam's, 157

Quennell, Peter, 152, 170

Ramonda, Karen Stevens, 170, 171–72
Red Cloud. *See* Nebraska
Reinhart, Charles Stanley, 219
Reynolds, Horace, 163
Robinson, Phyllis, 16, 41, 53, 56, 58, 68,
  70, 83, 88, 97, 123, 167–68, 177,
  182, 193–94, 196, 210–11, 214, 215,
  217, 236, 238, 241, 245, 255, 260,
  261, 267
Rosowski, Susan, 23, 25, 47, 89, 102,
  103, 105, 110, 129, 137, 149, 151,
  152, 169, 170, 181, 187, 208, 221,
  223, 245, 250, 251, 264
Rossetti, Christina, 61, 63, 220, 262
  "Goblin Market," 61, 62
Rossetti, Dante Gabriel, 39
  "Eden Bower," 39
Rossetti, W. M., 121
  Keats, 121
Rubin, Larry, 190
Ryder, Mary Ruth, 5, 8, 24, 27, 43, 67,
  69, 71, 115, 118, 119, 127, 129, 148,
  149, 150, 151, 154, 173, 250

Sadilek, Francis, 194
Sappho, 182
Saturday Evening Post, 120, 123
Schneider, Sister Lucy, 22, 35, 88, 89, 97,
  131, 133, 153, 263
Schroeter, James, 136, 162
Schweider, Nancy, 245
Scipio, 250
Scribner's, 59, 218
Selene (goddess), 24
Sergeant, Elizabeth Shepley, 20, 125
Shakespeare, William, 235, 247, 251
  Hamlet, 30, 85, 231
  Julius Caesar, 65
  Romeo and Juliet, 246
  Tempest, The, 246
Slote, Bernice, 4, 24, 27, 28, 37, 38, 44,
  46, 47, 51, 63, 74, 75, 78, 83, 95, 103,
  109, 118, 157, 158, 167,